Basic Science for FRCS
(Trauma & Orthopaedics)
3rd edition

Edited by

Dr V N Cassar-Pullicino LRCP, MRCS, DMRD, FRCR, MD (Malta)
and
Professor J B Richardson MChB, FRCS, MD

A Teaching Manual for
FRCS (Trauma & Orthopaedics) Trainees

Institute of Orthopaedics (Oswestry) Publishing Group
Institute of Orthopaedics
Robert Jones & Agnes Hunt
Orthopaedic & District Hospital NHS Trust
Oswestry
Shropshire SY10 7AG

January 2007

First published in 2001 by
Institute of Orthopaedics (Oswestry) Publishing Group, The Institute of Orthopaedics,
Robert Jones & Agnes Hunt Orthopaedic & District Hospital NHS Trust, Oswestry,
Shropshire SY10 7AG

British Library Cataloguing in Publication data
A catalogue record for this book is available from the British Library

ISBN : 978-0-9539982-6-5

Foreward

The role of the Institute of Orthopaedics is to support orthopaedic research and to foster orthopaedic education in every way that it can throughout the English speaking world.

The re-publishing of this book expands the Institute's teaching role by addressing the requirements of orthopaedic education. The authors of each section are noted experts in their respective fields. They support the work of the Institute and use its services for raising the funds they need for the programmes of research conducted in their departments.

I commend the excellent teaching material they have provided to all serious students who wish to improve their knowledge of orthopaedics and who face examinations in the future.

Richard Burbidge OBE, BA

Chairman

Institute of Orthopaedics

22nd February 2006

Preface

"Basic science" denotes the starting point and foundation that defines the necessary prerequisite before embarking on further clinical studies on patient care. In the past the subject was covered in an unstructured manner, its importance under-rated, and more often than not, knowledge was presumed to have been obtained but rarely confirmed. The FRCS (Trauma & Orthopaedics) examination requirements have re-ignited the interest and importance of the various facets of basic science, ensuring that trainees devote time to this area of orthopaedics. Although termed "basic", the subject is far from static but rather dynamic and constantly developing. Medicine as a whole is a constantly evolving and ever-changing discipline. As orthopaedics increasingly becomes sub-specialised, the basic science platform is also broadening. Basic science courses in orthopaedics were initially held in Leicester at the suggestion of Professor Paul Gregg, some ten years ago. Over the years the clinical examination techniques have been separated and Oswestry now provides three annual courses in clinical examination.

This book is co-authored by respected experts in their field who regularly contribute to the FRCS (Trauma & Orthopaedics) courses in Oswestry. It unifies the underlying principles and applications of current orthopaedic practice. It is specifically designed with the trainee in mind, providing a guide on the expected standard of knowledge. The approach is on a "what you must know" basis, is presented in a concise format, and is not designed to replace the excellent standard textbooks. The approach is streamlined, guiding the reader through quanta of knowledge with the help of relevant diagrams, illustrations, and suggested references for further reading. We have tried to make this educational experience as painless as possible in the hope that it will prove interesting, enjoyable, and satisfying.

Preparation of this book required the co-operation and efforts of many individuals. We are indebted to our co-author colleagues for their dedication, energy and enthusiasm as well as their secretarial staff who were often caught in the line of fire, having to meet unrealistic expectations and deadlines. Judy Harris has taken on the difficult work of organising us all and Marie Carter has been the proof reader. Alun Jones and Andrew Biggs deserve special mention for their input and assistance in providing the high quality medical photographs and illustrations and in this third edition have developed all the skills of page setting and printing. We are grateful to the Institute of Orthopaedics for its continued support and dedication to education and research under the Chairmanship of Richard Burbidge.

Dr Victor N Cassar-Pullicino
Consultant Radiologist, Clinical Director,
The Institute of Orthopaedics

Professor James B Richardson
Director
The Institute of Orthopaedics

Contributors

Dr R Allcock FRCA
Consultant Anaesthetist
RJAH, Oswestry

Dr S Bajada MD
Research Fellow
RJAH, Oswestry

Mr R Bindra MS Orth, D Orth, FRCS, MCh Orth
Consultant Orthopaedic Surgeon
Pulvertaft Hand Centre, Derbyshire Royal
Infirmary, London Road, Derby, DE1 2QY

Dr R Butler MD, FRCP
Consultant Rheumatologist
RJAH, Oswestry

Dr V N Cassar-Pullicino LRCP, MRCS, DMRD, FRCR, MD (Malta)
Consultant Radiologist, Clinical Director,
Senior Honorary Lecturer in University of
Keele
RJAH, Oswestry

Mr P Cool, Arts MMedSc(Res), FRCS (Ed), FRCS (Trauma & Orthopaedics)
Consultant Orthopaedic & Oncological
Surgeon
RJAH, Oswestry

Dr A Darby FRCPath
Consultant Histopathologist
RJAH, Oswestry

Mr G R Gordon, MBAPO
Orthotic Services Manager
Department of Orthotics
RJAH, Oswestry

Mr M J Haddaway Btech, MIPEM
Medical Physicist
RJAH, Oswestry

Mr S Hay FRCS
Consultant Orthopaedic Surgeon
RJAH, Oswestry

Mr N Kiely B Med Sci,BMBS,FRCS, MSc(Orth)
Consultant Orthopaedic Surgeon
RJAH, Oswestry

Dr J H Kuiper PhD
Biomechanical Engineer
RJAH, Oswestry

Dr A J C Lee BSc,PhD,CEng, MIPEM, FRSA
Honorary University Fellow
University of Exeter,
School of Engineering & Computer Science
Harrison Engineering Building,
North Park Road, Exeter, EX4 4QF

Dr D C Mangham, BSc,MB,ChB,FRCPath
Professor J McClure,BSc,MD,FRCPath
Consultant Histopathologists
RJAH, Oswestry

Mr J H Patrick FRCS
Consultant Orthopaedic Surgeon,
Director ORLAU/Movement Analysis
Service
RJAH, Oswestry

Dr R Quinlivan FRCPH,FRCP
Consultant in Paediatrics and
Neuromuscular Disorders
RJAH, Oswestry

Mr W J Ribbans MB BS,BSc,FRCSEd(Orth), MChOrth,FRCS
Consultant Orthopaedic Surgeon
Northampton General Hospital
Northampton.

Professor J B Richardson MChB, FRCS, MD
Professor of Orthopaedics
Director of The Institute of Orthopaedics,
RJAH, Oswestry

Mr A Roberts FRCS, DM
Consultant Orthopaedic Surgeon
RJAH, Oswestry

Dr S Roberts BSc PhD
Senior Research Scientist
RJAH, Oswestry

Mr S N J Roberts MA, FRCS (Orth)
Consultant Orthopaedic and Sports Injury
Surgeon
RJAH, Oswestry

Mr G D Smith MB,ChB,MRCS
Specialist Registrar
Nuffield Orthopaedic Centre
Oxford

Dr T Staunton MB, MRCP (UK), FRCP(C)
Consultant Neurologist
Norfolk & Norwich Healthcare NHS Trust
Brunswick Road, Norwich, NR1 3SR

Mr J Trivedi Mch Orth, FRCS (Orth)
Consultant Spinal Surgeon
RJAH, Oswestry

Dr P N M Tyrrell MB, Bch, BAO, MRCPI, FRCR
Consultant Radiologist
RJAH, Oswestry

Dr R Warren MB BChir, MA, FRCPath
Consultant Microbiologist
Royal Shrewsbury Hospital
Shrewsbury

Mr JP Whittaker FRCS, Mr R Roache FRCS, (Trauma & Orthopaedics)
Oswestry Trainees

Mr D Williams, FRCS
Consultant Orthopaedic Surgeon
RJAH, Oswestry

Note:- RJAH, Oswestry -
Robert Jones & Agnes Hunt Orthopaedic & District Hospital NHS Trust, Oswestry,
Shropshire. SY10 7AG

Contents

SKELETAL DEVELOPMENT AND STRUCTURE

Dr D C Mangham and Professor J McClure

Consultant Histopathologists
Robert Jones & Agnes Hunt Orthopaedic Hospital
Oswestry

Skeletal Development

Bone tissue formation, both during development and in adult life, is performed by osteoblasts which are formed by differentiation of primitive mesenchymal cells and which participate in two types of bone formation: *intramembranous* and *endochondral* ossification.

Intramembranous Ossification

This process forms the flat bones of the skull and parts of the mandible and the clavicle. Periosteal bone formation is also a form of intramembranous ossification. Precursor cells in loose vascular connective tissue enlarge, differentiate and secrete thin strands of osteoid. The cells, now committed osteoblasts, line the surface of these strands and lay down more osteoid. Within a few days mineralisation begins and the tissue is now primitive woven bone. The strands thicken to form recognisable trabeculae and eventually remodel to form mature lamellar bone. The fibrous tissue between the trabeculae is replaced by marrow.

Endochondral Ossification

In this process ossification is preceded by the formation of a cartilage template or anlage. At a genetically predetermined time and site (*primary ossification centre*) cartilage cells hypertrophy and secrete matrix vesicles into the surrounding matrix. The matrix calcifies and the hypertrophic chondrocytes die. Blood vessels penetrate the space left by the chondrocytes and bring with them osteoblast precursors which differentiate and lay down rapidly mineralising osteoid on the already mineralised cartilage matrix. At about the same time as ossification of the primary centre begins, the periosteal sleeve is laying down an outer shell of bone which will become the cortex.

In a long bone this process starts in the centre of the diaphysis (shaft) and rapidly spreads along the shaft leaving only the ends of the bone (epiphyses) as cartilage. At the junction of the cartilage and the bone the cartilage is organised to form a specialised structure: the *growth plate (physis)*.

The growth plate consists of four zones.

i) The *reserve* or *resting zone*, closest to and merging with the epiphysis.

ii) The *proliferative zone* of active cell proliferation where cells begin to line up in columns ("piles of coins").

iii) The *hypertrophic zone* associated with secretion of collagen type X, matrix vesicles and matrix calcification.

iv) The *"degenerative" zone* where vascular penetration of chondrocyte columns is followed by osteoblasts which lay down osteoid on the adjacent calcified cartilage matrix. These newly formed trabeculae of osteoid and bone, surrounding a core of cartilage, are termed the *primary spongiosa*. Further remodelling of the spongiosa (coupled resorption and formation) leads to formation of bony trabeculae without a cartilaginous core.

At varying times throughout the skeleton, *secondary centres of ossification* are formed in the epiphyses in a similar fashion to the primary centres. Growth of the bony epiphysis takes place by endochondral ossification at the junction of bone and articular cartilage (the "secondary growth plate").

Bone Modelling

This is defined as the process whereby the size and shape of bones and contained tissue change during development and in the mature skeleton.

Growth in length of a bone takes place by the mechanism of endochondral ossification.

Increasing width of a bone is achieved by periosteal bone formation.

Increasing width of the medullary cavity is the result of a programmed excess of osteoclastic over osteoblastic activity at the endosteal surface.

The shape of bones is maintained by co-ordination of waves of osteoclastic and osteoblastic activity, particularly in the metaphyseal regions.

In the adult skeletal alterations in the spatial disposition of trabecular (cancellous) bone may occur in response to altered mechanical loading of bones or the presence of space occupying lesions in the marrow. When bone resorption and formation occur at separate sites on the trabecular structure but at the same time then resorption/formation is said to be coupled in the *temporal* sense. Simultaneous resorption and bone formation on the opposite surfaces of the trabecular structure will result in the structure moving in the direction of the formation surface.

Regulation of Skeletal Development

Significant progress has been made in the elucidation of the genetic control and regulation of skeletal development.

A large number of genes are essential for the development of the craniofacial bones which derive from the neural crest and which arise by intramembranous ossification. The genes include patterning genes (e.g. *Hox, Pax*), genes encoding for several cytokines and growth factors and those encoding for matrix metalloproteinases (MMPs) and their physiological (tissue) inhibitors (TIMPs).

The axial skeleton derives from paraxial mesoderm which segments into somites under regulation of genes such as *hairy1* and *lunatic fringe*. The somites lead to the development of the vertebrae and the dorsolateral portion of the ribs again under gene regulation (e.g. *sonic hedgehog*). Mutations in these genes may lead to significant skeletal defects.

The skeletal elements of the limbs are formed from cells derived from the lateral plate mesoderm. Differentiation is again controlled by genes and the shaping of the limb bones is due to the interaction between mesenchyme and the overlying epithelium via, for example, *fibroblast growth factor, sonic hedgehog and Wnt7a*. Each gene controls a different stage in development of the cartilage elements of the limbs.

Structure

Bone has three functions: structural support, support of haematopoiesis within the marrow space, and as a reservoir for calcium and phosphate.
There are four types of bone cell - osteoblasts, osteocytes, bone lining cells, osteoclasts.

The mature skeleton is designed to provide maximum mechanical strength for minimum weight. Its structure reflects these properties.

Within any particular bone, the bone can be described by its

(a) site:
    (i)   subperiosteal
    (ii) cortical
    (iii) endosteal
    (iv) and medullary

(b) type:
    (i)   compact
    (ii) trabecular

(c) microscopic nature:
    (i)   lamellar
    (ii) woven

Compact bone is defined as bone that is sufficiently thick that it possesses an internal blood supply. Normal cortical bone is of compact type with concentric bone formation enveloping the vessel-containing Volkmann's canals. In contrast, trabecular (or cancellous) bone does not require, and therefore lacks, an internal blood supply. Its nutrition is derived from adjacent vessels.

The microscopic nature of bone is either lamellar or woven. Lamellar bone (i.e. plates of bone) is deposited by an orderly and co-ordinated sheet of osteoblasts forming successive waves of matrix. On the other hand, the rapid, slightly disorganized formation of bone produces so-called woven bone. Woven bone lacks a lamellar structure, contains slightly larger and less evenly distributed osteocytes than lamellar bone, and, when being formed, has a surface lined by active osteoblasts.

Woven bone deposition occurs as an early, rapid response to insult and, over time and with resolution of the stimulus, is replaced by lamellar bone.

The presence of woven bone in the mature adult skeleton is always abnormal.

Calcified bone contains about 25% organic matrix, including cells (2.5%), 5% water and 70% inorganic mineral (hydroxyapatite)

Normal bone matrix is laid down in layers (lamellae) for maximal mechanical strength and although mainly collagen, there are important non-collagenous proteins and other compounds. The major collagen present in bone is type I collagen and the minor collagen is type XI. These are both fibrillar collagens. Type I collagen has three subunits formed from type I procollagen which form a triple helix. The type I collagen molecules are assembled into fibrils. Type XI regulates the overall fibril diameter and links other molecules, such as proteoglycans, to the fibrillar structure. Other proteins, some unique to bone, such as osteocalcin, are embedded in the extracellular matrix and although small in quantity have important signalling functions (bone morphogenetic proteins, growth factors, cytokines, adhesion molecules) or play a role during mineralisation (osteopontin, osteonectin, matrix-gla protein). The use of knockout mice lacking the ability to synthesise these proteins has shed light on the individual functions of some of these proteins. Osteocalcin-deficient mice, for example, display increased bone formation whereas mice lacking osteonectin are osteopaenic due to reduced bone remodelling.

Osteoblasts lay down collagen in organised lamellae to form an osteoid seam about 10 μm thick. 10-15% of osteoblasts eventually become entombed in lacunae as *osteocytes*. The remainder die or become endosteal surface *lining cells*.

Mineralisation: the osteoid seam begins to mineralise after about 20 days. An initial rapid phase (75%) lasting a few days can be visualised (calcification front) by *tetracycline labelling* (usually given *in vivo* although the calcification front can be stained by a tetracycline solution). The calcification front is the site of action of the active metabolites of vitamin D. The calcification front can complex metallic ions such as aluminium causing an osteomalacic phenomenon.

Bone mineral is generically referred to as hydroxyapatite [$Ca_{10}(PO_4)_6(OH)_2$], a plate-like crystal 20-80nm in length and 2-5nm thick. It is four times smaller than naturally occurring apatites and less perfect in crystal structure. This makes it more reactive and soluble and facilitates chemical turnover. Almost 100% mineralisation is only achieved after one year.

A *canalicular system* connects osteocytes to one another and to lining cells and osteoblasts. This is now believed to be an important network. It is postulated that mechanical stresses within trabecular bone can cause deformation of the walls of lacunar spaces detectable by the resident osteocytes. Information passed via the canalicular network to the endosteal surface initiates modelling and/or remodelling sequences which may alter the shape, size and disposition of the trabecular structure.

Osteoclasts are multinucleated cells derived from the precursors of the monocyte/macrophage series which resorb bone surfaces.

Remodelling - microscopically both compact and cancellous bone are seen to be composed of individual basic multicellular units (packets) separated by *cement (reversal) lines*. This pattern is the result of bone remodelling activity involving not individual bone cells but organised cohorts of osteoclasts and osteoblasts.

The remodelling sequence is: Activation → Resorption → Reversal → Formation and lasts about six months. The linked processes of resorption and formation occurring in sequence at a single site are said to be coupled in a *spatial* sense.

In cortical bone, following an activation stimulus, a group of osteoclasts (the "*cutting cone*") tunnels through the compact bone for up to 2.5mm. This resorption activity is followed by a brief reversal phase when macrophages remove any debris. Then a group of osteoblasts lays down concentric lamellae of osteoid on the previously resorbed bone surface. The end result is the mature, fully mineralised, Haversian system (osteon) with a central vascular canal.

In trabecular (cancellous) bone a similar sequence occurs on the surface of a bone trabecula. Osteoclastic resorption to a depth of about 50μm is followed by osteoblastic activity to replace the resorbed bone. The resulting bone packet is bounded by a cement (reversal) line and the trabecular surface.

There are considered to be three functions of remodelling; replacement/repair of aged/damaged bone, reinforcement related to stress, and calcium and other ion homeostasis.

The control of the remodelling sequence is very precise. The amount of bone formed in each remodelling unit must match exactly that which has been resorbed otherwise the trabecular bone volume will change.

The bone lining cells are stimulated by molecules such as parathormone for which they express surface receptors (osteoclasts do not express such receptors). The lining cells secrete a collagenase which digests a very thin superficial layer of unmineralised type I collagen. The removal of this layer is necessary to expose a fully mineralised surface to osteoclasts which are incapable of secreting the appropriate collagenase.

Osteoclasts resorb mineralised bone at sites called Howship's lacunae in the remodelling sequence. They are derived from haemopoietic stem cells and are highly motile, multinucleated and contain a large amount of lysosomal enzymes. The cells have an apical membrane which adheres to the calcified matrix forming a tight seal. A resorption bay formed beneath the cell allows the secretion of lytic enzymes across the convoluted (ruffled) border to interact with the mineralised surface. Proton pumps add hydrogen ions to create a very low (acid) pH.

The co-ordination of osteoclastic and osteoblastic activities is co-ordinated by molecular cross-talk between these cells. RANK-L (receptor/activator of NF-kB ligand) is a transmembrane receptor on the surface of mature osteoblasts which can interact with transmembranous RANK receptor on the surface of mature osteoclast precursor cells. This induces proliferation and differentiation of osteoclasts in the presence of a permissive factor (macrophage colony-stimulating factor, M-CSF). This cross-talk mechanism appears to be the action endpoint for several calciotropic hormones and cytokines (1,25 dihydroxyvitamin D_3, parathormone, oestrogen, prostaglandin E_2, interleukins, TNF-α). Osteoprotegerin (OPG) can combine with RANK-L to inhibit osteoclastic differentiation. The importance of understanding these molecular messaging systems is illustrated by the fact that OPG has been considered as a possible therapeutic agent for osteoporosis.

Disordered Remodelling

This is involved in metabolic and other bone diseases, e.g. hyperparathyroidism, osteomalacia, osteopaenia, osteosclerosis and Paget's disease.

In hyperparathyroidism there is an overdrive of osteoclasis. In osteomalacia the mineralisation process in the newly formed bone is inhibited. In osteoporosis there is a continuing slight excess of resorption over formation and in osteosclerosis there is excess of formation over resorption. In Paget's disease both resorption and formation are stepped up to give the characteristic endpoint of thickened irregular "mosaic patterned" bone.

Notes

Notes

ARTICULAR CARTILAGE

Dr S Roberts

Senior Research Scientist
Robert Jones & Agnes Hunt Orthopaedic Hospital
Oswestry

Articular cartilage is a shock absorbing tissue that protects the more rigid underlying bone (Fig.1) and provides the smooth articulation in the bending joints during physical activity. Damage to and loss of this tissue in the arthritic diseases is responsible for a large proportion of the orthopaedic surgeons' workload and hence this tissue warrants study by them! This chapter provides a description of the biology of normal adult articular cartilage which it is hoped will be a useful groundwork for understanding cartilage pathologies including osteoarthritis. Articular cartilage is a specialised hyaline cartilage which ranges in thickness from about 1-4 mm depending on the joint and location within the joint. Different regions can be seen in the cartilage from the upper superficial zone to the mid-zone and then the deep zone. This can be differentiated at the tidemark from the calcified cartilage which leads into the subchondral bone (Fig.2).

The physiological and mechanical properties of cartilage depend on the physical properties of the tissue matrix, a resilient and elastic structure with a high content of very soluble large molecules (proteoglycans) which are entrapped in an insoluble network of fibres (collagen). This matrix, in turn, is a product of the cartilage cells, or chondrocytes, which are also capable of controlling and maintaining the extracellular matrix (ecm) by replacing molecules which are degraded and have lost functionality. Since the tissue is dependent for its existence and composition upon the chondrocytes, they will form the first subject within this chapter.

1. Chondrocytes

Function of Cartilage Cells:

- synthesise matrix components

- organise and incorporate these into the extracellular matrix

- degrade and enable the breakdown of matrix components for remodelling

- respond via mechanotransduction to changes in the cell environment

The cell density of cartilage is low in comparison to most other localities in the body with the chondrocytes comprising approximately 5% of the tissue volume. (The adult human femoral condylar cartilage, for example, has 15×10^3 cells/ mm^3.) There appear to be distinct subpopulations of cells found in the different

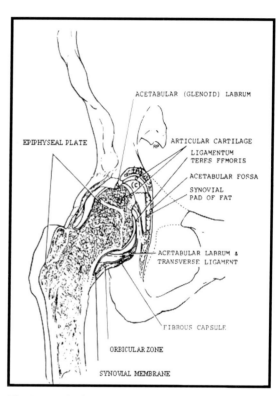

Fig.1. Articular cartilage lines the ends of the bones but is only one of many tissues making up the synovial joint.

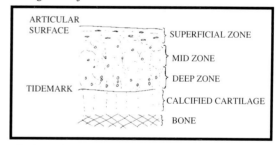

Fig.2. The matrix within articular cartilage is organised differently through its depth from the uppermost superficial zone (SZ), through the mid zone (MZ) to the deep zone (DZ) and underlying calcified cartilage and bone. The cells tend to follow the alignment of the matrix.

zones of the cartilage whose properties differ in terms of their morphology, metabolism, phenotypic stability and their response to cytokines such as interleukin-1 (IL-1).

1.1 Morphology

Cells in the uppermost, superficial zone are elongated, and lie parallel to the articular surface. There are approximately three times as many cells in this region compared to the deeper zones, probably reflecting the nutritive conditions within the superficial zone where there is better access for solute exchange. The cells in the mid and deep zones occur not only at a lower density but they are also more rounded or oval. Sometimes in the deeper zone they are arranged in columns, reflecting the articular cartilage's role in growth of the epiphyses. These columns are more prevalent in weight bearing joints than non-weight bearing regions. Chondrocytes, at least in mature cartilage, are encompassed within a fine fibrillar network or capsule, the whole unit constituting a chondron.

1.2. Cell Density and Proliferation

In human articular cartilage the cell density changes with age, being maximal in the young individual, decreasing slightly to skeletal maturity, but thereon remaining constant, for example between 25 and 84 years. There appears to be an inverse relationship between cartilage thickness and cell density, seen in different species and in different sized joints. This is such that there are approximately constant numbers of cells under a unit surface area of cartilage, regardless of its depth. Local physiological and mechanical factors are likely to influence the volume of matrix produced and maintained by the cells.

In the healthy adult cartilage there is little, if any, cell division. However, cell division can undoubtedly be induced under certain abnormal conditions, such as injury or altered loading. Similarly, if chondrocytes are removed from the matrix and grown in the laboratory they can proliferate extensively, but at different rates according to their origin within the tissue. Deep zone chondrocytes proliferate much faster than those from the superficial zone.

Chondrocyte metabolism is modulated by alterations in cell shape or changes in the organisation of the cytoskeletal microfilaments. Differences in sub-populations of chondrocytes seen in newly extracted cells will thus often diminish with time in culture as culture conditions alter the cell morphology.

1.3 Chondrocyte metabolism

Chondrocytes have a slow metabolic rate and low oxygen uptake, about 1/50th of that of liver or kidney cells, although the rate of glycolysis is comparable. There is zonal variation in cartilage with the cells of the superficial zone less metabolically active than those of the deeper zones. Synthesis of matrix molecules has been studied mostly via incorporation of radioactively labelled substrates, such as ^{35}S for proteoglycan synthesis and ^{3}H proline for collagen synthesis. Estimates of turnover times in normal adult matrices are one year for proteoglycan in rabbits and 360 years for collagen in human. However, in abnormal or traumatised tissue this capacity is greatly enhanced but although synthesis is significantly increased it remains too low to be of any measurable role in replacing damaged collagen. Thus the collagen you have as a

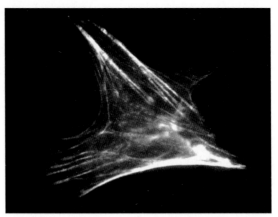

Fig.3. Human chondrocyte stained to demonstrate the actin microfilament component of the cell's cytoskeleton (courtesy of Dr WEB Johnson, Oswestry).

teenager normally stays with you for life. Chondrocytes also have the capability of producing proteases which can break down and degrade the matrix components. This is a pre-requisite for normal matrix turnover in growth and remodelling but an over-production can be deleterious in pathological states.

1.4 Mechanotransduction

The cytoskeletal system of the chondrocytes, consisting of microfilaments and their associated proteins such as actin, vinculin, gelsolin and talin, which are attached to the cell membrane via integrins, provide a means whereby the cell can respond to load or deformational changes in its local environment (Fig.3).

Chondrocytes express several integrins including the collagen receptor, $\alpha_2\beta_1$ and the fibronectin receptor, $\alpha_5\beta_1$. In addition, they have hyaluronan (HA) receptors (CD44) on their cell surface which contribute to the cell's ability to organise its pericellular matrix by binding to HA. CD44 may also be involved in transmitting mechanical information to the cell via its association with the intracellular cytoskeleton. If cartilage is loaded and the matrix deforms, the cells within that matrix will be deformed. This will result in changes at the cell membrane which can transfer forces via the cytoskeleton to the nucleus to induce changes in gene expression and result in increased or decreased synthesis of matrix components, whether the 'building blocks' such as collagen and proteoglycan, or the 'demolition squad' such as proteases of one sort or another. Mechanotransduction is likely to involve many parameters including stretch-activated channels, G-proteins, stimulation of phospholipase C and membrane transporters. The application of mechanical stress to cartilage also influences the concentration of intracellular ionic calcium, induces the expression of heat shock protein and the expression of various kinases. Other gene products which are influenced include IL-4, IL-6, NO, PGE$_2$ as well as growth factors such as TGFβ and cytokines. The complexities and interactions of all the factors involved in mechanotransduction remain to be elucidated.

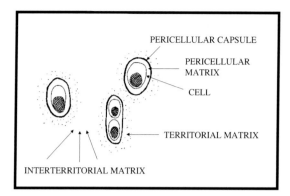

Fig.4. Terms used to describe the zones within the cartilage matrix relative to the location of the cell.

2 Extracellular Matrix
2.1 Morphology

Articular cartilage in the young, normal healthy state appears glassy (hence 'hyaline'), glistening and slightly bluish to the naked eye. The extracellular cartilage matrix comprises specialised regions including that immediately surrounding the chondrocytes, the pericellular matrix, the area beyond this, the territorial matrix, and thirdly the remaining intercellular or interterritorial matrix (Fig.4).

Throughout the depth of the cartilage the matrix organisation differs and can be crudely divided into 4 zones according to its image under polarised light:

(i) The upper superficial zone where the collagen fibrous component lies predominantly parallel to the articulating surface. This region is often thin in comparison to the rest and the collagen fibres are approximately 30 microns thick

(ii) The mid-zone, where the collagen fibres are more randomly organised (sometimes described as having 'Benninghoff's loops').

(iii)The deep zone, where the fibres become orientated perpendicular to the underlying bone and sometimes, depending on age and load, the cells will align in columns in this region and

(iv) The calcified layer of cartilage, commencing with the 'tidemark' (a basophilic line marking the precipitation of calcium salts), which joins directly into the underlying bone.

2.2 Biochemistry

Cartilage, like the rest of the body, is predominantly water (Table 1) which is attracted and retained there by the ionic pressure created by the high level of negative charges on glycosaminoglycan (GAG) chains on proteoglycan molecules. Inevitably these attract cations to neutralise their charge. This ionic pressure creates a 'swelling pressure' which will keep imbibing water until it is resisted by the tension in the fibrous component of cartilage, the collagen fibres. The cartilage matrix is thus a composite structure - the physical properties of the whole being far more than the sum of the individuals'.

2.2.1. Collagen

Collagen, the most common protein in the human body, is really a family of proteins consisting of at least nineteen members. The prerequisite to be a member is that at least part of the molecular structure must be composed of a triple helix made up of 3 helical α chains twisted round each other to form a superhelix. Cartilage consists of several types of collagen including types II, III, VI, IX, X, XI,XII,XIV and I (Table 2). However the most ubiquitous in cartilage is type II collagen, which constitutes about 80% of the collagen in cartilage. It is a fibrillar collagen and responsible for resisting swelling pressure within the matrix. Its triple helix structure is made up of three amino acid chains with a repeating tripeptide pattern: glycine-X-Y, where X is mostly proline and Y mostly hydroxyproline.

Table 1 Main Components of Articular cartilage

Component	Approx Content (/wet wt)
Water	60-85%
Proteoglycan (aggrecan)	4-7%
Collagen II	15-22%
Less than 5%: link protein hyaluronan biglycan decorin fibromodulin	collagens I, III, VI,IX,X,XI, XII,XIV & COMP

Table 2 Collagens found in Articular Cartilage

Type	Molecular Structure	Class	Distribution
II	$[\alpha_1(II)_3]$	fibrillar	throughout
XI	$[\alpha_1(XI)\ \alpha_2(XI)\ \alpha_3(XI)]$		fibrillar throughout
I	$[\alpha_1(I)]_2\alpha_2$	fibrillar	thin, surface zone
III	$[\alpha_1(III)_3]$	fibrillar	pericellularly
VI	$[\alpha_1(VI)\ \alpha_2(VI)\ \alpha_3(VI)]$	short helix	pericellularly
IX	$[\alpha_1(IX)\ \alpha_2(IX)\alpha_3(IX)]$	FACIT	on collagen II fibrils
X	$[\alpha_1(X)_3]$	short helix	calcified cartilage

Table 3 Known Cross-Links in Fibrillar Collagen in Cartilage

Reducible	hydroxylysino-5-norleucine	(HLNL),
	dihydroxylysinonorleucine	(DHLNH)
Mature	hydroxylysylpyridinoline	(HL-Pyr)
	histidinohydroxylysinonorleucine	(HHL)
Glycation Products	Pentosidine	

The molecules coil round each other, because glycine is always at the centre of the helix. These then align in rows of parallel sheets of molecules, each sheet shifting ¼ of the collagen molecule's length. This leads to alternating areas with a regular gap, which under the electron microscope, produces a lighter band compared to the rest which is darker.

Further chemical bonding between collagen molecules occurs in the form of cross-links, both within and between collagen fibrils leading to stabilisation of the collagen fibres and producing their mechanical strength. There are different groups of identifiable cross-links. Two are enzyme mediated, one being divalent reducible cross-links which are formed soon after the molecule is formed (either the ketoimine, hydroxylysino-5-norleucine (HLNL), or the aldimine, dihydroxylysinonorleucine (DHLNL; Table 3). As their name suggests they can be reduced or broken, perhaps allowing for growth within the fibrils and tissue.

With time these progress into non-reducible, stable and mature cross-links, hydroxylysylpyridinoline (HL-Pyr) and histidinohydroxylysinonorleucine (HHL), respectively. In addition to these enzymatic cross-links, there is another group which are glycation products and accumulate with age, such as pentosidine. These cross-links can all be measured in tissue, serum or urine and sometimes used as metabolic indicators.

Collagen is synthesised as a larger precursor molecule, procollagen, made up of the 3 constituent α chains. The genetic control of collagen is complex with the 19 known collagen types being coded for by at least 30 distinct genes. Types II and X collagen are each derived from 1 gene, whereas types VI, IX and XI are

Table 4 Collagen Metabolites which can be assayed and used as indicators of Collagen Turnover

Metabolite Measured	Indicator of:
C-propeptide	Collagen synthesis
COL2-3/4m	Collagen degradation
N-telopeptide	Collagen degradation
DHLN/HLN	reducible collagen cross-links - Collagen turnover
Hydoxypyridinium	mature collagen cross-links Collagen turnover
Pentosidine	level of glycation

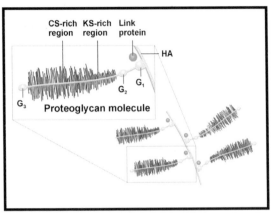

Fig.5. Schematic diagram showing molecular structure of the proteoglycan most commonly found in cartilage, aggrecan

formed from the gene products of 3 different genes (see Table 2). The synthesis is typical of secreted glycoproteins ie specific mRNAs are transcribed and translated to the a chains. They are post-transationally modified in the endoplasmic reticulum, where they are hydroxylated and glycosylated. The triple helix forms, disulphide bonds form and the procollagen is secreted. This has large globular C and N terminal domains which are enzymatically cleaved and removed when the procollagen is secreted from the cell. The procollagen telopeptides can be measured also and used as markers of synthesis.

2.2.1 Proteoglycans

Proteoglycans (PG) comprise the second largest component of the dry weight of articular cartilage. They are complex molecules comprising a central protein core to which the GAG chains, either keratan sulphate or chondroitin sulphate, are attached (Fig.5). The ratio of protein to carbohydrate is approximately 1:9. The GAGs have a high density of negatively charged ions, due to carboxyl or sulphate groups, which attract cations into the matrix to neutralise them (Fig.6). Thus a high osmotic or swelling pressure is created, leading to the matrix continually attempting to draw in water. This will occur until it is resisted by the tension arising in the fibrous network, thus establishing an equilibrium. The main proteoglycan in cartilage is aggrecan, which is a large aggregating proteoglycan. Each molecule has a molecular weight of approximately 1.5 to 2.5 million kDa, but many molecules bind to hyaluronan (HA), formally known as hyaluronic acid, creating large aggregates, hence the name. These can be enormous molecules.

There are other types of proteoglycans in cartilage, but they only constitute a small proportion. Only one other aggregating

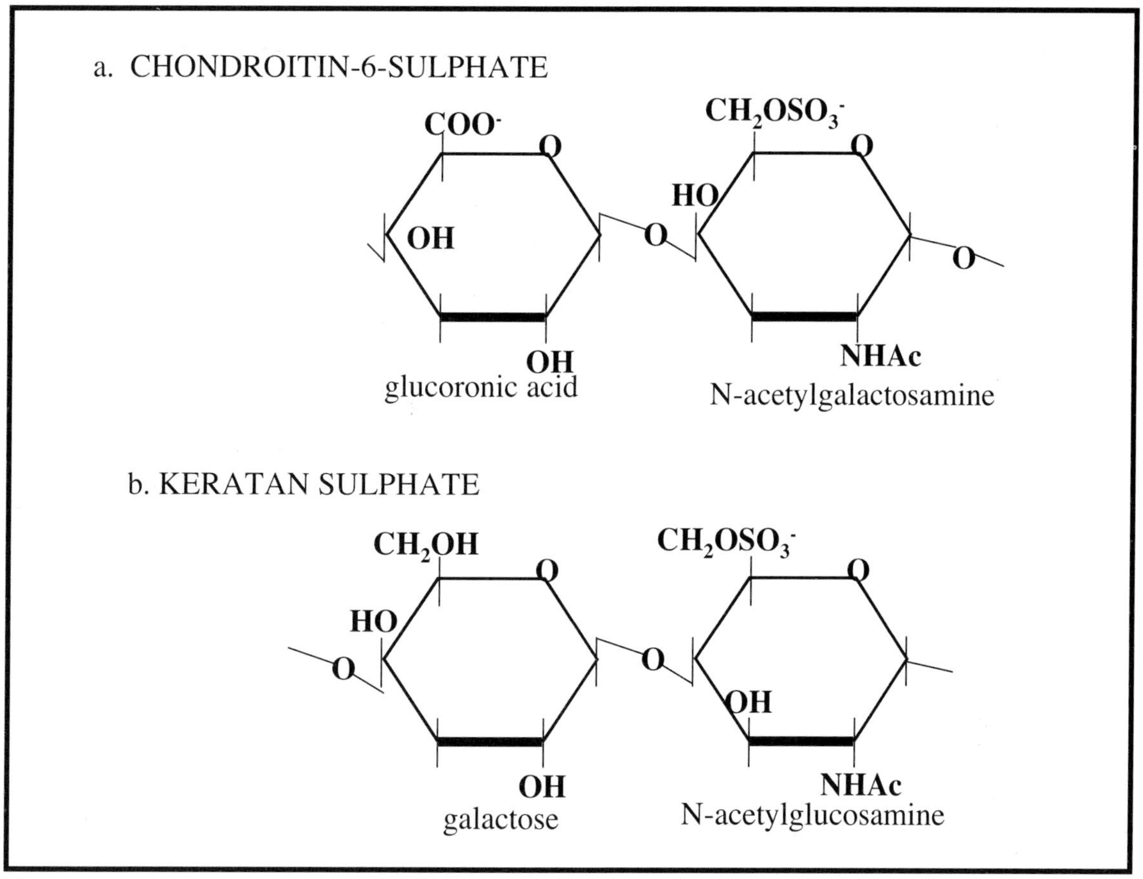

a. CHONDROITIN-6-SULPHATE

glucoronic acid   N-acetylgalactosamine

b. KERATAN SULPHATE

galactose   N-acetylglucosamine

Fig.6. Chemical composition of glycosaminoglycans in cartilage proteoglycans.

proteoglycan has been identified in cartilage to date, versican, and it is usually restricted to the upper zone. There are however, several smaller proteoglycans which are much simpler with only one or two glycosaminoglycan chains attached. These include decorin (so called because it is found "decorating" collagen fibrils), lumican, fibromodulin and biglycan. Their molecular weights are much smaller and their protein core consists of a high degree of leucine. Their functions are still being characterised but many of them appear to control collagen fibrillogenesis, their presence inhibiting the size and diameter of fibrils formed. Decorin also has the capability to bind growth factors and this may be an important function of it. More recently another proteoglycan has been identified - superficial zone protein, which occurs only at the very surface of cartilage. It may have several functions, including possibly that of lubrication since it has a mucin-like motif.

The protein component of proteoglycans is synthesised as other proteins and the carbohydrate attached in the vesicular compartment of the Golgi, the whole process, including secretion from the cell, taking only about 30 minutes. Link protein is a separate gene product from aggrecan, but is usually synthesised at a similar rate. The third component of aggrecan, HA, is synthesised at the cell membrane. Hence formation of PG aggregates only occurs in the extracellular matrix.

2.2.3 Water

Approximately 70% of articular cartilage is water, the exact amount varying with location, age etc. Because of the swelling pressure created by the glycosaminoglycans of aggrecan, the water content of cartilage generally follows trends seen in glycosaminoglycan content. A small proportion of this water is contained within the collagen fibrils (appprox 1-1.3 gm for every gm of collagen). These two fractions of water behave differently in the mechanical functioning of the tissue (section 4).

2.2.4 Minor Components

There are several other matrix molecules in cartilage which, although present in small quantities, may be important in modulating things such as cell attachment, or collagen fibre organisation or synthesis.

Some, such as fibronectin, are widespread throughout the body, whilst others such as cartilage oligomeric protein (COMP) and cartilage matrix protein are restricted more to cartilage.

3. Physico-Chemical Properties

The main function of articular cartilage is mechanical. It is able to carry out its functional role, primarily that of load bearing, dissipation of incident loads and lubrication and sliding of one surface over another, by virtue of the physico-chemical properties of its matrix.

These will be described below before going on to discuss the mechanical properties themselves.

3.1. Fixed charge density and swelling of cartilage

Physical interaction with the charged glycosaminoglycans chains in proteoglycans of cartilage occur by virtue of the requirement for electroneutrality and the electrostatic repulsion which occurs when like charges are brought together. Hence the fixed negative charges (carboxyl and sulphate groups on the GAG chains) are held at approximately 10-15Å apart in cartilage. They are restricted from repulsing each other further, and reaching their free solution volume, by the collagen network.

In the absence of the collagen it is estimated that the proteoglycans would expand to five times their volume in collagen if they had unlimited water and if they were allowed to swell freely. Normal adult cartilage has a fixed charged density of appproximately 0.05-0.2 mEq/g wet weight. Since each negative charge requires a counter ion to achieve electroneutrality, a high ionic concentration occurs in the cartilage matrix which is greater than the external bathing solution. This therefore creates an osmotic gradient between the interstitial fluid and the bathing fluid which is the physico-chemical force for cartilage to swell, and is described as the Donnan osmotic pressure. Fixed charge density therefore affects the mechanical functioning of the tissue via its influence on osmotic pressure and hence tissue hydration. In addition it is likely to influence the functioning of the cells within the matrix as they are very sensitive to concentration of ions in their environment.

3.2 Permeability and Diffusion - their influence on nutrition.

Nutrients can move through the cartilage matrix by two mechanisms: by diffusion and by entrapment in fluid that moves through the cartilage in response to changing loads. The rate of solute transport by diffusion is affected by properties of the solute, such as its molecular weight and shape. Long thin molecules, eg tropocollagen, can weave their way and diffuse faster than more globular molecules eg dextran. It is also affected by properties of the matrix through which it is moving and is hindered by the 'tortuosity' imposed by the non-aqueous components in the matrix, leading to longer diffusional path lengths.

The pore size within cartilage will obviously influence the permeability of the tissue. Since proteoglycans predominantly affect the pore size, loss of proteoglycan will diminish resistance to fluid flow and increase hydrostatic permeability. Solutes trapped within the cartilage fluid phase will move in and out of the cartilage in response to pressure gradients. It appears that the rate of transport for small solutes is much less by convection than by diffusion. For large solutes, however, convection may be more important.

4. Mechanical Properties of Cartilage

Articular cartilage is an homogeneous and anisotropic tissue by virtue of the way in which the collagen fibre network varies throughout its depth. This in turn results in differences in its mechanical properties. For example, in the superficial zone where the fibres lie parallel to the surface, the tensile strength, when tested in that plane, is greater in comparison to the matrix below in the mid and deep zones.

However, the dominant loading pattern in diarthrodial joints is compression and, in this, cartilage demonstrates flow-dependent viscoelastic behaviour. One can consider cartilage to be biphasic whereby there is a solid matrix which is porous and permeable, with an interstitial fluid phase. The two of these together form an intrinsically incompressible structure so that volume changes can only be achieved if the fluid is extruded or imbibed. This biphasic model embodies many features of poroelastic theories which have been developed from the study of soils.

5. Lubrication

There may be several factors aiding lubrication at the articular surface. Firstly the biphasic nature of the cartilage itself (a) the fluid phase of water and electrolyte and (b) the porous-solid phase of collagen and proteoglycan means the pressurization across the articular cartilage during joint loading causes the interstitial fluid to flow towards the 'leading and trailing' edges of the moving load as the joint moves. Hence a fluid-film can be created for lubrication during loading when joint pressures of up to 20MPa have been measured, resulting in fluid efflux across the surface of 1.0-10 µm/s.

Secondly ultra filtration contributes to lubrication. If a load is sustained, there will be a prolonged squeeze-film action such that the synovial fluid will be ultrafiltered across the fine collagen network at the articular surface. This will produce a concentration of very viscous hyaluronan protein gel between the articulating surfaces.

Thirdly the structure of the cartilage matrix itself may contribute to lubrication. Recently a particular type of proteoglycan, surface zone protein, has beeen identified to occur in this locality. Its molecular composition includes a region which is particularly suited to low friction lubrication.

6 Nutrition

Since adult articular cartilage has no direct blood supply of its own, it must rely for its supply of nutrients by diffusion from adjacent tissues. There are two possible routes, one being from the underlying bone. However, because of the relative impermeability of calcified matrices this is likely to be less important than from the synovial fluid bathing the surface of the articular cartilage. The synovial fluid contains approximately the same constituents as plasma but some, such as high molecular weight proteins, are at a lower concentration. Since molecules travel to the cells within the cartilage matrix mainly by diffusion concentration differences, the subsequent gradients that arise across the depth of cartilage are an important driving force for solute transport. Cellular metabolites, or waste products, are cleared by the same mechanism, with reverse gradients. The shape and size of the molecules will influence the rate of transport across the concentration gradient. Larger solutes may also reach the cell, via convection of the interstitial fluid of the cartilage which occurs during loading and the resultant creep behaviour.

Acknowledgements

Thanks to Mrs J Menage for help in the preparation of this manuscript and endless forbearance.

BIBLIOGRAPHY

1. Buckwalter, JA. (1998) Articular cartilage: injuries and potential for healing. J Orthop Sports Phys Ther 1998, 28:192-202.

2. Cohen, NP, Foster, RJ and Mow, VC. (1998) Composition and Dynamics of Articular Cartilage: Structure, Function and Maintaining Healthy State. J Orthp Sports Phys Ther 1998; 28:203-215.

3. Eyre, D. Collagen of articular cartilage. Arthritis Res 2002; 4:30-5.

4. Goldring, MB. The role of the chondrocyte in osteoarthritis. Arthritis and Rheum 2000; 43:1916-1926.

5. Hardingham, T. Articular Cartilage. In: PJ Madison editor. Oxford Textbook of Rheumatology. Oxford; 2nd edition, editors DA Isenberg, P Woo, DN Glass. Oxford Medical Publications, Oxford; Blackwell, 1997. p405-20.

6. Ratcliffe,A and Mow, VC. Articular Cartilage. In: Comper WD editor. Extracellular Matrix. Vol 1 Tissue Function. Harwood Academic,1996 pp234-302.

7. Stockwell, RA and Meachim, G. The Chondrocyte. In: Freeman MAR editor.Adult Articular Cartilage. London: Pitman Medical,1979. p69-144.

Notes

The Growth Plate

Mr A Roberts

Consultant Orthopaedic Surgeon
Robert Jones & Agnes Hunt Orthopaedic Hospital
Oswestry

Primary and secondary centres of ossification

Bones are formed by either intramembranous or enchondral ossification. Intramembranous ossification occurs in the flat bones of the skull as a result of direct transformation of mesenchymal cells into osteoblasts. The vast majority of the skeleton, however, is formed by a process of chondral proliferation, maturation and hypertrophy. A typical long bone has a central primary ossific centre and secondary ossific centres usually at each end. Early during skeletal development, the arrangement of the chondrocytes responsible for bone growth is columnar however by about 18 months post partum in the human the columnar arrangement recedes and is replaced by chondral nests in the growth zone around the secondary ossific centres.[1] The columnar arrangement persists in the growth plates of the primary centres until epiphyseal closure at skeletal maturity with chondrocytes taking about 24 hours to pass from the resting zone down to the terminal hypertrophic zone – their day of glory!

Growth plate development

During early foetal development Bone Morphogenic Proteins (BMPs) are responsible for producing the ossific centres. Noggin acts as an antagonist of BMPs and rabbit knockout studies have demonstrated that mesenchymal condensations are enlarged where BMPs act unopposed. A family of proteins known as Sox* proteins are responsible for mesenchymal cells becoming committed chondrocytes during limb bud formation. The formation of joint cavities in chondral mesenchymal condensates is induced by apoptosis promoted by GDF5†.

Noggin knockout rabbits fail to form joint cavities properly through an inhibition of GDF5 expression.[2]

Growth plates represent the interface between primary and secondary centres with a striking columnar organisation. With growth, the primary ossific centre becomes elongated and forms the diaphysis as the growth plates contribute new bone at each end in the metaphyseal region. A characteristic orientation exists where a reserve zone of stem-cell like cells on the side adjacent to the secondary centre (epiphysis) contribute cells into columns.[3] The cells within each column then proliferate and form flattened plates perpendicular to the column.

---

* *Absence of Sox9 leads to a rhizomelic deformity of curved bones known as camptomelic dysplasia. This is usually fatal.*

† *Null mutation produces acromesomelic chondrodysplasia of the Grebe and Hunter-Thompson type. Not surprisingly these GDF5 deficient phenotypes show loss of joints peripherally*

Fig. 1

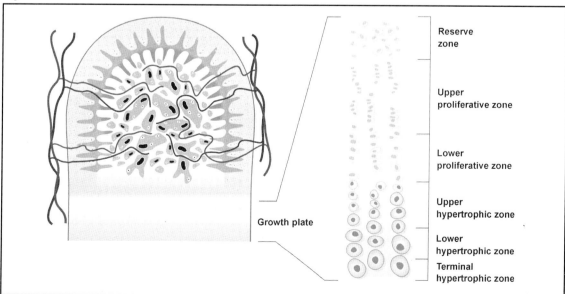

Growth plate

Reserve zone

Upper proliferative zone

Lower proliferative zone

Upper hypertrophic zone

Lower hypertrophic zone

Terminal hypertrophic zone

Local control

Further down the column the cells cease to proliferate and begin to secrete matrix material and vesicles. Sox9 and two other dependent Sox proteins (5 & 6) promote proliferation and inhibit hypertrophy. They are also essential for the production of cartilage matrix, notably collagen type II, IX and XI as well as aggrecan.[4] In the upper portion of the hypertrophic zone matrix increases progressively. It is at this point in the growth plate that matrix vesicles bud off and then become progressively separated from the hypertrophic columns by further matrix. In the middle portion of the hypertrophic zone the chondrocytes become increasingly large and there is an apparent reduction in matrix. The matrix vesicles during this time demonstrate an increase in their calcium content and become PAS positive. Type X collagen also appears around the middle of the hypertrophic zone. Separation of the primary and secondary centres occurs because of the hydraulic effect of the enlarged hypertrophic chondrocytes with the rate of growth being equivalent to the number of proliferated chondrocytes multiplied by the height of the terminal hypertrophic chondrocytes.[5]

The variation in growth is quite remarkable with intrauterine rates of 100cm/Yr slowing progressively throughout childhood with the exception of the adolescent growth spurt. In the lower hypertrophic zone the vesicles become disrupted and aggrecan and type II collagen are degraded. The calcium released from the vesicles forms the mineralised precursor of the primary trabeculae. Blood vessel invasion promoted by VEGF (see below) occurs leading to removal of the apoptotic chondrocytes. At the same time the cells become hypertrophic and rectangular.

Mechanical forces acting across the growth plate obey the Hueter-Volkmann principle[6] with a potential for significant realignment of deformity particularly in the direction of normal joint motion. The stress exerted by the physes at the knee have been calculated to be in the region of 1MPa[7] with a threshold for decompensation occurring once 4MPa has been exceeded.[8] This principle affects the proliferative zone by increasing the number of cells inserted into the top of the hypertrophic column rather than altering the height of the terminal chondrocyte. Excessive loads however do not lead to an increase but a slowdown or even cessation of growth as seen with severe angular deformity or epiphyseodesis by means of staples, plates or screws. Histologically, chronically compressed physeal plate shows an increased thickness to the hypertrophic zone with some disorganisation and a reduced thickness in the proliferative zone.[9]

A process of vascular invasion, matrix vesicle rupture and chondrocyte apoptosis characterise the edge of the growth plate adjacent to the (metaphyseal) primary ossific centre. From here on, Wolff's law[10] prevails both in the modelling of the trabeculi that initially follow the bars of calcification that result from matrix vesicle disruption as well as the cortical modelling.[11] The growth plate forms a barrier to infection as well as tumour owing to the lack of vessels penetrating the growth plate. In early life however some vessels do cross the physis including a central vessel in the distal femur that, when breached by infection, leads to a characteristic central tether and fishtail deformity where the condyles tilt inwards towards each other.

The regular nature of growth is taken for granted however the underlying mechanism producing this precision is currently unknown. Each growth plate has its own growth potential as shown by physeal transplantation studies both from one site to another in the same individual as well as from one individual to another of a different age.[12] Kember suggests that variation in the contribution of different growth plates to growth lies in the size of the proliferative zone. The size of the proliferative zone is set by the recruitment of cells from the stem-like cell reserve and the number of cell divisions allowed before maturation.[13] More recently Wilsman has highlighted the role of variation in the height of the terminal chondrocyte in explaining 40 to 50% of the variability in growth rate.[14]

Telomere restriction would offer a precise mechanism however mouse studies suggest that, in that species at least, telemorase knockout individuals have normal growth plate function even though their telomeres shorten progressively from generation to generation.[15] Speculation remains whether loss of DNA methylation or Cyclin-Dependent Kinases and their inhibitors[16] are the controlling factor in the human.

Systemic control

The progressive reduction in growth first seen by de Montbeilliard[17] when he plotted the growth of his own son ends with closure of the physis with bone replacing the whole of the plate thus connecting the epiphyseal trabecular bone with that of the metaphysis. Unlike many mammals, humans have a period of growth acceleration during sexual maturation known as the adolescent growth spurt. Sex hormones play a distinctive role in the growth spurt and closure of the epiphysis. Human mutations of either the oestrogen receptor á (ER-á)[18] or of the gene encoding for aromatase[19] lead to a continuation of growth beyond the 14 years in girls and 16 years in boys when limb growth normally ceases. The converse situation where precocious female puberty occurs does not however lead to immediate closure of the physis rather an earlier closure. It seems that the vigour of the physis in early childhood allows continued growth in spite of drive for closure from the prematurely high levels of oestrogen. It is suggested that oestrogen promotes closure indirectly by driving proliferation and thus exhausting the pool of chondrocytes contributed to the columns with ossification occurring across the physis once no further new cartilage is presented.[20]

Testosterone in the male is converted to oestrogen[21] thus promoting proliferation and advancing the end of chondrocyte production and physeal closure. Both growth hormone and insulin like growth factor (IGF-1) are increased as a result of testosterone with subsequent increases in proliferation of chondrocytes independent of testosterone's direct effect.[22,23] The effect of an increase in IGF-1 production is further intensified by upregulation of its receptor gene by testosterone. An absence of testosterone does not appear to have a direct effect on apoptosis in terminal chondrocytes but does lead to a reduction in proliferation with consequent delayed senescence of the growth plate.[24]

Systemic factors other than sex hormones influence growth and interact with the local physeal control mechanisms. Insulin like Growth Factors (IGFs) form a mediator of a number of hormones including growth hormone, glucocorticoids, insulin, leptin and sex hormones. Foetal growth mediated by IGF-I and IGF-II occurs independently of growth hormone. After birth until the adolescent growth spurt, growth hormone becomes an important driver of IGF mediated growth but absence of growth hormone does not lead to absence of growth because of all the other drivers.[25] The effect of growth hormone is predominantly seen in the proliferative zone with little effect on the hypertrophic zone. Hyperthyroidism leads to increased growth but this is predominantly due to effects on the hypertrophic zone and in particular the height of the terminal chondrocyte. Hypothyroidism leads to abnormal matrix deposition in the hypertrophic zone with disorganisation of the chondrocyte columns and an increase in vascular invasion.

Growth is reduced by glucocorticoids as a result of reduced height in the growth plate and an increase in apoptotic change in the lower hypertrophic zone. With juvenile idiopathic arthritis and transplant patients receiving large doses of glucocorticoid potential for alteration of growth is an important complication.[26]

Dramatic radiological abnormalities of the growth plate are seen in rickets underlining the importance of vitamin D in growth. Widened physeal plates with expanded cup like metaphyses characterise the macroscopic changes of vitamin D deficiency. Both 1,25 hydroxy vitamin D3 and 24,25 dihydroxy vitamin D3 act directly on the physeal chondrocyte.[27] Matrix protein elaboration and mineralization of matrix vesicles are specific effects of vitamin D. In rickets, the matrix vesicles exhibit much reduced alkaline phosphatase and metalloproteinase activity and mineralization in the lower hypertrophic zone is reduced or absent.

A complex interplay of local and systemic growth factors regulates enchondral bone development. Fibroblast growth factors (FGF) act on a family of four FGF receptors (FGFR) by binding with a heparin sulphate proteoglycan. The activated FGFR is a transmembrane structure that has tyrosine kinase activity on its intracellular aspect. FGFR3‡ is the key receptor found in the growth plate expressed in the proliferative zone. The main role for FGF is in the proliferative zone. Indian human hedgehog (Ihh)§ is a protein that is crucial in embryonic development. It is also present abundantly at the junction of the proliferative and hypertrophic zones as well as in the upper portion of the hypertrophic zone. A complex feedback loop exists between Ihh and parathyroid hormone related peptide (PTHrP), Runx2, FGFs and BMPs to maintain the position of the proliferative-hypertrophic boundary.

Parathyroid hormone-related peptide is a ubiquitous signalling factor in soft tissue and has a key role within the growth plate. Much work has focused on mouse models with increased or decreased expression of PTHrP. The parathyroid hormone/PTHrP receptor acts as a common target for parathyroid hormone and PTHrP and forms a common point where calcium homeostasis interacts with the local action of PTHrP. Mutations of PTHrP result in devastating and lethal skeletal malformations** suggesting a key role in normal function and development. It appears that mutations which cause the PTH/PTHrP receptor to be "always on" lead to short limbs with severe growth plate abnormalities and hypercalcaemia. Where mutations of PTH/PTHrP lead to a loss of function the proliferative zone within the affected growth plates is very much reduced with resultant abnormalities in ossification and limb length. Other mutations of the PTH/PTH RP receptor have been found in solitary and multiple enchondromas. Effectively, PTHrP maintains the proliferative phase of the growth plate.

‡ *A mutation in the FGFR3 gene leads to a receptor that is always on. The clinical consequence is achondroplasia. Other less common mutations of this gene result in hypochondroplasia and*

thanotrophic dwarfism. These mutations are usually spontaneous mutations of an autosomal dominant form. Homozygotes for achondroplasia are usually stillborn.

§ *Indian human hedgehog gene mutations are responsible for brachydactyly type A-1 which is autosomal dominant.*

** *Jansen's metaphyseal chondrodysplasia and Blomstrand's lethal chondrodysplasia.*

Indian human hedgehog has a similar role to PTHrP but on the hypertrophic zone acting to maintain hypertrophic chondrocytes and delayed mineralisation. Ihh induces PTHrP and PTHrP in turn delays the onset of hypertrophy and thus the expression of Ihh. BMPs and fibroblast growth factors FGFs have balanced actions on the proliferation-hypertrophy divide with BMPs stimulating proliferation and retarding hypertrophy FGFs stimulating hypertrophy and retarding proliferation. Whilst FGFs have a suppressing function on Ihh BMPs have a stimulating effect. A useful analogy is to think of a seesaw with Ihh as the pivot and proliferation on one end and hypertrophy on the other. PTHrP and BMPs favour proliferation whilst FGFs and Runx2 favour hypertrophy. The full subtleties of this mechanism have yet to be defined. Runx2 [††] is one of the Runt proteins originally thought to enable osteoblast differentiation but recently its role in the growth plate has become more widely recognised.[28] Runx2 produces expression of a number of matrix products from hypertrophic chondrocytes including collagen type X with the other Runx proteins also involved in this process.

Bone scan studies in children demonstrate the very high blood flow in the region around the growth plate and in particular on the epiphyseal side. Microscopically however the growth plate is avascular and thus a degree of hypoxia exists in the hypertrophic zone particularly in the foetal growth plate. Human tissue responds to hypoxia by means of the hypoxia-inducible factor HIF. HIF-1 is composed of an unstable á and ß sub unit. The von Hippel-Landau protein (VHL) directs the á sub unit to the proteasome for destruction but in the presence of hypoxia the sub unit binds to the nucleus leading to up regulation of genes that produce products necessary to manage the hypoxic environment, notably vascular endothelial growth factor (VEGF).

†† *Mutations leading to inactivity of Runx2 produce cleidocranial dysplasia.*

The role of the periosteum

Whilst the physis(es) is contributing to the longitudinal growth of bone, a number of factors constrain growth leading to a degree of control and defining eventual skeletal shape and proportion. The periosteum connecting the physes at each end of long bones contributes increased cortex to produce radial growth by an intramembranous mechanism to the diaphysis and metaphysis through the activity of the inner cambial layer. The outer fibrous layer however acts as a mechanical constraint on elongation. Transverse surgical incision of the periosteum adjacent to the physis leads to separation of the cut edges revealing the inherent tension in the periosteal sleeve.[29] Radial expansion of the physis is constrained by a ring of bone at the level of the growth plate first descrbed by LaCroix and by a condensation of the periosteum at the level of the growth plate termed the groove of Ranvier.[30] Further constraint occurs from muscle and ligaments as well as pressure from the growth of adjacent bones. Closure of a growth plate at one end of a long bone is associated with a small compensatory increase in growth at the other end.

Clinical Aspects

Fractures through the growth plate

Fracture occurs through the hypertrophic layer in slipped upper capital epiphysis however we are now aware of a more untidy pattern of failure of the physis in trauma. John Ogden[31] has undertaken both post mortem studies and zoological studies and shown that the classical notion of the hypertrophic zone being the single plane of a fracture is incorrect. Poland's[32] classification is of historical interest. The Salter Harris classification[33] remains the mainstay of plain radiological assessment of injuries although further extensions to accommodate crushing injuries (type V) and so called mower injuries (type VI) have been added subsequently.

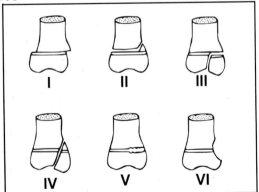

Salter Harris classification of epiphyseal injuries

1 – Benign. Often seen in young children where the growth plate is planar.

2 - Thurston-Holland metaphyseal fragment. Generally benign but may be associated with growth arrest in distal femur or tibia in the older child.3 – Articular. Requires accurate reduction (<2mm) as it is an intra-articular fracture.

4 – Tether. Requires precise reduction (0mm) as it is both intra-articular and has the potential for creating a bar between the metaphysis and the epiphysis.

5 - Crush injury can lead to 'spot welds' across the physis leading to cessation of growth but more than 10% of the surface of the growth plate has to be destroyed to lead to this.

6 – Mower. Any injury to the perichondral ring has a very high chance of leading to a unilateral cessation of growth and progressive angular deformity.

Salter Harris type IV, V and VI injuries frequently cause long term problems with either a cessation of linear growth or progressive angular deformity. Whilst linear growth loss can usually be dealt with by contra lateral epiphyseodesis an angular deformity requires either total ablation of the remaining growth plate or a resection of the tethering bony bar. Langenskiold reported the efficacy of physeal bar resection as a method of restoring growth and allowing some correction of angular deformity.[34] Full correction of a significant angular deformity requires concomitant correction of the angular deformity at the time of the release. The principle is that the bony connection between the metaphysis and epiphysis is resected and some mechanically weak but conforming substance is inserted into the defect to prevent haematoma organising into a recurrent bar. A variety of materials have been used with fat being the classical substance. Bone wax is an acceptable substitute that does not require a donor site. The growth plate should be visible as a complete ring at the site of the bar excision.

Tension across the growth plate will eventually lead to a disruption of the plate and this was thought to be a useful way of lengthening long bones without the need for an open corticotomy. The term chondrodiatasis was coined by de Bastiani.[35]

Chondrodiatasis probably does not occur in the sense that de Bastiani thought initially and if it does it does not appear to be clinically useful. The preferred term is epiphyseolysis consisting of fracture of growth plate +/- bar. With progressive distraction starting at the time of fixator application fracture occurs at 5 - 10 days. Unfortunately this leads to a high chance of premature closure restricting this technique to the last two years of growth. When compared with conventional callotasis the complications are such that it does not offer a great advantage over techniques further away from the joint.[36]

Surgical stimulation of growth can be produced by means of periosteal release. A circumferential division of the periosteum produces a 2cm growth spurt under the age of 6 years and can be repeated up to 12 years of age however it becomes less effective later on in childhood.[28] Because the growth gain is unpredictable it is very useful where the final discrepancy is large as part of a long term management strategy. Hemi-periosteal release can be used for angular correction.

Epiphyseodesis is the term reserved for surgical ablation of growth plate activity. By mimicking physeal closure it acts in a physiological fashion. Traditionally performed by an open method as described by Phemister[37] an open incision on either side of the growth plate was required with a block of bone containing the growth plate, towards one side, being removed and rotated through 180 degrees to create fusion between the epiphysis and the metaphysis. Less invasive percutaneous methods have been used recently using curettes/reamers[38] or screws (Metaizeau),[39] staples (Blount)[40] or plates (Stevens).[41] Success depends upon timing and requires the individual to have adequate potential stature. After epiphyseodesis the patient should be followed through to maturity. Successful epiphyseodesis depends on the accurate assessment of skeletal maturity. A variety of methods have been employed based on chronological age or ossific patterns at specific joints and anatomical regions. The Menelaus method has the virtue of simplicity depending on chronological age. In boys skeletal maturity is assumed to occur at 16 years of age and in girls 14 years of age. Growth at the knee during adolescence contributes 9 mm per year to the distal femur and 6 mm per year to the proximal tibia. Reasonable accuracy in predicting the timing of epiphyseodesis can be obtained by using these facts.[42]

Traditionally Green and Anderson's data from a group of Boston patients was used to demonstrate growth remaining[43] at the distal femur and proximal tibia by skeletal age as measured by the Gruelich and Pyle hand bone age atlas. Colin Moseley straightened out the Green Anderson charts and constructed a straight line method[44]. More recently Paley has published extensively on the use of growth coefficients in predicting future growth.[45]

Conclusion

Growth in long bones is a combination of enchondral and intramembranous processes. The primary ossific centre develops well-defined growth plates, usually at each end, with a columnar organisation to the chondrocytes. The secondary ossific centres have chondrocytes nest, losing the columnar organisation early during infancy. Intramembranous bone deposition is necessary to contribute circumferential growth in the metaphysis and diaphysis.

Stem-like cells in the resting zone proliferate and mature into columns of hypertrophic chondrocytes with associated matrix and vesicle production. Vascular invasion, mineralisation of matrix and apoptotic death of the terminal hypertrophic chondrocytes is followed by remodelling of primary trabeculae according to Wolff's law. A complex web of systemic and local control interacts with mechanical forces to determine the pattern of growth.

Injuries of the growth plate lead to either beneficial correction of deformity or troublesome cessation of growth or progressive angular deformity. Accurate identification of the nature of growth plate injury enables families to be counselled as to the likely effects on growth and provisional management strategies to be formulated. Assessment of bone age and progress towards skeletal maturity is generally necessary when planning physeal surgery with the objective of achieving a predictable alteration in the length at the skeletal maturity.

References

1. Ogden JA, Ganey TM, Light TR, Greene TL and Belsole RJ. Nonepiphyseal ossification and pseudoepiphysis formation. J Pediatr Orthop 1994;14: 78-82.

2. Mankin HJ. Localisation of tritiated thymidine in articular cartilage of rabbits. II. Repair in immature cartilage. J Bone Joint Surg 1962;44A:688-98.

3. Abad V, Meyers JL, Weise M, Gafni RI, Barnes KM, Nilsson O, Bacher JD, Baron J. The role of the resting zone in growth plate chondrogenesis. Endocrinology 2002;143: 1851–57.

4. Smits P, Li P, Mandel J, Zhang Z, Deng JM, Behringer R, de Crombrugghe B, Lefebvre V. The transcription factors L-Sox5 and Sox6 are essential for cartilage formation. Dev.Cell 2001;1: 277–90.

5. Walker KV, Kember NF. Cell kinetics of growth cartilage in the rat tibia. II. Measurements during ageing. Cell Tissue Kinet. 1972;5: 409–19.

6. Mehlman CT, Araghi A, Roy DR. Hyphenated history: the Hueter-Volkmann law. Am J Orthop. 1997;26 :798-800.

7. Bylski-Austrow DI, Wall EJ, Rupert MP, Roy DR, Crawford AH. Growth plate forces in the adolescent human knee: A radiographic and mechanical study of epiphyseal staples. J Pediatr Orthop 2001;21: 817-23.

8. Cook SD, Lavernia CJ, Burke SW, Skinner HB, Haddad RJ. A biomechanical analysis of the etiology of tibia vara. J Pediatr Orthop. 1983;3: 449-54.

9. Arriola F, Forriol F, Canadell J. Histomorphometric study of growth plate subjected to different mechanical conditions (compression, tension and neutralization): an experimental study in lambs. Mechanical growth plate behavior. J Pediatr Orthop B. 2001;10 :334-38.

10. Wolff J. Das Gesetz der Transformation der Knochen. Berlin; Hirschwald 1892.

11. Tanck E, Hannink G, Ruimerman R, Buma P, Burger EH and Huiskes R. Cortical bone development under the growth plate is regulated by mechanical load transfer. J Anat. 2006;208 : 73-79.

12. Stevens DG, Boyer MI, Bowen CV. Transplantation of epiphyseal plate allografts between animals of different ages. J. Pediatr. Orthop. 1999;19: 398–403.

13. Kember N. Cell Tissue Kinet Cell kinetics and the control of growth in long bones. 1978;11: 477-85.

14. Wilsman NJ, Farnum Ce, Lieferman EM, Fry M, Barreto C. differential growth by growth plates as a function of multiple parameters of chondrocyte kinetics. J Orthop Res 1996;14: 927-36.

15. Herrera E, Samper E, Martin-Cabalero J, flores JM,Lee HW, Blasco MA. Disease states associated with telomerase deficiency appear earlier in mice with short telomeres. EMBO J. 1999;18: 1950–60

16. Nilsson O, Baron J. Fundamental limits on longitudinal bown growth: growth plate senescence and epiphyseal fusion. Trends Endocr. Metab. 2004;15: 370-74

17. Scammon RE. The first seriatim study of human growth. Am J Phys Anthrop 1927;10:329-36.

Basic Science for FRCS (Trauma and Orthopaedics)

18. Smith EP, Boyd J, Frank GR, Takahashi H, Cohen RM, Specker B, Williams TC, Lubahn DB, Korach KS. Estrogen resistance caused by a mutation in the estrogen-receptor gene in a man. N. Engl. J. Med. 1994;331:1056–61.

19. Morishima A, Grumbach MM, Simpson ER, Fisher C, Qin K. Aromatase deficiency in male and female siblings caused by a novel mutation and the physiological role of estrogens. J. Clin. Endocrinol. Metab. 1995;80: 3689–98.

20. Weise M, De-Levi S, Barnes KM, Gafni RI, Abad V, Baron J. Effects of estrogen on growth plate senescence and epiphyseal fusion. Proc Natl Acad Sci U S A. 2001;98: 6871-6.

21. Frank GR. Role of estrogen and androgen in pubertal skeletal physiology. Med Pediatr Oncol. 2003;41: 217-21.

22. Phillip M, Maor G, Assa S, Silbergeld A, Segev Y. Testosterone stimulates growth of tibial epiphyseal growth plate and insulin like growth factor-1 receptor abundance in hypophysectomized and castrated rats. Endocrine 2001;16: 1-6.

23. Zung A, Phillip M, Chalew SA, Palese T, Kowarski AA, Zadik Z. Testosterone effect on growth and growth mediators of the GH-IGF-1 axis in the liver and epiphyseal growth plate of juvenile rats. J Mol Endocrinol 1999;23: 209-21.

24. Irie T, Aizawa T, Kokubun S. The role of sex hormones in the kinetics of chondrocytes in the growth plate. A study in the rabbit. J Bone Joint Surg. 2005;87B: 1278-84.

25. Philip M, Moran O, Lazar L.Growth without growth hormone. J Pediatr Endocrinol Metab. 2002; :1267-72. 15 (Suppl 5):

26. Hochberg Z, Mechanisms of steroid impairment of growth. Horm Res. 2002;58 1:33-38. (Suppl 1):

27. Boyan BD, Sylvia VL, Dean DD, Schwartz Z. 24,25(OH)2D(3) regulates cartilage and bone via autocrine and endocrine mechanisms. Steroids 2001;66: 363-74.

28. Kim IS, Otto F, Zabel B,. Mundlos S. Regulation of chondrocyte differentiation by Cbfa1. Mech. Dev. 1990;80: 159–70.

29. Wilde GP, Baker GC. Circumferential periosteal release in the treatment of children with leg-length inequality. J Bone Joint Surg Br. 1987;69: 817-21.

30. Langenskiold A: Role of the ossification groove of Ranvier in normal and pathologic bone growth: a review. J Pediatr Orthop 1998;18: 173-77

31. Ogden JA. Injury to the growth mechanisms of the immature skeleton. Skeletal Radiol. 1981;6: 237-53.

32. Poland J: Traumatic separation of the epiphyses in general. Clin Orthop 1985;41: 7-18.

33. Salter RB, Harris WR: Injuries involving the epiphyseal plate. J Bone Joint Surg 1963;45A: 587-622.

34. Langenskiold A. Partial closure of the epiphyseal plate. Principles of treatment. 1978.Clin Orthop. 1993; 297: 4-6.

35. De Bastiani G, Aldegheri R, Renzi Brivio L, Trivella G. Chondrodiatasis-controlled symmetrical distraction of the epiphyseal plate. Limb lengthening in children. J Bone Joint Surg. 1986;68: 68B: 550-6.

36. Reichel H, Haunschild M, Kruger T, Hein W. Tibial lengthening. Epiphyseal and callus distraction compared in 39 patients with 3-14 years follow-up. Acta Orthop Scand. 1996;67: 355-8.

37. Phemister D: Operative arrestment of longitudinal growth of bones in the treatment of bones in the treatment of deformities. J Bone Joint Surg. 1933; 15: 1-15.

38. Bowen JR, Johnson WJ: Percutaneous epiphysiodesis. Clin Orthop 1984;190:170-73.

39. Metaizeau JP, Wong-Chung J, Bertrand H, Pasquier P. Percutaneous epiphysiodesis using transphyseal screws (PETS). J Pediatr Orthop. 1998;18: 363-9.

40. Blount WP, Clarke GR. The classic. Control of bone growth by epiphyseal stapling. A preliminary report. Journal of Bone and Joint Surgery, July, 1949. Clin Orthop. 1971;77: 4-17.

41. Stevens PM, Pease F. Hemiepiphysiodesis for posttraumatic tibial valgus. J Pediatr Orthop. 2006;26: 385-92.

42. Little DG, Nigo L, Aiona MD. Deficiencies of current methods for the timing of epiphysiodesis. J Pediatr Orthop. 1996;16: 173-79.

43. Anderson M, Messner MB, Green WT. Distribution of lengths of the normal femur and tibia in children from one to eighteen years of age. J Bone Joint Surg. 1964;46A:1197-202.

44. Moseley CF. A straight-line graph for leg-length discrepancies. J Bone Joint Surg Am. 1977;59A: 174-9.

45. Paley D, Bhave A, Herzenberg JE, Bowen JR. Multiplier method for predicting limb-length discrepancy. J Bone Joint Surg. 2000;82A:1432-46.

Notes

Paediatric Inherited Neuromuscular Disease Presenting to Orthopaedic Surgeons

Dr. R. Quinlivan
Consultant in Paediatrics and Neuromuscular Disorders

A major breakthrough in our understanding of muscle disease was the discovery of dystrophin in 1989. This large molecular weight protein is absent in Duchenne Muscular Dystrophy (DMD) as a consequence of a deletion or mutation in the dystrophin gene at Xp21. Dystrophin was found to form part of a complex of proteins in the sarcolemmal membrane, forming the muscle fibre cytoskeleton (figure 1).

The classification of the muscular dystrophies is based upon the identification of other sarcolemmal and nuclear envelope proteins (table 1)

Inherited neuromuscular disease is relatively common affecting 1:3500 of the population, however individual conditions are rare. These conditions can present at any age. Early diagnosis is important for effective management and genetic counselling. Many patients, particularly children present initially to orthopaedic clinics.

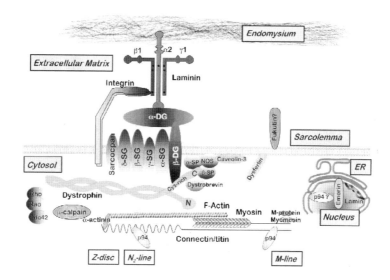

Figure 1: Sarcolemmal proteins

Table 1: Classification of Muscular Dystrophies

Condition	Gene / protein product	Inheritance
LGMD 1A	Myotilin 5q31	AD
LGMD 1B	LMNA 1q21	AD
LGMD 1C	Calveolin 3 3p25	AD
ADEDMD	LMNA 1q21	AD
FSHd	4q35	AD
DMD	Dystrophin Xp21	XR
DMD	Dystrophin Xp21	XR
EDMD	Emerin Xq28	XR
LDMD 2A	Calpain 3 15q15.1	AR
LGMD 2B	Dysferlin 2p13	AR
LGMD 2C	SG 13q12	AR
LGMD 2D	SG 17q12-q21.33	AR
LGMD 2E	SG 4q12	AR
LGMD 2F	SG 5q33	AR
LGMD 2G	Telethonin 17q12	AR
LGMD 2H	TRIM32 9q31-q34	AR
LGMD 2I	FKRP 19q13.3	AR
LGMD 2J	Titin 2q31	AR

Age and clinical features of neuromuscular disease at presentation:

♦ Neonatal: Arthrogryposis, congenital hip dysplasia, talipes
♦ Infancy: Motor delay, poor motor skills, toe walking flat feet
♦ Childhood: Pes cavus, toe walking, scoliosis, muscle weakness, clumsiness
♦ Puberty: Scoliosis, scapular winging / shoulder weakness / painful shoulders, pes cavus, muscle weakness, contractures, clumsiness
♦ Adulthood: Proximal weakness, facial weakness, distal weakness, scapular winging, muscle pains, pes cavus. Tripping over, falls

Progress:

♦ Improving: Congenital Myopathy
♦ Stable/Slowly progressive: Congenital Muscular Dystrophy(CMD), Congenital Myopathy, Spinal Muscular Atrophy (SMA), Charcot Marie Tooth Disease (CMT)
♦ Progressive: Muscular Dystrophy (Limb girdle, Becker, Duchenne, FSH), Myotonic dystrophy

Investigation:

Creatine kinase (CK)
♦ CK markedly raised in Duchenne Muscular Dystrophy (DMD), Becker Muscular Dystrophy (BMD), Limb Girdle Muscular Dystrophy (LGMD)
♦ Moderately raised: Congenital Muscular Dystrophy (CMD), Emery Dreiffuss Muscular Dystrophy (EDMD), SMA Type 3
♦ Normal or mildly raised: Congenital Myopathy, CMT, SMA 1 and 2, CMD, Fascio Scapulo Humeral Muscular Dystrophy (FSHd)

Neurophysiology:

♦ Nerve conduction slowed in type 1 CMT
♦ Motor and sensory action potentials reduced in CMT type 2. Nerve conduction is normal.
♦ Normal nerve conduction studies in SMA but denervation pattern on EMG
♦ EMG unpleasant, limit use in children to those with suspected distal SMA, Myasthenia and myotonias

Specific DNA studies availible:

♦ SMA deletion SMN gene type 1, 2 and 3
♦ DMD and BMD deletion Xp21 in 60 % cases, the remainder will have a duplication or point mutation
♦ LGMD selective DNA studies available through the NSCAG service in Newcastle.
♦ FSHD small fragment chromosome 4q
♦ CMT DNA studies available for CMT1a (PMP 22), CMT1b (MPZ) and CMT1X (CX32). There are at least 26 other genetic loci which cannot be excluded by DNA studies
♦ Myotonic Dystrophy DNA studies detect an expansion in the DMPK gene 19q13.

Muscle biopsy:

♦ H & E to detect variation in fibre size, internal nuclei, dystrophic features, vacuoles.
♦ Specific histochemical stains for sarcolemmal proteins involved in muscular dystrophies.
♦ Identification of structural defects in congenital myopathies: rods, cores, central nuclei.
♦ Electron Microscopy: identification of structural defects
♦ Metabolic studies for enzyme analysis

Duchenne Muscular Dystrophy (DMD)

Affects 1:3500 live male births, inheritance is sex linked recessive. Only boys are affected, mothers and sisters are carriers (figure 2). A frame-shift deletion in the dystrophin gene at Xp21 results in complete absence of the dystrophin protein, which can be confirmed with a muscle biopsy (figure 3). Genetic studies confirm a deletion, point mutation or duplication in the gene.

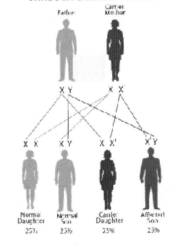

INHERITANCE OF X-LINKED RECESSIVE TRAIT THROUGH CARRIER MOTHER

Figure 2

Muscle biopsy   Dystrophin staining

Normal

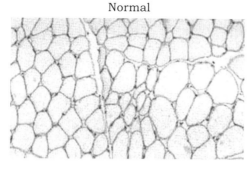

DMD Complete absence of Dystrophin

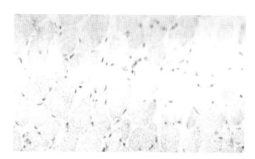

DMD

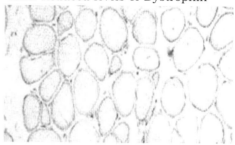

BMD Reduced levels of Dystrophin

Figure 3

Figure 4

The features include: delayed walking to 18 months or later. Affected children are unlikely to ever achieve walking, jumping or hopping. One third have learning difficulty. Presentation to the clinic is either because of motor delay and flat feet between the ages of 18 months to 3 years or later because of toe walking, clumsiness or muscle weakness usually between 5-7 years of age.

The condition is relentlessly progressive all children lose independent walking between 6-13 years, the average age to lose walking is 9.5 years. Steroid treatment commenced between 5-7 years may prolong independent walking by up to two years.

Wheelchair dependent children quickly develop contractures and rapidly progressive scoliosis requiring spinal fusion. Regular physiotherapy at all ages is essential to maintain range of joint movement. Vital capacity and cardiac function should be monitored regularly.

The mean age of death due to respiratory failure was 19 years before the introduction of non-invasive night -time ventilation (BIPAP), the mean life-expctancy is now at least 25 years and probably longer. Early intervention with ACE inhibitors may improve cardiac outcome. In all affected children, there is a risk of malignant hyperthermia with inhalational anaesthetics and muscle relaxants.

Learning point:
Check CK for every boy presenting with delayed motor development, learning difficulty or toe walking

Becker Muscular Dystrophy
Less common than DMD (prevalence is 1:28,000), the condition is milder with slower progression. Inheritance is sex-linked. The disorder is caused by an in-frame deletion in the dystrophin gene. Muscle biopsy shows a reduction in dystrophin staining (fig 4)

Presentation:

Weakness is slowly progressive, affected boys are never wheelchair dependent before 16 years of age. The condition may present with toe walking in mid-childhood. Leg pains and exercise induced myoglobinuria (red-black discolouration of the urine) are common presentations. Acute rhabdomyolysis following routine surgery is another common presentation. Otherwise the presentation is of gradual onset pelvic girdle weakness. Respiratory function is preserved in middle-age but a third may develop cardiomyopathy which is disproportionate to the muscle weakness.

Why are DMD and BMD different in presentation:

This relates to the reading frame of the gene. Normally DNA is read in groups of 3 amino acids:

THE LAW MAY LIE AND LET MEN DIE
THELAWMAYLIEANDLETMENDIE

When there is a 7 base pair deletion for example:

THE LAW MAY LIE AND LET MEN DIE

THE LAW MAE TEM END IE

The result is a nonsense mutation, which does not produce a functional protein as in DMD. This is known as a frame-shift mutation

When there is a nine base pair deletion:

THE LAW MAY LIE AND LET MEN DIE

THELAWMAYMENDIE

The result is a semi-functional protein, this is
known as an in-frame deletion.

Future potential treatment:

The use of antisense oligo-nucleides to put a "patch" on the deletion which will induce exon
skipping of the reading frame are currently undergoing phase 1 and 2 clinical trials. The objective
of treatment is to reduce the severity of the condition to a Becker phenotype by converting a
frame-shift deletion to an in-frame deletion

Notes

Notes

SKELETAL DYSPLASIA

Mr N. Kiely

Consultant Orthopaedic Surgeon
Robert Jones & Agnes Hunt Orthopaedic Hospital
Oswestry

Introduction

A skeletal dysplasia is a generalized condition affecting growth of the skeleton. The dysplasias are a diverse range of conditions that can affect the joints, epiphysis, metaphysis or diaphysis of the bone. The spine can also be involved. The aetiologies are diverse, but commonly have a recognized genetic origin. With new genetic studies, the underlying pathology of many dysplasias is becoming understood.

Presentation

Skeletal dysplasias can present with:

Presentation	Example
Short stature	Achondroplasia
Tall stature	Marfan's syndrome
Increased bone density	Osteopetrosis
Decreased bone density	Osteogenesis Imperfecta
Symmetrical limb deformity	Achondroplasia
Asymmetric limb deformity	Diaphyseal aclasis

Common conditions and Gene defects

Several conditions have a known gene defect:

CONDITION	GENE DEFECT
Achrondoplasia	FGFR3 (fibroblast growth factor receptor 3)
Pseudoachondroplasia and MED	COMP (cartilage oligomeric matrix protein)
Hereditary Multiple Exostoses	EXT 1 and 2
Leri Weil Dwarfism	SHOX Gene
Morquios- (Mucopolysaccharidosis IV)	2 Enzyme defects

One gene defect can result in several conditions or a spectrum of disease dependant on mutation.

Gene Defect	Condition
Type 2 collagen defects	Spondylo-epiphyseal Dysplasia, achondrogenesis, Stickler's syndrome; Kneist's, or premature OA hips
Sulphate transporter gene defects	Diastrophic dysplasia, Multiple Epiphyseal Dysplasia with Clubfoot
Type 1 collagen	Osteogenesis Imperfecta – very variable phenotype

An approach to the patient with a skeletal dysplasia

History

Family history
Developmental history
Symptoms- functional, pain, neurological, systemic, psychological.

Examination

Height- percentile chart.

Head circumference.

Proportion
- Proportionate or disproportionate
- rhizomelic (proximal segment), mesomelic (distal segment) , acromelic (hands and feet) shortening.

Limb alignment / length.

Hands and feet. e.g. trident hands in achondroplasia, hitchhiker thumb and clubfoot in diastrophic dysplasia.

Facial appearance. e.g. frontal bossing in achondroplasia.

Spine- kyphosis, scoliosis.

Other features. e.g. cataracts in Morquios, skin lesions in Neurofibromatosis, joint laxity in pseudoachondroplasia.
Joint movements- mobile , stiff, fixed deformity. Joint subluxations especially radial head.

Radiology

Skeletal survey- pelvis, spine including cervical spine, skull, knees, hands.

What is involved? Epiphysis, metaphysis, diaphysis or a combination.

Is the spine involved ? especially Thoraco-Lumbar junction wedging, platyspondoly, kyphosis, scoliosis.
From this information, the examiner can then give a general description of condition.

E.g. spondylo – epiphyseal dysplasia, multiple epiphyseal dysplasia.

NB is there atlanto axial instability?

Approach to treatment

The orthopaedic surgeon can only alter the secondary manifestations of the disease.
A multidisciplinary team approach is required including
Orthopaedic surgeon.
Geneticist.
Paediatrician.
ENT / ophthalmologist.
Physiotherapist.
Orthotist.

The orthopaedic surgeon can treat the following aspects
Spine- stabilize cervical spine, scoliosis correction.

Contain subluxed joints. e.g. chiari osteotomy.

Realign painful joints into a functional position. e.g. valgus femoral ostoeotmy.

Correct aligment or deformity.

Lengthen limbs- functional and cosmetic.

Notes

Notes

Fracture Healing

Professor J B Richardson, Dr S Bajada
Director, Institute of Orthopaedics, Research Fellow
Robert Jones & Agnes Hunt Orthopaedic Hospital
Oswestry

Function of Bone

Stiffness is the main function of bone. Healing is therefore the restoration of that function of stiffness (Perren). Osteoblasts have evolved to provide this highly specialised function and are adapted to the very low cyclic strain environment of the stiff skeleton. Fracture healing can be seen as the process by which this low strain environment returns.

One problem is also an advantage: following fracture there is naturally a high cyclic strain environment. Healing has therefore to proceed through a sequence of tissue formation until the cyclic strains are low enough for osteoblasts to thrive. These tissues form in a sequence of phases defined by the pattern of rising stiffness and falling cyclic micromovements at the fracture site. These dramatic change in the mechanical environment provide the cues that direct the orchestra of biological signalling.

Four Phases of Fracture Healing

John Hunter described four phases of fracture healing which I have combined with the pattern of rising stiffness to provide a biomechanical paradigm of fracture healing.

Phase 1 - Inflammation

In any injury an inflammatory phase commences with local prostaglandin release, neurologically mediated vascular changes and for fractures a pronounced cellular activity throughout the periosteum of the fractured bone. In the deep cambial layer of periosteum, osteoblasts and their precursors move out of the resting phase and begin to divide.
In the fracture thrombus, platelet derived growth factor is released (PDGF). Cytokines encourage vascular buds to form and begin to invade the fracture site.

Fetuin production by the liver falls at the time of major injury and will stay low for 2 months. Fetuin is a major system inhibitor of Bone Morphogenetic Protein type 2 (BMP2) and also interferes with the crystallisation of hydroxyapatite. Noggin acts as a local BMP inhibitor. This loss of a systemic inhibitor of fracture healing may be as important as the release of stimulant factors. In biological processes there is always a balance between stimulators and inhibitors. Other serum factors for stimulation of cell division (as yet unknown) increase in fractures that are not rigidly fixed.

Phase 2 - Growth

In phase 2 the periosteal response becomes localised to the fracture site and if the periosteum is intact then ***intramembranous*** bone is laid down adjacent to the bony cortex. Where periosteum is injured larger amounts of granulation tissue grow through the stimulation of applied cyclic micromovements. The optimum size of these movements is in the order of 1mm.

Movements result from loads being applied, and thus early activity is of use in callus growth. Rigid fixation will diminish the movements, as will the progress of callus formation. Bulky callus increases the stiffness in bending in proportion to the fourth power of its diameter

In the presence of flexible fixation, loss of pain after the first week makes it possible for increasing applied loads to maintain the level of micromovement to the level that callus stimulation is maintained. For a tibial fracture in an adult of average weight I recommend the patient is not allowed home until loads of 20 to 40Kg are applied, whether in cast, nailed or in external fixation. If there is a concern for stability, it is more logical to use a stronger method of stabilisation than to limit loading, for two reasons.

Firstly it is never possible to be sure the patient can limit their loads, particularly in the elderly and the optimistic younger patient.

Secondly, if loading is avoided then the lack of cyclic micromovement will result in small amounts of callus formation. This will lead to slow healing, and the possibility of a late failure of a fixation device. If callus forms, then this will protect the device at a later time when patients are often keen to undertake high levels of activity. This callus is also an advantage if infection supervenes. The internal fixation device (with its surface layer of Glycoclayx) can be removed and the fracture possibly be managed in a splint.

Cartilage slowly forms in a wedge shaped area at the fracture site in the process of **endochondral** bone formation, usually where the periosteum has been torn on the tension side of the injury. Periosteum can bridge the gap and in the later part of phase 2 bone will encroach from one side to the other across the fracture gap, replacing the collagen type II of cartilage with the type I necessary for bone to form. This bridging of the callus announces the end of phase 2.

Phase 3   Maturation

The high cyclic movements seen during phase 2 are replaced by increasing stiffness at the fracture site and progressive lessening of cyclic micro-movement. Osteoblasts can survive well in this environment, as they are adapted to very low strains (they are only happy with strains under 1% of their length). Increasing bulk and stiffness of callus reduces movements to allow conversion of the cartilage at the fracture site to woven bone. Calcification progresses through the release of small packets of calcium and phosphate in a precise ratio. The strict orientation and quarter offset of strands of collagen I leave spaces for calcium deposition to begin. These deposits are passed out of the cell through long processes that extend through the developing matrix. The processes remain and as the osteoblast becomes encased in calcified matrix as an

osteocyte, these extensions remain as an important communication system.

Inverted Pattern of Weight Bearing
For diaphyseal fractures is the Oswestry Weight Bearing sequence

1. Start with rest in Phase 1.
2. Insist on micromotion by weight bearing (or an applied load) in Phase 2
3. Phase 3 - Once callus growth is considered sufficient, (or stiffness > 6 Nm/degree for a tibial fracture). Then reduce weight bearing.
♦   Tell your patient to use their crutches, partial weight bearing staying at home while maturation proceeds. This will only be for 4 - 8 weeks.
♦   Stiffen the fixation device. Apply some compression to an axial fixation, check the wires of an Ilizarov are tight, consider dynamisation (Type II).
4. To allow remodelling under normal loading then Phase 4 calls for normal activity.

Phase 4   Remodelling

In this final phase the poorly organised woven bone of the final callus is remodelled back towards the normal contours of the bone. Wolff's law pertains now that the repair process has generated bone to be remodelled: cutting cones of bone remodelling units first remove woven bone then lay down Haversian canals behind. Bone is removed from areas of low stress and laid down in areas of high stress.

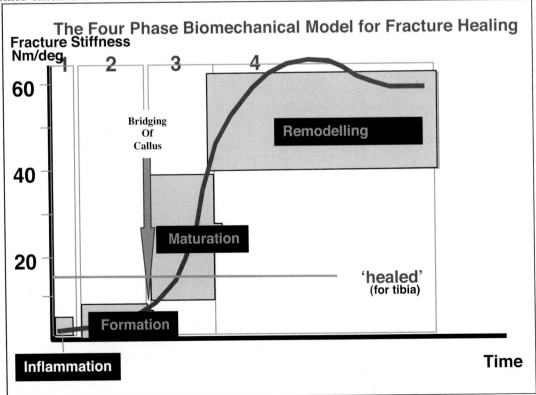

The Four Phase Biomechanical Model for Fracture Healing

The extensions that remained after calcium phosphate deposition in Phase 2 now become the communication system that allows osteocytes to continually monitor stresses in the intact bone. Gradually bone becomes more efficient in managing the loads of daily activity. This drive to efficiency was identified by Kummer to occur at every level of evolved life. In our skeletons this eventually becomes a risk as the highly remodelled skeleton can be 'caught out' in later life by unexpected directions of load that exceed the yield strength of the bone and 'osteoporotic' fractures occur.

Direct entry to Phase 4 - 'Primary Healing'

Healing is possible in phase 4 by applying a rigid environment using a plate or similar strong device. This allows direct healing by remodelling. A previous generation of Orthopaedic Surgeons argued hotly as to whether primary (rigid fixation) or secondary healing (through callus formation) was most appropriate. The implication was that these were mutually exclusive processes. One benefit of this biomechanical paradigm is to reconcile that apparent conflict as different phases of the same process. Callus is the 'biological plate' which allows remodelling and conversely a steel plate can be considered as a 'prosthetic callus' to allow healing by remodelling.

Repair is a very different process to remodelling and is the response to injury.

Remodelling is a process by which all tissues in the body are being redefined and undergo a turnover under local controls. It is repair that involves the production of new tissue.

How will you manage this fracture of the...?

Management = Assessment + Treatment

There are 889 different methods of classification of fractures in the British JBJS from 1984 to 1998. A useful classification should either predict prognosis or direct management. I have designed and used a universal system that directs management and can be used for virtually any fracture. It attempts to answer the common three questions about any fracture:

1. Is this fracture significantly displaced such that it requires reduction?
2. Will it remain reduced with conservative treatment, or will it need to be surgically stabilised?
3. Will it heal? Are there biological factors, local or general, which will significantly slow healing?

This 'Wizard of Os' will rationalise your understanding of fracture management.

Step 1. Define Displacement

A fracture healing in a particular position can be defined as functionally displaced if this leads to a functional disability for that individual. A great deal of common sense can be applied to the x-ray and clinical assessment of malalignment or mal-rotation on this basis. Evidently if a fracture is displaced then to avoid a functional disability a reduction of the fracture must be undertaken. The best way to achieve this is directed by the second step, stabilising the reduced fracture.

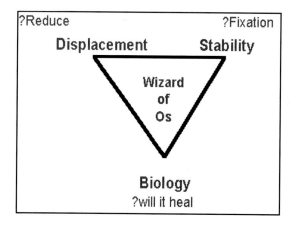

Displacement

'a fracture is significantly displaced where a functional disability will result if it heals in that position'

I chose this definition as it drives the need to clearly identify the commonest indication for reduction under anaesthesia. It is not an answer in itself, as the patient and surgeon must decide what disability is acceptable for any one fracture. Step one in fracture management can be broken down into its parts as follows:

Is there an accurate diagnosis? ABC then D and E

A methodical approach is needed, and the ABC taught by ATLS obviously takes precedence in all cases other than the 'walking wounded'. A careful examination for fracture begins with an accurate history of the injury from patient and any available observers.

With children please begin with palpation of a site that is definitely not injured with exaggerated concern so that confidence is maintained.

Test neurovascular competence distal to the injured part and remember that there may be more than one injury! One fracture masks the pain from another, and despite successful treatment of multiple major fractures, a patient with a missed little toe dislocation will find that is the thing preventing their return to work six months later!

Wounds
Even a tiny skin wound can afford entry of organisms and there may be a nutritious soup of injured avascular tissue hidden below - so for any compound wound ensure an appropriate antibiotic and tetanus prophylaxis. The best timing for antibiotic is immediately prior to injury...the closest you can get is as soon as the patient enters the accident department.

Remote Tenderness
Remotely evoked tenderness is the most useful sign of a bony injury - set yourself the test of predicting what the x-rays will show. Rib fractures can be life-threatening and you may have to depend on clinical examination as radiology may not confirm your diagnosis. Know how each projection is taken and ensure two views are taken of limbs and joints. In the shoulder arrange for your radiographers to always take an apical oblique - this is the best way of painlessly picking up a posterior dislocation, glenoid rim fractures and also confirming normal location (Richardson JB et al, 1988).

Specialised Investigations are Justified
A suspected scaphoid fracture is best diagnosed on CT or MRI and my practice is to routinely use a CT through plaster at 1 week. This confirms there is no fracture in 40% of cases and allows early rehabilitation. When the scaphoid is fractured the CT gives information on displacement so that early grafting or internal fixation can be considered.

Injuries in the hind-foot and mid-foot can similarly benefit from early CT scan and in the spine from MRI scan. If you suspect a fracture may have occurred in the cervical spine then you are duty bound to ensure that good x-rays are obtained down to T1. In any doubt discuss the x-rays with colleagues and radiologists, and ensure you get sufficient information for an accurate diagnosis.

Your patient is often young and otherwise fit. Mobilise resources and you will have a cost-effective result. Fail and that patient may need to find long-term financial support from you!

Infection
Finally, if you suspected a fracture on clinical examination, but find none on x-ray, consider infection...

Assessment of Severity of Displacement
How can one know if a disability will result from a particular displacement? Displacement must be analysed in terms of its direction, the anatomical site, and the functional requirements of the individual.

Direction
Displacement at any point can be considered as 3 rotations and 3 translations. These are in the sagittal and coronal planes, and also along the long axis of the limbs. Translations similarly are anterior/posterior, medial/lateral and shortening (rarely lengthening).

Anatomical Site: Upper v lower limb
We walk on legs within 10mm of equal length. Maintaining equal length within this range is therefore important. In the upper limb this is not nearly so important, unless perhaps the patient is an acrobat! Length becomes more important where there are two bones in parallel, such as the forearm. In the adult even a few millimetres of shortening of the radius can cause some dysfunction.

Upper limb joints and healing fractures are misnamed as 'non-weight-bearing' and therefore given different management from the lower limb fractures. The principle forces on the skeleton come from muscle action, each joint and bone being adapted to a size to give the same pressures (force per unit size or area).

Difference in the management of upper and lower limb relate more to the fact that an upper limb injury can be more protected from overuse during healing, or from sudden unexpected forces, than a lower limb. In effect, forces are more controllable, rather than intrinsically smaller.

Extra-articular Fractures
Angular deformity will affect function in the lower limb from its effects on length, knee moment and ankle angle. The level of the angulation is actually more important than the size of the angle, as there is a complex relationship between these three aspects of malunion (Wade et al, 1999).

This allowed the construction of nomograms to assess the effects of angle and level on the length, knee moment and ankle angle.

Intra-articular fractures
Alignment here has to be good as otherwise osteoarthritis can ensue. Cartilage does not heal significantly and remodelling of a step in an articular surface is only possible up to the thickness of the cartilage at that point. Gaps in the articular surface are better tolerated

and several millimetres will often cause no long-term disability.

Malalignment in a highly congruous joint such as the ankle can cause problems as a small displacement will cause a large increase in joint loading.

Functional Requirements

Each individual has different requirements. A labourer may prefer an amputation of a crushed finger tip but a musician may wish to consider prolonged reconstruction to maintain length - and do not assume an individual may not be both labourer and musician! Someone with profound neurological deficit in a limb may be safer allowing a fracture to heal with shortening, as the main requirement may be to fit in a wheelchair. A short life expectancy may remove the consideration of arthritis developing in a joint for instance.

Stability

A fracture is stable if it will not lose its position to the point of becoming displaced (or re-displaced if it has been reduced) when managed by a simple conservative method.

In many fractures this might be a plaster splint or strapping to an adjacent digit etc. It is obviously difficult to predict the future, but an educated guess regarding stability allows a decision to be made on whether fixation of a fracture is appropriate. Orthopaedics has suffered from this being a poorly defined term, being used in a different way in each of 1170 articles in the JBJS(B) from 1984 to 1998!

Displaced fractures that have to be reduced are usually unstable as they have a tendency to return to their original displacement. It is likewise true that an undisplaced fracture is unlikely to become displaced with conservative treatment unless it is subjected to a greater force than that which occurred at the original injury. (Although I accept that the displacement at the time of injury may be much greater than that shown on x-ray).

The methods of fixation are numerous and include internal and external fixation devices, but it is important to have a clear approach to fixation as this can interfere with the third part of this 'wizard', biology.

Stability of a fracture is generally due to its soft tissue attachments - and these are surprisingly strong. Plaster of Paris casts generally rely on these soft tissue attachments to maintain length as the cast can only really control angulation, not shortening.

Predicting the future

Life is not so simple when it comes to predicting the future. Allowing only yes/no answers to the questions of displacement and stability help to force a certain discipline of decision-making. Stability was based on the old teaching we had in physics at school. An object is either stable or unstable in an environment of varying loads. Of course even a stable fracture will displace further if a major force is applied - even the most careful patient can fall while under treatment.

Some fractures can not be predicted to be stable on day 1 with confidence. It is a good thing to explain the situation to the patient. Would they rather have the fracture fixed now, or check it carefully each week and perhaps avoid an operation?

These unpredictable fractures include the undisplaced lateral malleolar fracture, the isolated ulnar fracture, the reduced colles fracture. Peter Thomas uses the term 'metastable' to describe this uncertainty. The most useful thing is to try and predict the instability as it allows early decisions on management. Assess fracture stability whenever you can get the opportunity, especially under anaesthesia and with x-ray control. Study the anatomy of the soft tissue attachments as along with the direction and size of the original deforming loads, these determine how the fragments displace.

Biology

Musculoskeletal motion came under strong evolutionary pressure when fish left the sea and began to walk. Powerful evolutionary processes have evolved to return the high strength and power of the skeleton following fracture. Bones are one of the few tissues which heal by forming the original tissue. Severe generalised disease, dietary deficiency or drugs all interfere with this specialised biological process, or a local cancer. It is probable that the recommended treatment will be powerful internal fixation. A certain mental cooperation is also needed to allow the biology to succeed. At one extreme the nervous intelligent patient will appear at he clinic in their carpet slippers and be slow to weight-bear. At the other extreme there is a dictum by my colleague David Jaffray that 'nae brains equals heavy metal'. Judicious assessment of your patient and their active collaboration must be sought in fracture care.

If fixation has been undertaken and is rigid then the main drive to callus growth, cyclic micromotion, will be absent and no significant callus will form. This may have advantages, but if infection develops then there will be difficulties in removing a rigid internal device.

Methods of Stabilisation

Methods of maintaining reduction require sufficient strength to achieve this goal, but will tend to be also stiff. The stiffness will reduce cyclic micromovements at he fracture site and so reduce callus formation. A load-displacement diagram below describes the alternative types of devices.

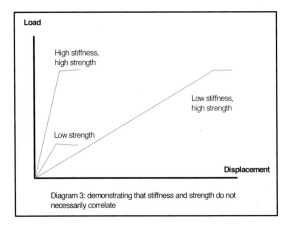

Diagram 3: demonstrating that stiffness and strength do not necessarily correlate

Combining a thick plate with compression of a transverse diaphyseal fracture provides good stability (reduction will not be lost) at the expense of high stiffness. Only minimal amounts of external callus will form and healing is slow through remodelling. Delaying fixation for two or three weeks will allow some of the stimulus for callus formation to have developed and this is the rationale for delayed internal fixation.

A heavy plate across a comminuted fracture with care to avoid degloving of the periosteum is promoted as **'biological plating'** and can work well if the biology is good and early mobilisation is encouraged. Further developments by Tepic of the AO group have been to make unicortical locking screws and plates that interfere as little as possible with venous drainage from the fracture site.

A flexible nail for the same fracture has the theoretical benefit of providing the same stability with a lower stiffness, so that healing is more likely to be through callus growth. Unilateral external fixation devices are relatively stiff and best used with applied movement. Orthofix have provided a device for this, the pro-callus, which produces 1mm of micromovement at the fracture site. This is particularly useful if a patient is unable to walk, or simply nervous of mobilising in weeks 2 to 6 after injury.

Circular frames with thin wire fixation have low axial stiffness but high strength and allow excellent axial micromovement, although care has to be taken to minimise soft tissue transfixion, and it may be difficult for the patient to use the limb in a functional way.

Casts do not provide significant axial stiffness, and provide stability (avoiding loss of reduction) largely by preventing angulation and mal-rotation. Axial stability depends either on a transverse fracture site or good residual soft tissue attachment.

Traction is generally an excellent way of maintaining reduction while allowing the greatest possible axial movements and a femoral fracture will piston 10 to 20mm in this situation and generate the largest possible volumes of callus. There are however costs both to the health service and also the individual which have limited this very safe method of treatment.

Fracture Site Cyclic Micromovements

Movement = Load
                    Stiffness

Cyclic Micromovement at the fracture site is a function of both stiffness and applied load, and the stiffness of the fracture site depends very much on the distribution of fixation material and bony contact at the fracture site. Thus an 'unreamed' nail may allow more movement because it is narrower but also because it is not a tight fit in the canal. A titanium nail will be less rigid than a stainless steel one. Distraction of the fracture site will reduce local strain at the fracture site by increasing the distance over which a movement is distributed (Strain is the percentage change in original length). Also there is the possibility of pre-stressing the fracture site in tension and so reduce micromovement.

Finally the amount of load applied in the early weeks following injury is the major determinant of micromovement and the no patient must be allowed discharge from hospital until they are weight-bearing. In my practice a load of 20Kg measured on a bathroom scale is the minimum for any lower limb fracture where callus growth is sought, and this will be sufficient for fixation by nail, external fixation or in cast. If there is concern that the fracture may be unstable with this load, then the method of fixation is not adequate.

An upper limit to the amount of weight depends on many factors, but for a tibial fracture the strongest predictor of the speed of union in my studies is the amount of weight-bearing at 6 weeks. After this point, or when a sufficient volume of callus has developed, and bridging is about to occur, then micromovements at the fracture site must be diminished. Reducing active use of the limb for 4 weeks will allow the appropriate biomechanical environment for the maturation process. Also the possibility of device failure (and pin loosening in external fixation) is reduced at patients are often keen to be very active at this stage and fatigue failure is a result of both high loads and a large number of applied cycles.

In a fracture of a joint surface then very accurate reduction is a priority of management and rarely is external callus required. In this circumstance accurate reduction and rigid fixation with systems of plates and screws is appropriate. Joint movement can then be encouraged. I find that concentrating on one maximal range of movement per day is sufficient to obtain a good range of movement in severe injuries.

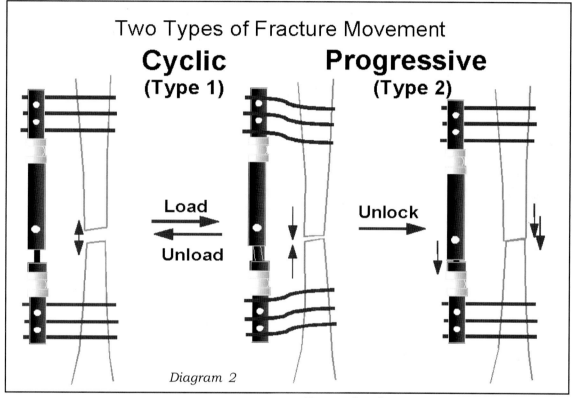

Diagram 2

This inverted pattern of loading can be augmented by unlocking an external fixator column or by removing locking screws from a nail (if the fracture is not transverse). Management of a hypertrophic non-union may be by applying external fixation in distraction or in compression, or by applying a heavy plate. The principle benefit of compression is simply to reduce the micromotion in the maturation or third phase of healing, although a secondary effect may be to promote calcification by providing a net compression across the tissue.

Controlling fracture site movement is the goal of fracture fixation and its aims are both to maintain reduction but allow cyclic micromovements where appropriate to generate callus. In a shaft fracture the production of callus is a very safe way to achieve union as if infection should ensue for then implant removal does not greatly compromise healing.

Dynamisation

Dynamisation is a rather sexy term. It is quoted in JBJS(B) in 367 articles between 1984 and 1998. De Bastiani was a physiologist and then Professor of Orthopaedics at Verona, Italy. He developed a method of using an external fixator where the axial loads taken by the fixator were reduced after callus formation by unlocking a central locking nut on the fixator. This allows the fracture to carry more normal loads, the fracture gap to close, and generally the cyclic movements at the fracture to decrease. This action is similar to removing the locking screws of a nail or using a sliding screw in a Dynamic Hip Screw (Dynamisation type II). Dynamos simply means 'force' and was the basis of the Italian use of the term.

A quite different type of Dynamisation (type I) is that developed by Kenwright and Goodship of applying cyclic loading of around 1mm at the fracture site of the tibia on a daily basis (Diagram 2).

This dose of micromovement speeded healing by 25% in a prospective randomised controlled trial of tibial fractures I ran when a research fellow at Oxford.

So this is the problem: Dynamisation is used to describe both types of movement.

- Type I - cyclic micromovement and
- Type II - progressive axial translation.

Cyclic vs. progressive movements

These two types of movement exist throughout orthopaedic clinical practice: cyclic movements and progressive ones. Immobilisation reduces cyclic and stabilisation controls progressive ones. If these two types of movement are not dealt with separately, then confusion reigns. A ship at anchor may move up and down with the waves - this is cyclic movement. If it drags the anchor, then a progressive displacement has occurred.

Dynamisation Type II

Unlocking a nail once bridging callus has formed has not been proven to be of benefit (although theoretically appropriate if the fracture surfaces prevent rotation around the nail). Unlocking a nail when fracture healing is slow and multifragemntary may be a disaster if severe shortening results.
Unlocking a unilateral fixator such as the Orthofix may reduce micromovement and encourage consolidation. (Richardson et al., 1995). The initial healing steps need to have happened, and then osteoblasts will thrive if micromotions are reduced below local strain of 1%.
Applying a compression plate to a hypertrophic non-union is a good example of the benefits of reducing micromotion in the presence of sufficient callus. I find these patients will have the most predictably successful outcome for their non-union.

New Advances - Mesenchymal Stem Cells

Tissue engineering is allowing the regeneration of cartilage as you will see in the chapter by Graham Smith. Mesenchymal stem cells cultured from bone marrow offer similar opportunities. I am fortunate at Oswestry in having the help of Paul Harrison and his team to provide the only NHS facility for culture of these cells. A randomised trial using this technique run by the Problem Fracture Service at Oswestry has a success rate of 11 non-unions healed out of 12, and these are all cases where several previous procedures have failed, including failure of BMP in 3 patients.

Mesenchymal Stem Cells (MSC)

Stem cells by definition have a capacity for self-renewal giving rise to more stem cells for long periods, and the ability of differentiation into tissues of different lineages under appropriate conditions. Adult stem cells are lower in the hierarchy of stem cells but maintain their differentiation potential throughout the life of the organism. Progenitor cells are derived from stem cells; they retain the differentiation potential and high proliferation capability, but they have lost the self-replication property. Mesenchymal stem cells are multipotent progenitor cells which are capable of differentiating into several connective tissue cells types, including osteocytes, chondrocytes, adipocytes, tenocytes and myocytes[1,2]. The argument for using stem cells to augment fracture healing is simply that these cells are what build bone or re-unite them - "Cells form bone" - so use them.

The first option is to stimulate stem cells present at the fracture site. The presence of osteogenic proteins in bone capable of inducing the formation of endochondral bone, was first described in 1965 by Urist. Bone-inductive proteins, present in the matrix of demineralised bone, have been shown to cause the differentiation and proliferation of mesenchymal stem cells to chondrogenic and osteogenic cells which are capable of participating in bony repair and osseous regeneration. In vivo studies have shown that bone morphogenetic proteins (BMPs), transforming growth factor (TGF) beta, insulin-like growth factor (IGF), fibroblast growth factor (FGF), platelet derived growth factor (PDGF) and vascular endothelial growth factor (VEGF) are all present during normal healing of fractures.
In addition to these agents, various hormones such as growth hormone and parathyroid hormone (PTH) have an effect on the repair of fractures. Growth hormone was shown to increase the ultimate load, stiffness and callus in a model of fracture repair. Statins have showed a potential to affect the healing of fractures; they showed induction of BMP-2 and VEGF in repair models[3]. These osteoinductive agents can have a clinical application in simple closed fractures, delayed healing, non-union or regeneration of large segmental defects. There is particular interest in the potential role of BMP-2 and BMP-7; both have been isolated, sequenced and synthesized using recombinant DNA technology. Recombinant human BMP-2 (rhBMP-2) and osteogenic protein-1 (rhBMP-7) have been used successfully to heal critical-sized defects in both the appendicular and the craniomaxillofacial skeleton in various animal

speices[4]. The use of growth factors in non-unions was studied; models of non-unions have demonstrated the influence of growth factors on their receptors and blood vessels which are present in varying degrees in the fracture gap, but not necessarily in the correct temporal and spatial arrangement. Also studies demonstrated that all components of the BMP-signalling pathway are present in the micro-environment of delayed unions and nonunons[5].

Even though growth factors have been demonstrated in trials to have a beneficial effect on the healing of non-unions and critically sized bone defects in humans, there is a need to use supra-physiologic doses of osteogenic factors to achieve success when compared to animal models[6,7]. This discrepancy between animal models and humans could be attributed to differences in numbers of responding cells and residence time of osteogenic factors. Higher doses in humans are thought to be required to maintain physiologic levels of osteogenic factors for the longer period of time required to recruit sufficient cells into the repair compared with those required in animal models.

The second option is to add cells to the fracture site. They can then produce the full range of osteogenic proteins needed for fracture healing. Cell based clinical therapies using MSC should involve a tissue-engineering approach in which MSC are incorporated into three-dimensional (3-D) scaffolds for the replacement of *in vivo* tissues with or without the use of osteoinductive agents. Each tissue and site requires a different 3-D scaffold and a different approach. The best appropriate scaffold for the different tissues still needs to be defined but a consensus regarding the properties needed is present. Caplan; 2005 states that the scaffold must[8]:

1. Allow for and encourage cell attachment.
2. Be porous for abundant and specialized extracellular matrix.
3. Allow bioactive molecules to have access to the cells.
4. Integrate into the neo-tissue or silently disappear.
5. Provide some cellular cueing.
6. Be mechanically sensitive to the site.

It is clear that successful bone tissue engineering will depend on an appropriate mechanical environment. A synergy between biological and physical stimuli will further enhance the effectiveness of tissue engineering strategies. Mechanical environment modulation can be successful applied to control the release of signalling molecules associated with fracture healing. Osteoblasts and osteocytes respond to fluid shear in vitro by increasing producing of nitric oxide, TGF-beta and prostaglandins. Electomagnetic field (EMF) is thought to cause fluid shear stress and electric potentials. *In vitro* exposure of osteoblasts to EMF induced secretion of growth factors including BMP-2, TGF-beta and insulin like growth factor-II. *In vitro* low intensity US LIUS stimulates expression of numerous genes involved in the fracture healing including aggrecan, IGF and TGF-Beta. Cellular attachment can also be amplified by specific physical cues. Integrin mediated attachment is vital for osteoblast and progenitor cell survival. It causes cytoskeletal rearrangement inducing mitogenesis to cellular proliferation anddifferentiation. Integrin attachment also inhibits cellular apoptosis. Osteoblasts were shown to alter their cytoskeleton, adhesion molecules and extracellular matrix due to strain forces in vitro[9]. LIUS was shown to upregulate integrin mediated attachment to several scaffolds. This leads to a possibility to enhance MSC integrin mediated attachment tissue-engineering scaffolds by prior ultrasound stimulation through integrin attachment.

Conclusion

Fracture healing is essentially all about reducing the cyclic micromotions - and yet as John Hunter explained, 'fractures heal by a species of necessity', and so the second phase of fracture healing does need micromotion.

References

Richardson J.B. Ramsay A Davidson JK Kelly IG. Radiographs in Shoulder Trauma. J Bone Joint Surg. (1988.) 457-60. 70B:

Kenwright J. Richardson J.B. Cunningham J.L. White S.H. Goodship A.E. Adams M.A. Magnussen P.A. Newman J.H. Axial Movement and Tibial Fractures. A Controlled Randomised Trial of Treatment. J Bone Joint Surg 1991; 73B: 654-59.

Perren S.M. Rahn B.A. Biomechanics of Fracture Healing Can J Surg. 1980; 23: 228 - 32.

Richardson J.B. Gardner T.N. Hardy J.R. Evans M. Kuiper J.H. Kenwright J. Dynamisation of Tibial Fractures. J Bone Joint Surg 1995; 77B: 412-6.

Wade R.H. New A.M.R. Tselentakis G. Kuiper J.H. Roberts A. Richardson J.B.Malunion in the Lower Limb - A Nomogram to Predict the Effects of Osteotomy. J Bone Joint Surg 1999; 81B: 312-16.

Richardson J.B. Cunningham J.L. Goodship A.E. O'Connor B.T. Kenwright J. Measuring Stiffness Can Define Healing of Tibial Fractures J Bone Joint Surg 1994; 76B: 389-94.

1. Friedenstein AJ, Piatetzky-Shapiro II, Petrakova KV. Osteogenesis in transplants of bone marrow cells. J Embryol Exp Morphol 1966;16: 381-90.

2. Caplan AI. Mesenchymal Stem Cells. J Orthop Res 1991;9:641-50.

3. Simpson AHRW, Mills L, Noble B. The role of growth factors and related agents in accelerating fracture healing. J Bone Joint Surg 2006; 88B: 701-5.

4. Cook SD, Wolfe MW, Salkeld SL, Rueger DC. Effect of recombinant human osteogenic protein-1 on healing of segmental defects in non-human primates. J Bone Joint Surg 1995;77A: 734-50.

5. Kloen P, Steven B, Gordon E, Rubel IF et al. Expression and activation of the BMP-signaling components in human fracture nonunions. J Bone Joint Surg 2002;84A: 1909-18.

6. Geesink RG, Hoefnagels NH, Bulstra SK. Osteogenic activity of OP-1 bone morphogenetic protein (BMP-7) in human fibular defect. J Bone Joint Surg 1999;81A: 710-8.

7. Friedlaender GE, Perry CR, Cole JD, Cook SD et al. Osteogenic protein-1 (bone morphogenetic protein-7) in the treatment of tibial nonunions. J Bone Joint Surg 2001;83A: (Suppl 1);S151-8.

8. Caplan AI. Mesenchymal Stem Cells: Cell-based reconstructive therapy in orthopaedics. Tissue Engineering 2005;11:1198-1211.

9. Mazzini MC, Toma CS, Schaffer JL et al. Osteoblast cytoskeletal modulation in response to mechanical strain in vitro. J Orthop Res 1998;16: 170-80.

Traction

Professor J B Richardson
Director, The Institute of Orthopaedics
Robert Jones & Agnes Hunt Orthopaedic Hospital
Oswestry

Each force has an equal and opposite reaction. Thus application of a force equal to the deforming forces at a fracture site will result in the reduction of its displacements and provide stability.

Traction is one of the original methods of fracture management. In a thesis on the subject of treating femoral fractures in the mid-nineteenth century, Lane (*not Arbuthnott*) detailed the techniques of traction. He also discussed and used recent innovations such as suture with silver wire. For him, the introduction of plaster-of-Paris was new and unproven. Thus traction can be considered the original and safe option for treating fractures.

Different types of traction have been developed, and each case requires appropriate traction loads. In gallows traction the child's own weight provides the force for reduction of the fracture, and skin traction is sufficient for these loads. In a young adult the initial muscle spasm requires 15 pounds of traction. From the third week the spasm ceases and muscle atrophies, so loads can be reduced to 10 pounds or so. Evidently the load can be titrated in each case to achieve sufficient reduction.

Daily care and attention is needed for the patient in traction. All pressure points have to be checked. Skin traction should be re-applied daily. Muscle exercises are important, as a lot of muscle atrophy will occur. Exercises also help apply the cyclic micromovements that stimulate callus formation.

Gallows Traction

Used in children up to two years of age for femoral fractures.

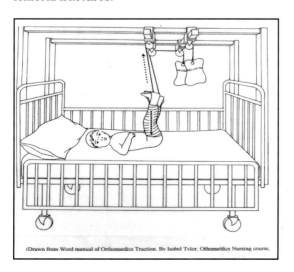

(Drawn from Word manual of Orthopaedics Traction. By Isobel Taylor. Othopaedics Nursing course.)

Thomas Splint

Developed by Hugh Owen Thomas for treatment of a variety of lower limb disorders. His nephew Robert Jones was in charge of medical services in the First World War and made use of the splint for compound femoral fractures. In North Africa, during the Second World War, they were used at Tobruk for transport by wrapping the splint in plaster cast.

The splint can be used as fixed traction where the counter force is taken as pressure on the ischium. In this mode the patient can be transported.

In sliding traction the traction in applied to the femur and the splint is there only as a resting splint.

In combined mode the fixed traction system is pulled away from the ischium by loads applied to the splint

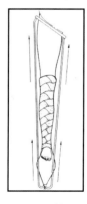

Hamilton-Russell Traction

This traction is useful resting traction following hip revision or similar procedures. It is cleverly designed to produce a vector of traction in the line of the femur, as shown in the diagram.

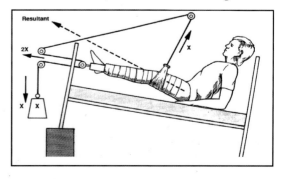

Perkins Traction

Perkins advocated the functional management of fractures and understood how micromovements could produce abundant callus growth. Traction is applied by a Steinmann pin and a special bed is used where the lower part of the mattress can be dropped or removed. Patients are encouraged to sit up and exercise the leg. It is widely used for the large numbers of femoral fractures in Africa where healing has been described at an average of 9 weeks.

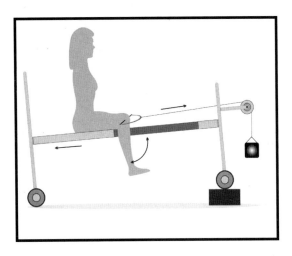

Skull Traction

Cones Callipers are applied by making a small skin incision under local anaesthetic, 1 inch above the top of the ear. They apply a controlled pressure by use of a torque screwdriver that allows the outer table of the skull only to be penetrated. A unifacet dislocation of the cervical spine may need high loads to be applied, but care must be taken where the injury is ligamentous, as wide separation of the vertebrae may be possible with only low loads.

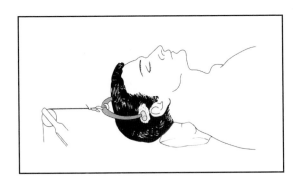

Dunlop Traction

Straight-arm traction is a very safe way to manage supracondylar fractures of the humerus in children. In traditional Dunlop traction a weight is applied as counter traction to the humerus. This can slip into the antecubital fossa and cause vascular problems, so I advise against this option.

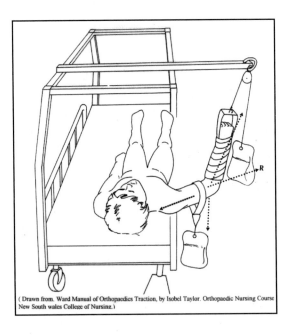

(Drawn from. Ward Manual of Orthopaedics Traction, by Isobel Taylor. Orthopaedic Nursing Course New South wales College of Nursing.)

Basic Science for FRCS (Trauma and Orthopaedics)

Notes

Notes

BONE GRAFTING
W.J. Ribbans
S.A.I. Chinchanwala
Northampton General Hospital

INTRODUCTION

Bone grafting is one of the oldest methods of reconstruction in orthopaedic surgery and represents the second most frequently transplanted tissue after blood.

In the U.S.A., over 426,000 bone grafts or bone implant procedures are undertaken each year (Boyce, 1999);

- 58% autografts
- 34% allografts
- 8% bone graft substitutes

Despite a familiarity with the application of bone grafting in clinical practice, there remains incomplete understanding concerning its subsequent action at molecular level.

Friedlander (1987) wrote: "The physiological and biological events that are crucial to the process of incorporation and the mechanisms that control these actions are crucial to the process of incorporation. Furthermore, the principles that maximise efficacy of bone grafts as well as circumstances that detract from their full potential may not be widely appreciated".

HISTORICAL PERSPECTIVE

- **Ancient Greeks:**
Understood that bone had considerable potential for healing
- **Europe 17th Century:**
Job van Meek'ren (Dutch surgeon, 1668) filled a small defect in the skull of a Russian soldier using a canine calvaria. The operation was a success - but the church would not recognise the graft as a Christian method of treatment. The implant was removed 2 years later under threat of ex-communication !
- **Europe 19th Century:**
Phillipe von Walther (1821) filled a cranial defect with autograft - unfortunately, patient developed osteomyelitis.

Ollier (1867) championed the concept of periosteum as "mother of bone". He beleived that bone and periosteum remained viable following grafting and that both contributed to the formation of new bone.

Barth (1893) challenged Ollier's theory. He beleived autogenous bone and periosteum died when transplanted and only adjacent cells of host contributed to osteoneogenesis. He thought donor cells merely acted as a scaffold on which new bone was built by host. Barth first used the term, "Creeping Substitution", but described only cortical surface resorption rather than complete necrotic bone resorption and its replacement with viable new bone.

MacEwen in Glasgow developed aseptic techniques and studied bone healing in dogs.He successfully treated a sequestered humerus. He transplanted wedges taken at the time of closing distal femoral osteotomies of four patients into the upper arm of a young girl.

- **America 19th Century:**
Senn (1899) used acid-treated antiseptic decalcified ox bone in the healing of osteomyelitis and other bone deformities.
- **20th Century:**
Axhausen (1909) described the fate of autogenous bone graft as we currently understand it.
He believed:

- Donor inner cambium layer of periosteum survives.
- Donor bone undergoes necrosis
- Need for intimacy between graft and vascular host tissue
- Necrotic bone resorbed and replaced by new tissues moving along channels made by invasive host blood vessels. Axhausen referred to this as "Schleichender Ersatz", which has been translated into creeping substitution.

By the early 20th century, the technique of bone grafting had become firmly established.

Albee (1923) reported 3,000 successful bone-grafting operations.

Urist (1965) first described the results of implanting lyophilized segments of bone matrix and the subsequent formation of bone matrix. Since then the osteoinductive potential of bone matrix has become well established.

CLASSIFICATION OF BONE GRAFTS

Bone grafts can be classified in a number of different ways. Since each of these factors will influence the subsequent biological, immunological and biomechanical properties of the graft, it is necessary to clearly state the type of graft being used in any communication.

TYPE	EXAMPLES
Tissue Composition	Cortical
	Cancellous
	Cortico-cancellous.
Anatomical	Donorsite
	Geometric configuration orthoptic(anatomically appropriate)heterotopic (anatomically inappropriate).
Genetic background	
	Autograft: between sites in same individual
	Isograft: between genetically identical individuals
	Allograft: between members of the same species
	Xenograft: between memebers of different species

Blood-supply	Vascularised
	Non-vascularised
Preservation method	Fresh
	Freeze dried
	Deep-frozen
Any additional chemical or physical manipulation	Irradiated
	Demineralised
	Chemical processing e.g. ethylene oxide, DMSO

GENERAL PRINCIPLES

Graft Function

Graft functions are either mechanical or biological. The two functions are often intimately related.

Mechanical functions of bone graft include:

♦ reconstruction and replacement of the skeletal defects,
♦ augmentation of fracture repair,
♦ augmenting arthrodeses,
♦ filling of defects after the excision of bone tumours.

Biological function refers to bone healing. The net biological activity of a graft is the summation of:

♦ Inherent biological activity (living cells and products)
♦ Capacity to activate surrounding tissues (mediated by bioactive factors)
♦ Ability to support the ingrowth of host tissue
♦ Structural integrity

In summary, bone graft expresses its activities through a combination of osteogenesis, osteoinduction, osteoconduction and structural integrity.

Graft Incorporation

Incorporation is the process by which host and donor material are united. It can occur regardless of the latter's origin and the amount of envelopment and admixture of necrotic and viable new bone.

It is dependent upon;

♦ Graft's biological properties
♦ Responsiveness of the host bed
♦ Graft fixation stability
♦ Graft mechanical loading

The success of incorporation of the graft can be gauged as the subsequent ability to function as well as the original surrounding tissue.

Osteogenesis

Osteogenesis refers to the bone formation with no indication of cellular origin. This may be of graft or host origin. Cancellous bone, with its large surface area covered by quiescent lining cells or active osteoblasts, has greater potential for new bone formation than cortical bone. Simplified, osteogenesis refers to augmentation of bone formation.

Osteoinduction

Osteoinduction refers to the recruitment from the surrounding bed of mesenchymal-type cells, which then differentiate into cartilage forming and bone forming cells.

Osteoinduction is mediated by graft-derived factors. Demineralised bone matrix (DBM) is osteoinductive. The agents responsible for osteoinduction include:

♦ Bone morphogenic proteins (BMP)
♦ Transforming growth factor beta (TGFß)
♦ Insulin-like growth Factor 1 & 2
♦ Acidic and basic fibroplast growth factors
♦ Platelet derived growth factor (PDGF)
♦ Interleukins

Bone morphogenic proteins deserve a special mention as much has been written about them. They were first described by Marshall Urist in 1965. BMP's are low molecular weight proteins that initiate endochondral bone formation, presumably by stimulating local progenitor cells of osteoblast lineage, and by enhancing bone collagen synthesis. Thirteen BMPs designated as BMP-1 through BMP-13, have been identified and each probably has a different target and effect. Each BMP probably acts on several cell types in the cascade. BMP-1 is a procallagen proteinase. BMP-2 and BMP-7 (OP-1) are the most investigated growth factors. There is plenty of animal data available and prospective human studies are underway.

There are at least forty BMP-like molecules within the TGFß super-family.

Biological Principles of Osteoinduction

Burwell (1964)

For new bone to be laid onto autograft, it needs:

a) Osteoblasts on surface of graft
b) Primitive osteogenic cells contained within marrow

Postulated:

Graft Necrosis>>	Osteo-inductive substances >>> released	Differentiation of reticulo- >>> endothelial cells into osteogenic cells	R-E cells also released osteo-inductive substances on death

Types of Osteogenic Precursor Cells:

Type	Name	Site and Action	Induction
D.O.P.C.	Determined Osteogenic Precursor cell	Found on bone surfaces and marrow. Differentiates into osteoblast	No inducing agent needed
I.O.P.C.	Iducible Osteogenic Precursor Cell	Mesenchymal cell capable of differentiating into osteoblast	Only in presence of inducing agent

3 Phases of Osteoinduction (Reddi, 1987):

Phase	Activity
Chemotaxis	Direct migration of cells in response to chemical gradient
Mitosis	Proliferation of newly attached mesenchymal cells
Differentiation	Cartilage differentiates >Vascular invasion >Bone differentiates

Contribution of Individual Substances to Osteoinductive Process

Substance	Activity
B.M.P.	Stimulates I.O.P.C. More easily released from demineralised bone than mineralised bone
Collagen	Provides structural framework for mineralisation. Collagen surface provides nucleation sites for mineral deposition
Osteonectin	Non-collagen matrix protein. Stimulates hydroxyapatite crystal deposition
Fibronectin	Matrix and cell membrane protein. Made by platelets, myofibroblasts and fibroblasts. Chemotactic and Mitogenic Binds mesenchymal cells to collagen matrix. Brings osteoinductors into contact with cell surface receptors.
Osteocalcin	Increases bone turnover, ? Chemotactic for osteoclasts and monocytes.

Osteoconduction

Osteoconduction refers to the three-dimensional process of ingrowth of sprouting capillaries, perivascular tissue and osteoprogenitor cells from the recipient bed into the structure of the graft. This may be an active or a passive process (most cortical allografts). Simplified, the graft functions as a result of a trellis, or a scaffold, for the ingrowth of new host bone.

Ideal Donor Graft

Possesses maximum osteogenic, osteoinductive and osteoconductive capacity.

"Gold Standard"

Autograft represents the "gold standard" for the evaluation of other potential donor materials.
Try to characterise the potential of all grafts, or graft substitutes, in terms of their precise contribution to bone forming mechanism.

AUTOGRAFTS

Non-vascularised Autogenous Bone

Autogenous cancellous bone is robustly osteogenic, easily revascularised and quickly enhances new bone formation. Autograft exhibits three of the four activities previously mentioned:

- hydroxyapatite and collagen elements are osteoconductive,

- stromal cells are osteogenic,

- growth factors, including BMP, are osteoconductive.

Autograft does not provide structural support but contributes to stability by the rapidity of its osteogenic potential. In other words, it rapidly changes.

The major site of autogenous cancellous bone is the iliac crest. This is associated with significant morbidity, as shown by numerous papers in the literature. The other disadvantages of autogenous cancellous graft include the limited quantity available, increased anaesthetic time and increased blood loss.

The biological activity results from its histocompatability, the large surface area covered with osteoblasts and their precursors, and the trabecular architecture.

Minced and morcellised autogenous cortical bone is not as biologically active but, when mixed with cancellous bone, helps extend the volume of the graft material.

The main advantage of non-vascularised cortical autograft is structural support.

Autograft Incorporation

When an autogenous bone graft is transplanted, there are 2 distinct phases:

Phase 1   0-2 weeks.
Analogous to fracture healing. Little difference between cortical and cancellous bone

Phase 2   2 weeks
Important differences between behaviour of cortical and cancellous bone

The host response is in five stages:

- Haemorrhage and inflammation.

- Infiltration of the porous graft by host vessels, osteoblast and osteoblast precursors (two days post-operatively).

- Osteoblastic activity and osteoid seam formation.

- Remodelling.

- Graft integration.

Initial Phase

Week 1.
1. Coagulum.
Prevents further blood loss

2. Intense inflammatory response.
Due to graft necrosis. Fibro-vascular stroma containing new vessels infiltrating donor bed. Exposed graft surfaces bathed in nutrients
Osteogenic precursor cells are taken to donor from host. Graft contribution is probably small.
Osteoconduction provided by graft architecture
Osteoinduction in part from cells within graft and major contribution from matrix of graft in form of B.M.P., etc.

3. Cells and connective tissue envelope transplant, including lymphocytes, plasma cells, osteoblasts and small amounts of fibrous conective tissue.

Week 2.
1. Decreased inflammatory response

2. Dominance of fibrous granualtion tissue

3. Early necrosis:
Osteoclasts numbers and activity increase. Conspicuous by 10th day (sometimes as early as 4th day)
Lacunae appear empty
Dead marrow tissue removed by invading macrophages.

4. Marrow Repopulation:
Host: Angioneogenesis supplies both differentiated and primitive mesenchymal cells.
Donor: Some peripheral cells survive by passive diffusion of nutrients from host.

Secondary Phase

The differences between cancellous and cortical bone grafts tend to become more apparent during the secondary phase.
The differences are mainly due to structural differences >> biological behavioural differences.

Main differences:

1. Rate of revascularisation
2. Mechanism of creeping substitution repair
3. Completeness of repair

Creeping substitution refers to the process whereby necrotic bone is resorbed and replaced by new tissue moving along the channels created by invasive host blood vessels. This is analogous to fracture healing. The process is well under way by six months and complete by one year.

Cancellous Bone Behaviour during Secondary Phase

2-4 Weeks

Marrow necrosis >> Large spaces>>		New vessels >Enter enter primitive mesenchymal cells
>> Differentiate >> into osteoblasts trabiculae	Osteoid seam lines dead trabeculae	>>By end of 2nd week all graft has appositional bone laid down on it.

X-rays: Early initial increase in density of transplanted bone.

4 Weeks

Osteoclasts appear >>	Re-absorb entrapped >> necrotic bone	Decrease overall density of transplanted area

EVENTUALLY ALL CANCELLOUS BONE IS REMOVED AND REPLACED
Haemopoietic elements redevelop within transplanted bone. Some donor cellular elements survive at trabecular surface and contribute to osteogenic response. Some osteo-inductive influence exerted.

1 Month +
Haematoma entirely removed
Fibrous union at host-graft junction
Peripheral callus at graft-host junction is frequently present and occasionally osteochondral bridging of both ends is seen.

3 Months +

Usually:
Bridging: Either osseous or osteochondral mature haemopoietic tissues in marrow spaces. Osteoneogenesis on trabecular surface + osteoclast re-absorption and re-modelling. Re-modelling > rough, irregular neo-cortex from surface callus.

Occasionally:

Fibrous of fibro-cartilage union
or
Complete re-absorption

Overall

Analogous to callus formation following fracture

Initial goal is restoration of stiffness
Fibrous >> Cartilaginous >> Osseous stages

Once bridging has occurred >> Increased remodelling >> Cortical consolidation >> Reduction in diameter of cortex >> Retubilisation of bone at graft level

Cortical Bone Behaviour during Secondary Phase

Main differences with cancellous bone are in terms of:
1. Rate of Revascularisation
2. Rate of Reabsorption of Graft

1. Revascularisation
Vascular buds are limited to central canals of Haversian systems.
Limited number of endothelial cells available to assist in formation of vascular anastomoses.

2. Reabsorption
Reverse situation to cancellous bone
Reabsorption of bone takes place before apposition of new viable bone.

0-2 weeks:
Reabsorption >> enlarging peripheral Haversian canals
3-4 weeks:
Reabsorption spreads to involve inner canals
Most of the interstitial lamellae remains.

As cortical bone is revascularised and then reabsorbed >> loses strength.
Cortical bone develops maximal weakness between 12-48 weeks. Strength may be only 60% of original strength.
Takes 2 years to regain former strength.

3. Later Bone Formation
Appositional bone repair does not begin for at least 3 months

Source of new bone:
a) Host: Primitive mesenchymal cells
          >>differentiate into osteoblasts
b) Donor: Few surviving osteoblasts

New bone seals off remaining necrotic bone, i.e. interstitial lamellae from further osteoclastic encroachment.

Summary of Autogenous Cortical and Cancellous Differences

Type of bone	Rate of Revascularisation	Mechanism and order of Repair	Completeness of repair
Cancellous	Rapid	Osteiod seam laid down on dead trabeculae. Donor bone later reabsorbed	All graft eventually reabsorbed
Cortical	Slower- because limited to Haversian canals	Donor bone reabsorbed proir to laying down of appositional new bone	Some necrotic bone remains

Vascularised Cortical Autograft

Sites include:
- Fibula is chosen commonly as a vascularised cortical autograft because of its accessibility and convenient vascular pedicle.
- Rib
- Mandible
- Iliac crest

Although there is limited structural support, the graft will heal quickly if stable. The turnover and remodelling resemble normal bone.

The advantages of using vascularised cortical autograft include:
- More than 90% of the osteocytes will survive transplantation, assuming a reasonable intraoperative ischaemic time, and resorption is not seen.
- Can bridge large defects.
- Can be used in compromised host beds, e.g. after radiotherapy or infection.
- Less articular chondral collapse.
- Systemic route for transportation of osteogenic cells.
- Early mechanical strength and stiffness as there is no unopposed matrix reabsorption.

Vascularised cortical autograft must be supported (internal or external fixation) until hypertrophy is achieved in response to load. Once this occurs, the graft will obey Wolff's law.

The disadvantages of using vascularised cortical autograft include:
- donor site morbidity
- prolonged operative times
- limited donor sites
- sacrifice of normal structures.

There is no doubt that vascularised cortical autograft is superior to nonvascularised cortical autograft when a bridging area of more than 12 cm is encountered.
The incidence of stress fractures is double in non-vascularised as opposed to vascularised cortical graft. Stress fractures of vascularised cortical autograft heal better than those of non-vascularised cortical autograft.
Initially, vascularlised cortical autograft is superior biomechanically to non-vascularised cortical graft but after six months no difference is seen as measured by torque, bending and tension studies.

Properties of Types of Autograft

Property	Cancellous	Non-vascularised Cortical	Vascularised Cortical
Osteoconduction	++++	+	+
Osteoinduction	++	+/-	+/-
Osteoprogenitor Cells	+++	-	+
Immediate strength	-	+++	+++
Strength at 6 Months	--	++	+++
Strength at 1 year	---	+++	++++

ALLOGRAFTS

Introduction

The genetic disparity between donor and recipient is reflected in the biological response. The greater the disparity, the greater the impact on graft incorporation. However, many allografts do survive despite being immunogenic. Revascularised allografts fail because the immune response is mounted against vascular endothelium and osteogenic cells. The development of allografts has focused upon non-vascularised allografts and different methods of preservation and sterilization, e.g. deep-frozen, freeze-dried.

Historical Perspective

Lexer (1908)	Knee allografts - 50% functioning
Herndon (1950s)	Freeze allografts > reduced immunogenecity
Mankin (1980s)	200 + allografts; 75% success rate; 10-15% non-union and infection rate

Allograft Types

Allogeneic grafts may be:
♦ fresh,
♦ frozen
♦ freeze dried (lyophilisation)
♦ demineralised

Fresh allografts are used soon after harvesting without being stored in a frozen or freeze-fried state or undergoing sterilisation.
Frozen allografting involves freezing to below -70°C or using liquid nitrogen at -196°C. Cryopreservatives have been used such as glycerol. Freezing diminishes enzyme degradation affording decreased immunogenicity without changes in the biomechanical properties. Frozen allograft is the commonest allograft in clinical use.
Freeze-drying (lyophilisation) involves removing the water from the frozen tissue and then vacuum packing the graft with storage

up to five years. This process decreases the antigenicity even further. It does not appear to affect the limited osteoconductive properties. The main disadvantage is biomechanical alteration on rehydration.

In all these techniques of preservation, the osteoprogenitor cells are destroyed. Hence allogeneic grafts are not osteogenic.

Forms of Allograft

Morcellised and Cancellous Allograft
Morcellised and cancellous allograft provides limited support (mostly resistance to compression) and is osteoinductive only. The chips may vary from 0.5 to 3 mm up to 1 cm in diameter. Morcellised allograft is freeze-dried. Porosity allows vascular ingrowth.

Corticocancellous and Cortical Allograft
Corticocancellous and Cortical Allografts provide structural support with limited osteoconduction. Corticocancellous grafts are harvested from a number of sites including the ilium, distal femur and proximal tibia, normally in "strut" form. The grafts are then deep-frozen to -70°C, which retain the mechanical properties, or freeze-dried (necessitating reconstitution). Implantation causes an inflammatory response and sensitisation of the host antigens.

Massive Allogeneic Osteochondral Graft
Massive allogeneic osteochondral grafts comprise cortical bone, metaphyseal cancellous bone and articular cartilage. There is minimal revascularisation of cortical bone.

The attachment of soft tissues is via a seam of appositional bone laid down on surface allograft. Common complications include non-union of the host graft interface. A major disadvantage is that only one end of the graft can be immobilised (the other end is weightbearing cartilage) and thus fixation is not only difficult, but also extremely important for stability.
The graft is stored at -80°C. The cartilage can be cryopreserved with dimethyl sulphoxide (DMSO) or glycerol. The viability of the cartilage is limited using these methods, as only the superficial chondrocytes survive. In an effort to limit chondrocyte damage, slower freezing with the cryopreservative has been used.

Immunogenicity of Allografts
Bone Allograft failure rates in different studies may vary from 10-50%. Both local and systemic immune responses are partially responsible.
The response of the host to any allograft is a cell-mediated response to cell surface antigens carried by allograft cells. The major antigens involved on the allograft are the Class 1 and Class 2 antigens, enoded by the genes of the major histocompatability complex (MHC).
However, the situation is more complex that this in that graft incorporation also relies on fixation stability and the mechanical loading of the graft.

2 distinct BUT simultaneous responses:

Response to any organ allograft:	T-lymphocytes and macrophages attack cells and vessels of transplanted tissue
Response specific to allograft bone:	Immune cells > Cytokines > Activate > Osteoclasts Reabsorption of allograft

Source of Allograft Antigens:

Major Antigens	Weaker Antigens
Bone Marrow	Collagen
	Proteoglycans
	Link Proteins
	Osteoblasts and other cells

Possible Outcomes of Allografting:

Outcome	Comments
"Acceptance" as autogenous graft	Reflects minimal /no genetic disparity- Rare
"Reluctantly accepted"due to genetic disparity	Most common. Possible outcomes: 1. Delayed or non-union at graft-host site 2. Increased incidence of fatigue fracture 3. Less internal repair than seen in autografts 4. Formation of a callus that bridges the transplanted segments
Rejection because of strong genetic differences	Allograft rapidly and completely rejected

Biological Response to Preserved Allografts

Early stages are similar to an autograft
-Inflammatory response at periphery of allograft (peaks at end of 2nd week)-1st maximal osteogenic peak at end of first week, but goes into reverse because of vascular shut down

Later, immunological response causes changes
New vessels > Occluded with inflammatory cells > Hyalinization of vessels

Progressive vascular shut-down >> Necrosis

Fibrous tissue envelope encapsulates graft

2nd maximal osteogenic peak at end of first month + Not as powerful as in autografts

Union between Bone Grafts and Host Bone

This incidence and speed of union is determined by two physical factors:
- stability of the construct
- contact between the host bone and the graft.

It has been shown in animal models that when the host-graft interfaces are intimately apposed and are stably fixed with compression plates, all interfaces will heal whether the graft is autogenous or allogeneic, fresh or frozen.

Observations on retrieved allografts

Several observers have reported the outcome of analyses on retrieved implanted allografts following the death of the recipients:

Enneking, A.O.A. Boston, 1990

Internal repair	Rarely extends more than a few mm into graft
Osteoinductive ability	Absent
Osteoconductive ability	Present
Union with host	Needs good fixation and close host-graft approximation
Fracture	More likely with plating than i.m. nailing
Cortical allograft physical properties	Like autograft
Cartilage preservation	Depends to great degree on soft-tissue stability and joint congruity
Soft-tissue	Firmly adheres to non-rejected specimens
Inflammatory rejection	Uncommon but did occur

Other workers have made the following observations:

Host-Graft Union	Callus both endosteal and periosteal
Creeping Substitution of necrotic bone	Limited, if not absent, in allografts
Host soft-tissue attachments to graft	Accomplished by formation of thin layer of tenuous bone

Complications of Allografting

Revascularisation of allografts is limited which explains the reported high fracture rate (16-50%) in massive allografts. Immune reactions are most often seen in fresh bone or bone frozen without complete debridement and cleansing. The complications of structural use of large allografts include:

- non-union (10% of cases).
- fracture (16-50%).
- infection (10-15%).
- Failure of soft-tissue attachment.
- Immune rejection.

The risks of disease transmission are covered in the section on Bone Banking.

BONE BANKING

Introduction

Bone banking should be set up along similar ethical lines as any other type of transplant programme. Informed consent is required from both the donor and recipient. Appropriate screening is required. Staff must be identified and trained in appropriate harvesting techniques, preservation methods and auditing. Appropriate safeguards must be established for every step of the process from harvesting to implanting.

Types of Bone Banks

Many forms of Bone Banks have developed. To ensure quality and safety local "cottage industry" banks are generally discouraged.

- "Cottage Industries"
- Surgical Unit Tissue Banks
- Regional Tissue Banks
- National Tissue Banks, e.g. American Association of Tissue Banks.

Donors

Donors may be living or cadaver.

Harvesting of allograft bone must be performed under strictly aseptic conditions. Deijkers et al (1997) found out of 200 cadaver donors, 50% grew organisms of low pathogenecity and 3% organisms of high pathogenecity. The major source of contamination appeared to be exogenous and strongly influenced by the care taken by the procurement team.

Risk of Disease Transmission

Pathogens of concern include human immunodeficiency virus (HIV), hepatitis B and hepatitis C. Most incidents of disease transmission have occurred when a pathogen had not yet been identified or the prevailing technology did not identify its presence in the donor. Furthermore, there has been the problem of the sero-negative period or "incubation window" from the date of infectivity.

Polymerise chain reaction assays enable one infected cell to be identified in a population of one million infected cells. These assays are a very sensitive and reliable way of identifying infection.

The American Association of Tissue Banks (AATB) has set the standards for bone banking. A detailed past medical and social history of the donor is obtained.

When screening potential donors, exclusions include:

- Any evidence of current symptomatic infection.

- History, or suspicion, of relevant past infections, e.g. TB, hepatitis, veneral disease.

- Malignancy.

- High-risk activities for HIV.

- Dementia.

- Long term steroid use.

- Metabolic Bone Disease (?)

Any condition with uncertain aetiology, where altered immune competence or viral involvement is suspected or implicated e.g. rheumatoid arthritis, C-JD, MS, post-transplantation.

Serological testing for the following is routinely carried out:

- Hepatitis B surface antigen.
- Hepatitis B core antibody.
- Hepatitis C antibody.
- Syphilis.
- Human T-lymphotropic virus I antibody.
- HIV-1 and HIV-2.
- HIV P24 antigen.

Some units have, at different times, suggested the following additional tests:

- CMV
- Toxoplasmosis
- Blood cultures
- ABO blood grouping
- HLA typing
- Lymph node sampling
- Femoral head histological examination
- Rhesus status

Infection Risks

HIV

The only documented incidents of disease transmission have involved frozen unprocessed grafts such as the patella tendon and femoral heads. The high marrow content of the latter makes these types of grafts a particular risk.

In 1992, a case was reported in which the donor's serum was negative. The 25 patients that received freeze-dried allograft did not develop HIV. However, 3 out of the 4 patients that received unprocessed deep-frozen allografts subsequently became HIV infected.

In 1995 the AATB reported that out of the three million tissue transplants, only two donors tissues were linked with the transmission of AIDS.

Using the AATB standards, the risk of transmission is summarised below.

Risk of HIV Disease Transmission according to graft types

Type of Graft	Risk of Transmission
Freeze-dried bone chips	Practically zero
Frozen unprocessed femoral head	Less than the risk of transfusion of one unit of blood
Musculo-skeletal graft	Low 1 in 10

Hepatitis

Hepatitis B was transmitted first in a frozen bone allograft in 1954. The first reported case of Hepatitis C transmission was reported in 1990. The learnt lessons are similar to HIV. Hepatitis may be transmitted in frozen bone and soft-tissues. Sterilisation and irradiation afford at least partial protection. Screening cannot eliminate all infected donors.

Processing, Preservation and Sterilisation

Processing, preservation and sterilisation must be evaluated carefully. For example autoclaving kills pathogens but is not functionally useful because the process denatures the graft reducing its biological potential. Likewise, irradiation reduces soft tissue graft strength and stiffness.

Processing

The purpose of processing is to reduce the potential of immune sensitisation of the recipient to the donor. Processing also reduces disease transmission; e.g. the very low incidence of HIV transmission.

Modern methods of processing include:
♦ Optional low dose irradiation (less than 20 kGy)
♦ Physical debridement
♦ Ultrasonic or pulsatile water washes
♦ Ethanol
♦ Antibiotic soak

Low dose irradiation destroys non-pathogenic bacteria. Physical debridement removes unwanted tissue and reduces the cellular load. Washing the graft removes the rest of the excess cells and blood. Alcohol denatures cellular proteins and kills some viruses and more bacteria. Finally, soaking in antibiotic kills the remaining bacteria.

Preservation Methods
Allograft Types and effects of Preservation Methods (adapted from Friedlander, 1983):

Method	Comment
Fresh	No preservation required. Viable articular cartilage. Vigourousinflammatory response; specific immune response; resorptive activity that may be overwhelming. Need and availibility may not coincide. Risk of disease transmission.
Deep frozen (-70°C)	Little change in biomechanics. Straight forward method of preservation but expensive. Needs rigid screening to reduce risks of disease transmission. Less immunogenic than fresh allograft. However they remain immunogenic, BUT take longer to evoke response and the reaction is less intense. Cartilage viability is limited. Cryo-protectors e.g. D.M.S.O. or glycerol > Chondrocyte preservation > Protects cell surface antigens > Increases immunogenecity. Needs to be maintained frozen during transport. For use as intercalary (diaphyseal) and osteoarticular allografting.
Freeze-dried	Less immunogenic than deep-frozen. Can be stored indefinitey at room temperature. Easy to transport. Can be secondary sterilised. Compatable with demineralisation. Expensive. Cannot preserve cartilage. Biomechanical weakened by preservation method. Less completely incorporated. For use in cystic and intercalary defects.

Sterilisation

If the harvesting is aseptic, then no further treatment is requires. If the harvest has been potentially contaminated, irradiation (less than 20 kGy) is effective. However, more than 30 kGy is required for viruses and this affects the material property of the graft. Ethylene oxide is not a recommended treatment for sterilisation as the residuals are inflammatory.

Summary of Allografts

Allografts are excellent for early structural integrity and reasonable for osteoconduction. However, osteoinduction potential is limited and osteogenic potential absent. Allografting results are poor when grafting on to an unfavourable bed, as in infected cases. Allografts require augmentation for the formation of new bone.

Comparison of Autografts and Allografts

	Autograft	Allograft
Immunogenic	-	+
Osteogenesis	+	-
Osteoconduction	+	+
Osteoinduction	++	+/-
Union	Rapid	Slow
Donor site	Morbidity	-
Quantity	Limited	Unlimited

OTHER ALTERNATIVES TO AUTOGENOUS BONE GRAFTING

There has been an obvious need for the development of bone graft substitutes to act as an 'off the shelf' alternative to autografts. Attention has turned to alternatives such as ceramics.

Ideally any alternative should satisfy the following criteria:
- unlimited volume,
- absence of donor site morbidity
- no risk of disease transmission
- decreased immunogenicity
- decreased anaesthetic and operative time

Ceramics

Ceramics are composed of hydroxyapatite ($Ca_{10}[PO_4]_6[OH]_2$) or tricalcium phosphate ($Ca_3[PO_4]_2$) or calcium sulphate ($Ca[So_4]$) or a combination. They are osteoconductive only and act as scaffolding. Their function is to bind directly to the host. Their volume is clearly unlimited and it is possible to have prescriptive configurations according to need. Hydroxyapatite is the major constituent of the inorganic component of bone, which is both biocompatible and nonimmunogenic. They are free of the risk of transmissible diseases seen in allografts and negate the problems of donor site morbidity seen in autografts.

The intellectual task has been to put the appropriate calcium salts into the correct three-dimensional form, so that bone can be guided into a prescribed location – otherwise it will dictate unnatural bone lealing pathways. Porosity allows soft tissue and bone to regenerate within the pore space. The optimal pore size is 150-500 µm. Ideally, they need tight interlocking with the host.

Ceramics are produced as porous implants, non-porous dense implants and granular particles with pores. The shape of ceramics is important. For example dense blocks with small surface areas degrade much slower. Calcium phosphate is sintered during processing. Tricalcium phosphate is more porous and biological degradation is ten to twenty times faster than hydroxyapatite. Hydroxyapatite is resorbed by foreign body-giant cells, which stop ingesting once 2-10 µm of hydroxyapatite has been consumed. Consequently, hydroxyapatite may remain in the body for up to ten years. Tricalcium phosphate, on the other hand, is better remodelled but weaker. For this reason, tricalcium phosphate is not ideal for compression.

Ceramics are brittle with little tensile strength and hence their applications are limited. They are biomechanically strongest in compression. However, the mechanical properties of porous calcium phosphate are comparable to those of cancellous bone once incorporated and modelled. Ceramics must be shielded from loading forces until ingrowth has occurred.

Ceramics are non-inflammatory and inert when in a structural arrangement. Small granules, however, may elicit a foreign body-giant cell reaction (this has been demonstrated in the rodent) and subsequent partial resorption.

Theoretically, they can be used as a transport agent for osteoinductive elements or antibiotics.

Coralline Ceramics

These may be natural coral or replamineform ceramics. Replamineform ceramics are porous hydroxyapatites derived from the calcium carbonate skeletal structure of sea coral. The replamineform process converts calcium carbonate to hydroxyapatite. These are produced from marine specimens by hydrothermal exchange replacement of coral carbonate with calcium phosphate replicas. The pore structure is highly organised and is similar to human cancellous bone.

Replamineform ceramics include those derived from Goniopora (large pores 500-600 µm) and Porites (pores of 200-250 µm). The trade name is Pro Osteon™. The number following the trade name designates the nominal pore diameter, either 500 or 200 µm. To be considered for commercialisation and amenable to conventional manufacturing methods, the corals must be naturally in abundance and grow in large hemispherical forms.

Generally, autograft is superior to ceramic for the majority of uses. Once incorporated, coralline ceramics obey Wolff's Law and do not stress-shield the regenerated bone. These grafts have mainly been used in dentistry and maxillo-facial surgery. However, there is one human study of tibial plateau fractures, which shows a favourable result.

Bone marrow grows well in ceramics, combining the properties of osteogenesis with osteoconduction. This combination has not yet been trialled in human beings. It may well prove that ceramics act well as a transport agent for elements such as inductive proteins and antibiotics.

Bioactive Glass

Bioactive glass are silicate-based bone graft substitutes. They promote hydroxyapatite formation and cell attachment.

Their main uses are as coatings on metallic implants or in particle form to fill defects.

Allogeneic Demineralised Bone Matrix (DBM)

Demineralised bone matrix is formed by the acid extraction of bone leaving non-collagenase proteins, bone growth factors and collagen in continuity in a composite. DBM is quickly revascularised (osteoconductive), moderately osteoinductive (due to bone morphogenic proteins), but offers no structural support. It thus enhances osteoinduction at the expense of mechanical strength. The processing process reduces the risk of disease transmission.

The process of incorporation involves inflammation, cellular differentiation of mesenchymal cells into chondrocytes (five days), a cartilagenous phase, mineralisation and eventual complete absorption of the DBM. If DBM is kept at room temperature for more than 24 hours it becomes biologically inactive. Ethylene oxide and radiation (more than 2.5 Mrad) reduces its osteoconductive potential. DBM is available as powder, crushed granules, chips, putties and pastes. The literature reports excellent results in clinical trials. DBM is most effective in conjunction with internal fixation and as an adjunct to other grafting materials. Its applications include augmentation of autogenous and traditional allogeneic bone grafts in the repair of cysts, fractures, non-unions and stable fusions.

Consistency of biological activity is a problem and the supplier should provide evidence of activity of the particular batch supplied.

Bone Marrow

Bone Marrow contains osteoprogenitor cells in the order of 1 per 50,000 nucleated cells, which decreases with age. Techniques have been developed to increase the number five-fold. These may be used with an inorganic matrix (to provide osteoconduction) and, additionally, have osteoinductive properties. Bone marrow grows well into ceramics. Studies have demonstrated that bone marrow will successfully treat non-unions when adequate amounts are utilised. They have also been used in the treatment of bone cysts and pseudoarthroses. Bone marrow is harvested by aspirating 2-3 mls from either the proximal humerus or the ilium, diluting with blood and using immediately. Naturally, morbidity is negligible when harvesting bone marrow. The best clinical indication for bone marrow use is when augmentation (osteogenesis) is required.

Composite Graft

Composite graft is a combination of materials including both an osteoconductive matric and an osteogenic or osteoinductive material. Collagraft™ is a bovine collagen and porous calcium ceramic combination. The combination is nonosteoinductive.Bone marrow must be added to induce osteogenesis. As yet research results are limited. However, one study has shown no significant difference in functional and radiographic results when Collagraft™

was used as a bone graft substitute compared to autograft. Composite graft has no structural support

Xenografts

Xenografts are bone grafts transplanted between different species. The graft is cut from animal bone, machined into the required shape and, finally processed.

The advantages of xenografts are that there is theoretically an unlimited supply, no osteotomy is required for graft harvest, the infection risk is low and the operative time shorter.

Kiel Bone Graft has been used in the past derived from young calves. It is a partially deproteinated and defatted xengraft. Its theoretical advantage is its reduced immunogenicity as it is derived from immature animal.

In orthopaedics and neurosurgery, xenografts have mainly been used in cervical spine surgery. There has been variable success in clinical trials. A xenograft will ossify and incorporate. Hence it is a promising alternative to autograft and allograft. Bone is laid down from the adjacent host bone via creeping substitution. Fusion is significantly slower than autograft. Non-ossification and defective ossification are common scenarios. Xenografts are neither osteogenic nor osteoinductive. Allegedly, there is improvement of new bone formation by the addition of bone marrow or cultured human osteoblasts. Salama (1973, 1978) demonstrated that when xenograft was implanted into bone defects or muscle pockets there was no osteogenesis unless autogenous bone graft was added.

It has been noted on x-ray that a radiographic halo forms around xenograft. The aetiology of the halo has been the cause of much debate. The halo may represent fibrotic tissue around the xenograft. Other authors believe that the halo is autogenous non-mineralised osteoid. Immunological reactions do occur with xenograft.The subsequent inflammatory response may inhibit new bone formation. Further research is required to assess the osteoconductive capacity of xenograft.

Type	Examples
Bovine Hydroxyapatite:	Bio-Oss
Synthetic Hydroxyapatite:	Osteograft/D, Allogran-N
Coralline-derived Hydroxyapatite:	ProOsteon
Other Calcium Phosphates:	Collagraft (Bovine collagen + HA + TCP), Healos
Calcium Sulphate:	Osteoset, Stimulan
Bioactive Glass:	Biogran; Perioglas
Demineralised bone matrix	AllogroGrafton (DBM+glycerol) Allomatrix = Allogro (DBM) + OsteoSet (calcium sulphate)

REFERENCES:

AATB Information Alter, 1995: 3 (6)

Axhausen G. Uebor den Vorgang Partieller sequuestrirung transplantierten Knochengewebes, nebst neuen histologischen Unterschangen uber Knochentransplantation an Menschen. Arch Klin Chir 1909;89: 281-302.

Barth F. Histologische Befunde nack Knochem implantation. Arch Klin Chir 1893;46:409-17.

Bone Grafting and Bone Grafting Substitutes. Orthop Clin of North Am 1999; 30 (4)

Boyce T, Edwards J, Scarborough N. Allograft Bone. The Influence of Processing on Safety and Performance. Orthop Clin of North Am 1999; 30: 571-81.

Bucholz RW, Carlton A, Holmes RB. Interporous Hydroxyapatite as a Bone Graft Substitute in Tibial Plateaux Fractures. Clini Orthop 1989; 240: 53-62

Burwell RG. Studies in the transplantation of Bone: VII. The Fresh Composite Homograft/ Autograft of Cancellous Bone. An analysis of factors leading to osteogenesis in marrow transplants and in marrow containing bone grafts. J Bone Joint Surg 1964; 46B: 110-40.

Cornell CN, Lane JM, Chapman MW Multicenter Trial of Collagraft as Bone Graft Substitute. J Orthop Trauma 1991; 5: 1-8.

Deijkers RLM, Bloem RM, Petit PLC, Brand R, Vehmeyer SBW, Veen MR. Contamination of bone allografts. J Bone Joint Surg 1997; 79B: 161-6.

Freidlander G. Immune response to osteochondral allografts. Current knowledge and future directions. Clin. Orthop. 1983;174: 58-68.

Freidlander G. Current Concepts Review. Bone Grafts. J Bone Joint Surg 187; 69A: 786-90.

Gazdag AR, Lane JM, Glaser D, Forster RA. Alternatives to Autogenous Bone Graft: Efficacy and Indications. J Am Acad Orthop Surg 1995; 3: 8

Kontinnen YT, Waris E, Xu J-W, Lassus J, Salo J, Nevalainen J, Santavira S. Bone Grafting. Curr Orthop 1998;12: 209-15.

Ollier L. Traite experimental et clinique de la regeneration des os et de la production artificielle du tissue osseoux. Paris: Masson, 1867.

Reddi AH et al. Biological Principles of Bone Induction. Orthp Clin North Am. 1987;18: 207.

Senn N. On the healing of aseptic bone cavities by implantation of antiseptic decalcified bone. Am J. Med. Sci. 1889;98: 219-43.

Tomford WW. (1995) Transmission of Disease through Transplantation of Musculoskeletal Allografts. J Bone Joint Surg 1995;77A: 1742-54

Urist MR. Bone formation by autoinduction. Science 1965;150: 893-9

Urist M.R., Silverman BF, Buring K, Dubuc FL, Rosenberg JM. The Bone Induction Principle. Clin Orthop 1967;53: 243-83.

Walther P. Widereinheilung Der Bei Der Trepanation Ausgebohrten Knochenscheibe. Journal Schir. Augench. 1821:2;571.

Weiland AJ. Current Concepts Review; Vascularised Free Bone Transplants. J.Bone Joint Surg 1981; 63A:166-9

Younger EM, Chapman MW. Morbidity at Bone Graft Donor Sites. J Orthop Trauma 1989; 3: 192-195.

Notes

Notes

X-Rays and Scintigraphy

Mr M Haddaway & Dr V N Cassar-Pullicino
Medical Physicist, Clinical Director
Robert Jones & Agnes Hunt Orthopaedic Hospital
Oswestry

X-rays

1. X-rays and gamma rays lie at the upper end of the electromagnetic spectrum (Figure 1), which also includes microwaves and radio frequency waves as used in MRI. There is a direct link between their energy, frequency and wavelength:

2. X-ray tube.
X-rays are produced when high speed electrons are stopped by a tungsten target **(Fig.2)**. Only about 1% of the electron's kinetic energy is converted to x-rays. The rest is dissipated as heat.

3. Exposure parameters
Different x-ray tube factors influence an exposure:

Factor	Means
Incr. kV	Incr. penetration
Incr. mA	Incr. exposure(film and patient)
Incr. time	Incr. exposure(film and patient)

4. Primary Radiation
Primary radiation contributes to the ideal image; scatter detracts from it (see table below)

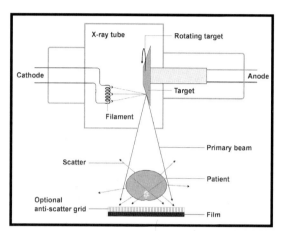

Fig.2.   Production of a radiograph

5. To reduce the effect of scatter on the x-ray image, anti-scatter **grids** may be used. These are either in the x-ray table itself or may be part of the x-ray film cassette. The grid is made up of a sandwich of lead and aluminium (or other x-ray lucent material). The lead acts to absorb the scattered radiation, by virtue of its non-primary direction.

6. Increasing kV of the primary x-ray beam produces **(Fig.3)**:
♦ a reduction in back scatter
♦ an increase in forward scatter.
This impacts on the scattered radiation dose to any staff in the vicinity (e.g. for fluoroscopy).

Primary radiation	Secondary(scattered) radiation
Direct from x-ray tube	Scattered from patient or surroundings
Energy as per machine setting	Reduced energy due to scattering process
In forward direction	Can occur in any direction
Produces x-ray image	Reduces quality of x-ray image
More penetrating	Reduced penetration
May penetrate lead gloves	Lead gloves protect

Fig.1.   Electromagnetic spectrum with position of typical medical uses.

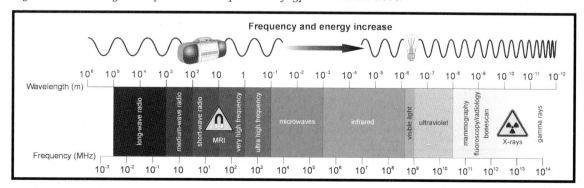

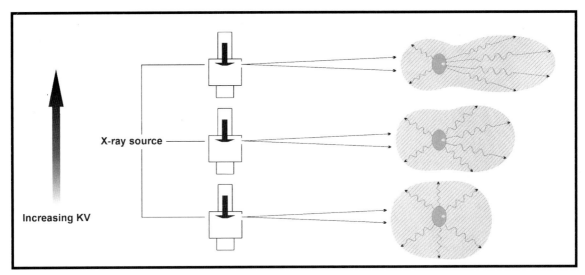

Fig.3. Effect of increasing kV on scatter distribution

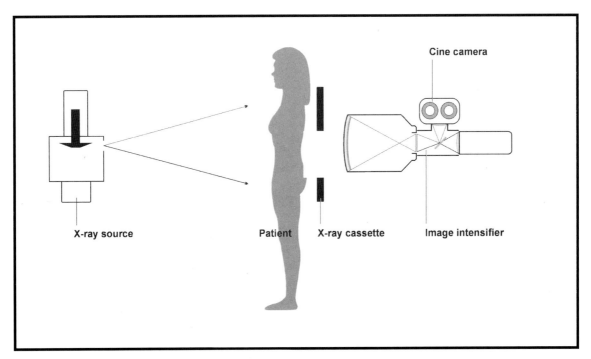

Fig.4. Different methods of recording x-ray images

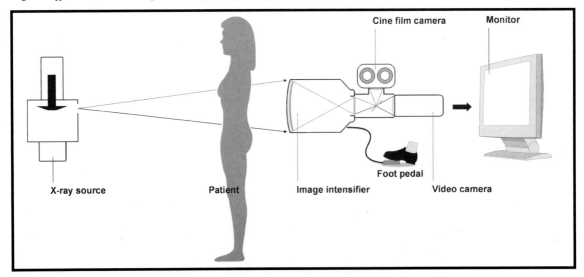

Fig.5a.   Different means of image production via image intensifier.

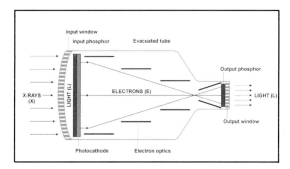

Fig. 5(b). Schematic of image intensifier

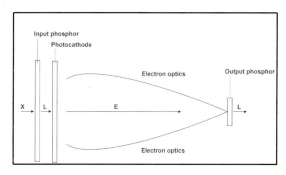

Fig. 5(c). Conversion processes involved in the image intensifier

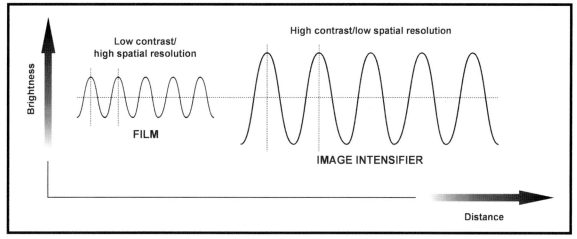

Fig.6. Interaction of contrast and spatial resolution.

Fig.7. Relative attenuation (whiter on x-ray film).

7. X-ray images are recorded via **(Fig.4)**:
- radiographic cassettes, containing film and intensifying screens(radiography)
- image intensifier monitor, in real time (fluoroscopy) or on cine film

7(a). Fluoroscopy, using the image intensifier produces an image **(Fig.5a) via:**
- a cine film camera
- video recorder (motion studies)
- directly on the display monitor

NB: The foot pedal is the final arbiter of dose to the patient!

7(b) Image intensifier:

The image intensification process converts the incident x-ray beam into a visible light image via the type of evacuated glass envelope illustrated above**(Fig.5b)**: This device involves a number of conversion processes, in order to intensify the x-ray image by a factor of between 5000 and 10,000. These are illustrated above **(Fig. 5c)**:

Incident x-ray (X) photons are converted first to light photons (L) within the input phosphor and then to electrons (E), which are focussed onto an output phosphor, thereby converting to a light image (L) which is intensified, inverted and greatly reduced in size.

8. Resolution and **Contrast** are important factors that contribute to the quality of the x-ray image **(Fig.6)**:
- Resolution is the ability to separate spatial detail(measured in line pairs per millimetre)
- Contrast is the ability to distinguish between different types of tissue
- Both are influenced by image noise

Typical relative values:

	Film	Cine Film	Image Intensifier
Resn.	10	5	1
Noise	20	25	high
Dose	10	1	very low(dose *rate*)

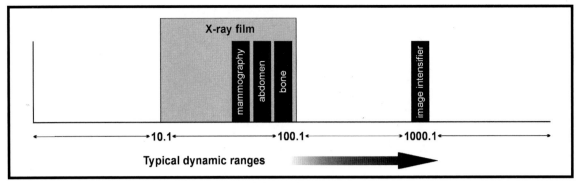

Fig. 8.   Typical dynamic ranges.

9. Contrast Medium is used to enhance natural radiographic contrast **(Fig.7)**:

♦   Contrast in radiography is a function of the differential attenuation of tissue.

♦   Soft tissue/vasculature is difficult to image using primary contrast (subject's own contrast), due to the poor discrimination, by conventional x-rays, of these tissues.

♦   Radiographic contrast media use materials with high atomic number (e.g. Barium or Iodine) to enhance the differential attenuation.

♦   Air and other gases enhance contrast by virtue of their low density.

10. Greyscale:-

♦ In conventional x-ray images, blackness represents objects that attenuate the x-ray beam less than dense objects (i.e. bone), which are presented as whiter on the film.

♦ **An analogue image** is defined as one that has an infinite number of different levels of film density, or blackness.

♦ **A digital image** presents these changes of blackness as a discrete number of levels (greyscale).

11.The dynamic range of an imaging system **(Fig.8)** is the ratio of:
x-ray intensity *NOT* attenuated (black)
TO
x-ray intensity *after maximum* attenuation(white)

12.'Freeze frame' is the ability of a digital x-ray system to store the last image of a fluoroscopic examination:-
Which means
extended viewing
Without
further patient exposure
Which means
reduced patient radiation dose

13. A radiograph is a 2-D representation of a 3-D object. 3-D information is most accurately conveyed, with plain radiography, from 2-D images taken at 90 degrees to each other (orthogonal) (Figure 9)

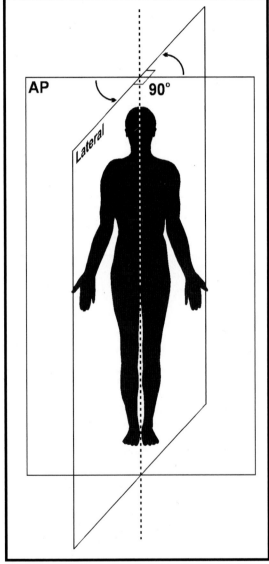

Fig.9. 3-D information from 2 orthogonal views.

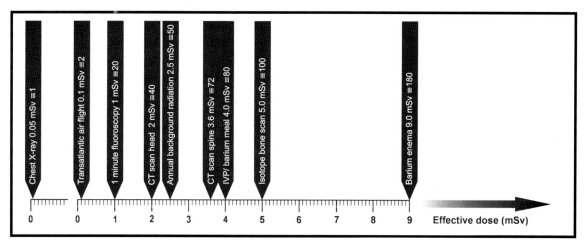

Fig.10. Effective doses from typical diagnostic exposures, compared with equivalent number of chest radiographs.

14. Relative dose:-

Effective dose (Figure 10) is a measure of the effective risk, whether all or part of the body is irradiated, enabling comparison of different procedures. It is presented in units of Sieverts, most usually given as milliSieverts (= 10-3 Sieverts).

15. Relationship between kV and radiation dose:-

- ♦ an x-ray beam contains a spectrum of energies(kv's)
- ♦ low energies contribute to skin dose and to image contrast
- ♦ high energies contribute to depth dose and to penetration of the object/patient

16. Digital imaging

Most medical imaging techniques, such as MRI, CT and Nuclear Medicine, now are able to store and transmit digital images. This is as a result of their requirement to process image data. This makes such imaging modalities suitable for use in Picture Archiving and Communication Systems(PACS), enhancing the transfer of medical images both within hospitals and between them.

This technological advancement has been much slower in conventional radiography, leading to a position where a number of different options may be found for recording the radiographic image.

- ♦ Conventional film/screen cassettes: analog images recorded on film and developed using a photographic process. These are viewed on a light box.
- ♦ Computed Radiography(CR): this technique uses a phosphor contained within a cassette, exposed as a conventional film and then removed to be by read remotely by a laser mechanism. ie cost is limited to replacement of cassettes as conventional cassette holding devices are used.
- ♦ Digital Radiography(DR)or Direct Digital Radiography(DDR): this technique uses a phosphor to record the latent image but this is linked directly to the read out device, therefore requiring much higher costs for replacing the x-ray imaging hardware.

CR and DR images are subsequently viewed on a monitor via the local PACS system.

Scintigraphy:

1. Radionuclides:-
Nuclides are different forms of the same element, having different properties
Radionuclides are unstable forms of an element which transform spontaneously, with accompanying emission of radiation(alpha, beta or gamma)
Gamma rays are emitted by some radionuclides, with discrete characteristic energies, and are employed in scintigraphy
Decay rate of radionuclides is characterised by their half life

2. Common radionuclides:-

Radionuclide	Energy	Physical half-life	Use
Technetium 99m	141 keV	6 hours	Bone & Lung scanning
Indium 111	173, 247 keV	67 hours	Infection
Gallium 67	185,300,394 keV	78 hours	Infection, oncology
Krypton 81m	190 keV	13 sec	Lung ventilation scan

3. Half-life
◆ The decay of a radionuclide in isolation is measured by its physical half-life
◆ The removal of a radionuclide from a patient environment, is measured by its biological half-life
◆ The radiation dose to the patient, of an administered radionuclide, is influenced by both its physical and biological half-life.
◆ In the case of a bone scan, the removal or excretion is via the urinary system

4. Radiopharmaceutical
The radiopharmaceutical is made up of 2 components:-

◆ the radionuclide is the means of detection
◆ the pharmaceutical controls the in vivo distribution and localisation
e.g.:-

Radionuclide +	Pharmaceutical =	Radiopharmaceutical	Used
Tc99m +	MDP(methylenediphosphonate) =	Tc99m MDP	for bone scan
Tc99m +	MAA(macroaggregated albumin) =	Tc99m MAA	for lung scan

5. The 'Ideal' Radionuclide has:

◆ a short half-life, equivalent to the investigation duration
◆ decay to stable or long lived daughter product
◆ only gamma emission(other emission, such as beta, contributes to radiation dose not image)
◆ energy which is high enough to leave patient, but low enough for efficient detection(about 150 keV)
◆ discrete single energy for optimal discrimination from scatter
◆ ready availability

6. The 'Ideal' Pharmaceutical has:-
◆ rapid and efficient localisation
◆ rapid elimination after investigation
◆ low cost
◆ low toxicity
◆ stability

7. Uptake is influenced by Bone Weight:-
◆ Organic: Cells, collagen, MPS, fluid - 35%
◆ Inorganic: Hydroxyapatite crystal - 65%

Basic Science for FRCS (Trauma and Orthopaedics)

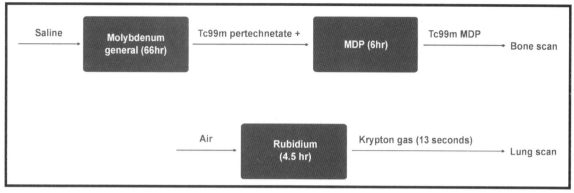

Figure 1.   Production of radionuclides from generators.

8.   Isotope Generators (Fig.1) :
♦   Technetium meets most requirements of the 'Ideal' radionuclide.
♦   It is produced daily by elution (passing saline through) of a molybdenum (parent) generator.
♦   Molybdenum has a half-life of 66 hours, allowing it to be 'milked' for several days (about 2 molybdenum generators would be required to produce daily Tc99m for a week).
♦   A similar process is used to produce the Krypton gas used for lung ventilation imaging, using a Rubidium generator.

9.   Bone scans:
The most widely used radiopharmaceuticals for bone imaging are the phosphate analogues, of which MDP is one.
Advantages:
♦   Rapid renal excretion
♦   High bone to soft tissue uptake
♦   Efficient localisation(50-60%)

10.   Physiological factors influencing uptake are:-
♦   Blood supply
♦   Rate of bone turnover
♦   Amount of mineralised bone
♦   Capillary permeability

Phosphates bind to bone first by active adsorption on to the bone and then binding to the crystalline lattice and matrix, particularly in newly formed crystals.
Scintigraphy is the primary investigation for the detection of regional abnormalities of skeletal function.

11.   Trans-capillary exchange:
♦   passive free diffusion
♦   solely dependent on molecular size
♦   requires fluid space(11ml per 100 gm) of bone

12.   Information is available at different stages following injection in a bone scan.
The various **phases** are:-

	Phase I	*Phase II*	*Phase III*	*Phase IV*
	Vascular	Blood pool (or diffusion or capillary)	Bone (or static or late or crystalline)	Delayed
Timing	1-2minutes	5minutes	3hours	24hours
Duration	Every few seconds for 2 minutes	about 3 minutes	20-40minutes	20minutes

13.   Gamma Camera
(i). In scintigraphy the injected patient is the source of radiation, detected and imaged by the **gamma camera** system **(Fig.2)**. The injection, which is systemic, allows imaging of any part or the entire skeleton.

14. The gamma camera via its components selects only primary gamma radiation **(Fig.3)**:

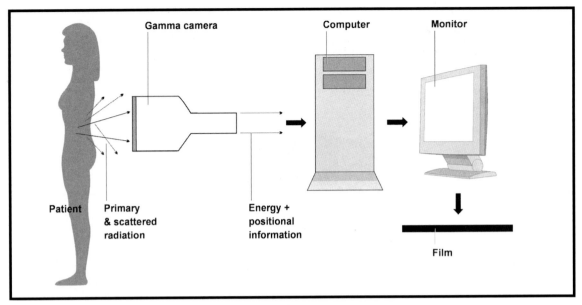

Figure 2.   *Producing a radioisotope scan with a gamma camera.*

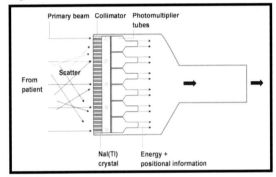

Figure 3. Components of the gamma camera.

Figure 4. Path of the gamma camera during SPECT acquisition.

15. *Choice of* collimator *affects the scan image:-*

Collimator	Advantage	Disadvantage
High Resolution	Better resolution	Longer scanning time
High sensitivity	Poorer resolution	Faster scanning
Pinhole	Enlarged image	Less uniform image

16. SPECT:-

Tomographic images can be obtained by rotating the camera to typically 60 positions around the patient. Data from each of the 60 images is processed by the computer to produce transaxial, coronal and sagittal sections.

17. The orbit of the camera

This is either circular or elliptical to match the body shape **(Figure 4)**.

Benefits of SPECT:-
- enhanced sensitivity
- improved anatomical location

18. Imaging for infection:-

Choice of scintigraphic imaging agents for infection are governed by many factors:-
- availability
- anatomical site
- ease of use
- type of infection - chronic or acute
- radiation dose

Agent	Advantage	Disadvantage
Tc99m MDP	Available and easy to use Low dose	Non-specific
Tc99m Sulesomab(Leukoscan)	In vivo labeling Low dose Same day scanning	Less sensitive for chronic disease
Tc99m HMPAO, labelled white cells	Tc99m readily availible	Labelling process requires time and patient's blood Short half-life not good for chronic infection
Indium 111, labelled white cells	Better for chronic infection	Less available Higher dose Labelling process requires time and patient's blood
Gallium 67 citrate	Requires no ex vivo labelling	Non-specific

19. Sensitivity of agents for infection imaging:Specificity and sensitivity for imaging infection can be improved by combining agents.

i.e. use of gallium AND MDP or MDP AND HMPAO improves the specificity of diagnosis.

20. Gallium uptake mechanism:

Gallium citrate is bound to plasma transferrin. Excretion is via the urinary system AND faeces, making abdominal imaging difficult without use of a laxative regimen. Skeletal uptake is related to reticulo-endothelial activity and bone turnover.

It may also be influenced by:

♦ entry via 'leaky' capillaries into inflamed tissue

♦ binding to lactoferrin in inflamed tissue

♦ longer residence time in blood linked to higher turnover in inflammation

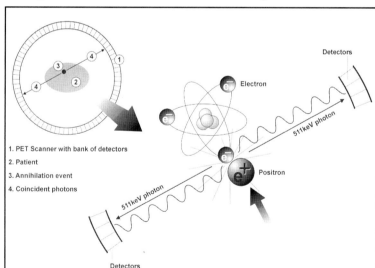

1. PET Scanner with bank of detectors
2. Patient
3. Annihilation event
4. Coincident photons

Figure 5. Picture of patient with bank of circular detectors around the thorax. Example of positron being emiited from body, colliding with electron, and consequent detection of simultaneous photons by banks of detectors.

21. PET(Positron Emission Tomography)

The principle of PET scanning involves the administration to the patient of a metabolically targeted radiopharmaceutical, labelled with a radionuclide that emits a positron as part of its decay process.

Positrons emitted within the patient, interact rapidly with orbiting electrons, after very short path lengths, to produce annihilation of the 2 particles, along with the production of two 511keV photons(same energy regardless of isotope). The significance of this event is that these 2 photons travel in opposite directions at, essentially, 180 degrees apart. This means that by use of coincident detection within the PET scanner, the fixed line (between the 2 detectors) along which the originating annihilation event occurred, is known (see figure 5).

Basic Science for FRCS (Trauma and Orthopaedics)

Positron emitters, such as 18F are used to label substrates such as deoxyglucose. This radiopharmaceutical, FDG is transported, via circulation and metabolism, to the organ of interest where it is incorporated. In the case of FDG the metabolic process is glucose utilisation. PET imaging activity is a measure of metabolic activity, rather than the size of a lesion. This makes active small lesions relatively easy to detect. Small inactive lesions are therefore diagnostically less significant. It also highlights the need for the anatomical localisation and structural detail, provided by hybrid PET/CT systems.

Because of the short half life of positron emitting radionuclides, proximity to cyclotron production is normally a requirement of PET imaging. Also, the higher energies involved create more significant implications regarding radiation protection, particularly for those handling(and therefore administering) the radiopharmaceutical.

PET radionuclides:

Radionuclide	Fluorine-18	Oxygen-15	Carbon-11	Nitrogen-13
Half-life	1.83hr	2.05min	20.4min	9.96min
Max. positron energy	0.64MeV	1.7MeV	0.96MeV	1.2MeV

NB: Compare above with Tc99m - Photon energy of 0.14MeV; half-life of 6hrs

Types of PET equipment:

♦ Gamma camera PET: Early PET was either with dedicated/expensive scanners or cheaper/compromised adapted gamma cameras(GC). GC detector crystal was not optimised for resultant higher energy photons from the annihilation events.
♦ Dedicated PET machines: have become more sensitive - scans quicker. More available with greater availability of cyclotrons.
♦ PET/CT: offers image fusion and faster attenuation correction via CT attenuation methods. Nowadays it is difficult to purchase PET scanners on their own.

PET resolution limitation (6-8mm)depends on:

♦ Energy of radionuclide(fluorine-18, carbon-11, nitrogen-13, oxygen-15.)
♦ Photons not emitted at exactly 180 degrees due to residual momentum of the original positron.
♦ Type of detector
♦ Origin of annihilation event with respect to the centre of the scanner.

Effective dose is of the order of 2-3 times that of a bone scan.

Notes

Notes

Basic Principles of CT, MRI and Ultrasound

Dr P N M Tyrrell & Dr V N Cassar-Pullicino

Consultant Radiologist and Clinical Director
Robert Jones & Agnes Hunt Orthopaedic Hospital
Oswestry

The plain radiograph (x-ray) provides imaging information in analogue form while CT (x-rays) and MRI (proton mapping) are based on the process of digitisation.

A digital image is one where information contained within the patient is received and converted into numerical data by a computer. A particular point within that part of the patient being imaged, referred to as a pixel (or picture element) can be identified by a number. The object plane (slice) is of variable width (the slice thickness - usually in terms of mms, for example 4mms) subdivided into a matrix of elements (pixels). Each slice can be considered as a matrix, where a matrix size of 256 x 256, corresponds to a pixel size of 1mm in a field of view of 25cm².

After the image has been obtained each pixel contains an identifying number, housing information about the imaging characteristics of that pixel (small piece of tissue) (Fig. 1). Computed tomography images a series of slices of the patient. The slice thickness and interslice distance is usually constant in a given examination. With helical (spiral) scanning the pitch ratio will also be chosen, which is defined as the ratio of the table increment per 360 degree gantry rotation to the collimation setting. From this numerical computerised data, images can be manipulated such that brightness and contrast can be altered, background subtraction enables tissues to be highlighted, and reformatting in different imaging planes can take place.

By computer analysis the information in all the pixels that make up the imaged slice can be reformed into the visual anatomical image with which we are familiar. That image can then be displayed on a console, stored on a floppy or hard disc and can be printed onto film for viewing on a film viewing light box. The digitised information can also be manipulated and viewed in different imaging planes (sagittal, coronal etc) and reconstructed into three dimensions (3D).

Computed Axial Tomography (CT scanning)

CT utilises x-rays from a single source to form the image. The current scanners consist of a gantry made up of the x-ray source (rotating) and a circle of detectors (stationary) to detect the attenuated beam once it has passed through the patient. Data is acquired as the x-ray tube rotates through 360° (Fig. 2). When patients are placed on the CT table, they are positioned according to the area to be scanned. Image reconstruction is carried out by a

Fig. 1 *Fan beam of x-rays passing through patient. Variable attenuation of each portion of the beam as it passes through different parts of the patient's tissues, and hence variable attenuation received by detectors.*

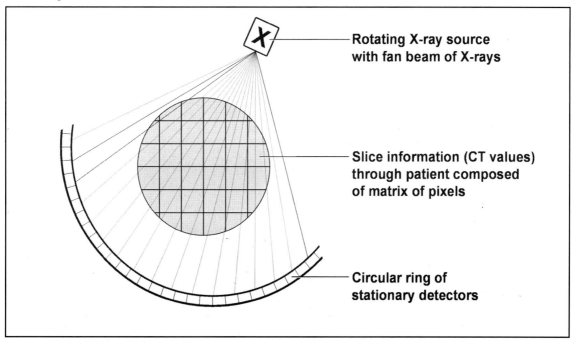

Rotating X-ray source with fan beam of X-rays

Slice information (CT values) through patient composed of matrix of pixels

Circular ring of stationary detectors

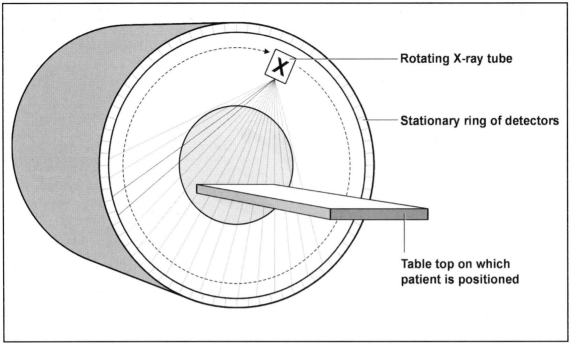

Fig. 2 *Schematic representation of a CT gantry with a rotating x-ray source and a stationary ring of detectors.*

Labels in figure:
- Rotating X-ray tube
- Stationary ring of detectors
- Table top on which patient is positioned

complex computerised mathematical process of Fourier transformation of back projection or reiteration (Figs.1,3).Early CT scanning of complete organs and volumes was done by sequential (incremental) scanning of consecutive slices. Spiral CT was later introduced as a mode for continuous volume scanning, facilitated by continuous patient transport through the scanner. Multi-slice spiral CT (MSCT), introduced in 1998, is associated with multi-row detectors which facilitate increased table feed per rotation according to the increased width of the x-ray fan beam and this has also been associated with improvements in z-axis resolution. These technological developments have resulted in greatly increased speed of image acquisition together with superior volume image reconstruction and image quality.

Windowing

By centring on a particular CT number or attenuation value, one can choose a window, and the grey scale can be compressed within this window (Fig. 4). Appropriate window widths and window centre values can be pre-set: bone, (a centre of 300 with a width of 1200); lung parenchyma (a centre of minus 500 with a width

of 2500, air having a very negative attenuation value). A single CT data set of the thorax can be 'windowed' sequentially to look at the lung parenchyma, the vertebrae and the ribs.

Resolution

Although the spatial resolution in CT is high, it is not as high as that on plain x-rays Spatial resolution can be reduced as a result of "partial volume averaging". This occurs because picture elements (pixels) or voxels (volume elements) (voxel = pixel x slice thickness) can interfere with the sharpness of a line edge in a line pair due to overlap. CT has a high intrinsic contrast resolution, much better than that of plain radiographs. Contrast resolution is again open to the problem of partial volume averaging.

Radiation Dose

There is significant radiation dose associated with CT as compared to radiography. Frequently comparisons are made between the dose received from a chest x-ray and that from a CT scan. Quantitatively a chest x-ray is associated with a typical skin radiation dose of 0.02 millisieverts (mSv), a 3 view radiograph of the lumbar spine is associated with a radiation dose of 2 mSv, whereas that of a CT . scan of the thorax is associated with a dose of 8 mS

Fig.3 *Schematic representation of equipment involved in CT.*

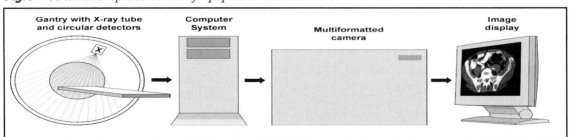

Labels in figure:
- Gantry with X-ray tube and circular detectors
- Computer System
- Multiformatted camera
- Image display

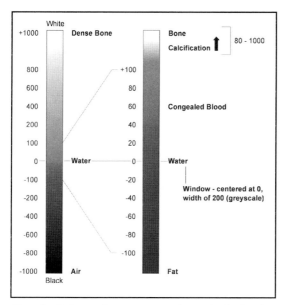

Fig. 4 *Schematic representation of windowing used in digital imaging, with an associated grey scale.*

Magnetic Resonance Imaging (MRI)

MRI does not depend on ionising radiation. It is similar to CT in that the image is digitally acquired, but the nature by which that information is obtained is quite different, requiring a uniform magnetic field, tissue magnetisation induced by the application of radio-frequency pulses, and measurement of relaxation of the tissue after the removal of the pulse and a return of magnetisation to base line level. The particular strength of MRI lies in its representation of the soft tissues with a superior soft tissue contrast compared with CT.

In MRI it is the protons (Hydrogen ions (H^+)) in individual atoms which participate in the imaging process and it is the mobile protons which are important. In tissues such as cortical bone the H^+s are tightly bound, unavailable to contribute to the signal, and appear black (or low signal) on all imaging sequences. In tissues such as fat, the H^+s are loosely bound and some may be free i.e. mobile. Thus mobile protons associated with fat are available to participate in production of the signal. Fat typically appears white on T1 weighted images (high signal).

Production of Signal

A proton is a positive charge and the protons within the nucleus move in a particular way known as precession (like a spinning top). The frequency with which the protons precess is equal to the strength of the external magnetic field (measured in Tesla) multiplied by the gyromagnetic ratio, which is a constant for individual protons (e.g. the proton of hydrogen has a gyromagnetic ratio of 42 MHz). This relationship is known as the ***Larmor equation.***

The radio frequency (RF) pulse used in MRI must have the same frequency as the protons and is calculated from the Larmor equation. Only when the radio frequency pulse and the protons are the same frequency can protons pick up some energy from the radio wave, a phenomenon known as resonance.

Fig. 5 *Schematic representation of a MR scanner, with patient lying within the scanner.*

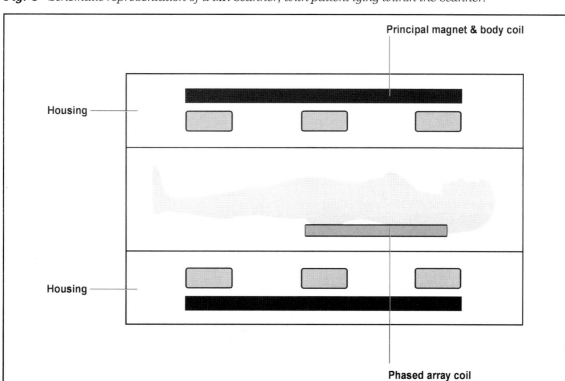

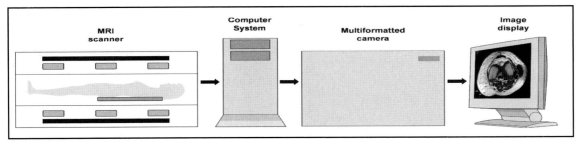

Fig. 6 *Schematic representation of equipment involved in MRI.*

A coil is put in place depending on the area to be scanned (a body coil for a large area or a smaller surface coil, as for the knee) (Figs.5,6). The surface coil is a radio-frequency antenna designed to be positioned near the surface of the tissue to be imaged to improve the signal to noise ratio (S/N) when imaging a localised area of the body. As high a S/N ratio as possible is required for good resolution of the image. When a patient is put into the scanner they are surrounded by the external magnetic field. Within this external magnetic field unpaired protons in atoms, with their associated magnetic fields line up with the external magnetic field.

When a radio frequency pulse is then switched on (as part of a pulse sequence) this induces magnetisation within unpaired protons within the scan field of view, lifting some protons to a higher energy level and decreasing their longitudinal magnetisation. It also causes the protons to precess or move or turn in phase together and induces a transversal magnetisation. When a radio frequency pulse is switched off two things occur:

(i) longitudinal magnetisation increases and is regained and
(ii) the protons get out of phase, the transverse magnetisation decreases.

Longitudinal relaxation (spin relaxation) has a time constant equalling **T1**.

The time constant **T2** is related to transverse relaxation time (spin relaxation).

The terms longitudinal and transverse relaxation can be replaced by the terms signal or signal intensity.

In biological tissues, T1 is approximately 300-2000 milliseconds and T2 is approximately 30-150 milliseconds.

The magnetic vectors reflecting longitudinal and transverse magnetisation directly determine the MRI signal and signal intensity by inducing electrical currents within the antennae.

When more than one radio frequency pulse is used, i.e. a succession of radio frequency pulses, this is called *a pulse sequence.* The TR is the repetition time, that is, the time between repetition of a pulse. The TE is the time between the administration of the pulse and the time at which the signal is measured or picked up by the antenna.

Different pulses can be employed (90° or 180° pulses) or alternatively the angle at which these are applied can be altered and different time intervals between repetition (TR) of the pulse and the time to measurement of the echo (TE) can be employed and thus many different pulse sequences are theoretically available. By the application of a variety of pulse sequences different types of contrast can be obtained.

Because each tissue has different relaxation values, it is possible to use sequences in order to specifically highlight contrast between different tissues. MR is not tissue specific, but it can give some indication as regards the nature of tissue present by assessment of how much water it contains, this being related to the high level of mobile protons in water. For example, acutely inflamed tissue is usually oedematous and this will be manifest by high signal on T2 weighted images.

Resolution

A similar grey scale is employed in imaging digital information as in CT. By convention, high signal intensity is white while low signal intensity appears black. To generate the image, the brightness of each pixel in the displayed image is proportional to the MR signal intensity emanating from the corresponding small volume of tissue.

In MRI, spatial resolution is achieved by the superimposition of various types of magnetic field gradients on top of the external magnetic field. These gradients are known as slice selecting, frequency encoding and phase encoding gradients. By a mathematical process known as Fourier transformation the image can be subsequently reconstructed such that, as in CT each pixel can be represented by an individual number. A higher spatial resolution will usually require a longer imaging time.

Contrast resolution between tissues can be accentuated by the application of appropriate pulse sequences. Maximising contrast resolution in MRI requires proper selection of imaging parameters in order to maximise the inherent contrast between different tissues. In addition the T1 properties of tissues are altered in the presence of administered intravenous Gadolinium chelates, improving the contrast

Basic Science for FRCS (Trauma and Orthopaedics)

differentiation of normal and pathological tissues.

Safety Considerations and Contra-indications to MRI

MRI utilises a high magnetic field. In view of this metallic objects are likely to undergo movement or an increase in temperature within the range of the magnetic field. While large fixed pieces of metal, such as a hip replacement, may cause significant artefact in the area being scanned, they are unlikely to move. Small pieces of metal however, such as that found in intra-ocular metal foreign bodies, with aneurysm clips and cardiac pacemakers are likely to move. Patients who have such pieces of metal in situ should not undergo a scan. Claustrophobia is also a contra-indication to MR, occuring in approximately 5-8% patients.

Ultrasound

A soundwave is a longitudinal pressure wave that produces compressions and rarefactions of the "particles" in the medium (a "particle" refers to a group of molecules in which the pressure and temperature is uniform and each particle is continuous with adjacent particles). The human ear can detect sound up to a frequency of approximately 20kHz. Ultrasound is any higher frequency wave that cannot be detected by the human ear and is used in medicine at a frequency between 1 to 15MHz.

Soundwaves travel at different velocities through different tissues, undergo partial reflection at the boundary between tissue interfaces and undergo diffraction, scattering and attenuation. Each medium through which an ultrasound beam passes is identified ultrasonically by its characteristic acoustic impedance.

The *acoustic impedance* for different materials is proportional to the density of that material/ medium and the speed of sound through that particular medium. As the ultrasound beam passes through a homogeneous medium, some of the ultrasound energy may be lost and converted into heat. Most media are not completely homogeneous and further ultrasound energy may be lost due to scatter from small regions in the tissue with a different acoustic impedance from the remainder of the tissue. Losses of energy due to scatter and heat production are collectively called attenuation. It is this diffuse reflection which gives different tissues their characteristic echogenic patterns. Ultrasound is particularly good at differentiating solid from cystic lesions as a result of the difference in density of the two media and subsequent different acoustic impedance.

Production of the Ultrasound Beam

An ultrasound transducer is a device that is capable of both converting an electrical signal into ultrasound waves and converting ultrasound waves back into electrical signals. The ultrasound wave is produced by an electric signal which causes the dimensions of the transducer to change rapidly, known as the *piezo electric effect*.

Fig. 7 Schematic representation of an ultrasound transducer probe.

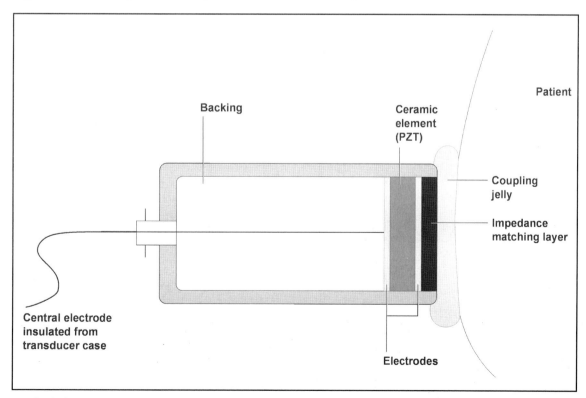

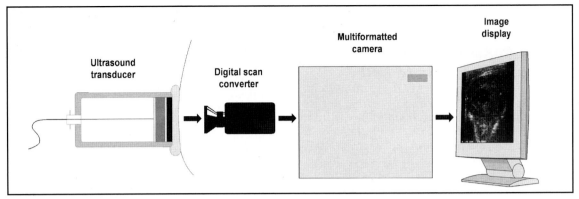

Fig. 8 *Schematic representation of ultrasound equipment.*

In piezo electric crystals, the electric charges bound within the lattice of the crystal can be considered to be in the form of dipoles. When an electric field is applied across the faces of the crystal, charges are repelled and the dipoles are compressed. This reduces the distance between the two faces of the crystal. When the polarity of the electric field is reversed, the dipoles are expanded and the distance between the two faces of the crystal is greater. If the polarity of the electric field changes in a sinusoidal manner, then a similar motion is produced in the crystal faces. This is transmitted to the air in contact with the face of the crystal, and an ultrasound wave is generated.

The crystal most commonly used for ultrasound transducers is lead zirconate titanate (PZT) which is a synthetic ceramic (Figs. 7+8). Being a ceramic, the transducer can be moulded and fired into any shape and can also be polarised in any direction. The most common shape produced is either a disc with flat faces or part of the surface of the sphere. The thickness of PZT must be the same over the transducer surface. A thin layer of silver is applied to each of the faces so that electric connections can be made. The transducer used to transmit the sound waves is also used to detect them after reflection. Some transducers have fixed focal distances and if areas of interest in a patient are at substantially different depths then a change in probe may be necessary. Varying focus probes can be produced using transducer arrays. A linear array (typically used in musculo-skeletal ultrasound) consists of many very small rectangular elements, typically 1-4mms wide.

The face of the transducer used to transmit and receive ultrasound must be coupled to the body in a way to achieve maximum transmission. The three materials involved in transmission are air, tissue and PZT.

A coupling oil or gel is used to ensure that there are no air gaps between the transducer and tissue. Transmission is further improved by inserting between the face of the transducer and the tissue, an intermediate layer of material with a characteristic impedance approximately mid way between tissue and PZT.

Real-Time Ultrasound

With real-time scanning it is possible to study movement of organs and vessels. This is carried out by utilising a number of small transducers within the scan head. Groups of transducers are then activated electronically in turn so that the pulses are scanned across the section and the picture is continuously updated with any interfaces that have moved since the last scan. The ultrasound pulses are scanned across the plane so quickly that a flicker-free image is produced which is continuously updated. Because of this real-time imaging, it is possible to dynamically evaluate structures by putting them through movements and examining the effect of that movement on the underlying structure.

Doppler Ultrasound

A moving surface can result in a change in frequency of the reflected ultrasound beam. This change in frequency can be used to measure the rate at which the reflecting surface is moving. Most real-time scanners will include the facility to carry out pulsed Doppler measurements with the same probe that is used to produce the real-time scan. The signal detected by the receiving transducer can detect the Doppler shifted frequency produced by moving interfaces and this can be extracted electronically from the returned signal.

Image display

Returned echoes from a real-time scan give positional information and also information on the strength of the echo and hence on the type of tissue reflecting the beam. The strength of the reflected signals is given in terms of shades of grey and the grey scale is used as elsewhere.

Musculo-Skeletal Ultrasound

In musculo-skeletal ultrasound high frequency probes (usually between 7 to 15MHz) are used. The frequency of the probe is directly proportional to the resolution that can be obtained. In ultrasound the frequency of the transmitted signal is inversely proportional to the depth of the tissue it can traverse and still produce a meaningful/visual signal. In musculo-skeletal work a high frequency probe will produce an image of high resolution especially at a low depth. The high frequency probes can be compared with a lower frequency 3-5MHz probe which is typically used for trans-abdominal scanning.

Basic Science for FRCS (Trauma and Orthopaedics)

Notes

Notes

Articular Cartilage Repair Techniques

Graham D Smith

Specialist Registrar, Nuffield Orthopaedic Centre, Oxford

It has been appreciated for centuries that the ability of cartilage to self-repair is limited[1,2]. Articular cartilage is avascular, alymphatic, and aneural. The surrounding extracellular matrix shields cartilage cells from even immunological recognition and the cellular response to injury within cartilage is minimal.

Damage to articular cartilage is a common problem and may lead to premature osteoarthritis[3]. At knee arthroscopy, the incidence of articular cartilage pathology has been found to be between 19% and 66%[4-6]. It is very difficult to predict the long term outcome of chondral injury. In some cases the amount of damage may be small and cartilage homeostasis may permit articular surface integrity to be maintained. If homeostasis is lost, the articular surface will break down, leading to further degenerative changes. The progression from chondral damage to osteoarthritis is slow and many people may be asymptomatic until the pathological process is advanced. In long-term follow-up of patients with chondral defects found at arthroscopy, radiological changes of osteoarthritis were seen in as many as 57% of patients, but few were symptomatic[7].

How should we approach these injuries? At present there is no evidence that any articular cartilage repair technique can reduce the risk of osteoarthritis occurring in the future. This evidence may come, but until it does, it would be reasonable not to treat asymptomatic lesions or incidental findings. In anterior cruciate ligament reconstruction, for example, the presence or absence of chondral damage has been shown not to affect the clinical outcome at a mean of 9 years[8]. An exception may be in the adult form of osteochondritis dissecans, where the incidence of premature osteoarthritis is as high as 80%[9]. In these patients it could be justified to repair the defect to reduce the risk of future degeneration.

What makes a joint painful is poorly understood. There are no pain receptors in articular cartilage, so pain arising from chondral defects must arise from elsewhere, most likely from bone. Articular cartilage is a tough, low friction interface, which allows the forces applied across a joint to be distributed over a wide area. Loss of integrity of articular cartilage may result in increased point pressure on underlying bone. Subchondral bone is usually protected from synovial fluid by intact articular cartilage. The action of hydrostatic forces from synovial fluid as well as increased point pressure may activate pain receptors in the subchondral bone

Cartilage repair techniques aim to treat damaged articular cartilage by replacing it with tissue that can restore the structure and function of the joint surface. The "holy grail" of cartilage repair would be to reliably repair lost cartilage with hyaline cartilage identical to that which was damaged. Unfortunately this has not yet been achieved. Articular cartilage has a unique and specialised structure. Its cellular content is low (2% by volume) and the metabolic rate of chondrocytes is also very low (1/50th that of a liver cell.) The fibrillar architecture of articular cartilage is complex, with arcades of type II collagen fibres, anchored to the underlying subchondral bone, held together with proteoglycans. The surface is smooth to allow gliding of the joint surfaces, and the matrix exerts a fixed negative charge, attracting water, resulting in a very resilient structure which can resist both sheer and compression forces.

A number of techniques have emerged which are used to repair articular cartilage. These techniques vary in complexity, but all of them result in filling of a defect to regain the integrity of the joint surface, protect the subchondral bone, and reduce pain. None of these techniques regenerate normal hyaline cartilage, but tissue may be generated which is structurally stable enough to give lasting benefit.

Microfracture.

This technique was introduced by Steadman some 20 years ago[10-15]. In this technique, debridement of unstable and damaged cartilage down to the subchondral plate is performed, creating a defect with a stable perpendicular edge of healthy cartilage. An arthroscopic awl is used to make multiple holes in the base of the defect (3-4 mm apart,) ensuring the structural integrity subchondral plate is maintained. When the tourniquet is released, elements of the bone marrow are seen to enter the defect, forming a "super clot," which provides an environment for the pluripotential marrow cells to differentiate into stable tissue[12]. The rehabilitation protocol is an important part of the microfracture procedure. The "superclot" in the defect is very friable and until it matures, may be dislodged if impacted. Early mobility of the joint with Continuous Passive Motion (CPM) is advocated in conjunction with reduced weight-bearing for an extended period.

Microfracture is a modification of the Pridie drilling technique[16;17]. Microfracture, drilling and debridement (abrasion arthroplasty) may all be considered as "marrow stimulation" techniques in that the chondral lesion is exposed to material moving from the bone marrow cavity through the subchondral plate. This layer is "unsealed" by removing the lower calcified layer of articular cartilage and by making holes which penetrate the subchondral plate. Theoretical advantages of microfracture include a reduction in thermal damage to subchondral bone caused by drilling, and a rougher surface which may make it easier for the repair tissue to adhere to. In addition, it is technically easier to penetrate the defect perpendicular to the surface at arthroscopy with an angled awl compared to a drill.

The histological results of Microfracture are mainly fibrocartilage, although in one series it has been shown that 11% of biopsies are predominantly hyaline cartilage and 17% a mixture of fibrocartilage and hyaline cartilage[18]

Mosaicplasty.

Mosaicplasty or Osteochondral Cylinder Transplantation (OCT) is a procedure where osteochondral plugs are taken with a cylindrical cutting device and used to fill a cartilage defect[19-24]. Plugs can be taken from the peripheries of the femoral condyles and the trochlear notch and are transplanted into a chondral defect as a "mosaic." Different sizes of plug can be used in order to maximise filling of the defect. The technique is usually done as an open procedure although it is possible to perform the surgery arthroscopically[25].

Advantages of mosaicplasty are that treated defects are immediately filled with mature hyaline cartilage and that both chondral and osteochondral defects can be treated. Donor site morbidity is a concern and the maximum recommended treatable area is $4cm^2$ [22]. There are technical difficulties in restoring the surfaces of cartilage and bone to produce a smooth convex joint surface. The thickness of the donor cartilage may differ from the area to be treated and reconstitution of the important subchondral bone layer may not occur. Lateral integration rarely develops[26], giving concern that synovial fluid may escape into the subchondral layer causing cyst formation. Perpendicular access to the cartilage surface by cylinder cutters is required in this technique which makes treatment of defects on the tibial plateau difficult.

Autologous Chondrocyte Implantation.

Autologous Chondrocyte Implantation was first performed by Peterson in Gothenburg in 1987 and was the first application of "cell engineering" in orthopaedic surgery. It is a two-stage procedure, (Fig 1.) and clinical results rated as good or excellent in 84% of patients have been recorded up to 11 years post-operatively[27].

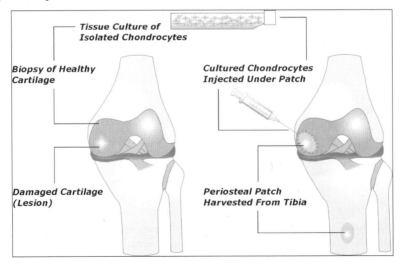

Fig 1. The Autologous chondrocyte Implantation Technique: Cells are harvested arthroscopically and grown in culture. Approximately three weeks later, an open procedure is performed where the defect is debrided and covered with a periosteal patch. The cultured chondrocyte suspension is injected under the patch.

Basic Science for FRCS (Trauma and Orthopaedics)

ACI Stage I: Cartilage harvest. This is done arthroscopically. The lesion to be treated is assessed, and cartilage is harvested from either the trochlea or the peripheral margin of the femoral condyle. A full thickness sample is taken which allows some healing of the harvest site by exposing subchondral bone.

In the laboratory, collagenase is used to release the cells from the matrix. The chondrocytes are collected by centrifugation and cultured. The patient's own serum is used as the culture medium. This process takes approximately 3 weeks until the cells are ready. Just before the second stage, the cells are suspended in a small volume of serum and delivered to the surgeon for implantation[28].

ACI Stage II: Chondrocyte Implantation. A parapatella approach is used and the lesion is debrided to stable margins. The size of the defect is measured and a patch of periosteum is taken from the proximal tibia (usually via a separate incision.) The patch is sutured onto the defect and fibrin sealant is used to make the pouch watertight. The cultured cells are injected under the patch. (Fig 2.) An alternative to periosteum is a synthetic patch derived from porcine collagen. This patch is easier to handle and can be used in a similar way to periosteum. In Matrix Assisted Chondrocyte Implantation (MACI), chondrocytes are seeded on the synthetic membrane instead of being injected under the patch[29].

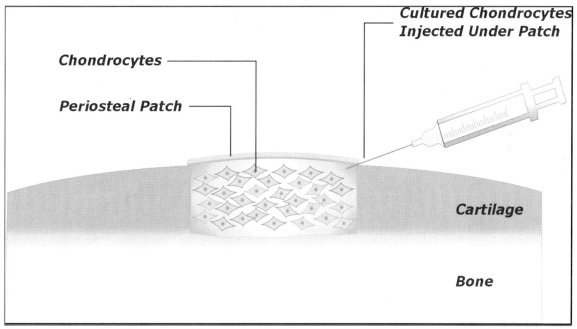

Fig 2. Cross-section of ACI treated lesion showing chondrocyte suspension being injected underneath a periosteal patch.

Similar to microfracture, the treated defect is fragile in the early stages and must be protected to prevent dislodgement. After ACI Stage II, the knee is splinted for 6 hours to allow cell attachment. Following the attachment phase, CPM continues for 48 hours. Weight bearing is limited for 8 weeks. Low impact exercise such as cycling is encouraged initially, with jogging allowed at 6 months and return to contact sports after a year[30].

ACI is capable of producing a tissue which is "hyaline-like" or "predominantly hyaline"[31]. However, the best repair tissue is not morphologically or histo-chemically identical to normal hyaline cartilage and the majority of samples are in the "mixed" or "fibrocartilage" category.

Comparative evidence.

Which technique is the best? At present there is no hard evidence to support one technique over the others. There have been a handful of randomised clinical trials comparing these methods. Two trials have compared ACI with mosaicplasty[26;32], one being in favour of ACI and the other mosaicplasty. A Norwegian group has performed a randomised study of ACI versus microfracture[18]. This trial identified no statistically significant difference at two year follow-up in all but one of the clinical outcome measures used. (The physical component of the SF-36 score was better in the microfracture group.) In this trial, the histological appearance of biopsies in the ACI group was better than the microfracture group, although the trend did not reach statistical significance.

It is possible that better histology may result in superior longevity of the graft, although so far there is no significant clinical difference at 5 years in this group of patients[33].

Clinical trials are ongoing, including the ACTIVE trial which is a multi-centre MRC funded study based in Oswestry. In this trial patients are randomised to receive either ACI or the "best alternative" treatment, (be it microfracture, mosaicplasty or other treatment based on the surgeon's choice.) This and other trials may be able to determine which treatment is better, but a difference may only be found after long-term follow-up when the durability of treated defects is compared.

The future of articular cartilage repair.

There is a lot of research aimed at improving techniques in cartilage repair. Modifications in the technique of ACI include using chondrocyte impregnated scaffolds for cell delivery[34]. A flexible scaffold or fleece can be rolled up, and delivered arthroscopically, removing the requirement for performing an arthrotomy[35,36].

Do we actually need to use chondrocytes? Some researchers have used cultured bone marrow mesenchymal stem cells which are capable of transforming into chondrocytes[37,38]. Using bone marrow derived cells instead of chondrocytes means that cartilage harvest would be unnecessary, eliminating the potential for donor site morbidity.

Do we need to use in vitro cultured cells? One group is using a hybrid procedure called Autologous Matrix Induced Chondrogenesis (AMIC,) which uses a collagen patch over a defect which has been microfractured[39]. The rationale of this treatment is to contain the marrow contents released from the base of the defect in microfracture, offering some protection of the clot in the early post-operative period. Other approaches include using growth factors to modulate cell growth kinetics and extracellular matrix production, and gene therapy techniques may be used in the future to turn on chondrogenesis where it is needed. Tissue engineering in cartilage repair is in its infancy and the techniques available at present are crude. Even the matrixes which are being developed come a long way from reproducing the complex structure of hyaline cartilage; all they do is act as biodegradable carriers to deliver cells to a cartilage defect. In the future, nano-technology could be used to engineer articular cartilage by assembling type II collagen and proteoglycans into a hyaline matrix which could be populated with chondrocytes and transplanted. This approach is still a long way off being a reality.

	Microfracture	Mosaicplasty	ACI
Procedure	Arthroscopic	Open	Stage I: arthroscopic Stage II: open (3 week interval
Technical difficulty	++	+++	++++
Specialist Equipment	Arthroscopic Awls	Cylinder cutters	Fibrin glue Cultured cells
Rehabilitation	Protected WB	Protected WB	Protected WB
Cost	+	++	++++

Table 1. Comparison of articular cartilage repair techniques

References.

1. Hunter W. Of the structure and disease of articulating cartilages. Philos Trans R Soc Lond 1743;42: 514-21.

2. Hunter W. Of the structure and disease of articulating cartilages. The classic. Clin Orthop 1995; 317: 3-6.

3. Mankin HJ. The response of articular cartilage to mechanical injury. J Bone Joint Surg 1982; 64B: 460-6.

4. Aroen A, Loken S, Heir S, Alvik E, Ekeland A, Granlund OG et al. Articular cartilage lesions in 993 consecutive knee arthroscopies. Am.J.Sports Med. 2004;32: 211-5.

5. Curl WW, Krome J, Gordon ES, Rushing J, Smith BP, Poehling GG. Cartilage injuries: a review of 31,516 knee arthroscopies. Arthroscopy 1997;13: 456-60.

6. Hjelle K, Solheim E, Strand T, Muri R, Brittberg M. Articular cartilage defects in 1,000 knee arthroscopies. Arthroscopy 2002;18:730-4.

7. Messner K,.Maletius W. The long-term prognosis for severe damage to weight-bearing cartilage in the knee: a 14-year clinical and radiographic follow-up in 28 young athletes. Acta Orthop.Scand. 1996;67:165-8.

8. Shelbourne KD, Jari S, Gray T. Outcome of untreated traumatic articular cartilage defects of the knee: a natural history study. J.Bone Joint Surg. 2003;85A: (Suppl 2.): 8-16.

9. Linden B. Osteochondritis dissecans of the femoral condyles: a long-term follow-up study. J.Bone Joint Surg 1977; 59A: 769-76.

10. Steadman JR, Rodkey WG, Singleton SB, Briggs KK. Microfracture technique for full-thickness chondral defects: technique and clinical results. Operative Tech in Orthop 1997;7: 300-4.

11. Blevins FT, Steadman JR, Rodrigo JJ, Silliman J. Treatment of articular cartilage defects in athletes: an analysis of functional outcome and lesion appearance. Orthopedics 1998;21: 761-7.

12. Steadman JR, Rodkey WG, Rodrigo JJ. Microfracture: surgical technique and rehabilitation to treat chondral defects. Clin.Orthop. 2001; 391 (Suppl) S362-9

13. Steadman JR, Briggs KK, Rodrigo JJ, Kocher MS, Gill TJ, Rodkey WG. Outcomes of microfracture for traumatic chondral defects of the knee: Average 11-year follow-up. Arthroscopy 2003;19: 477-84.

14. Steadman JR, Miller BS, Karas SG, Schlegel TF, Briggs KK, Hawkins RJ. The microfracture technique in the treatment of full-thickness chondral lesions of the knee in National Football League players. J.Knee.Surg. 2003;16: 83-6.

15. Miller BS, Steadman JR, Briggs KK, Rodrigo JJ, Rodkey WG. Patient satisfaction and outcome after microfracture of the degenerative knee. J.Knee.Surg. 2004;17: 13-7.

16. Pridie, K. H. A method for resurfacing the osteoarthritic knee joint. J.Bone Joint Surg 1959; 41B: 618-19.

17. Insall J. The Pridie debridement operation for osteoarthritis of the knee. Clin.Orthop Relat Res 1974; 56: 61-7.

18. Knutsen G, Engebretsen L, Ludvigsen TC, Drogset JO, Grontvedt T, Solheim E et al. Autologous chondrocyte implantation compared with microfracture in the knee. A randomized trial. J.Bone Joint Surg 2004;86A: 455-64.

19. Bobic V. Arthroscopic osteochondral autograft transplantation in anterior cruciate ligament reconstruction: a preliminary clinical study. Knee.Surg.Sports Traumatol.Arthrosc. 1996;3:262-4.

20. Gudas R, Kalesinskas RJ, Monastyreckiene E, Valanciute A, Trumpickas V. [Osteochondral transplantation for the treatment of femoral condyle defects]. Medicina (Kaunas.) 2003;39: 469-75.

21. Hangody L, Kish G, Karpati Z, Szerb I, Udvarhelyi I. Arthroscopic autogenous osteochondral mosaicplasty for the treatment of femoral condylar articular defects. A preliminary report. Knee.Surg.Sports Traumatol.Arthrosc. 1997;5: 262-7.

22. Hangody L,.Fules P. Autologous Osteochondral Mosaicplasty for the Treatment of Full-Thickness Defects of Weight-Bearing Joints: Ten Years of Experimental and Clinical Experience. J.Bone Joint Surg 2003; 85A: 25-32.

23. Morelli M, Nagamori J, Miniaci A. Management of chondral injuries of the knee by osteochondral autogenous transfer (mosaicplasty). J.Knee.Surg. 2002;15:185-90.

24. Solheim E. [Mosaicplasty in articular cartilage injuries of the knee]. Tidsskr.Nor Laegeforen. 1999;119: 4022-5.

25. Huang H, Yin Q, Zhang Y, Zhang Y, Cao Z, Li J et al. Mosaicplasty osteochondral grafting to repair cartilaginous defects under arthroscopy. Zhonghua Wai KeZa Zhi, 2002;40: 662-4.

26. Horas U, Pelinkovic D, Herr G, Aigner T, Schnettler R. Autologous chondrocyte implantation and osteochondral cylinder transplantation in cartilage repair of the knee joint. A prospective, comparative trial. J.Bone Joint Surg 2003; 85A:185-92.

27. Peterson L, Brittberg M, Kiviranta I, Akerlund EL, Lindahl A. Autologous chondrocyte transplantation. Biomechanics and long-term durability. Am J Sports Med 2002;30: 2-12.

28. Harrison P.E., Ashton I.K., Johnson W.E.B., Turner S.L., Richardson J.B., Ashton B.A. The in Vitro Growth of Human Chondrocytes. Cell Tissue Banking 2000;1: 255-60.

29. Bartlett W, Skinner JA, Gooding CR, Carrington RW, Flanagan AM, Briggs TW et al. Autologous chondrocyte implantation versus matrix-induced autologous chondrocyte implantation for osteochondral defects of the knee: a prospective, randomised study. J Bone Joint Surg 2005; 87B: 640-5.

30. Bailey A, Goodstone N, Roberts S. Rehabilitation after Oswestry autologous chondrocyte implantation: the OsCell protocol. J.Sports Rehabil. 2003;12:104-18.

31. Roberts S, McCall IW, Darby AJ, Menage J, Evans H, Harrison PE et al. Autologous chondrocyte implantation for cartilage repair: monitoring its success by magnetic resonance imaging and histology. Arthritis Res.Ther. 2003;5: R60-R73.

32. Bentley G, Biant LC, Carrington RW, Akmal M, Goldberg A, Williams AM et al. A prospective, randomised comparison of autologous chondrocyte implantation versus mosaicplasty for osteochondral defects in the knee. J.Bone Joint Surg 2003;85B: 223-30.

33. Knutsen G, Drogset J, Engebretsen L, Grontvedt T, Isaksen, V., Ludvigsen T, Roberts, S, Solheim E, Strand, T., and Johansen, O. ACI v Microfracture - the picture at 5 years. 193. 31-10-2005. Sports Knee Surg 2005; 193: Abstract.

34. Ochi M, Uchio Y, Kawasaki K, Wakitani S, Iwasa J. Transplantation of cartilage-like tissue made by tissue engineering in the treatment of cartilage defects of the knee. J.Bone Joint Surg 2002;84B: 571-8.

35. Ochi M, Adachi N, Nobuto H, Yanada S, Ito Y, Agung M. Articular cartilage repair using tissue engineering technique--novel approach with minimally invasive procedure. Artif.Organs 2004;28:28-32.

36. Erggelet C, Sittinger M, Lahm A. The arthroscopic implantation of autologous chondrocytes for the treatment of full-thickness cartilage defects of the knee joint. Arthroscopy 2003;19:108-10.

37. Wakitani S, Imoto K, Yamamoto T, Saito M, Murata N, Yoneda M. Human autologous culture expanded bone marrow mesenchymal cell transplantation for repair of cartilage defects in osteoarthritic knees. Osteoarthritis Cartilage 2002;10:199-206.

38. Wakitani S, Mitsuoka T, Nakamura N, Toritsuka Y, Nakamura Y, Horibe S. Autologous bone marrow stromal cell transplantation for repair of full-thickness articular cartilage defects in human patellae: two case reports. Cell Transplant. 2004;13: 595-600.

39. Anders, S., Gellissen, J., Zoch, W., Lobenhoffer, P., Grifka, J., and Behrens, P. Autologous Matrix Induced Chondrogenesis (AMIC) for focal chondral defects of the knee - first clinical and MRI results. ICRS 2006 . Abstract

Osteoarthritis

Dr S Roberts

Senior Research Scientist
Robert Jones & Agnes Hunt Orthopaedic Hospital
Oswestry

Osteoarthritis is the most common joint disorder in the UK affecting more than 1 million people. It is an expensive disorder costing 1.1% of the gross national product in western societies. Osteoarthritis is characterised by altered joint anatomy, especially loss of articular cartilage and formation of osteophytes. These changes are clearly seen radiologically as joint narrowing and bone growth and sometimes sclerosis or cyst formation (Fig.1). In most cases the aetiology is unknown and it is generally considered to be a multifunctional disorder with many possible routes to a common endpoint (Table 1). It is less inflammatory than some other arthritides such as rheumatoid arthritis but there can be some signs of inflammation. Of the two hundred or so synovial joints in the human body those most frequently affected are the knee, elbow, distal interphalangeal, hip and acromio-clavicular. The incidence in all joints increases with advancing age.

1. Classifications

Over the years there have been many attempts at classification systems to group similar osteoarthritis patients together, eg

- **familial/non-familial**

- **primary idiopathic/secondary osteoarthritis**

- **atrophic/hypertrophic osteoarthritis**

- **nodal/generalised.**

2. Joint Changes in Articular Cartilage in Osteoarthritis

Although most studies of osteoarthritis concentrate on changes in the cartilage or bone, all the tissues within the joint can be affected by the disease. Hence muscles can atrophy,

Table 1 Factors Implicated in the Aetiopathogenesis of Oseoarthritis

Mechanical insult (wear/tear)
Joint shape
Occupational and recreational activities
Genetic predisposition
Antecedent condition,
    eg Perthes, Paget's disease,
    hip dysplasia, infection (present in
        approximately 20% of cases)

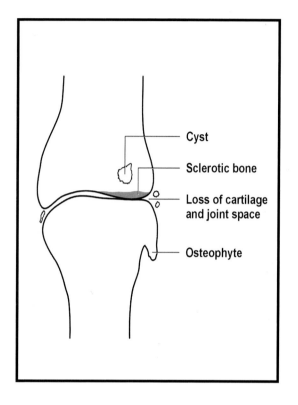

Fig.1 Typical features used in defining osteoarthritis radiologically.

synovia can become hyperplastic, the joint capsule can become fibrotic and bursitis can occur in the joint bursae.

Whilst there are almost always changes in the bone, they are variable, ranging from sclerosis and eburnation of the subchondral bone to excessive new bone growth at the rim of the joint or osteophytes and often severe localised loss of bone in cysts. Articular cartilage changes however, are more consistent, in that it becomes softer, damaged or fibrillated at the surface and becomes progressively thinner and worn away, particularly in weight bearing regions.

Perhaps it is this consistency that has made cartilage the focus of much study in the aetiopathogenesis of osteoarthritis of the last few decades. Whilst we know now much detail about the matrix changes in cartilage, all of this study has not elucidated the aetiology of osteoarthritis and there remains much debate and conjecture on this matter. For the bulk of this chapter most discussion will relate to properties of articular cartilage and how they change in the disease.

(a)

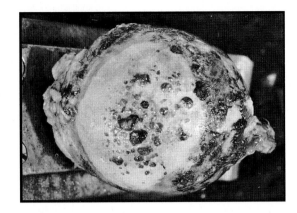

(b)

Fig.2 Islands of fibrocartilage can be found 'mushrooming' up through the subchondral bone in some individuals with late-stage osteoarthritis. Femoral head from (a) a 77 year old female and (b) a 73 year old male removed at surgery for arthroplasty.

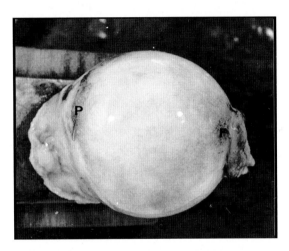

(3a)

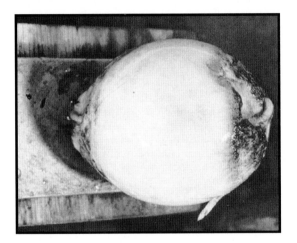

(3b)

Fig.3 Apparently normal areas of cartilage can be demonstrated to have early fibrillation when brushed gently with Indian ink. Femoral heads from
(a) 17 year old female and
(b) 67 year old female.
Note the extensive fibrillation demonstrated by this technique in (c) from a 90 year old female.

2.1 Morphological changes in osteoarthritis

The most significant features of an osteoarthritic joint removed at surgery or autopsy are alterations in the shape of the joint, full-thickness cartilage loss, bone exposure and eburnation, remodelling and osteophytosis and cyst formation. Sometimes small areas of fibrocartilage 'mushroom' up from the denuded bone (Fig.2).

Cartilage damage begins with fibrillation or microscopic disruption of the surface layer. In certain locations, such as around the insertion point of the ligamentum fovea, it is a normal feature of ageing. In the weight bearing regions of the joint, however, such as the zenith of the femoral head, it is indicative of osteoarthritis. Areas that may initially appear normal macroscopically can often be demonstrated to be fibrillated by brushing the surface with Indian ink (Fig.3).

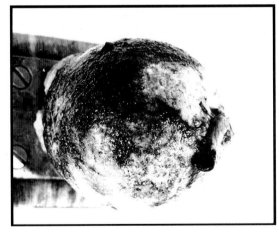

(3c)

Microscopically this early fibrillation can be seen as superficial clefts. As osteoarthritis progresses these clefts become deeper, cartilage is lost and chondrocyte clusters are common in the remaining cartilage. There is substantial reduction in metachromasia and glycosaminoglycan or proteoglycan staining (eg with toluidine or alcian blue or safranin O) in the cartilage matrix (Fig.4), which can be seen even before any surface damage is apparent. Ultrastructurally, electron microscopy studies demonstrate that collagen fibrils become

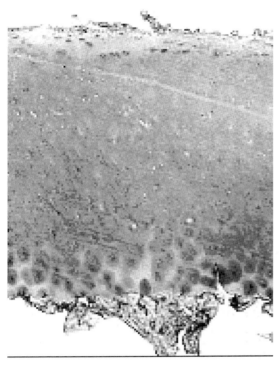

Fig.4 Histological section of articular cartilage stained with safranin O. This has only slight surface damage in the very upper region with a small amount of loss of proteoglycan here.

increasingly disorganised: the fibril diameter becomes more variable and initially there is an increase in interfibrillar matrix and water and sometimes matrix vesicle formation. In early osteoarthritis the chondrocytes retain their metabolic activity. At this stage and when clefts first appear, the cells are capable of proliferation and increased matrix synthesis. However, when the collagen microskeleton is destroyed, such cell activity does not continue. As fibrillation advances, structureless electron dense material accumulates in the superficial matrix. Chondrocytes degenerate further, chromatin condenses, the cells become apoptotic and cell numbers decrease.

2.2 Biochemical changes

As with the morphology there is a chronological sequence of alterations to the composition of articular cartilage as osteoarthritis progresses. Quantitatively, the most significant finding is in the proteoglycan and water component.

2.2.1 Collagen - The weak link

Early osteoarthritis (where structural changes to the cartilage are not visible to the naked eye) is characterised by an increased swelling potential of the matrix and increased water content. This is thought to result from disruption of the collagen matrix, reducing its ability to resist the swelling pressure of the glycosaminoglycan population present. Disruption of the collagen structure might result from enzymatic activity or possibly trauma, either of which could arise from altered loading. There is, however, little quantitative change to the overall collagen content of osteoarthritic cartilage as measured by hydroxyproline despite many qualitative changes to the collagen, such as crosslinking or type of collagen present. The population of minor collagens change with disease progression, for example types I, III, VI and X can be seen increasingly.

2.2.2 Proteoglycan - The prime mover

The most consistent and severe change in the biochemistry of osteoarthritic cartilage is loss of the large aggregating proteoglycan, aggrecan (responsible for the loss of metachromasia morphologically). The decrease of aggrecan and glycosaminoglycans (GAGs) is directly proportional to the severity of the lesion. The changes are not uniform throughout the depth and the region of maximum change alters as the disease progresses. As well as a change in the total proteoglycan content, there are many alterations to the proteoglycan quality as well (Table 2). In general the large aggrecan, becomes more fragmented, smaller and leaches out of the tissue.

2.2.3. Enzymes

The eventual biochemical composition in cartilage matrix is the result of the synthetic or anabolic capability of the cells countered by the degradative process or catabolism of the cells. In osteoarthritis and other arthritides the normal equilibrium becomes shifted more towards catabolism. This is primarily mediated by an increase in degradative enzymes.

Matrix metalloproteinases (MMPs) are a family of enzymes which are zinc and calcium dependent. Several members are active on cartilage components and can be present in synovial fluid as well as being produced by chondrocytes. They are found in increased quantities in osteoarthritis. Whilst many enzymes can degrade proteoglycans, it is only the collagenases which can degrade the helical collagen molecule. Hence these are very important potentially in 'loosening the collagen matrix' in early osteoarthritis. MMP-13 is the most potent collagenase, being very reactive against type II collagen and it has been found

Table 2 Changes in Proteoglycan populations in Osteoarthritis

- ♦ Loss of glycosaminoglycan and aggrecan content
- ♦ Decrease in the ratio of keratan sulphate:chondroitin sulphate
- ♦ Increase in chondroitin-4-sulphate relative to chondroitin-6-sulphate, particularly in patients in early OA (indicating new synthesis of glycosaminoglycan)
- ♦ Overall decrease in glycosaminoglycan chain length in late stage OA (early OA may have increased glycosaminoglycan length due to initial new synthesis of GAGs)
- ♦ Decrease of proteoglycan aggregates and size of aggregate
- ♦ Decrease of hyaluronan (HA).

Table 3 *Metalloproteinase Enzymes capable of degrading Cartilage Components*

Matrix MetalloProteinase	Common name	Substrate
MMP 1	collagenase 1	helical collagen, aggrecan
MMP 8	collagenase 2	helical collagen, aggrecan
MMP13	collagenase 3	helical collagen, aggrecan
MMP 2	gelatinase A	collagen fragments or gelatin
MMP 9	gelatinase B	or elastin or fibronectin
MMP 3	stromelysin 1	aggrecan, gelatin, fibronectin
MMP 10	stromelysin 2	aggrecan, gelatin, fibronectin
MMP 11	stromelysin 3	aggrecan, gelatin, fibronectin
MMP 12	macrophage metalloelastase	
MMP14	membrane bound MMP	
ADAMTS		
Adamts -4 and -5	aggrecanase -1 and -2	aggrecan

to be increased in osteoarthritis. Matrix metalloproteinases have naturally occurring inhibitors, tissue inhibitors of matrix metalloproteinases or TIMPs. The quantity of these is reduced in osteoarthritis, further tipping the balance towards matrix degradation.

Proteoglycans can be degraded by many enzymes. There has been much interest recently in a group of enzymes called aggrecanases which belong to the ADAMs (A Disintegrin And Metalloproteinase) family. Aggrecanase degradation products have been found frequently in synovial fluid and cartilage in osteoarthritic patients. It appears that both aggrecanases and MMPs are important in aggrecan breakdown, the two groups of enzymes perhaps having different chronological expression.

2.2.4 Cytokines and Growth Factors

Cytokines or cellular messengers, such as the interleukins, are thought to be important in the progression of the arthritides. Some, such as IL-4, may be chondroprotective. However, most of them are implicated in osteoarthritis, such as IL-1 and IL-6 and appear to increase catabolism (via increased production of matrix metalloproteinases) and decrease anabolism (via decreased proteoglycan synthesis by chondrocytes), resulting in a net loss of matrix components, such as aggrecan. Various growth factors have been investigated, mainly in tissue

culture systems. A summary of their influence here and their supposed role in osteoarthritis can be seen in Table 4. It is the balance between the milieu of cytokines present in a joint which will determine the status of the cartilage.

3. Markers of Osteoarthritis

Osteoarthritis is not usually a fast-progressing degenerative disease. Longitudinal monitoring is thus important in assessing the status quo of the patient. Our improved understanding of the aetiopathogenesis has lead to a better capability for monitoring the disease progression in the individual patient via the use of markers (Table 5).

3.1 Anabolic markers

Since normal adult cartilage demonstrates little propensitity for type II collagen production *in vivo*, any increase in this must indicate anabolism. Type II collagen production can be measured via the level of the C-propeptide (CP-II) of type II collagen (which is cleaved from newly synthesised procollagen to produce type II collagen). It can be measured in either the synovial fluid or the serum.

3.2 Catabolic markers

These include degradation products of either the proteoglycan or collagen population, eg aggrecan, cleaved by either matrix

Table 4 *Cytokines and Growth Factors*

Name	Effector Mechanism	Primary Effect
FGF	chondrocytes/ fibroblast	proliferation
IGF-1	chondrocytes	proliferation and ↑glycosaminoglycan synthesis
TGFb	chondrocytes	proliferation, ↑matrix synthesis, ↑ TIMPs
IL-1	chondrocytes	↑MMPs, ↑PGE$_2$, ↓glycosaminoglycan synthesis
IL-6	chondrocytes	↑TIMPs, ↑ proliferation ↑MMPs, ↓glycosaminoglycan synthesis
TNFα	chondrocytes	as IL-1
IL-4	chondrocytes	chondroprotective
IL-10	chondrocytes	chondroprotective

Table 5 Metabolites with Potential for use as Markers of OA

MARKER	TISSUE	INDICATE:	CHANGES IN OA: SERUM/SYNOVIAL FLUID	
Hyaluronan	synovial fluid	synovitis	↑	ND
C-propeptide collagen II	cartilage	collagen synthesis	↑	↑
COMP	cartilage	synthesis ± degradation	ND	↑
Collagen X-links	cart/bone	synthesis ± degradation		↑(urine)
KS	cartilage	synthesis/deg of aggrecan	↑	↑
core protein	cartilage	degradation		↑
CS epitopes	cartilage	?synthesis		↑
osteocalcin	bone	bone synthesis	↑	↑

(ND = not detected)

metalloproteinases or aggrecanase. Degeneration products of collagen (CTX-2) have been measured in serum and urine and appear to correlate with disease progression.

However, as with all markers, understanding their metabolism of potential markers is vital to understanding the relevance of levels measured and their reliability in different tissue fluids.

4. Aetiology of Osteoarthritis

Whatever the primary cause of the disease it would appear that there is an initial response within the joint to attempt to repair or counter the immediate damage or insult.

4.1 Repair

There seems to be several primary or initiating factors for osteoarthritis which can be superimposed on the ageing process and lead to a faster degeneration of the cartilage and bony changes. In the cartilage this is seen as cell proliferation or cloning, often accompanied by increased metachromasia, representing greater proteoglycan production. This is termed intrinsic repair. When the metabolically active contribute to the problem, for example, osteophyte formation or extrinsic repair can lead to further change and development of process fails to match the triggering insults then joint failure, or endstage osteoarthritis results. The repair process may eventually lead to abnormal joint shape and hence further altered loading.

4.2. Inflammation

There are intermittent phases of inflammation in osteoarthritis, possibly due to separated fragments of cartilage and bone or 'loose bodies' causing a response from the synovium or capsule; crystals of sodium pyrophosphate in the synovial fluid or hydroxyapatite from cartilage can also be responsible. However, the inflammmatory reponse is not consistent and much less marked than, for example, in rheumatoid arthritis. Indeed for many years there was much debate as to whether '....itis' should even feature in the name and there was a tendency then to call the disorder osteoarthr*osis*.

4.3 Cartilage versus bone for initial change

Whilst most studies in osteoarthritis have focussed on cartilage as the prime tissue, there has been increasing debate over recent years as to whether the initial changes occur here or in the underlying bone. Normally the thin cartilage lamina is protected from the effects of repeated impact by the energy absorbing capacity of the bone. If, however, this becomes increased in stiffness, the cartilage may be more liable to damage and trauma caused by impact. It has been suggested that bone may contribute to osteoarthritis by undergoing stiffening as a

Figure 5 Possible factors involved in the Aetiopathogenesis of OA

		Compensation with no symptoms	↗
Insults:	Trauma	}	**Repair process:**
	Metabolic abnormality	}	Chondrocyte metabolism
	Instability	}⇨ ⇨	Osteophyte remodelling
	Ageing	}	Synovial response
	Other factors	}	Capsular response
		↘	
		Decompensation with symptoms, disability	

Table 6 Genetic Polymorphisms demonstrated in OA

Structural defect - eg	collagen II
	fibrillin
	collagen V
Interleukin - 8 receptor	
Vitamin D receptor	

result of numerous microfractures sustained before cartilage disorder is obvious.

4.4 Genetics

There are certain populations in which the incidence of osteoarthritis is markedly lower than that, for example, in western populations. Similarly, certain families appear to have a preponderance to osteoarthritis. Identical twins are twice as likely to develop osteoarthritis if one has it, than occurs in non-identical twins. These observations have led to the suggestion that there are genetic influences in the disease although the exact level of the influence remains unclear and with some studies suggesting that it may be as ahigh as 60%. Possible prime candidates can be seen in Table 6.

4.5 Ageing versus osteoathritis

Whilst there is no doubt that the incidence of osteoarthritis increases with increasing age and some of the changes seen with both processes are similar, it is clear that they are not one and the same process. Whatever causes osteoarthritis can be superimposed on ageing changes, or ageing changes may lead to a more rapid progression of osteoarthritis. The differences between ageing and osteoarthritis can be seen in Table 7.

5. Animal Models

Animal models of any disease are important not only in trying to unravel its aetiopathogenesis, but also as systems in which to test pharmaceutical or alternative therapies which are at a developmental stage. Whilst they are no doubt useful in these aspects they have limitations and results cannot be assumed to be exactly the same in humans as in the animal models. Models can be divided crudely into two groups:

(a) those that focus on certain specific parameters, the effect of which can be assessed in a defined system to learn more about their role in the complex pathology and

(b) those which attempt to mimic the complex situation found in humans by the use of genetically predisposed models. The most commonly used models are discussed briefly below.

5.1 Genetic Predisposition

5.1.1 Canine hip dysplasia

Selective breeding has produced a population of labrador dogs with enhanced susceptibility to hip dysplasia and osteoarthritis. The osteoarthritis is not restricted to the hip but can also be found in the knee and shoulder joints. At the morphological and biochemical level the canine and human osteoarthritic tissues are very similar and this group has provided an instructive model of early events in the osteoarthritic process.

5.1.2. Rhesus macaque

Both calcium pyrophosphate dihydrate crystal (CPPD) arthopathy and non-crystal associated degenerative arthritis are found in a colony of rhesus macaque monkeys in Puerto Rico. The degenerative arthritis is similar to osteoarthritis in humans and changes in the cartilage can be observed before any changes in the bone are seen. The knee joint of these animals resemble those of human in both form and function and are large enough to allow arthroscopy in addition to histological and biochemical study.

Table 7 Differences between Ageing and OA

	OSTEOARTHRITIS	AGEING
CHONDROCYTES	Cloning of cells forming clusters	↓ number in superficial zone ↑ in numbers in DZ
ECM	↑ hydration early, ↓ late-stage more reducible crosslinks: (early OA)	↓ hydration ↑ stable collagen crosslinks
PGS	↓ PG aggrecan content ↑ C-4-S:C-6-S ratio ↓ KS:CS ratio	↓ aggrecan content ↑ KS:CS ratio ↑ HA binding region domain ↑ decorin,
HA AND LP	↓ HA	↑ HA content, but shorter chains ↑ proteolytic degeneration of LP

5.1.3 Hartley guinea pig

Spontaneous cartilage degeneration develops in the femoro-tibial joint in the male Hartley guinea pigs between 60 and 90 days of age. By 12 months there is bilateral fibrillation over 50% of the medial tibial surface. Cartilage lesions occur which become increasingly severe and resemble tissue seen in human osteoarthritis.

5.1.4. Spontaneous osteoarthritis in mouse

Spontaneous arthritis arises in the C57 black mouse. In this strain of mice characteristic osteoarthritis-like changes take place, progressing from about six months of age, most prominently in the knee joint due to a distal shift in the patella, leading to altered joint congruity. Other strains of mice with spontaneous osteoarthritis include YBR/Wi and STR/ORT strains which have anatomical anomalies leading to osteoarthritis.

5.2 Altered loading models of osteoarthritis

Whilst there is evidence that genetic factors predispose to osteoarthritis it is also clear that work, sports and lifestyle in general contribute to the development of the disease. By understanding the regulation of articular cartilage matrix to joint loading, certain factors may be identified.

Restriction of movement and weight bearing by splinting the knee in several species of animals (eg sheep, dog, rabbit, rat, mouse, guinea pig) have been used as models of reduced joint load, with deleterious effects to the articular cartilage. These changes begin with loss of proteoglycan and surface fibrillation within two and seven days, respectively, in the rabbit and dog. Biochemical changes resembled those seen in human osteoarthritis.

Increased loading has also been used in an attempt to produce osteoarthritis, for example, the contralateral joint to that immobilised or splinted as described above. Alternatively, excess exercise regimes (treadmills etc) have been used. These models produced mixed results, sometimes giving alterations similar to those seen in osteoarthritis but often not. Changes which may be induced by some regimes can be reversed. Study of features such as this may give a better insight into repair possibilities for cartilage.

5.2.1 Rabbit Meniscectomy

Surgical damage of other tissues in the joints, such as, the menisci or ligaments in the knee, will also lead to altered function and loading. For example, a partial, lateral meniscectomy, by sectioning the fibular collateral and sesamoid ligaments and removing 4-5 mm of the anterior lateral meniscus, results in osteoarthritis-like changes in joints of rabbits within six weeks of surgery. There is loss of both tibial and femoral cartilage and bone lesions in the operated joints whereas the contralateral control, sham operated joints remain normal.

5.2.2 Pond-Nuki Dog Model

This model has been generated by sectioning the anterior cruciate ligament of the dog knee, creating instability and laxity and so altering the biomechanics of the joint. The biochemical changes that occur initially in the cartilage are increased hydration, particularly in the superficial layer, loss of tensile strength, increased cell activity, together with osteoarthritic-like changes of the underlying subchondral bone. The long term progression to full blown OA, beyond 2 years post-surgery, is not always inevitable, however, in this model.

6. Future Therapies

Whilst arthroplasty as a treatment for osteoarthritis must be considered one of the great successes in orthopaedics in the last century there remain problems with it. Not least of these is the finite and relatively short life of the prosthesis which is particularly pertinent in an increasingly aged population. A more biological approach to treating osteoarthritis and utilising the body's own cells to reverse and repair the disease process may provide a suitable alternative. There are several aspects of this being investigated currently.

6.1 Pharmacology

There are obviously many pharmaceutical agents currently available to decrease pain and inflammation in the arthritides. However, areas showing potential for development include antagonists of catabolic agents, such as interleukins-1, 6, TNFα aggregates only occurs in the extracellular matrix. and enzymes, such as matrix metalloproteinases or aggrecanases. Clinical trials are underway with several candidates. Infliximab and other TNFα antagonists, are showing great promise in diminishing pain and inflammation in arthritis patients although side effects and contraindications are not insignificant. Another class of drugs now widely available are the cyclo-oxygenase (COX)-2 inhibitors, such as celecoxib. COX-2 is an enzyme which encourages the inflammatory cascade from arachodonic acid, resulting in local prostanoid release in addition to peripheral nociceptor sensitisation. It is upregulated in arthritis, hence the use of COX-2 inhibitors leads to diminution of symptoms. As well as developing new therapies we can improve our understanding of the action of old remedies. For example, it appears that the action of cod liver oil and other fish oil extracts(containing 3-omega fatty acids) also inhibit COX-2 (and lipo-oxygenase) enzymes and thence inhibit aggrecanase and MMP production, diminishing the loss of proteoglycan from cartilage matrix.

Chondroprotective agents are another area of development.

Components such as hyaluronan, glucosamine and chondroitin sulphate are purported to have potential in this respect.

However convincing studies for this particular parameter, at least for long term efficacy are lacking. Other factors such as IL-4 which can decrease the activity of the cytokines associated with catabolism may prove to be more useful.

6.2 Biological repair

Various techniques have and are being used to stimulate the body's own cells to produce a replacement tissue for the articular cartilage lost in osteoarthritis. These incude microfracture and drilling of the subchondral bone, when precursor cells within the mesenchymal stem cell in bone marrow are thought to give rise to fibrocartilage production at the surface. More recently much interest has been focussed on culturing various autologous cell types in the laboratory before returning them to the patient either with or without some type of scaffold, such as polylactic or polyglycolic acid or a collagen and hyaluronan mesh. One such technique, autologous chondrocyte implantation, involves using the patient's chondrocytes and returning them to the damaged area under a layer of periosteum which is stitched, and sometimes glued, into position. Whilst this particular technique is restricted to being suitable for relatively small areas, variants of the technique are being developed which it is hoped could lead ultimately to 'resurfacing' of an osteoarthritic joint.

6.3 Genetic engineering

With the establishment of the human genome it is to be expected that genetic engineering will become a most powerful tool in treating many diseases, including osteoarthritis. In the short term, however, there are many obstacles to overcome, including ethical objections.

A small trial has been carried out in the US, where patients' synovial cells were transfected with a gene for IL-1 receptor antagonist via retroviruses. (IL-1 Ra blocks the receptor for IL-1, so diminishing its catabolic effects.) Transfected cells were then injected into the patients' arthritic metacarpopharyngeal joints. This study was very preliminary and involved few individuals and there remain many technical difficulties including obtaining an efficient transfection rate and sustaining the genetically engineered cell population in vivo. In addition, one must have absolute confidence in being able to contain the genetic engineering. With time, and resolution of these problems, however, genetic engineering could prove to be a very powerful tool.

Summary

With the changing demographic trends and increasingly aged population, an age related disorder such as osteoarthritis will become ever more important. Hence it is likely to remain a major part of the orthopaedic surgeons' workload for a long time to come. Whilst the problem may remain constant, the way the orthopaedic clinician is likely to approach treatment will almost certainly change significantly over the working life of the reader. Instead of a 'hammer and chisel' approach, the tools of the trade are likely to get more subtle, ie more chemical and biological, and hopefully more long lasting.

SUGGESTED READING:

Bullough, PG. Orthopaedic Pathology, 3rd edition. Mosby-Wolfe, (London) 1997.

Curtis,CL.Rees,S.G. Little,C.B. Flannery,C.R. Hughes,C.E. Wilson,C. Dent,C.M. Otterness,I.G. Harwood,J.L. Caterson,B. Pathologic Indicators of Degradation and Inflammation in Human Osteoarthritic Cartilage Are Abrogated by Exposure to n-3 Fatty Acids. Arthritis Rheum 2002; 46:1544-53.

DeLise, AM. Fischer, L. Tuan, RS. (2000) Cellular interactions and signalling in cartilage development. Osteoarthritis and Cartilage 8: 309-34.

Doherty, M. Jones, A. Cawston TE. Osteoarthritis. In: Maddison PJ editor,Oxford textbook of rheumatology 2nd ed. Oxford University Press, 1998; 1515-33.

Ghosh, P. Smith, M. Osteoarthritis, genetic and molecular mechanisms. Biorheology 2002; 3: 85-88.

Hascall, V. and Kuettner, KE. Many Faces of Osteoarthritis. (Boston) Birkhauser, 2002.

Hunziker, EB. Articular cartilage repair: basic science and clinical progress. Osteoarthritis Cartilage 2002; 10:432-63.

O'Driscoll, SW. The healing and regeneration of articular cartilage. J Bone Joint Surg 1998; 80A: 1795-1812.

Roughley, PJ. Articular cartilage and changes in arthritis: non-collagenous proteins and proteoglycans in extracellular matrix of cartilage. Arthritis Research 2001;3:342-7.

Notes

Notes

The Biomechanics of Hip Joint Replacement

Dr A.J.C.Lee

*Honorary Research Fellow
Department of Engineering
University of Exeter,
Exeter, England*

*Honorary Consultant Clinical Scientist
Royal Devon and Exeter Hospital
Exeter, England*

This chapter will consider three aspects of the biomechanics of the hip joint and should lead, in the end, to a much greater understanding of hip joint replacement. The topics to be considered are:

- The biomechanics of the natural hip aspects of particular importance with regard to total hip replacement.
- Conventional models of the hip ? unless models of the hip are available for use in the laboratory, for use in finite element analysis, etc, it is not possible to assess devices before they are used clinically.
- Biomechanics of total hip replacements ? there are a number of devices currently in use; the biomechanics of these devices is not identical, it is important to understand how existing devices function.

The chapter will concentrate on the biomechanics/fixation of total hip joint femoral stems, the biomechanics/fixation of acetabular cups will be considered very briefly. The use of cemented or cementless cups in clinical practice varies in different clinics and in different areas of the world, and is a somewhat controversial matter: it is beyond the scope of this short chapter to cover the topic fully

Biomechanics of the natural hip

This paper is concerned with the biomechanics of hip joint replacement and, as such, is aiming to consider those biomechanical factors which influence the design, development and testing of hip implants. The biomechanics of the normal joint will be considered, but only in as much as it helps the understanding of the artificial joint.

Any biomechanical study concerned with joint replacement needs to determine the magnitude and direction of the forces that act on the implants and in the bones into which the implants fit. It is necessary to see how these forces arise - that means that we have to study some aspects of the physical anatomy of the bones and muscles around the joint, and it is necessary to investigate how forces are transmitted from the implant components to the surrounding bones and tissues

Forces acting at the hip joint

The usual starting point for the analysis of forces acting at the hip joint is the skeleton, in this case the bones of the pelvis and leg .

The structure is easy to understand, it is easy to see with X-rays and has been studied for many years. However, a study of the skeleton only tells part of the story and must be supplemented by an understanding of the forces transmitted by the muscles if hip biomechanics is to be understood.

Initially, three general points need to be made:

- Joints are virtually friction free; consequently joints only transmit compressive forces.
- Bones transmit bending, compression and torsion in a variable combination.
- Muscles and ligaments transmit tension.

Looking more closely at muscles and their function, again three points need to be made:

- Muscles stabilise the skeleton against gravitational and inertial forces
- Muscles initiate and maintain movement
- Muscles control the placement/position of limbs

It is useful to look at three contrasting ways in which the problem of determining hip joint forces have been considered: the 'historical' methods used by Pauwels[1], the gait analysis methods used by Berme and Paul[2] and the direct measurement method used by Bergmann et al[3].

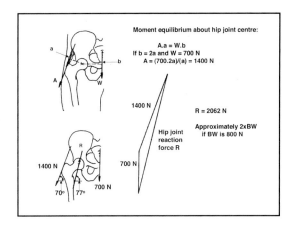

Moment equilibrium about hip joint centre:

$$A.a = W.b$$
If $b = 2a$ and $W = 700$ N
$$A = (700.2a)/(a) = 1400 \text{ N}$$

1400 N

$R = 2062$ N

Approximately 2xBW if BW is 800 N

Hip joint reaction force R

1400 N   700 N

700 N

70°   77°

Fig 1:
Simple Model of the hip joint and hip joint forces

Pauwels proposed a very simple model of the hip joint as shown in Fig.1. The hip is considered in two dimensions only and a single abductor represents musculature.

Equations of static equilibrium (forces up equal forces down; forces to the right equal forces to the left and anticlockwise moments equal clockwise moments) are applied, resulting in a prediction of the hip joint resultant force R to be about 2.5 x body weight (BW). The magnitude of the force turns out to be about right but cannot give an accurate assessment of stresses in the femur as the analysis exists only in two dimensions (no torsion or stress in the anterior/ posterior direction).

A number of investigators have used gait analysis to predict joint forces in the lower limb, the group in Strathclyde led by Professor JP Paul[2] being one of the best known. Patients with normal and abnormal hips were asked to walk or run along a walkway in the laboratory and step on a force plate which could record all forces and moments imposed on it, from heel strike to toe off, during the walking/running cycle. The results from Paul's group rely on a mathematical model of the bones and muscles to translate the forces measured at the foot/ground interface to the forces at the hip joint and indicated that the maximum value of the vertical component of the joint force, J_y, during a walking cycle is about 2.25 x BW, that there is a significant anterior/ posterior force, J_x, with a maximum value of about ± 1.8 x BW, and a medial/lateral force J_z with a maximum value of about 0.8 x BW. The three dimensional nature of the hip joint force revealed by gait analysis is clearly shown by this work.

Perhaps the most accurate determination of hip joint forces to date comes from Bergmann et al[3] in Berlin. They have developed a replacement hip joint with a radio telemetry device built to the neck of the femoral component. Their paper reports that the telemetry hip has been implanted into two hips of a male patient and one hip of a female patient. Results from measurements made in these patients are shown in summarised in Table 1.

	Walking	Jogging	Stumbling
Max. hip joint force (BW)	3	5	7
Frontal plane moment (%BW*m)	5	8	14
Torsion (%BW*m)	1	4	5

Table 1: Telemetry hip joint test results

It can be seen that forces and torques are very large (a torque of 4% BW*m is approximately equal to a torque of 32 Nm for a Body Weight of 800N).

Structure of the hip joint

Having established the magnitude and direction of the forces at the hip joint, it is possible to extend the analysis to see how the forces and induced moments and torques are controlled and reacted around the hip. Looking at a plain X-ray of the top of the femur (Fig.2), a number of points become clear. The cortical shell covering the head of the femur is very thin and

has to be supported by the underlying trabecular bone, forces put onto the head of the femur are transmitted to the structural parts of the bone (the cortical bone) by the trabeculae.

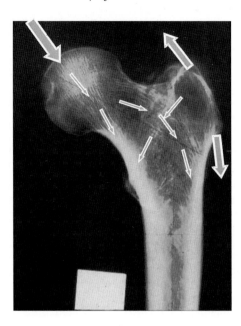

Figure 2 : Transmission of force from the head of the femur into trabecular bone

The cortical bone of the femur thickens as it receives load, the increase in thickness is gradual, therefore the cortex absorbs load over a significant length of the femur (not at a single, identifiable level) and the load is taken into the cortical bone from the inside of the bone. By the mid diaphysis, the medial and lateral cortices are of nearly equal thickness, indicating that they are loaded by forces of similar type and magnitude and not by forces resulting from simple bending (simple bending would give tension in the lateral cortex, compression in the medial cortex - significant tension is not normally resisted by bone but by tendons and ligaments). Finally, the musculature attaches to the outside of the cortical bone and reacts the forces, moments and torques between the bones of the joint (primarily the femur and pelvis) to complete the force path, as originally proposed by Pauwels and illustrated in Fig.1. As will be discussed later, the nature of the forces in the trabeculae, whether they are tensile or compressive, is important.

Laboratory and computer models of the hip joint

There are a significant number of replacement hip joints in clinical use that are functioning successfully after many years in use in patients, for more than twenty five years in a number of instances[4]. It is clear that any new hip joint replacement has at least to equal this level of function and should, if possible, exceed it. Consequently, there has to be a method of evaluating a proposed new device, using physical models in a laboratory or numerical models in a computer, before the new device is used in people. The evaluation model has to be able to

Basic Science for FRCS (Trauma and Orthopaedics)

accelerate the testing time - testing a device for twenty years to predict performance at twenty years is clearly not acceptable. So, the models that are used to carry out the initial design of a new device, or its evaluation, must be properly representative of the natural joint into which the device is implanted and reflect the forces, moments, torques, musculature and support conditions of the natural joint as well as providing a test regime that can predict performance using accelerated tests.

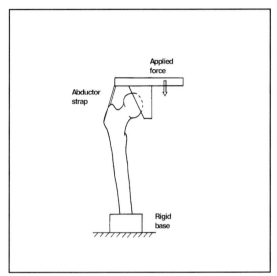

Fig 3: Simple laboratory model of loaded femur

It is useful to look at a typical laboratory model to see how representative it is - the typical model is shown in Fig.3. It consists of the proximal half of a femur articulating with a half pelvis - represented by a rigid horizontal bar. A single abductor strap connecting the greater trochanter to the pelvis represents musculature. The whole assembly is fixed into a rigid support at the lower end of the femur. In this set up the femur is acting as a simple cantilever - nothing like the situation in-vivo. Is it any surprise, therefore, if results from tests carried out in such apparatus are poor: garbage in, garbage out! Indeed, many tests with apparatus which is very similar to that illustrated (and which are reported in the literature) show strains of the order of 2000µε for an applied load of about 1.25 x BW. The strain recorded in the tibia of a live patient running on a treadmill (thus applying about 4 x BW) was 743µε tensile, 2000me shear and 1226µε compression[5], the maximum strain ever recorded in bone, in a racehorse, was 4750µε[6]; above 3000µε fatigue damage will occur. Consequently, for a test apparatus to record a strain of 2000µε at such low values of applied load indicates that something is seriously wrong with the design of the apparatus.

Applying the vertical equilibrium equation to the simplistic laboratory model gives the result that the vertical support reaction at the built-in base of the bone equals the vertical component of the applied load. Evidence from measurements taken from patients with strain gauged and telemeterised proximal femoral

prostheses undergoing simultaneous readings of telemetry, EMG and ground reaction forces show this is not true[7]. Moment equilibrium on the model will give the result that the medial cortex is in compression while the lateral cortex is in tension - again, not true. The conclusion is that models must be improved and, in particular, muscle activity must be modelled properly if predictions from models are to be realistic.

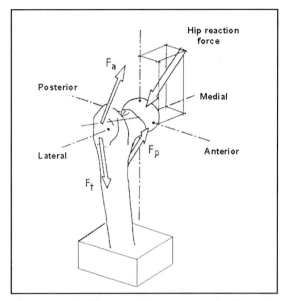

Fig4: Model of femur with some muscles for Finite Element Analysis

Are computer models any better? A computer model is only a numerical version of a physical model, so if the computer model is a numerical version of figure 3, then it too will be seriously flawed. Most models used in computer analysis are better than the simple one shown in figure 3; a more typical model was developed in the author's laboratory in the mid eighties. A numerical model of the proximal end of the femur was constructed[8] for finite element analysis, with a representation of a small number of muscles (Fig.4).

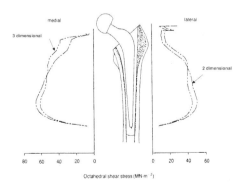

Fig 5: Stress at the centre of the medial and lateral faces of the stem from 2- and 3-dimensional models

The numerical model itself was built-in at the mid-diaphysis level (bad!). Octahedral shear stress* contours on the medial and lateral faces of the stem for a two-dimensional and three dimensional analyses are shown in Fig. 5 and the effect of muscle forces on the axial stress in the bone is shown in Fig.6. Clearly there is a difference between the predicted stresses - it can be concluded that two-dimensional models are definitely not accurate and the influence of muscle forces is significant. It must be stated that computer models in particular are getting better very rapidly; the increased power of modern computers means that more and more realistic models can be constructed[9]. It may well be that, in the near future, numerical models used for finite element analysis will be accurate enough to start to predict clinical results - not possible at the present state of development. The strength of finite element analysis of hip joints, as of any other joint, is the ease with which different factors can be compared and the relative importance of the factors established.

* Octahedral shear stress.
$$s = . \{ (.1 - .2)^2 + (.2 - .3)^2 + (.3 - .1)^2 \}^{1/2}$$

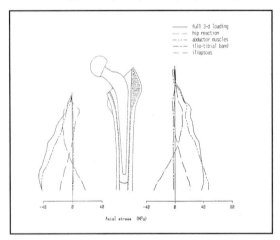

Fig 6: Variation of axial stress in the bone produced by full 3-d loading, hip reaction force and individual muscle forces.

The transmission of forces within the distal part of natural femora.

The structure of the hip joint has already been discussed and the bone of the top of the femur illustrated in Fig.2. It is important to establish whether the trabecular bone structure of the distal end of the femur is in tension or compression - a replacement joint femoral stem has to engage with and interlock into the trabecular bone and it is very much easier to construct a reliable compression interlock than a tensile one. It can be shown[10] that the trabeculae are nearly always in compression, consequently, the stem of the femoral component has to achieve a compressive interface with the bone, this is likely to be the only reliable interface that can be routinely achieved. Under the action of the hip joint reaction force and the muscle forces (particularly those of the ilio-tibial tract and the vastus

lateralis) around the greater trochanter of the femur, a tension band effect on the femur is produced, which reduces bending and increases compression in the cortical bone.

Design of femoral stems for total hip replacement

When considering load transmission between stem and bone, the 'design philosophy' of the stem must be recognised. Broadly, there are three commonly used modes of fixation:

- Cementless fixation
- Cemented, all interfaces fixed
- Cemented, stem cement interface free to slip, cement bone interface fixed

These fixation philosophies are described in more detail in the papers by Shen[11] and Lee[12]. The important conclusion from consideration of the different stem fixation modes is that the stress regime at the vital implant-bone interface (NB cement is 'implant') is similar in nature for fixation modes 1 and 2, different for mode 3. For cementless fixation and for cemented fixation with all interfaces fixed, the interface stresses at the implant-bone interface give rise to high shear stresses, low compressive stresses and the possibility of some tensile stresses. For the cemented, taper-slip, fixation, the stresses at the cement bone interface are significantly different -low shear stresses, high compressive stresses and almost zero tensile stresses. The long-term properties of bone cement, particularly creep and stress relaxation, are primarily responsible for the 'conversion' of tensile stress into compressive stress at the cement bone interface[12]. There is an easily visible difference in clinical behaviour between the two types of cemented fixation, the 'all interfaces fixed' type should not show visible subsidence on plain X-rays, indeed subsidence of more than 2 mm is a clear indicator of impending failure. The 'taper slip' type will be seen to move inside the cement mantle, with an average movement of about 1.3mm in two years, followed by stability. The subsidence of the 'taper slip' implant is not a precursor to loosening, indeed it indicates tightening inside the cement mantle.

Stem surface finish

Load transmission from stem to bone is a function of stem shape, stem surface finish and (for cemented devices) cement properties and cementing technique. The influence of stem shape on load transmission is described by Shen[11] and Lee[12]; these papers indicate the major differences between, for example, stems with and without collars; such differences were referred to above and will not be considered in more detail here. The effect of cement properties and technique will be considered in another chapter in this book - "The role, properties and use of bone cement in total joint replacement". However, it is appropriate to consider briefly the effect of stem surface finish on stem function.

The long term survival of total hip replacement stems is affected by the production of debis at the interfaces and by osteolysis of the femur. Debris production is significantly affected by the surface finish of the stem, whether it is matt or polished. The dividing line between what is considered a matt surface and a polished surface is not an absolute quantity; from numerous observations of many different types of stem it has been deduced that a surface acts as a matt (rough) surface when S_a is above about 0.3mm and a surface acts as a polished (smooth) surface when S_a is below about 0.04mm (see note at the end of this section for definition of S_a). A matt finish stem produces wear debris by an abrasive mechanism, giving rise to particles of metal and cement that are released into the joint space and can lead to osteolysis, expansion of the stem mantle and, maybe, loosening of the implant. A polished surface produces wear by fretting of the surface, leading to loss of metal below the level of the original surface, with the stem-cement interface and the cement surrounding the worn surface remaining undisturbed[13, 14]

NOTE: S_a is a surface roughness assessment and is the 3D equivalent of R_a. Surface roughness parameters are defined in comparison with a plane obtained through levelling of the mean square plane of the measured surface and then through centreing of heights around the mean. S_a is the arithmetic mean of the deviations from the mean plane.

Acetabular cups ~ design and fixation

There is no doubt that acetabular cups present a greater long-term problem than stems. Loosening of cups is more common and often occurs relatively late, typically between ten and fifteen years after implantation. The fixation of cups is controversial - whether to use cemented or cementless techniques. In Sweden, as a result of the information contained in the Swedish National Hip Register, cemented cups are most commonly used[15]. In the USA, for other reasons including aggressive marketing, cementless cups are almost always used. The biomechanical situation is also complex, the pelvis is a flexible structure loaded by a complex array of muscles. Accurate insertion of cups is difficult. Optimal materials are not yet determined - whether to use 'conventional' or highly cross-linked ultra high molecular weight high density polyethylene, whether to use metal-on-metal couples or one of the ceramic alternatives that are becoming available. There will continue to be much laboratory and clinical research in this area; at present, in the absence of convincing long-term clinical results, the best acetabular cup system cannot be defined.

Conclusions

1. Forces, moments and torques acting around the hip joint are large. They have been accurately measured at the hip joint itself for cases where the joints have been totally replaced. Detailed descriptions of the way in which the forces, moments and torques are transmitted around the hip, from femur to pelvis, by muscles and ligaments are not known accurately.

2. Laboratory models and computer models are never perfect, they are only as good as the assumptions and simplifications made in their design. In any study of the biomechanics of hip joint replacement, it is necessary to use a model of the hip joint that is firmly based on clinical reality - it must work from the foot/ground contact up and include the musculature that transfers the hip joint loads around the pelvic area. The model may then be able to describe more accurately the performance of existing devices and be useful in predicting the performance of new devices before they are inserted into patients.

3. The design philosophy of the stem fixation system is important and will effect the stress regime at the implant bone interface

References

1.Pauwels F. Biomechanics of the normal and diseased hip. Publ. Springer -Verlag, 1976.

2.Berme N and Paul J P. Load actions transmitted by implants. J.Biomed.Eng. 1979; 1: 268-72.

3.Bergmann G, Graichen F and Rohlmann A. Hip joint loading during walking and running measured in two patients. J.Biomech 1993;26: 969-90.

4.Callaghan JJ, Albright JC, Goetz DD, Olejniczak JP and Johnson RC. Charnley total hip arthroplasty with cement: a minimum 25 year follow-up. J Bone Joint Surg 200; 82A: 487-97.

5.Burr DB, Milgrom C, Fyhrie D, Forwood M, Nysaka M, Finestone A, Hoshaw S, Saiag E and Simkin A. In-vivo measurement of human tibial strains during vigorous activity. Bone 1996; 18: 405-10.

6.Nunamaker DM, Butterweck DM and Provost MT. Fatigue fractures in thoroughbred racehorses: relationship with age, peak bone strain and training. J Orthop Res 1990; 8: 604-11.

7.Lu T -W, Taylor S J G, O'Connor J J and Walker P S. The influence of muscle activity on the forces in the femur: an in-vivo study. J Biomech 1997; 30: 1101-06.

8.Fagan M J and Lee A J C. The loading of cemented femoral hip stems: a finite element investigation. Chapter 14 in: Yettram,AL editor. Material properties and stress analysis in biomechanics. Manchester University, Press, 1986; 188-202.

10. St Clair Strange The Hip, publ W Heinemann Medical Books Ltd, London, 1965.

11. Shen G. Topic for debate: Femoral stem fixation. J Bone Joint Surg 1998;80B: 754-56.

12 Lee A.J.C. The time dependent properties of polymethymethacrylate bone cement: the interaction of shape of femoral stems, surface finish and bone cement. In: Learmonth I D editor. Interfaces in total hip arthroplasty. Berlin: Springer 2000. p11-19.

13 Howell JR, Blunt LA, Lee AJC, Hoper RM, Gie GA, Timperley AJ and Ling RSM. An investigation of the fretting wear seen on explanted hip replacement femoral stems. J.Bone Joint Surg 2000; 82B: (Supp I): 52.

14 Howell, J.R., Blunt, L.A., Doyle, C., Hooper, R.M., Lee, A.J.C., Ling, R.S.M. In vivo surface wear mechanisms of femoral components of cemented total hip arthroplasties: the influence of wear mechanism on clinical outcome. J. Arthroplasty 2004; 19: 88-101.

15 Malchau H, Herberts P, Garellick G, Soderman P and Eisler T. Prognosis of total hip replacement: update of results and risk-ratio analysis for revision and re-revision from theSwedish National Hip Register 1979-2000. Scientific exhibition, 69th Annual Meeting of the AAOS, Dallas, USA, February, 2002.

The Role, Properties and Use of Bone Cement in Total Joint Replacement

Dr A.J.C.Lee

Honorary Research Fellow
Department of Engineering
University of Exeter,
Exeter, England

Honorary Consultant Clinical Scientist
Royal Devon and Exeter Hospital
Exeter, England

Introduction

We are concerned with a material, bone cement, that has been in clinical use in orthopaedic surgery for more than forty years, has been used in patients many millions of times and has, in the vast majority of cases, been extremely effective. However, in too large a number of cases, the material has been reported as being not good enough and has been (wrongly) blamed for clinical failures. If bone cement is functioning well in a large number of cases and functioning poorly in others, there must be some reason, probably connected with the properties or use of the cement that leads to the variation in performance. Consequently, it is the aim of this paper to review the properties and use of bone cement, and to give some clinical results, to see if a proper understanding of the characteristics of bone cement can lead to improved results in patients.

Role of bone cement

The role of bone cement in a primary or revision total joint replacement can be described under three headings:

1 to locate the implant component in bone

2 to transmit load from the component into bone

3 to encourage maintenance or restoration of bone stock.

Bone cement needs to have particular characteristics to enable it to function properly and fulfil the long-term requirements of a total joint replacement. These characteristics will be discussed as this paper progresses, but it is clear that certain commercially available cements function better than others. In the results of the Swedish National Hip Arthroplasty Register[1] the following risk ratios were given:

Type of Cement	Risk Ratio
SulfixÒ	1.00
CMWÒ	0.73
SimplexÒ	0.60
PalacosÒ	0.51
Palacos GentamicinÒ	0.49

The reasons why these differences exist have to be discussed.

Mechanical properties of bone cements.

Most bone cements in clinical use today are variants on a very common polymer, polymethylmethacrylate (PMMA). As there are currently about forty different PMMA bone cements on the market, it is important to choose a cement with a long clinical history that is known to have adequate strength. Details of the properties of the various cements are given in the book by Kühn[2], in this paper typical properties will be given.

The physical properties of bone cement may conveniently be described under two headings: short-term properties and long-term properties. Short-term properties are those properties that can be found experimentally by taking a sample of material into a laboratory and testing in a conventional materials testing machine. Typical properties[3,4] will be found as:

Tensile strength	25	MPa
Shear strength	40	MPa
Compressive strength	90	MPa
Modulus of elasticity	2400	MPa

It is clearly seen that bone cement is weak in tension, strong in compression and has a low modulus of elasticity (often called Young's modulus and given the symbol E). Comparing the Young's modulus of PMMA with that of other materials found in total joint replacements

$$E_{metal} = 10x \; E_{cortical \; bone}$$

$$E_{metal} = 100x \; E_{PMMA}$$

it is seen that there is an order of magnitude difference between the moduli of the various materials used in a total joint replacement.

The long-term properties of bone cement are equally as important as the short-term properties - if a material is required to function for 25+ years, we should know how the material is likely to behave over such long time periods. The long-term properties that are of particular concern are Creep, Stress Relaxation and Fatigue[5,6]

Creep

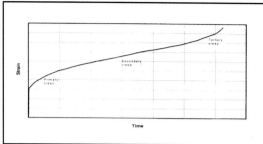

Fig 1: Creep ~ time dependant deformation under constant load

Creep is defined as time dependent deformation under constant load (Figure 1). It can be seen that a specimen of viscoelastic material will deflect by a certain amount (proportional to the applied load/stress) at time zero. As time passes, with the material under constant load, the deflection increases until, in an unconstrained specimen, failure takes place. The deflection regimes can be divided into three stages,

stage 1   primary creep
stage 2   secondary creep and
stage 3   tertiary creep.

Stage 1, primary creep, sees deformation change rapidly; stage 2, secondary creep, sees deformation take place almost linearly with time; and stage 3, tertiary creep, sees rapid deformation, leading to failure. In the context of PMMA bone cement as used in total joint replacement, the cement is normally constrained by cortical bone and the tertiary creep stage which leads to failure, is not reached. Although the definition of creep implies the load should be constant, creep still takes place under variable loads as experienced by bone cement in joint replacements. Creep is important for PMMA bone cement at body temperature (37°C) but is not important for the metals used in joint replacements as the stresses and temperatures are too low for creep to occur in them. As a result of a significant number of investigations[5,6] it can be confirmed that all conventional bone cements creep, that the creep rate reduces with time after polymerisation, that creep rate is influenced by the environment surrounding the cement (rate in intralipid is 2.3x rate in saline), that creep rate increases with temperature (rate at 37°C is 3.5x rate at 20°C) and, in common with all materials, creep rate increases with stress level.

Stress relaxation

Stress Relaxation is the second long-term time dependent property that must be considered. Stress relaxation is defined as the change in stress with time under constant strain. (Figure 2)
Suppose a specimen of bone cement is put in a testing machine and loaded in tension so that

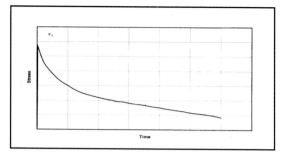

Fig 2: Stress relaxation ~ the change in stress with time under constant deformation (tension shown)

it is strained and develops a stress s_0 over its cross section. If the grips of the testing machine are clamped and held at that instant so that the deflection (strain) of the specimen is maintained constant, it will be found that the load needed to maintain the deformation changes with time (load reduces in the case of a tensile test). As the load changes, so the stress changes. Stress relaxation occurs in all bone cements at body temperature, it occurs most easily under conditions of tensile loading and is caused by a similar mechanism in the structure of the polymer as that which causes creep - the side chains of the long chain molecules which make up the polymer flick and slide over each other, causing the specimen to extend under creep conditions and reducing tensile stress under stress relaxation conditions. Both creep and stress relaxation will take place under tensile, compressive or shear conditions, but will take place preferentially under tensile conditions.

Fatigue

Fatigue is the final long-term time dependent property to be considered. Fatigue is the effect of repeated load cycles below the level needed to fail the material in a single application of the load cycle (Figure 3).

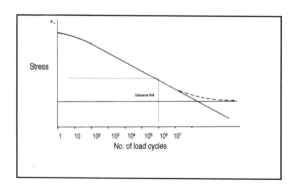

Fig 3: Fatigue ~ the effect of repeated load cycles below the level needed to fail the material in a single application.

Suppose a load cycle that takes a specimen up to a given stress and back to zero is imposed upon the specimen. If the given stress is the ultimate stress s_u then the specimen will fail at s_u at the peak load of the first cycle. If the given stress is about half the ultimate stress, then the load cycle has to be repeated about 10^6 times before failure takes place in the material represented by figure 3. For most metals there is a stress level, known as the 'endurance limit', such that, if the stress developed is less than the endurance limit, then the material will never fail. There is no endurance limit for polymers like PMMA bone cement; these polymers will all eventually fail if loaded continuously for many millions of load cycles. It is important to note two facts:

1. The time axis is a logarithmic axis, so it only takes a small reduction in stress level to extend the life of a specimen by a very large amount.

2. Virtually all reported fatigue tests which end up by quoting a fatigue life, are tests where the load cycles are applied continuously, with no rest periods. For example, a test may apply 10^7 load cycles at 4 Hz continuously to a specimen and report failure. Such a test would take about 29 days to complete; in life 10^7 load cycles would take about 10 years to be put on the cement - patients are not active for 24 hours every day!

The extended time of reality is important; during the patient's rest periods stress relaxation can take place, reducing the tensile stress level in the cement. Since fatigue failure is primarily a tensile mode of failure, it can be seen that bone cement, in a patient, has a 'self-protection' mechanism built into its material characteristic.

Significance of long term properties

The long-term properties of bone cement have a substantial effect on the stresses set up in the cement because loads are put into the cement in a variable pattern. In a relatively simplistic way, loads can be described as a pattern of high loading during the day when a patient is active followed by low loading during the night when the patient is asleep. This pattern repeats day after day. The effect on stresses is described in detail in Lee[7] - briefly, tensile stresses set up as a result of creep during loading periods are significantly reduced by stress relaxation during unloading periods, leaving the residual stress at the cement/bone interface as mostly compression.

The use of bone cement in clinical practice.

The use of bone cement will be considered under five headings:
1 Choice of cement
2 Mixing cement
3 Preparation of the bone cavity
4 Creation of the interface between cement and bone
5 Definition of a modern cementing technique

Clinical results from Exeter and the Swedish National Hip Arthroplasty Register will then be described to answer the question "Is cementing technique important?"

Choice of bone cement

It is assumed that commercially available PMMA bone cement will be used. Such cements can be classified according to a number of variables, the most important being the presence or absence of antibiotics in the cement and the viscosity-time curve of the cement during the mixing/insertion phase.
There are three antibiotics containing bone cements commonly available:

(a) PalacosÒ with 0.5g of gentamicin

(b) SimplexÒ with 0.74g of erythromycin and 0.24g of colistin

(c) SimplexÒ with 1.0g of tobramicin

These cements all have mechanical properties that are marginally (i.e. about 4%) less than the plain versions of the cement[8] and they all have similar viscosity-time characteristics to the plain cements. The choice (antibiotic or plain) of cement is entirely a matter for the individual surgeon who must be guided by the patient's clinical history, particularly whether the procedure is a primary replacement or a revision. Most surgeons use antibiotic cement for revision procedures. If it is decided that a specific antibiotic needs to be used in the cement, other than those in (a), (b) or (c) above, then the antibiotic must be in powder form (never use liquid antibiotics) and must be stable at the temperatures reached during cement polymerisation. Hand mixing antibiotics into cement will produce a greater reduction in mechanical properties than with commercially available cements.

The different commercially available cements have different viscosity-time curves during mixing. These differences are shown diagrammatically in Figure 4.

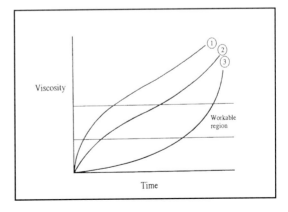

Fig 4: Viscosity - time curves for three types of cement

Cement 1 becomes relatively stiff (viscous) early, cement 2 has a smoother transition between low, medium and high viscosity, while cement 3 remains at low viscosity until just before polymerisation. The workable region where cement may be handled and the implant inserted is shown on the diagram, only cement 2 has an extended working region. Cement 3 (low viscosity cement) is difficult to handle and any cement with such a characteristic should be used with caution and only by experienced joint replacement surgeons.

Mixing bone cement.

Bone cement can be mixed in a number of ways:

(a) by hand in an open bowl,
(b) by hand in a closed bowl or cement gun syringe
(c) .... plus vacuum
(d) .... plus centrifugation
(e) .... plus pressure

Most joint replacement teams now use a closed bowl/syringe system with a degree of vacuum, either with low vacuum to control the cement fumes (which some people find unpleasant) or with higher vacuum to control porosity in the cement. The Swedish National Hip Arthroplasty Register[1] has examined the statistics to attempt to determine the clinical effect of vacuum mixing cement (to remove porosity) but, while recommending its use, has demonstrated a higher risk ratio in the first four/five years after the operation and a lower risk ratio at about eight years after the operation. It is not clear why this occurs. Other authors[9] do not believe that porosity in the cement is clinically significant, so each surgeon must determine whether or not to use this mixing technique

Scientific basis for modern cementing technique.

A number of projects in Exeter in the seventies and eighties investigated the various factors that are now regarded as significant in modern cementing technique. Five studies will be referred to in this paper that define the scientific basic of modern cementing technique. These papers are:

• Lee et al[8] , Arch. Orth. Tr. Surg., 1978, 1-18
• Halawa et al[10] , Arch. Orth. Tr. Surg., 1978, 19-30
• Heyse-Moore and Ling[11] , Exerpta Medica, 1981, 71-86
• Benjamin et al[12] , J.B.J.S.[Br], 1987, 69-B, 620-624
• Fagan M[13] , PhD Thesis, Exeter, 1984

Preparation of the bony cavity and creation of the interface between cement and bone.

Lee et al[8] determined that the cement should be physically constrained by good quality bone, that laminations of blood and tissue debris should be minimised in the cement dough and that, as far as possible, cement should be loaded in compression.

(a)   Constraint around bone cement

As has been noted earlier, bone cement is weak in tension and strong in compression. It is therefore desirable to load cement so that it can develop compressive stress - in order to do this the cement must be surrounded and supported by constraining material (good quality cortical bone) against which it can react. If cement is not constrained, then bending stresses will frequently be set up in the unsupported material, leading to excessive tensile stress in the cement and to failure.

(b)   Blood and tissue debris.

Laboratory experiments show that inclusions of blood, bone or tissue debris in cement can significantly affect both shear and tensile strength (giving a reduction of about 60%) by the formation of debris laminations in the cement. Compressive strength is not affected significantly in constrained specimens. If an attempt is made to remove debris by brushing and use of a pressure lavage, two effects can be seen: firstly the debris is removed, reducing the likelihood of contamination of cement and, secondly, the bone surface itself is cleaned, opening up spaces in the cancellous bone structure into which the cement can penetrate. This penetration (mechanical interlock) into bone can increase the strength of the cement-bone interface by about 4x. A third effect of removal of debris is a reduction in the incidence of serious pulmonary embolism when cement is forced into the bony spaces - the debris is not present so cannot be forced into the blood stream.

(c)   Stress raisers

Bone cement is a notch sensitive material - being weak in tension, the stress magnification found at the ends of sharp corners or cracks in the cement are sufficient to cause the cement to fail. Consequently, sharp corners on implant components, sharp corners at the edges of drill holes in the acetabulum, etc., are to be avoided.

Halawa et al[10] used shear strength tests on cylindrical specimens of cadaveric bone trepanned from the femur to include cortical and cancellous bone together with cement that had been put onto the cancellous bone with varying pressure. The tests showed that the strongest cancellous bone in the femur is always close to the cortico-cancellous junction and that intrusion of cement into bone was advantageous. They also tested push-out strength of cement inside the medullary canal of femoral bone, pushing-out against and with the generally conical shape (figure 5).

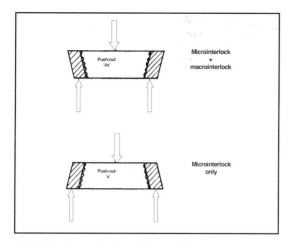

Fig 5: Push-out tests : effect of shape

The effect of shape is to increase the force needed to push-out cement when pushing cement into the generally conical shape of the bone. The conclusion of the shear tests by Halawa et al was that a fourfold increase in the strength of the cement/bone junction can be achieved by exposure of strong bone, cleaning the bone surface using pressure lavage and pressurising relatively low viscosity cement into the clean bone.

In addition to improving the strength of the cement/bone interface, putting pressure on the cement improves the cement strength by reducing voids in the cement, giving a more consistent material.

The penetration of cancellous bone by cement is most easily accomplished when the cement is at relatively low viscosity - flow is proportional to pressure divided by viscosity - therefore greatest flow/bone penetration will occur when cement is put under high pressure at low viscosity. However, while relatively low pressures will force low viscosity cement into bone, low pressures will also force low viscosity cement out of bone - such relatively low pressures can be generated by the bleeding pressure of blood in the bone. Halawa et al used cadaveric bone; cadaveric bone does not bleed. In consequence, the effects of bleeding and bleeding pressure in the bone had to be considered.

Heyse-Moore and Ling[11] found that bleeding pressures of between 0 and 36 cms of saline could be measured at the time of preparation of the femoral cavity and that bleeding pressure in the femur influenced the appearance of the post operative X-rays (good cement/bone interfaces with low bleeding pressures, poor interfaces with high bleeding pressures).

Benjamin et al[12] found that bleeding pressure in the femoral cavity was sufficient to displace SimplexÒ bone cement at 20^{0} C until 6 minutes after the start of mixing. They also determined that keeping pressure on the cement using specially designed instrumentation until the viscosity of the cement had increased sufficiently to enable it to resist the bleeding pressure and remain in place in the cancellous bone, counters the effects of bleeding. They recommended that, if correct instrumentation to control and pressurise cement while it is at relatively low viscosity is not available, then the cement should be inserted and pressurised by hand at a higher viscosity.

Fagan[13] carried out a series of tests using models of the femur and cement. He confirmed that pressure on the cement and consequent intrusion of cement into bone, could only be achieved reliably using specially designed seals and pressurising instruments - insertion of the stem itself generated low pressures and cement intrusion into bone, especially at the proximal end of the femur.

Modern cementing technique

As a result of the series of investigations described above, a 'modern cementing technique' was developed in Exeter that has been in use for a number of years. Such techniques were also developed in other places in parallel with the Exeter technique and have been summarised by the Swedish National Hip Arthroplasty Register[14]. The Register defined cementing technique in terms of the use of a number of devices/techniques as follows:

	Old technique	Early technique	Modern technique
Distal femoral plug	No	Yes	Yes
Proximal seal in femur	No	No	Yes
Acetabular compression	No	No	Yes
Hand mixing of cement	Yes	Yes	No
Vacuum mixing of cement	No	No	Yes
Brush	No	Yes	Yes
Pulsatile lavage	No	No	Yes

Is using a modern cementing technique important?

The question "Is cementing technique important?" has to be answered - i.e. will the use of a modern technique improve long-term clinical results?

In order to answer the above question, clinical results from two groups of Exeter patients will be considered and then the results from the Swedish Hip register will be reviewed.

The Exeter results come from a retrospective analysis of 72 hips, 33 in patients whose hips were operated upon in 1976 using an 'old' cementing technique and 39 in patients whose hips were operated upon in 1983 using the 'modem' technique. Results of both series are reported at an average follow-up of ten years. The clinical details of the patients in the two series are shown in the table below

The surgical technique used in the 'old' series for the femur involved no lavage for bone cleaning, no distal plug (therefore no cement pressurisation) and a thumb down cement insertion technique. In the 'new' series, lavage, a distal plug, cement gun and cement pressurisation with a proximal femoral seal was used. In the acetabulum, the 'old' series involved complete decortication of the socket, no lavage and short (1 minute) pressurisation. The 'new' series preserved the subchondral bone, used lavage and pressurisation for a longer time (5 minutes).

The clinical outcome at five years is similar for both series:

Table 2 - Clinical details of patients

	Old Series	**New Series**
Diagnosis	70% OA	77% OA
Average age	61 years	59 years
Sex: male	16	16
Sex: female	17	23
Average follow-up	10 years	10 years

First Series		**Second Series**	
in-situ	27	in-situ	36
Stem revised	2	Stem revised	2
Cup revised	4	Cup revised	1

A single surgeon performed all the operations in both series using the posterior approach with an Exeter hip and SimplexÒ P bone cement. The series were matched for average age, sex, diagnosis, pro-operative clinical assessment and length of follow-up.

Clinical assessment shows all patients were initially severely incapacitated but had good quality results at ten years, as assessed by Charnley's modification of the D'Aubigne-Postel scales for pain, function and movement (A is fit for age, B has both hips affected, C has inbuilt limitations in addition to the hips; 6.00 is a perfect score).

		'Old' pre-op	'Old' 10 years	'New' pre-op	'New' 10 years
A	Pain	2.09	5.80	2.75	5.60
	Function	2.45	5.80	2.33	5.80
	Movement	3.18	5.60	3.33	5.40
B	Pain	1.90	5.57	2.36	5.96
	Function	2.38	5.70	1.86	5.65
	Movement	2.38	5.75	3.00	5.67
C	Pain	3.00	5.70	1.80	6.00
	Function	2.38	5.70	1.20	4.00
	Movement	2.00	4.91	2.60	5.20

An extensive radiological assessment was carried out on the femur and acetabulum of the two series. For the femur, post-operative assessment of canal diameter, cement fill, mantle thickness, stem position and radiolucencies was made. At ten years the films were assessed for canal diameter, diaphyseal hypertrophy, stem position, bone lysis, cement fracture, stem sinkage, calcar resorption and radiolucencies. The acetabular socket films were assessed post-operatively for cup angle, cup cover, mantle thickness, centre of rotation and radiolucencies; at ten years they were assessed for cup angle, cup migration, radiolucencies and socket wear.

While the detailed results are outside the scope of this paper, it was concluded that, for the femur, the effect of changes in surgical technique (use of lavage, cement gun, distal plug and femoral seal) gave significant radiological improvements with respect to cement fill, production of a complete cement mantle, cement fractures, post-operative radiolucencies, ten year radiolucencies, bone lysis and stem engagement within the cement mantle. For the acetabulum, assuming that the change in acetabular bone preparation (retaining subchondral bone or removing it) was not of primary importance, lavage and prolonged socket pressurisation produced radiological improvements with respect to line free sockets, demarcated sockets, progressive radiolucency and cup migration. Evidence from another series of Exeter hips[15] showed that the use of the acetabular pressuriser produced a 3.8x reduction in clinical loosening rate at an average follow-up of 16.4 years, but the difference in migration rates shown at the 5-10 year review was lost at the 10-16 year review.

Current cementing technique in Exeter

In Exeter, the current cementing technique in the femur is as follows:

- prepare the bone
- insert a distal plug
- clean the bone with pressure lavage
- insert a suction catheter and pack the cavity with ribbon gauze soaked in 10% H_2O_2 until the cement is ready for insertion
- retrograde fill the cavity with reduced viscosity bone cement using a cement gun,
- pressurise the cement until its viscosity has increased sufficiently to resist bleeding
- insert a pre-warmed implant
- pressurise the cement until it polymerises using the 'horsecollar' seal.

It is important not to remove too much cancellous bone (a layer of strong cancellous bone should remain on the cortical bone), it is important not to use reduced viscosity bone cement unless all seals and pressurising instruments are available and it is important not to insert the stem too soon as that would lead to an increased risk of blood at the interface and/or a displaced component.

In the acetabulum, current technique in Exeter is as follows:

- remove the articular cartilage, locate the true medial wall (osteophyte) and remove the sub-chondral bone with a reamer to expose bleeding bone
- make pits and drill holes for fixation
- lavage to clean bone
- place a superior sucker in iliac wing
- graft medial wall and any cysts
- lavage again, protecting grafts with a spoon.
- pack with H_2O_2 soaked swab, with suction on iliac wing sucker
- mix cement, remove swab and place cement, by hand, into cavity at appropriate time
- pressurise until ready to insert cup
- insert cup, hold in place with pusher until cement polymerises, trimming excess cement around cup as necessary.

Results from the Swedish National Hip Arthroplasty Register

The year 2000 publication of the Swedish National Hip Arthroplasty Register[1] reviews 169,419 primary hips and 13,562 revisions. The register published risk ratios using appropriate statistical models and identified the effects of cementing technique. It showed that using a pulsatile lavage reduces the risk ratio to 0.93 compared with no lavage, a proximal femoral seal reduces the risk ratio to 0.88 compared to no seal and using a distal femoral plug reduces the risk ratio to 0.88 compared to not using a plug. Risk ratios for various brands of cement were given in the introduction to this chapter. The use of vacuum mixing of cement produces a risk ratio higher than 1.0 for the first four years of use, thereafter, a lower risk ratio until it reaches 0.74 at eight years. The authors conclude that the use of vacuum mixing seems to be justified. An earlier publication of results from the Register[16] showed that introducing cement into the acetabulum by hand and into the femur, retrograde, using a cement gun produced a risk ratio of 0.54 compared to hand cementing in both acetabulum and femur. It should be noted that the continued use and publication of results from the Swedish register has improved results overall in Sweden, presumably by encouraging all surgeons to adopt better techniques. The cumulative frequency of revision is reducing as years pass for cemented implants, but not for uncemented implants (it should also be noted that relatively few uncemented implants are used).

Conclusion

A proper understanding of the nature and use of bone cement is important. Theoretical work, experimental work in the laboratory and clinical results all show that modern cementing techniques can lead to improved results in patients. The simplest and cheapest way of improving long-term results of cemented hip arthroplasties is to use modern cementing techniques.

References

1. Malchau H, Herberts P, Söderman P and Odén A. Prognosis of total hip replacement, Scientific exhibit presented at the 67th Annual Meeting of the AAOS, March 2000, Orlando, U.S.A.

2. Kühn, K-D Bone Cements. Berlin: Springer 2000.

3. Saha S and Pal S. Mechanical properties of bone cement: a review. J Biomed Mater Res, 1984; 18: 435-62.

4. Lewis G. Properties of acrylic bone cement: state of the art review. J Biomed Mater Res 1997; 38: 157-82.

5. Lee A J C, Perkins R D and Ling R S M. Time-dependent properties of polymethylmethacrylate bone cement. In: Older J editor. Implant Bone Interface. Berlin: Springer 1990. 85-90.

6. Lee A J C, Ling R S M, Gheduzzi S, Simon J-P and Renfro R J. Factors affecting the mechanical and viscoelastic properties of acrylic bone cement. J Mater Sci Mater in Med 2002; 13: 723-33.

7. Lee A J C. The time-dependent properties of polymethylmethacrylate bone cement: the interaction of shape of femoral stems, surface finish and bone cement. In: Learmonth I D editor Interfaces in Total Hip Arthroplasty. Berlin: Springer 2000. 11-19.

8.Lee A J C, Ling R S M and Vangala S S. Some clinically relevant variables affecting the mechanical behaviour of bone cement. Arch Orthop Trauma Surg 1978; 92: 1-18.

9. Ling R S M and Lee A J C. Porosity reduction in acrylic cement is clinically irrelevant. Clin Orthop 1998; 335: 249-55.

10. M.Halawa, A.J.C. Lee, R.S.M. Ling and S.S. Vangala. The shear strength of trabecular bone from the femur, and some factors affecting the shear strength of the cement-bone interface. Arch Orthop Trauma Surg 1978; 92: 19-30.

11. Heyse-Moore G H and Ling R S M. Current cement techniques. In: Marti R K. editor.Progress in Cemented Hip Surgery and Revision. Amsterdam: Exerpta Medica, 1983. 71-86.

12. J B Benjamin, G A Gie, A J C Lee, R S M Ling and R G Voltz. Cementing Technique and the effects of bleeding. J Bone Joint Surg 1987; 69B: 620-24.

13. Fagan M J. PhD thesis: A finite element analysis of femoral stem design in cemented total hip replacements. University of Exeter, 1984.14. Malchau H and Herberts P. Prognosis of total hip replacement, Scientific exhibit presented at the 63rd Annual Meeting of the AAOS, February 1996, Atlanta, U.S.A.

15. Fowler J L, Gie G A, Lee A J C and Ling R S M. Experience with the Exeter Hip since 1970. Orthop Clin of North Am 1988; 19: 477-89.

16. Malchau H and Herberts P. Prognosis of total hip replacement,. Scientific exhibit presented at the 65th Annual Meeting of the AAOS, February 1998, New Orleans, U.S.

Friction, Lubrication, and Wear in Joint Replacements

Dr J H Kuiper

Biomechanical Engineer
Robert Jones & Agnes Hunt Orthopaedic Hospital
Oswestry

Contents

- Friction
- Lubrication
- Wear
  - Adhesive/abrasive wear
  - Fatigue wear
  - Wear rate
  - Consequences
- What to do?

Questions

- How are wear particles generated?
- Where do wear particles go?
- What is the effect of wear?
- How important is wear in the loosening process?
- How does a change of material affect wear volume?
- What is the effect of head size?
- **What should I do?**

Friction

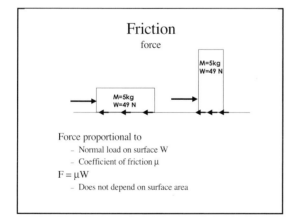

force

Force proportional to
  - Normal load on surface W
  - Coefficient of friction μ

$F = \mu W$
  - Does not depend on surface area

Friction

- Initiate sliding: static coefficient μ_s
- Continue sliding: dynamic coefficient μ_d

Combination	μ_s	μ_d
Rubber/concrete	1.0	0.7
Steel/steel	0.7	0.5
Steel/UHMWPE	0.5	0.3

Whenever surfaces are in contact, friction can be generated. Frictional force can be measured by trying to slide or sliding a body over a surface. The force is proportional to the normal load on the surface and the coefficient of friction. It does not depend on the surface area. So, if you try to move a chest is does not matter whether it lies flat or stands upright.

The coefficient of friction depends partly on the material combination that is making contact. Some combinations give a high coefficient of friction (e.g. rubber on concrete or tarmac), and are partly used for that reason.

To initiate sliding requires more force than to continue sliding. Therefore, two coefficients of friction exist: the static coefficient and the dynamic coefficient. The value of the dynamic coefficient of friction is about 70% of that of the static.

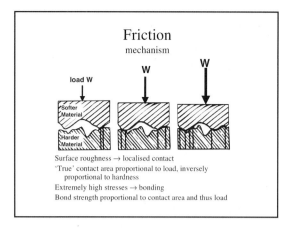

Friction
mechanism

load W

W

W

Softer
Material

Harder
Material

Surface roughness → localised contact
'True' contact area proportional to load, inversely
proportional to hardness
Extremely high stresses → bonding
Bond strength proportional to contact area and thus load

The frictional force does not depend on the contact area. However, the contact area we see is the 'apparent' contact area. Surfaces are never completely smooth, and therefore always have asperities. True contact only takes place where asperities from both surfaces touch. When the normal load is increased, the material at the top of the asperities deforms, and therefore the true contact area is proportional to the load. The harder the materials, the less deformation occurs, and therefore the true contact area is inversely proportional to the hardness of the materials.

The true contact area is typically far less than 1% of the apparent contact area, so at the areas of true contact the stresses are extremely high. Such high stresses are sufficient to cause bonding between the surfaces. The strength of the bonds is proportional to the true contact area, and depends on the material combination. Static friction is generated by the bonds: the stronger the bond strength the higher the friction. During sliding, bonds are continuously generated and broken, a process that requires slightly less force than to initiate sliding. This explains why the dynamic coefficient of friction is smaller than the static one.

implants. John Charnley was sufficiently worried about this to decide for a small-headed prosthesis. Given that the failure torque of a cemented cup is about 40 Nm, his worry was understandable. However, in reality the frictional torque is much lower due to lubrication, which reduces the coefficient of friction for metal-on-plastic about 10-fold.

Lubrication
Principle

- Film between surfaces
- Low shear strength, motion *within* film
- Reduction of friction
- Reduction of wear

Combination	dry	lubricated
Rubber/concrete	0.7	0.5
Steel/UHMWPE	0.5	0.05
Natural hip joint		0.002

Lubrication occurs when a film of low shear strength is present between the two surfaces. Ideally, the film prevents direct contact between the surfaces, thus reducing bonding between the surfaces. The low shear strength means that motion between the two contacting surfaces can occur within the film. The effect of it all is a reduction in friction and, as we will see, wear. Amongst others, the efficiency of the lubrication depends on the material combination and the viscosity of the lubricant. Luckily, water is not a very good lubricant for rubber tyres on the road. However, synovial fluid is a good lubricant for steel on polyethylene, reducing friction 10-fold

Friction
effect

- Increase load on implant
  e.g. frictional torque on acetabular cup (unit Nm)
  Proportional to:
  – coefficient of friction μ
  – head diameter D

	D = 22 mm	D = 32 mm
μ=0.5	17 Nm	25 Nm
μ=0.05	1.7 Nm	2.5 Nm

Friction increases the effort required to move the joint, and increases the load on the implant. For instance, the femoral head will generate a frictional torque on the acetabular cup. Assuming a patient of similar weight, this torque is proportional to the coefficient of friction and the diameter of the femoral head. For steel on polyethelene, the frictional torque could be as much as 25 Nm for large-headed

Lubrication
Mechanisms and film thickness

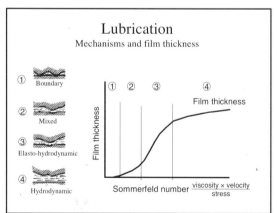

① Boundary
② Mixed
③ Elasto-hydrodynamic
④ Hydrodynamic

Film thickness

Film thickness

Sommerfeld number $\frac{viscosity \times velocity}{stress}$

Lubrication varies between boundary lubrication, where a layer of only a few molecules thick separates the surfaces where the asperities touch, and hydrodynamic lubrication, where a fluid film completely separates the surfaces. Hydrodynamic lubrication is often separated in two regimes, elasto-hydrodynamic and hydrodynamic lubrication. Elasto-hydrodynamic lubrication occurs when the bearing surfaces are not conforming and deform elastically, such as in artificial joints or gears. Hydrodynamic lubrication occurs when the surfaces are conforming, such as in natural joints or journal bearings. Boundary lubrication usually occurs, if only because it is difficult to keep surfaces completely clean. For instance, artificial joints will readily absorb proteins on their surface. In natural joints, chondrocytes produce a specific boundary lubrication protein, appropriately named 'lubricin'.

The thickness of the lubrication film depends on several factors, summarised in the 'Sommerfeld number'. The higher this number, the thicker the film. Firstly, the number is proportional to viscosity of the film: the larger the viscosity, the more difficult the fluid is squeezed-out. This makes oil or synovial fluid a better lubricant than water. The number is also proportional to the 'entraining velocity', which is the velocity at which fluid is forced into the gap. For sliding bearings, this is the sliding velocity. The higher the velocity, the better the skier can ride the water. Likewise, the thicker the fluid film becomes. Everybody who has water-skied (or watched water-skiers) is familiar with this phenomenon.

Finally, the number is inversely proportional to the applied stress over the bearing. This is the 'apparent stress', i.e. the force divided by the apparent area. This is obvious: the harder you press, the more you squeeze the film.

Mixed lubrication is the transition stage between boundary lubrication (low Sommerfeld number) and fluid film lubrication (high Sommerfeld number), during which both mechanisms occur simultaneously.

However, when the Sommerfeld number is sufficiently large to start fluid lubrication, less and less asperities will touch, and the coefficient of friction drops rapidly. This process of mixed lubrication occurs until a full fluid film separates the surfaces. At this point, the coefficient of friction is minimal. Further increasing the Sommerfeld number will lead to an increasing in friction due to the viscous effect in the film.

When the surface asperities are higher, or the roughness of the surfaces is larger, a thicker film is required for complete separation of the surfaces. The Sommerfeld number where transition between mixed and (elasto)-hydrodynamic lubrication occurs therefore depends on the ratio of film thickness to roughness, the lambda-ratio". The critical lambda-ratio is about 2-3. Conversely, for similar viscosity, velocity and stress the surface roughness can profoundly influence the lubrication regime.

Under typical conditions, artificial joints operate in boundary and mixed lubrication mode (lambda-ratio < 3), although full-film elastohydrodynamic lubrication may just be achievable for ceramic-on-ceramic or metal-on-metal implants. A particular case is a hip prosthesis with large head size, such as a resurfacing prosthesis. The large head size gives a relatively high sliding velocity, and therefore a relatively large Sommerfeld number. When they are smooth (such as after the wearing-in period), and they may therefore have a large ë-value, hydrodynamic fluid film lubrication may be possible. Natural joints operate within all four lubrication regimes.

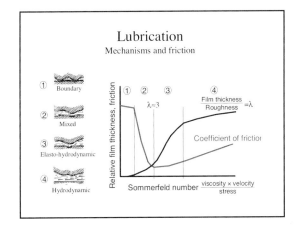

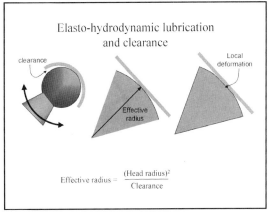

Friction is caused by adhesion at the tops of asperities, which form the true contact between bearing surfaces. The film in boundary lubrication is only a few molecules thick, but influences adhesion between the surfaces and therefore the frictional properties. As long as boundary lubrication is the only mechanism, friction will not depend much on Sommerfeld number.

Elasto-hydrodynamic lubrication occurs at non-conforming surfaces. At the point of contact, the surfaces deform elastically and become more conform. These conform surfaces allow hydrodynamic lubrication, hence elasto-hydrodynamic lubrication. Apart from velocity, sliding speed and stress, the 'effective radius' is the important determinant of fluid film thickness. A large effective radius increases the contact area and decreases the contact stress.

For a hip implant, the effective radius depends on the stiffness of the materials, the radius of the head and the clearance, i.e. the mismatch between head and socket. Large heads with a small clearance give a large effective radius, a large contact area, and therefore a large film thickness. Soft materials deform more, and therefore also generate a larger contact area and thicker film. However, only ceramic or metal surfaces can be made smooth enough for this film thickness to be larger than the surface asperities large lambda-ratio). Therefore, elasto-hydrodynamic lubrication is only feasible for metal-on-metal or ceramic-on-ceramic bearing combinations

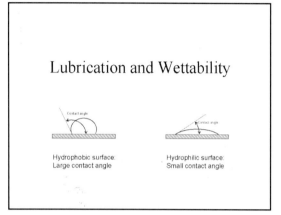

An extra variable that places a role in lubrication of joint implants is the wettability of the bearing surfaces. Wettability is measured by the contact angle, the angle that the tangent to a drop makes with the surface. This angle characterises the surfaces of different materials. Based on the angle, they can be divided in highly hydrophilic (angle<45°) and highly hydrophobic (angle>90°). All being equal, a surface with a larger wettability (i.e. a small contact angle) will have a better lubrication. Ceramics have a smaller contact angle (i.e. better wettability) than metals, and will therefore have a larger fluid film thickness for equal Somerfeld numbers.

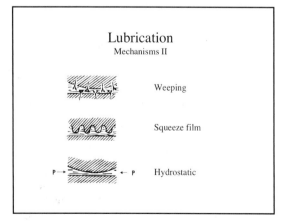

Three further lubrication mechanisms exist. Weeping and squeeze film lubrication are two mechanisms occurring in natural joints. Weeping lubrication occurs when the fluid

pressure inside the cartilage caused by joint loading is high enough to force out fluid, giving extra fluid for lubrication. The same principle has been tried for joint implants by using foam materials. Although these had very low coefficients of friction and minimal wear, reliable fixation proved impossible. Squeeze film lubrication can occurs when a thick fluid layer is brought between the joint surfaces during periods of zero load or positive load, such as during the swing phase of walking. Due to the high joint fluid viscosity and large conformity of the surfaces, it requires seconds to squeeze out the fluid during the stance phase. Squeeze film lubrication is probably the most important mechanism in natural joints.

Hydrostatic lubrication maintains a thick fluid layer by using a pump to generate high pressure inside the fluid. This is unlike hydrodynamic lubrication, which relied on moving surfaces to generate pressure. Hydrostatic lubrication does not occur in nature.

Wear in artificial joints

- Mechanical wear
  - Adhesive & abrasive wear
    - Often occur simultaneously
    - Mild (fatigue and damage accumulation)
    - Severe (ploughing and cutting)
  - Surface fatigue (pitting, delamination)
    - Non-conforming contacts
  - Fretting wear
    - Small-amplitude oscillations (< 100 micron)
- Chemical wear
  - Formation of new substances that wear more readily than original material
    - E.g. corrosive wear, oxidative wear
  - Can enhance mechanical wear

Wear occurs whenever contact and relative motion coincide. It leads to changes in the size and shape of objects, and production of debris. In general, the softest and weakest material wears. Wear is still poorly understood, and maybe because of this several classifications exist in the literature. The main distinction is between mechanical and chemical wear. For artificial joints, adhesive, abrasive, fatigue and fretting wear are the most important mechanical wear mechanisms.

Adhesive and abrasive wear

During sliding, bonds are created and broken at local contacts at top of asperities.

1. Bond weaker than both materials
   - Bond breaks so little adhesive wear
   - Depending on roughness, mild or severe abrasive wear
2. Material I weaker than bond and material II
   - Material I breaks and forms film on material II
   - Continuous wear of material I on material I
3. Bond stronger than both materials
   - Fragments break from either materials
   - Continuous wear of both materials

Friction occurs because during sliding bonds are continuously created and broken at local contacts at the tops of asperities. The balance of strength between material I, material II and the bond determine where fracture occurs, and the likelihood of wear.

If the bond is weaker than both materials, the bond will break which means there is little adhesive wear. This is an ideal situation. However, depending on the roughness of the hardest surface there will be mild or severe abrasive wear due to polishing or ploughing.

If one material is weaker than the bond and the other material, fragments of the weakest material will be removed. They are likely to remain attached to the stronger material, leaving a film of weaker material on the stronger material. This creates a new situation where identical materials slide over each other. In such a situation the bond strength is often similar to the strength of the material. Breakage of bonds and material will then alternate, giving a process of moderate wear. When the bond strength is smaller than the material strength, little adhesive wear occurs. When the bond strength is larger, material will be removed continuously, resulting in severe wear.

If the bond is stronger than both materials, fragments will be removed from both parts and severe wear occurs.

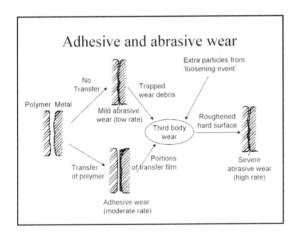

For example, mechanical wear of polymer-on-metal normally proceeds with little transfer of polymer. In that case, wear is caused by abrasion of the softer material by the asperities of the harder material. Smooth abrasive surfaces generate large elastic and plastic strains in the softer material, leading to failure by local fatigue or straining beyond the point of failure. This is a slow wear process.

Mild abrasive wear can proceed for a long time, but the wear process can suddenly accelerate when third body particles roughen the harder surface. Particles released by loosening of the implant are the most likely source of such particles, but trapped wear debris could also be a source. Small increases in surface roughness can transform mild abrasive wear into severe abrasive wear, generating debris by ploughing and cutting.

The polymers used as bearing surfaces in artificial joints (UHMWP or POM (i.e. polyoxymethylene or Delrin) will in general produce a very thin transfer film, which has no noticeable effect on the wear process. However, under appropriate conditions a thicker film may form, completely covering the asperities of the harder surface. Effectively, this leads to polymer-on-polymer wear with increased adhesion between the two surfaces, generating wear particles by pulling out material on both sides.

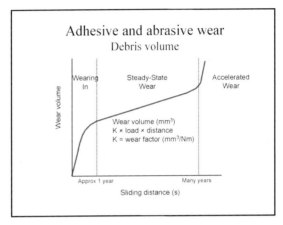

Debris production by adhesive and abrasive wear in artificial joints can be divided in two or three stages. For a large part in the lifetime of a component, wear occurs at a low rate. During this stage of steady-state wear, the debris volume is proportional to the product of joint load, sliding distance and a wear factor K. Similar to frictional force, wear volume is independent of the apparent contact area, and therefore independent of the applied stress. Instead, it is related to the true contact area.

Before the stage of steady-state wear, a process of wearing-in occurs normally. During this process, transfer films may form or some sharper asperities may be deformed or removed. At the end of the lifetime, a period of accelerated wear is often observed. In the case of joint implants, this often follows implant loosening. When the steady state wear rate is however large, implant failure is associated directly with the wear debris and therefore the final stage never occurs.

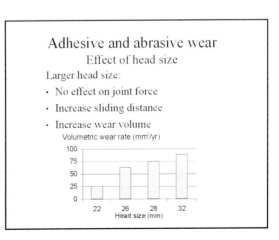

One implication of the dependence of wear volume on joint force and sliding distance, but not on joint stress, is the effect of femoral head size on wear volume. Increasing head size has no effect on joint force, but does increase the sliding distance. Wear volume therefore increases with increasing head size.

To minimise wear volume, the femoral head should be made as small as possible. However, smaller femoral heads increase the risk of impingementand polythylene penetration. In practice, a 28 mm head is regarded a reasonable compromise.

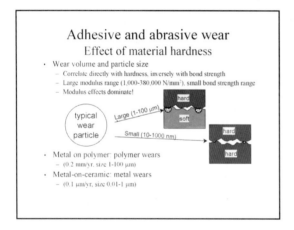

During adhesive and mild abrasive wear, particle size and wear volume inversely correlate with the hardness and modulus of materials, and directly correlate with their bonding strength at the interface.

Harder materials have a smaller true contact area, giving smaller wear particles. Stronger bonds increase the change that material fragments are removed. The range of material stiffnesses is very large compared to the range of bond strengths. Because of this, the largest differences in wear particle size and volume are caused by changes in material stiffness.

Typically, for a metal on polymer combination, the polymer wears at a rate of 0.2 mm/year, producing particles between 1 and 100 micron. For a metal-on-ceramic bearing, the metal wears at a rate of 0.1 micron per year, producing much smaller particles between 0.01 and 1 micron.

Besides stiffness and interface bond strength, many other factors determine wear volume. The local environment at the contact, in particular the lubrication, is very important. When the fluid film is about 2-3 times thicker than the surface roughness, no wear occurs. In practice, only metal and ceramic surfaces could be made so smooth that the fluid film is thick enough to have a noticeable effect on wear. In addition, it needs accurate manufacturing to produce small clearances. At current technical standards, accurate manufacturing seems a more important factor determining wear in hard-on-hard surfaces than other factors, such as metallurgy.

During sliding, large plastic deformations are generated. Tough materials can sustain these large deformations before failure. They therefore tend to show better wear performance than brittle materials, although brittle materials may be stronger. These large deformations cause plastic with long linear molecules (UHMWPE or delrin) to align itself along the sliding direction. Alignment makes these plastic stronger and tougher, giving very good wear resistance during rectilinear sliding, such as occurs in knee implants. However, in hip implants sliding is not rectilinear, giving larger wear for otherwise similar circumstances. Cross-linking polyethylene to improve wear properties is a delicate act, because although it increases strength it can also increase brittleness. Hylamer is an example of a strong but brittle polymer that had poor wear performance. Accidental embrittlement of polyethylene was caused by oxidation, following irradiation and subsequent storage in oxygen-containing air. This made shelf life an import determinant of wear resistance.

Finally, the surface roughness of the hardest material plays an important part. Small asperities may only cause elastic deformation of the smooth surface, causing mild abrasive wear due to fatigue, whereas larger asperities may plough and cut, causing severe wear.Hence, small changes in roughness may have disproportionate effects on wear. Scratches from third-body particles are an important cause of changes in surface roughness. Scratches in ceramic, which is brittle, only cause cuts that do not change roughness much. Scratches in metal, which

Basic Science for FRCS (Trauma and Orthopaedics)

is plastic, have little ridges where the material was pushed upwards. These can have a large effect on roughness: ceramic heads should thus be less scratch-sensitive. Evidence from clinical studies is mixed: for metal-backed cups, differences are small (Sychterz et al., JBJS-Br 2000), but for all-polyethylene cups ceramic heads may indeed reduce wear (Urban et al., JBJS_Am 2001

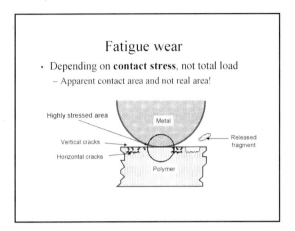

Fatigue wear is a second important cause of debris generation. It is related to high stresses inside materials at the area of contact. These stresses will cycle during movement. If they are high enough, they cause fatigue cracks in the material, eventually leading to breaking out of fragments. The risk of fatigue wear is related to the contact stress, which is a function of the 'apparent contact area'. Unlike adhesive and abrasive wear, fatigue wear is therefore not related to the high, localised stresses at asperities

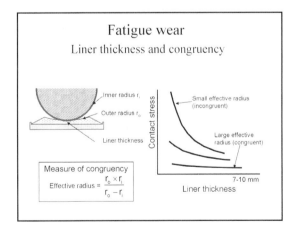

Fatigue wear occurs particularly in metal-backed plastic liners. Contact stresses for those liners are determined by liner thickness and congruency.

Thin liners lead to larger contact stresses, in much the same way that thin mattresses can be very hard. This is simply because a thick liner or mattress masks the effect of the underlying hard surface, whereas a thin liner cannot do that.

Incongruent surfaces also create larger contact stresses. Congruency is measured by the effective radius, which was also important for elasto-hydrodynamic lubrication. Surfaces that are more congruent have a larger effective radius, a larger contact area and a smaller contact stress.

Non-congruent tibial components of knee implants with thin liners are particularly at risk. For such implants, maximum shear stresses occur 1-2 mm below the surface, potentially causing delamination. This was particularly a problem with cold-pressed polythene liners, which had a low fatigue strength. Embrittlement caused by oxidation following irradiation in air also greatly reduces the fatigue strength of polyethylene. Metal-backed acetabular cups are congruent, giving smaller contact stresses than knee implants. Fatigue wear is therefore less likely to play an important role in those implants. However, acetabular cups with thin liners will have a thinner fluid film from elasto-hydrodynamic lubrication, increasing adhesive and abrasive wear.

Adhesive/abrasive versus fatigue wear

- Adhesive/abrasive wear in hip implants and congruent knee implants
  - Dominated by local contact at asperities
  - More small (<0.5 μm), less large (>1μm) particles
- Fatigue in non-congruent knee implants
  - Less small, more large particles

Wear in hip implants and congruent knee implants is mainly by adhesion and abrasion. This wear type is dominated by local contact at asperities. It produces many relatively small particles (<1 micron) and few relatively large.

Wear in non-congruent knee implants with thin liners is mainly by fatigue. This wear type is dominated by high stresses inside the bulk material. It produces less small and more relatively large particles. It can completely wear through the liner.

Fatigue wear as a mechanism is related to stresses at the contact area and inside the material. However, fatigue can also be an important mechanism during mild adhesive and abrasive wear. Fatigue failure then occurs at the level of asperities. These are loaded cyclically, and will fail given sufficient loading cycles.

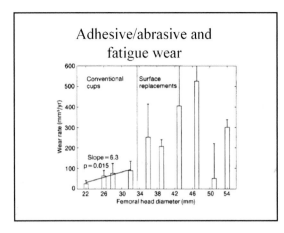

Adhesive/abrasive and fatigue wear

For conventional cups, wear volume increases with head diameter because the sliding distance increases whereas the joint load remains constant. However, surface replacements often show excessive wear rates, suggesting that larger sliding distance from increased head size is not the single explanatory factor. Use of thin liners may lead to smaller contact areas and larger contact stresses. This may increase the likelihood of fatigue failure and reduce film thickness from hydrodynamic lubrication. In addition, surface replacements may be more susceptible to third-body wear.

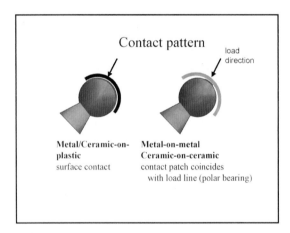

Contact pattern

Hard-on-plastic and hard-on-hard hip implants have very different contact patterns. Due to the soft plastic, hard-on-plastic implants make contact over a large part of the joint surface, although for metal-backed prostheses this may depend on liner thickness. Hard-on-hard hip implants deform only little, creating a small contact patch coinciding with the load line. These implants are therefore 'polar bearing'. If the head were larger than the cup, these implants become 'rim bearing', leading to seizure and early failure. This has happened with older designs metal-on-metal hips.

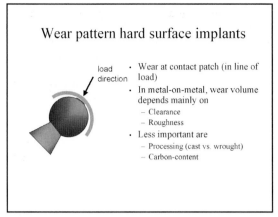

Wear pattern hard surface implants

Wear of hard surface hip implants is restricted to the limited area where contact occurs. Relative to the femur, the joint load has an almost constant direction. This means the location of the constant patch is almost constant, giving a very small wear patch. Relative to the pelvis, the load moves more. This means the acetabulum wears over a larger area.

Wear of hard-on-hard surface implants depends strongly on the effective radius of the implant, which determines fluid film thickness, and the roughness, which should be smaller than the film thickness. Parameters such as material processing and carbon content are less important.

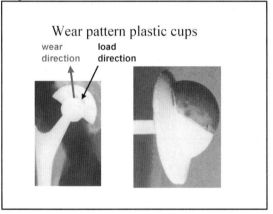

Wear pattern plastic cups

Plastic cups are contacting the head over a large part of the surface. Since wear is related to load and sliding distance, the direction of largest wear is determined by a combination of loading direction and the area of largest movement. In practice, this means most plastic cups where upwards.

In-vivo wear measurement

- Non-retrieved
  - Radiography
    Using template: 95% confidence limits ±0.6 mm
    Better accuracy needs computer-aided analysis, stereography or tomography
  - Impossible for hard-on-hard due to small wear rates
- Retrieved
  - Shadow graph
    For polyethylene
  - Co-ordinate Measuring Machine
    For hard-on-hard
  - Gravimetric measurements
    Least accurate

In-vivo wear measurement on non-retrieved specimens is only possible from radiographs. Using standard AP X-rays, templates will give 95% confidence limits of ±0.56 mm. Typical reasons for the inaccuracy are e.g. that wear is not necessarily in the plane of the X-ray, that the projection of the X-rays make the head appear elliptic. More accuracy requires 3-dimensional analysis. Wear of hard-on-hard surfaces is typically only 0.01 mm/year and cannot be measured on non-retrieved implants, unless there is a serious problem.

To measure wear on retrieved implants, shadow graphs of casts are often used. This method is probably best suited for polyethylene cups. Alternatively, a co-ordinate measuring machine will produce a 3-D reconstruction of the worn cup, which can be compared with the unworn. This is a good method for hard-on-hard surfaces. Gravimetric methods (weighing) are less suitable for retrievals. Plastic cups would require a control to correct for uptake of fluid, and metal implants lose so little weight from wear that damage during removal would have to much of an effect.

Wear rate

Combination	Material worn	Wear rate (mm/yr)	(mm³/yr)
Metal/polymer	Polymer	0.07-0.19	40-80
Metal/composite	Composite	0.03-0.09	
Ceramic/Polymer	Polymer	0.008	
Ceramic/ceramic	Ceramic	0.003	
Metal/metal	Metal	0.0003	1-5

The table gives typical wear rates of hip implants for different material combinations. Note the large difference between hard-on-plastic and hard-on-hard wear rates.

Other wear mechanisms

- Fretting wear
  - Relative motion over small range (< 50 μm)
  - Large amount of trapped debris
  - example: modular connections
- Corrosive wear
  - Increased corrosion due to wear
    - Removes or damages passivation layer
    - Large local deformations increasing internal energy
  - Increased wear due to corrosion
    - Increases number of surface crack initiation sites
    - Decreases strength of material at crack tips

Fretting wear is the third mechanical wear mechanism that plays a role in artificial joints.It occurs when surfaces slide over small distances, from 50 microns down to 0.01 microns. The debris produced is often trapped, making the situation worse by increasing third-body wear.Thus fretting wear often produces a far larger volume of debris than expected from the small sliding distance. It typically occurs at modular connections, such as at the back of polythene liners, but also between implant and cement.

Corrosive wear is a form of chemical wear. It occurs when corrosion acts in synergy with mechanical wear. On the one hand, mechanical wear removes or damages the passivation layer which normally protects metals, and the large deformations over 100% associated with adhesive/abrasive wear increase the internal energy. Both these factors cause increased corrosion. On the other hand, corrosion increases the number of crack initiation sites and decreases the strength of material at crack tips, two factors which increase mechanical wear. The embrittlement of polymer following irradiation in air is an example of corrosive wear. The oxygen causing embrittlement can only diffuse over a small distance into the plastic. However, the ongoing wear ensures the oxygen front continues to penetrate into the plastic, causing further embrittlement and thus maintaining a high wear rate.

Linear vs. volumetric wear

- Linear: head penetration, can be seen on X-ray
  - mm or mm/year
- Volumetric: wear volume, can be calculated
  - mm³ or mm³/year
- Simplified calculation
  - head produces cylindrical bore
  - Volume = Area*linear wear = $\pi/4$ * (head diameter)² * linear

Linear wear relates to a distance. It is the head penetration into the socket, can be measured directly on an X-ray, and is expressed in mm or mm/year.

Volumetric wear relates to the volume of debris produced, and is expressed in mm³ or mm³ per year. It cannot be measured from an X-ray but must be calculated from the linear wear. A simple formula assumes that the head produces a cylindrical bore. In that case the wear volume is the product of cross-sectional area of the cylinder times the linear wear:

$V = \pi/4$ * (head diameter)² * linear wear

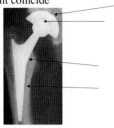
Wear occurs at all surfaces wear contact and movement coincides. It obviously occurs at the bearing surfaces, but also at the interfaces between modular connections (e.g. backside wear), between prosthesis and cement, and between cement and bone.

Pathways of wear particles

- 'Large' particles (micron-size) remain local
  - Fibrous capsule bone-implant interface
  - Cement-metal interface
  - Cement cracks
  - Acetabular notch
- 'Small' particles (nanometer size) spread throughout body
  - Lymph system
  - Blood
  - Urine

The wear particles escape wherever they can find a path. Relatively large (micron-size) particles such as generated from polyethylene remain locally at the joint.They migrate into the fibrous capsule that often forms the bone-implant interface. They can also find their way along the cement-metal interface, through cracks, into the bone-cement interface. The acetabular notch can form a specific entry point for wear particles, as are screw holes.

Small particles such as generated from metal spread throughout the body. They are often transported by the lymph system or are taken into the bloodstream. They can be detected in urine or blood.

Local tissue reactions

- Osteolysis
- Particle size specific, not material-specific
- Phagocytosable particles (0.5-10 μm) cause reactions, smaller or larger do not
  - osteoblasts: function impaired by 1 μm particles, not by 20 μm
  - macrophages: induction of cytokine and PGE_2 production, inducing bone resorption
- Critical levels
  - 10 billion (10^{10}) particles/g wet tissue
  - 150 mm^3 PE per year
- Combination of movement and particles synergetic

The micron-sized particles have a local effect, namely bone resorption or osteolysis around the implant. The effect is size-specific: only particles in the range of 0.5-10 ?m, which are phagocytosable, cause reactions. The main reactions are the induction of macrophages to produce cytokines and prostaglandins leading to bone resorption, and a reduction of osteoblast activity reducing bone formation. Interestingly, non-congruent knee prostheses wear by fatigue and produce particles larger than 10 micron. Congruent knee prostheses with mobile bearings, such as the LCS, wear by adhesion/abrasion and produce smaller wear particles. It was reported recently (Huang et al., J Orthop Res 2002) that osteolysis was observed far more often around conforming knee prostheses than non-conforming. It seems that the body can copy with small amounts of such particles. A critical level appears to be 10 billion particles per gram of wet tissue. In practice, wear rates below 150 mm^3 per year seem to avoid that critical level.

The situation is exacerbated if wear particles coincide with relative movement between bone and prosthesis.

Wear particles

- Metal-on-Polymer
  - Linear rate 0.10 mm/year
  - Volumetric rate 40-80 mm^3/year
- Assumption: 1 μm particles
- 250-500 billion particles/year
  - Sufficient for 2.5-5 gram tissue!!
- 250-500 thousand particles /step
- Metal-on-metal (1 mm^3/yr, 0.01 μm)
  20 billion particles/step,
  every week surface area of 1 prosthesis!

To see things in perspective, one can roughly calculate the implications of typical wear rates. It turns out that each step produces 250-500 thousand plastic particles in a metal-on-plastic replacement. Each step produces even 20 billion metal particles in a metal-on-metal hip, which each week adds a surface-area equivalent to one prosthesis. Not surprisingly, metal ion levels in patients with metal-on-metal implants are high compared to controls.

Particle size distribution

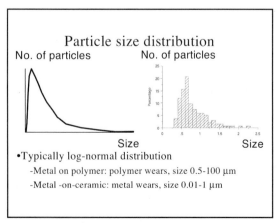

- Typically log-normal distribution
  - Metal on polymer: polymer wears, size 0.5-100 μm
  - Metal -on-ceramic: metal wears, size 0.01-1 μm

Almost every mechanical process that produces particles leads to a log-normal particle size distribution. In other words, there are very many small particles and few large particles. For example, a metal-on-plastic combination produces particles between from 0.5-100 micron. By far the majority of these are about 1 micron, exactly the phagocytosable size which leads to increased bone resorptionand decreased bone formation. Hard-on-hard bearings produce wear particles between 0.01 and 1 micron. This means there are only few micron-sized particles, but very many particles of 10 nm.

Systemic reactions

- Chronic increase metal in tissues
- Metal-on-Metal 5 times more metal release
- Sensitisation of immune response
- Overall cancer incidence after joint replacement
  - THR: no influence (95% CI of odds ratio 0.99-1.03)
  - TKR: no influence (95% CI of odds ratio 0.98-1.08)
- Metal-on-Metal vs. Metal-on-Plastic
  - Increased risk overall cancer (OR 1.25)
    same OR for lung cancer of non-smoking spouses of smokers
  - In particular increased risk leukaemia (OR 2.3), uterus (OR 2.0) and prostate (OR 1.5)

Metal wear particles are typically 10 nm, too small to be phagocytosed and to cause harm locally around the joint. However, the small particles give an enormous surface area, from which metal ions dissolve easily. These ions are transported throughout the body in the blood stream and the lymph system, and lead to a chronic increase in metal ion levels. Compared to metal-on-plastic, metal-on-metal implants release about five times more metal. The main effect is a sensitisation of the immune system. However, mostly feared is an increased risk of cancer. A metal-on-plastic hip or knee implant has probably no influence on cancer incidence (typical odds ratio 1.01 to 1.03). Compared to metal-on-plastic implants, the cancer incidence of metal-on-metal implants may be about 1.25, mainly due to larger numbers of leukaemia, uterus and prostate cancers. This odds ratio is similar to that of passive smoking. However, all data are for older type metal-on-metal implants which may have worn more. No data is available for current implants.

The real question is how much wear contributes to osteolysis and to implant loosening. A recent meta-study of compiling studies of acetabular wear rate versuspercentage osteolysis found a tentative relation between the two. Three kinds of cups and wear behaviour appeared. Group I: cups with large heads and thin liners. These produced much debris (400 mm³/yr), causing general osteolysis after 10 years.
Group II: cups with smaller heads (22-28 mm) and metal backing. These produced intermediate amounts of debris (200 mm³/yr), and had smaller osteolysis rates (about 50% after 10 years).
Group III: cups with smaller heads (22-28 mm) and no metal backing. These had low wear rates (75 mm³/yr), and low rats of osteolysis. In this group of cups, osteolysis typically occurs after loosening first causes a dramatic increase of wear rate by roughening the head.

This analysis suggests that cups with high wear rates (large heads or metal-backed) have wear rates above the critical level of 150 mm³/yr, giving a large chance of osteolysis. Cups with low wear rates (smaller heads, not metal-backed) have wear rates below the critical level, giving a small chance of osteolysis unless something changes.

Loosening, wear and osteolysis

- Roentgen Stereophotogrammetry:
  Early migration predicts late loosening
- Insufficient early fixation/Early loss of fixation
- Cyclic motion ↑
- Wear generation at interfaces ↑
- Wear transport ↑
- Third body wear ↑
- Resorption ↑
- Contribution secondary, but significant

If implants with large heads or metal backing are left aside, what is the contribution of wear to loosening? RSA studies suggest that early migration is a good predictor of late loosening. This suggests that implants that loosen late had either insufficient early fixation or early loss of fixation. Loose prostheses increase wear generation at the various interfaces, increase wear particle transport, and increase the risk of third-body particle generation. This may roughen the bearing surfaces, thus increasing wear rates and making matters even worse. For these prostheses, the primary event seems mechanical loosening, and increased wear followed by osteolysis a secondary event. The open question is how much wear debris contributes to the process that turns a "mechanically loose" prosthesis into a "clinically loose" prosthesis.

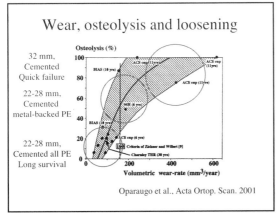

Wear, osteolysis and loosening

32 mm, Cemented Quick failure

22-28 mm, Cemented metal-backed PE

22-28 mm, Cemented all PE Long survival

Oparaugo et al., Acta Ortop. Scan. 2001

What to do?

- Slooff (1999)

  "[..] more attention and care should be paid to perfect the operative technique of the individual surgeon. With this I mean optimising the initial fixation for cemented and cementless implants, producing a strong fixation between the components a the bone. [..]"

What then should a surgeon do? As far as hip implants go, it seems wise to avoid implants with large femoral heads or metal-backed implants, in particular with thin liners. As for knee implants, it seems again wise to avoid modular designs with thin liners. Experience with alternative bearing materials is patchy at best. So, the best advise seems to be that given by Slooff, namely to perfect the operative technique.

Who wants to be a millionaire?

1. Do modern metal-on-metal implants increase cancer risk?

2. Will modern cross-linked polyethylene have small long-term wear rates?

3. If mechanical loosening is the event triggering increased wear and subsequent osteolysis in slow-wearing implants, how much longer can a mechanically loose implant survive when wear is eliminated?

Some open million-pound questions.

Summary

- Friction
  - 'Welding' at localised contact
- Lubrication
  - Fluid film: speed, viscosity, force
  - Boundary → Mixed → Elasto-hydrodynamic → Hydrodynamic
- Wear
  - Mechanism: Abrasive/Adhesive wear ↔ Fatigue wear
  - Stiffer materials: ↓ wear volume & particles size
  - Plastic → 1μm particles → local tissue reaction
    - Critical level 100 mm^3/year or 10 billion particles/gr tissue
  - Metal → 0.01 μm particles → systemic reaction
    - Possible worry about cancer, but no evidence to support

Some literature to finish off. I found the following very useful:

Black J, Orthopaedic biomaterials in research and practice. Edinburgh Churchill Livingstone, 1988. *Although a bit old, it has a clear chapter on wear.*

Scholes SC, Unsworth A. Comparison of friction and lubrication of different hip prostheses, Proc Inst Mech Eng [H] 2000; 214: 49-57. *Clear experimental and theoretical analysis of friction and wear in hard-on-plastic, metal-on-metal and ceramic-on-ceramic hips.*

Oparaugo PC, Clarke IC, Malchau H, Herberts P. Correlation of wear debris-induced osteolysis and revision with volumetric wear-rates of polyethylene: a survey of 8 reports in the literature., Acta Orthop Scand. 2001; 72: 22-8. *Good overview of relation between wear, osteolysis and loosening.*

J Elfick AP, Smith SL, Unsworth A. Variation in the wear rate during the life of a total hip arthroplasty: a simulator and retrieval study. J Arthroplasty. 2000;15: 901-8.

Wan Z, Dorr LD. Natural history of femoral focal osteolysis with proximal ingrowth smooth stem implant. J Arthroplasty. 11 (1996):718-25. *The above two studies demonstrate that in little-wearing implants loosening precedes wear precedes osteolysis.*

Archibeck MJ, Jacobs JJ, Black J. Alternate bearing surfaces in total joint arthroplasty: biologic considerations. Clin Orthop 2000; 379:12-21. *Balanced review of the pro's and con's of alternative bearing combinations.*

Notes

Notes

Basic Science for FRCS (Trauma and Orthopaedics)

Clinical Shoulder Biomechanics

Mr S N J Roberts

Consultant Orthopaedic & Sports Injury Surgeon
Robert Jones & Agnes Hunt Orthopaedic Hospital
Oswestry

The human shoulder has an enormous range of movement and serves primarily to position the arm and therefore hand in space. It was first described as a complex by Cleland in 1881 and may be considered as consisting of five joints:

> steronoclavicular,
>
> acromioclavicular,
>
> scapulothoracic,
>
> subacromial and
>
> glenohumeral.

Normal shoulder movement requires the coordinated contraction of nearly 30 muscles acting across these joints. Biomechanically, it may be simplified and considered as a two-bar chain consisting of the clavicle and humerus, with elevation occurring at the sternoclavicular and glenohumeral joints in varying proportions (Figs.1, 2 & 3).

It is possible to elevate the humerus from the side to above the horizontal after glenohumeral arthrodesis with a combination of scapulothoracic movement and lateral flexion of the spine. Similarly, after scapulohumeral fusion, isolated glenohumeral elevation also allows a good range of movement. Normal movement requires the glenoid to rotate in a coordinated fashion so that the glenoid articular surface is best placed to "catch" the humeral head in its "palm" (or to, like a performing seal, balance the ball of the humeral head on its "nose")(Fig 4), and also to elevate the acromion and avoid impingement.

The coordinated elevation of the humerus occurs throughout the range of motion approximately two-thirds in the glenohumeral joint and one third in the scapulothoracic joint (Figs. 5-6). Interestingly, the pattern is clearly seen to be different in elevating the arm from that lowering the arm to the side.

More scapulothoracic movements occur in the high arc than the low arc perhaps explaining the high painful arc in acromioclavicular pathology. This scapulohumeral rhythm (Codman 1934) is disturbed by a number of

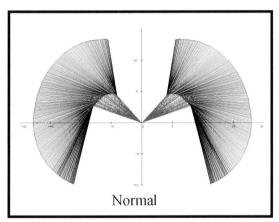

Normal

Fig.1

Fig.2

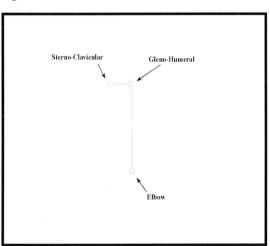

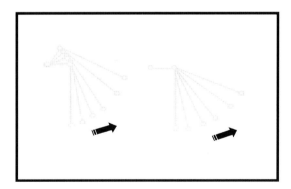

Fig.3

Fig.4 Warner, JJP et al Crit Rev Rhys Rehab Med 1992 4 145-198

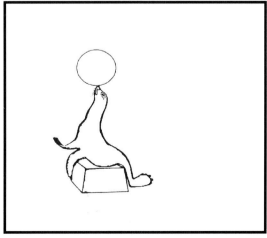

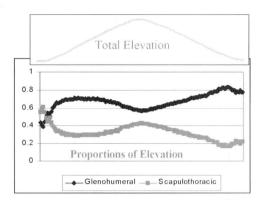

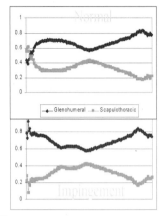

Fig.5

Fig.6

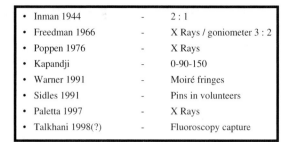

• Inman 1944	-	2 : 1
• Freedman 1966	-	X Rays / goniometer 3 : 2
• Poppen 1976	-	X Rays
• Kapandji	-	0-90-150
• Warner 1991	-	Moiré fringes
• Sidles 1991	-	Pins in volunteers
• Paletta 1997	-	X Rays
• Talkhani 1998(?)	-	Fluoroscopy capture

Fig.7

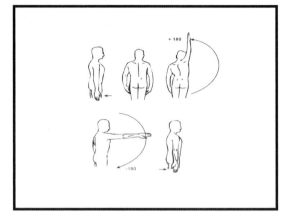

Fig.8

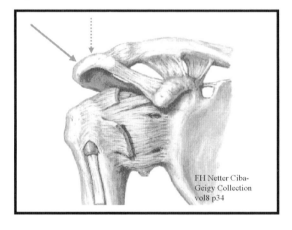

FH Netter Ciba-Geigy Collection vol8 p34

Fig.9

conditions affecting the shoulder, most commonly subacromial impingement but also instability, and may be either cause or effect in both conditions.

It is much easier to observe than describe or quantify this rhythm, but numerous attempts have been made (Fig 7) to analyse the relative contributions from the scapulothoracic and glenohumeral joints or alternatively describe the locus of the instantaneous centre of rotation[3]. Attempts have been made with fluoroscopy, video and various motion analysis systems, including markers attached to pins driven into the scapula and humerus of volunteers!

Codman's paradox causes much more confusion than it deserves. It is a function of sequential rotation about orthogonal axes and is of interest to mathematicians more than surgeons. Sequential abduction of the adducted arm by 180° followed by extension forwards to replace the arm by the side leaves the humerus having rotated about its longitudinal axis by 180° (Fig 8). This is described by Eulerian geometry not biomechanics.

Shoulder Anatomy

The clavicle is the only bony connection between the upper limb and trunk, forming unusual and incongruous synovial joints at either end, each with a fibrocartilaginous intra-articular meniscus. Both joints are stabilised by strong extra-articular ligaments which lie some distance from the joints themselves and connect the clavicle to the first rib (which it can articulate with) medially, and the coracoid process of the scapula laterally.

These ligaments constrain both joints to undergo gliding movements with all but axial rotations, since the instantaneous centre of rotation does not coincide with the centre of curvature of the articular surface. The amount and significance of axial rotation of the clavicle is debated, with estimates of its magnitude varying from over 45° to less than 10°.

Laterally, the coracoclavicular ligaments are of great clinical interest, consisting of the conoid and trapezoid components. The latter is stronger & runs superiorly and laterally, serving to oppose medialisation of the acromion with respect to clavicle. This is important as the usual mechanism of injury to the acromioclavicular joint is a direct blow to the point of the shoulder – a blow whose force is directed medially as well as having the inferior component which is usually recognised (Fig 9). The angle of inclination of acromioclavicular joint to the sagittal plane is also variable and this is of relevance in the incidence and pattern of injuries to the joint.

Fig.10

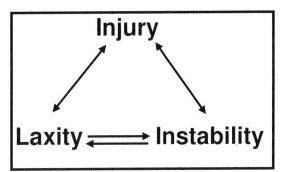

Fig.11

Matsen

Traumatic	Atraumatic
Unidirectional	Multidirectional
(Unilateral)	Bilateral
	Rehabilitation
Bankart Lesion	Inferior Capsular Shift
Surgery	(Interval Closure)

Fig.12

Longitudinally, the clavicle's S-shape allows the middle third to clear the thoracic outlet, where its tubular cross-section helps to protect the neurovascular bundles. Laterally the section is flat to allow attachment of the large deltoid and trapezius muscles to maximum mechanical advantage, while medially the triangular section resists axial compression.

The coracoacromial ligament completes the coracoacromial arch over the humeral head and inserts into the inferior surface of the acromion. Its anatomy is somewhat variable, but does make it impossible to perform an anterior acromioplasty without at least elevating the ligament. The deltoid muscle predominantly attaches to the peripheral and superior surface of the acromion and clavicle but does have an element of insertion inferiorly leaving it also vulnerable during acromioplasty.

Viewed from above the humeral head lies in front of the acromion and the subacromial bursa is related to the humeral head as opposed to the acromion. This can easily be seen in the presence of bursal effusion or after inflation of the subacromial bursa, when the swelling is seen to extend anteriorly in front of the acromial margin.

It has been shown that the centre of the humeral head lies significantly behind the axis of the humeral shaft and that its retroversion is only 20-25° (Fig 10). Some of the previously described retroversion was misinterpreted posterior offset.

Clinical Problems

The two Topics of interest clinically with respect to Shoulder Biomechanics are[1]: -

Shoulder Instability and

Disorders of the Rotator Cuff.

1. Instability

There is a big difference in the aetiopathology and treatment of shoulders which are "torn" loose as opposed to "born" loose. There is a wide variation in the amount of glenohumeral translation which occurs in normal shoulders making it important to compare one side with the other during clinical examination. Laxity is not the same as instability: Laxity is a clinical sign; instability is the symptom clinically attributed to increased joint laxity (Fig.11).

In assessing a potentially unstable shoulder it is, therefore, vitally important to take an adequate history of the injury and symptoms as well as examining both shoulders to elicit the relevant clinical signs. Matsen clarified the probably continuous spectrum from "TUBS" to "AMBRI" shoulders (from Traumatic Unidirectionally unstable shoulders with Bankart lesions and requiring Surgical reconstruction, to the Atraumatic Multi-directional Bilaterally unstable shoulders, best treated with Rehabilitation and if absolutely necessary, an Inferior capsular shift with closure of the rotator Interval) (Fig.12).

Factors contributing to glenohumeral stability[2]

Articular congruity is limited in the shoulder since the glenoid only covers about a quarter of the articular surface of the humeral head. There may be congenital deficiency in congruity or acquired deficiencies such as a bony or soft tissue Bankart lesion or an impression defect from dislocation as in a posterior Hill Sach's lesion.

Articular depth. The bony glenoid forms a shallow saucer rather than a true socket for the humerus to articulate with. The bony depth is increased by the articular cartilage being thicker peripherally than centrally and also by the fibrous glenoid labrum (Fig 13).

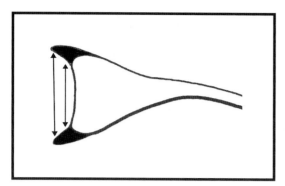

Fig.13 .

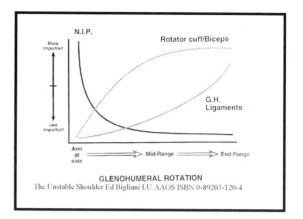

Fig.15

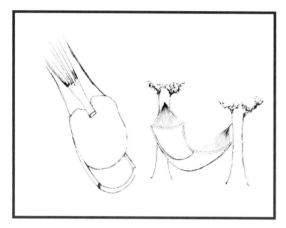

Fig.14

Articular version. Static and dynamic orientation of the glenoid socket which implies adequate control of scapulothoracic movement as well as glenohumeral. Proper scapulothoracic kinematics allow the glenoid socket to be orientated so as to be as nearly as possible normal (perpendicular) to the compressive force across the glenohumeral joint, minimising the shear component. Static alteration in the glenoid version in any plane may contribute to glenohumeral instability. **Humeral retroversion** has been reported as being altered in patients with instability and proximal humeral rotational osteotomy has been recommended as a treatment. This surgery is not currently recommended unless a major abnormality is demonstrated.

The primary static restraints to glenohumeral subluxation are the capsulo-ligamentous complex and the most important static restraint to anteroinferior subluxation is the anterior band of the inferior glenohumeral ligament. This band undergoes plastic deformation during anterior shoulder dislocation with or without Bankart lesion. The inferior ligament has both anterior and posterior bands with a lax hammock-like arrangement in between in the infraglenoid pouch (Fig 14). The more superior ligaments, the superior and middle glenohumeral ligaments may be more important with the arm in less abduction since they are rendered relatively lax in glenohumeral abduction.

The dynamic restraints to glenohumeral subluxation include:

Negative intra-articular pressure. A suction effect which is contributed to by the seal formed

by the glenoid labrum forming a suction cup effect. The maximum effect of this negative intra-articular pressure is with the glenohumeral joint adducted, it may be that lesions of the rotator interval allow this negative intra-articular pressure to be lost as a soft tissues are sucked into the defect (Fig 15) with anteroinferior translation.

Proprioception and proper muscular strength and coordination is important not only of the rotator cuff muscles but also particularly the long head of biceps and the periscapular muscles, ensuring that scapular orientation is optimal. The rotator cuff muscles help the static restraint by dynamizing the ligaments, tensing them in various positions. There is also a concept of concavity compression whereby mass action of the rotator cuff holds the humeral head snugly in the depths of the glenoid fossa. There is conflicting evidence regarding the importance of proprioception in the shoulder, since Lephart showed in 1996 that there were alterations in both threshold to detection of passive movement and the ability to reproduce passive positioning in traumatically unstable shoulders which was improved by surgical reconstruction.

2. Subacromial impingement.

The scapulothoracic joint may also contribute to subacromial impingement. In the presence of thoracic kyphosis the scapula is rotated anteriorly to lie along the posterior chest wall making anterior subacromial impingement more likely in elevation.

Anterior acromioplasty was popularised by Neer nearly thirty years ago and it was suggested at that time that there were three progressive grades from reversible inflammation through chronic fibrosis to rotator cuff tear. More recently, there is increasing evidence of a primary tendonopathy with a secondary change in shape of the acromion, as it becomes more "curved" or "hooked" (Bigliani's types II & III). It is probable that a primary tendonopathy of the supraspinatus leads to impaired glenohumeral kinematics allowing the humeral head to ride superiorly causing a secondary compression and a vicious cycle leading to progressive tendonopathy and eventual rotator cuff tear[4].

Basic Science for FRCS (Trauma and Orthopaedics)

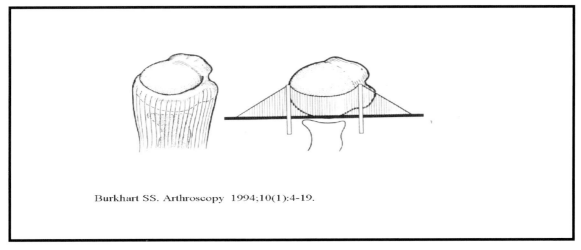

Burkhart SS. Arthroscopy 1994;10(1):4-19.

Fig. 16 Burkhart SS Arthroscopy 1994 10 (1) 4-19

Subacromial impingement simply refers to the squashing of the subacromial tendon between the humeral head and the acromion and this may be caused either by a spur from above, a spur from below, increased volume of the subacromial soft tissues or upward migration of the humeral head. Probably all of these contribute in various proportions.

Certainly, supraspinatus tendonosis is commonly seen before there are changes in the coracoacromial ligament and before the change in acromial morphology. A degree of fatiguability of glenohumeral centering has been demonstrated and it would be expected that overuse may lead to superior migration of the humeral head and consequent reduction in the space available for the supraspinatus tendon.

At exploration for rotator cuff tear, lamination of the rotator cuff is often seen and partial thickness cuff tears are more commonly seen on the glenohumeral as opposed to bursal side, again making it appear more likely that the pathology is not simple abrasion of the superior surface of the supraspinatus.

Our current concept of subacromial impingement is that the clinical syndrome occurring in patients aged under 35 is probably secondary to glenohumeral instability and poor glenohumeral centring allowing the subacromial distance to be reduced by the humeral head.

Between 35 and 55 may well be an intrinsic tendonosis leading to a secondary impingement. In patients over aged 55, it should be remembered that a small full-thickness rotator cuff tear may be a normal variant. A number of studies have shown that the prevalence of full thickness rotator cuff in totally asymptomatic patients over the age of 60 is around 25% and partial thickness 50%.

The reason that these patients are asymptomatic may well be explained by Burkhart's concept of a "cable and crescent" arrangement of the rotator cuff in that if the cuff is well anchored anteriorly and posteriorly there is a flaccid segment in between which may not contribute to either glenohumeral stability or elevation[5]. This is analogous to suspension bridge which is able to support a high load with compression on each pylon and tension in the cable sagging between (Fig.16).

Provided the anterior and posterior struts are intact and balanced, the central segment (which is often seen to be lax from the glenohumeral side at arthroscopy) may be redundant.

Concepts are also changing from the classical description of supraspinatus as the initiator of abduction and deltoid as the mid-range motor. The muscles work synergistically throughout the range of movement.

Summary

In summary, the biomechanics of the shoulder are complex and concepts have changed considerably over the last 20 years. Coordination and synergism between the large number of glenohumeral and periscapular muscles leads to the normal kinematic pattern.

Static and dynamic factors contribute to glenohumeral stability, so that there is no "essential lesion".

Rotator cuff disease may be at least partly an intrinsic tendinosis rather than primarily a mechanical abrasion.

References

1. Matsen FA; Fu FH; Hawkins RJ. The shoulder: A balance of mobility and stability. Rosemount: American Academy of Orthopaedics Surgeons. 1993.
2. Bigliani LU. editor.The Unstable Shoulder. American Academy of Orthopaedics Surgeons. 1996.
3. An KN, Browne AO, Korinek S, Tanaka S, Morrey BF. Three-dimensional kinematics of glenohumeral elevation. J.Orthop.Res. 1991;9:143-9.
4. Budoff JE, Nirschl RP, Guidi EJ. Debridement of partial-thickness tears of the rotator cuff without acromioplasty. Long-term follow-up and review of the literature. [Review] [58 refs]. J.Bone Joint Surg. 1998;80B: 733-48.
5. Burkhart SS. Reconciling the paradox of rotator cuff repair versus debridement: a unified biomechanical rationale for the treatment of rotator cuff tears. [Review]. Arthroscopy 1994;10:4-19.
6. Morrey BF, Itoi E, An K-N. Biomechanics of the shoulder. In: Rockwood, CA editor. The shoulder. Philadelphia: Saunders, 1998: p233-76.

Notes

The Elbow

Mr S Hay

Consultant Orthopaedic Surgeon
Robert Jones & Agnes Hunt Orthopaedic Hospital
Oswestry

THE ELBOW

The elbow joint provides a vitally important functional linkage between the shoulder and the hand. Without normal elbow mobility and stability, it is difficult to place the hand precisely in space and the functional activities of the individual may be limited, thereby compromising independence.

The biomechanics of this complex articulation have been investigated in depth and have helped us to understand both how it works normally and why sometimes it functions abnormally. A detailed description of the complexity of elbow movement is beyond the scope of this text, but some points are worthy of consideration.

The elbow joint is a synovial joint of the hinge variety, created by the articular confluence of the distal humerus, the proximal radius and the proximal ulna. *(Fig.1.)* It has 3 areas of articulation between 1) the articular surface of the olecranon and the trochlear component of the humerus 2) the radial head and the capitellar process of the humerus and 3) the circumferential articular surface of the radial head and the sigmoid notch of the proximal ulna. The major components of elbow movement include flexion/extension and rotation. The alternative terminology applied to rotation is "pronation and supination". Full supination is represented by the position adopted by the forearm and hand with the arm held in the anatomical position ie. palm forwards. Pronation describes the rotation of the forearm such that the palm faces backwards.

The normal range of movement in flexion/ extension is 0 – 142 °, where zero represents full extension(1).

Hyperextension is common and more commonly seen in females, but greater than 10° is generally regarded as abnormal.

Rotational movements are described relative to a neutral position with the extended thumb pointing vertically, and the elbow flexed to 90°. Supination normally occurs to approximately 85° and pronation to approximately 75°.

During these rotational movements the thumb can act as a useful goniometer.(Fig 2) The axis of rotation passes distally through the centre of the wrist and interestingly Ray et al (2) have shown that during rotation, a varus/valgus movement of approximately 9° is also happening at the humeroulnar joint. This collateral movement reflects the small but important accommodating slackness of the collateral ligaments, and for which the joint is sometimes referred to as a sloppy hinge. Newton (3), using an Isotrak system to investigate the patterns of movement in cadaveric specimens has also shown that varus/valgus movement occurs at the humeroulnar joint during flexion/extension. In addition he has also shown that the ulna pronates and supinates on the humerus during flexion/extension. The extent of this pattern of movement was seen to be variable between subjects, but supports the contention that the early loosening seen in the congruous elbow prostheses, is probably related to the torsional forces which are imparted during movement. Nowadays such devices are deliberately designed to include some degrees of freedom of movement in the form of either unlinked, non congruous surfaces, or as sloppy hinged prostheses. Such devices attempt to mimic the natural predisposition of the elbow towards slight valgus-varus and rotational movements at the humeroulnar articulation, which of course is where the components are fitted

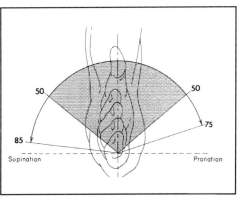

Fig 1 The bony components of the Elbow joint   *Fig 2 The range of supination and pronation.*

Elbow Stability

Stability for this joint is conferred by several components, which include the bony configuration, the capsule, the medial and lateral collateral ligaments and the surrounding musculature. The medial ligament has an anterior band, a posterior band and a central band. The lateral ligament is comprised of the radial ligament, the ulna band of the lateral ligament and the annular ligament. *Figs 3a and b*. O'Driscoll (4) has performed cadaveric studies to investigate elbow stability and has postulated that the ulna band of the lateral ligament has an extremely important role.

He suggests that damage to this ligament is an important process in elbow dislocation and as the radial head and ulna rotate out of joint the injury progresses circumferentially both anteriorly and posteriorly towards the medial ligament.*Fig4* Dislocation can occur although the anterior band of the medial ligament may remain intact. He suggests that in posterolateral rotatory instability, the ulna band of the lateral ligament is damaged and the pivot shift test which assesses rotational instability, is positive. Reconstruction using the palmaris longus tendon can restore stability.

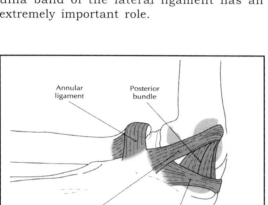

Fig 3a) The medial collateral ligament of the elbow

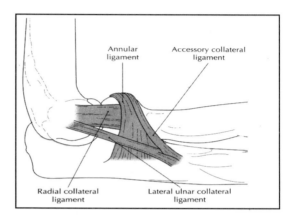

Fig 3b)The lateral collateral ligament

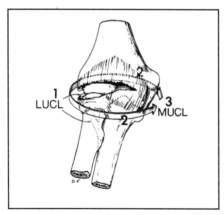

Fig 4 The pattern of injury in elbow dislocation.

Carrying Angle

The "carrying angle" is a term commonly used in description of the elbow and refers to the lateral deviation of the forearm relative to the sagittal plane of the humerus, with the elbow in full extension. In adult males it averages 11° and in females 14°, whilst in childhood it averages 6°. *(Fig 5)* The carrying angle arises because the articular surface of the distal humerus lies in approximately 6° of valgus and as flexion progresses, so the forearm will gradually come to overlie the upper arm. In addition to valgus angulation, the humeral articular surface is also seen to be angulated 30° anteriorly and is internally rotated by 5°.

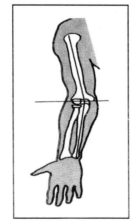

Fig 5 The carrying angle

Basic Science for FRCS (Trauma and Orthopaedics)

Forces across the Joint

Forces in Flexion

Amis and Miller (5) have investigated this, taking into account the directions of those muscles which cross the elbow and could therefore influence this. The most important of the flexor group include, brachioradialis, biceps and pronator teres. The joint forces were predicted to act primarily in the sagittal plane and were seen to be similar in magnitude on both the radial head and on the coronoid. *Fig 6* Large forces were seen to act axially on the distal aspect of the humerus as the elbow approached extension, but these diminished with flexion. The balance of forces results primarily from the distribution of influential muscles, the humeroulnar joint being compressed by the brachialis and the common flexor muscles, whilst the radius has biceps, pronator teres and brachioradialis inserting into it.

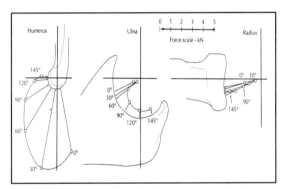

Fig 6 Forces acting on the humerus, radial head and coronoid during maximal isometric elbow flexion efforts in adult male subject. From ref. 5 with permission.

Forces in Extension

The triceps muscle is responsible for most of the force required to extend the elbow. This force is generated predominantly through the olecranon and therefore acts into the trochlear notch. It can exceed 3kN and peaks as extension occurs through 120°. In addition however, the lateral head of triceps dissipates force in the fascia overlying the supinator muscle and this, coupled with those forearm muscles stabilising the wrist, contributes to a humeroradial force peaking at approximately 1kN. Triceps has a small moment arm, acting through the olecranon and consequently the muscle forces are high. With a stabilising influence from biceps, the humeroulnar force exceeds 20 times the load in the hand, sometimes reaching 24 times the external load.

Radial Head Excision

Occasionally, in the context of trauma, where fractures of the radial head are unreconstructible (ie Mason type 3) and in the presence of rheumatoid disease affecting the radiocapitellar joint, it is necessary to excise the radial head. This reduces the effective width of the articulation and greater forces are concentrated on the lateral edge of the coronoid process. Valgus angulation of the elbow may occur, and is balanced by increasing tension in the medial collateral ligament which may become attenuated or disrupted as a result. In those trauma cases where a comminuted radial head fracture is associated with elbow instability or in association with disruption of the radio-ulna interosseus membrane (Essex-Lopresti lesion) there is a good argument to replace the radial head, (6) usually with a metallic prosthesis and recently several such devices have become available. In the absence of associated instability however, radial head excision remains the treatment of choice for the comminuted radial head fracture.

Elbow Arthroplasty

The first elbow replacement was performed by Robineau in 1927 and consisted of a hemiarthroplasty for the distal humerus. The popularity of total elbow arthroplasty has gradually increased since that time and particularly within the last 30 years. This is in keeping with an upsurge in clinical and biomechanical research in this field and with the experience gained in other joints, notably the hip. The failings of the earlier constrained, hinged elbow prostheses was largely due to loosening, reflecting the complex pattern of movement of the elbow, as discussed above. Large torsional forces were transmitted to the bone cement interface and loosening was the inevitable consequence. Unlinked, incongruous varieties such as the Kudo and iBP systems and sloppy hinged varieties such as the GSB and Coonrad-Morrey systems have been designed to overcome this although each has its own shortcomings

The primary indication for elbow replacement is pain relief and the secondary indications include 1)restoration of stability in the presence of painful instability and 2)improvement in motion. The main absolute contraindication is sepsis either locally or distally and relative contraindications include arthrodesis, the neuropathic elbow, paralysis of biceps/triceps, ectopic ossification and degenerative change in the young fit manual worker. It is most frequently undertaken in rheumatoid disease and the results have generally been good.

A recent article from Kudo's own group in Japan showed acceptable long term results for the type III Kudo prosthesis in rheumatoid disease, with a prosthesis survival rate of 90% at 16 years. (7)

In the presence of primary osteoarthritis of the elbow, the role of arthroplasty is limited and it is discouraged in the young manual worker with isolated disease where loosening and wear is likely to occur rapidly. Arthroscopic or open debridement in the form of an Outerbridge-Kashiwagi (OK) procedure (8) has been helpful in slowing the symptomatic progression of osteoarthritis. In this procedure, via a posterior approach, osteophytes are removed from the olecranon and the olecranon fossa and loose bodies can simultaneously be removed. A fenestration of approximately 1cm is then drilled between the olecranon and coronoid fossae and further loose bodies can be removed from the anterior compartment. At the same time it may be possible to release the anterior capsular structures and to remove osteophytes from the coronoid tip.

Arthroscopic surgery in the Elbow.

In recent years we have generally seen a huge increase in the successful introduction of minimally invasive surgery for a variety of joints and the elbow is no exception. However, it is not without significant neurovascular risk and although the risk is low, it reflects the very close proximity of these important structures. The most common neurological injury is probably to the radial nerve and generally reflects surgical inexperience. Several portals have been described for arthroscopy of the elbow and these include the following: (10)

Anterolateral - This is established in the sulcus between the radial head and the capitellum anteriorly, situated approximately 3 cm distal and 2 cm anterior to the lateral humeral epicondyle. It is valuable for viewing the anterior compartment, especially the medial side.

Superomedial - This is located 2 cm proximal to the medial humeral epicondyle. The trochar and cannula must be directed anterior to the medial intermuscular septum and aimed towards the middle of the joint. It is often used as the initial portal and is useful for viewing the anterior compartment, especially the lateral side.

Direct Lateral - This portal is situated at the centre of an isoceles triangle created by the radial head, the lateral epicondyle of the humerus and the subcutaneous tip of the olecranon. It is the site through which the joint is distended, by injecting 20-30 mls of saline, before arthroscopy is performed. The advantages of joint distension are as follows; a)It pushes important neurovascular structures away from the joint, b)It provides

a larger target towards which the trochar and cannula can be aimed, c)It can be felt as a resistance which gives way as it is penetrated, d)Fluid is seen to issue from the cannula when the trochar is withdrawn. This portal can be used for viewing the olecranon fossa, the humeroulnar joint, the proximal radio-ulnar joint and the posterior aspect of the radio-capitellar joint.

Straight posterior - The straight posterior portal is created 3cm proximal to the subcutaneous olecranon tip. It is useful as a viewing or a working portal for the olecranon fossa.

Posterolateral - This is established approximately 2 cm lateral to the posterior portal. Its uses are similar to the posterior portal

The ulna nerve, whilst in its anatomical position lies on the postero-medial aspect of the joint and because of the potential risk to this nerve, posteromedial portals are not made. Indeed, where the position of the neurovascular structures has been disturbed either by injury or by previous surgery, arthroscopy should not be attempted.

The indications for elbow arthroscopy have gradually increased and include both diagnostic and therapeutic. In our own series of 100 therapeutic arthroscopies, the procedures included the removal of loose bodies, excision of osteophytes, removal of impinging soft tissue and bone, treatment of osteochondral lesions and synovectomy for rheumatoid disease. Within this group, 74% were sportsmen and when a follow up assessment was made, 88% of patients felt their surgery had been worthwhile. (10)

References

1)Amis AA, Miller JH The Elbow. Measurement of joint movement. Clin Rheum Dis 1982; 8: 571-93.

2)Ray RD, Johnson RJ, Jameson RM Rotation of the forearm: an experimental study of pronation and supination. J Bone Joint Surg 1951; 33A: 993-6.

3)Newton SD: A study of elbow joint anatomy and biomechanics in relation to the implantation of an unlinked replacement arthroplasty. B Med Sci Thesis University of Newcastle Upon Tyne, UK, 1992.

4)O'Driscoll SW, Morrey BF, Korinek S, An K. Elbow Subluxation and Dislocation A Spectrum of Disability. Clin Orthop 1992; 280: 186-96.

5)Amis AA, Miller JH Design, development and clinical trial of a modular elbow replacement incorporating cement-free fixation. Eng Med 1984: 13 175-9.

6)Edwards GSJ, Jupiter JB Radial head fractures with acute distal radioulnar dislocation: Essex-lopresti revisited. Clin Orthop 1988; 234: 61-9.

7)Tanaka N, Kudo H, Iwano K, Sakahashi H, Sato E and Ishii S. Kudo Total Elbow Arthroplasty in Patients with Rheumatoid Arthritis. A Long-Term Follow-up Study. J Bone Joint Surg Am. 2001 83A: 10: 1506-13.

8)Stanley D, Winson IG A surgical approach to the elbow. J. Bone Joint Surg 1990; 72B 728-9.

9)Stanley D and Kay NRM. Arthroscopy. In Surgery of The Elbow – Practical and Scientific aspects. London: Arnold, 1998, 71-81.

10)Hay SM and Bell SJ. Therapeutic Elbow Arthroscopy – A Review of 100 patients. Presented at the British Elbow and Shoulder Society Annual Meeting1999. (unpublished data) Legends.

Acknowledgements

I gratefully acknowledge the Times Mirror/Mosby College Publishing group for permission to use fig 1, W.B.Saunders publishers for permission to use figs 2 and 5, The Arnold publishing group for permission to use figs 3a and 3b and the Engineering Medical Journal for permission to use fig 6. I would also like to thank the Medical Illustration Department at the Robert Jones and Agnes Hunt Orthopaedic Hospital for their help in preparing the manuscript.

Notes

Nerve Injury and Healing and the Brachial Plexus

Mr R Bindra
Consultant Orthopaedic Surgeon
Pulvertaft Hand Centre, Derbyshire Royal Infirmary

Relevant Anatomy

The 5th to 8th cervical and 1st thoracic nerve roots contribute to the brachial plexus. The roots emerge from behind the scalenus anterior muscle and in the posterior triangle of the neck, combine to form the trunks. The upper trunk is formed by the 5th and 6th cervical roots, the middle trunk is a continuation of the 7th root and the 8th cervical and 1st thoracic roots form the lower trunk.

At the level of the clavicle, the trunks divide into anterior and posterior divisions. The three posterior divisions form the posterior cord. The anterior divisions of the upper and middle trunks form the lateral cord and the anterior division of the lower trunk forms the medial cord. The nomenclature of the cords is based on their relationship to the axillary artery behind the pectoralis minor muscle.

Relevant Physiology

Proximal nerve segment:
The severity of injuries and proximity to the cell bodies result in chromatolysis and even death of cell bodies.

Site of nerve injury:
Proximal to the injury, axons degenerate for a distance of one or several internodal segments. After an initial delay, a single nerve fibre will sprout into a regenerating unit containing many nerve fibres. At the distal portion of each axon sprout, there is a growth cone consisting of filopodia, constantly moving, exploring the local microenvironment. The axons that make connections with peripheral targets mature and myelinate, the rest (majority) disappear.

Distal segment:
Rapid disintegration occurs- 'Wallerian degeneration'. The myelin disintegrates and is phagocytosed by Schwann cells and macrophages.

Axonal regrowth rates vary –the average regrowth in adults is 1-2mm/day.

End organs

1. Sensory receptors
Denervation of the encapsulated sensory receptors occurs. Reinnervation is possible even after many years following injury. In pre-ganglionic injuries, the sensory cell is intact, and degeneration does not occur.

2. Motor-end plate
Normal muscle has a random arrangement of type I and II fibers. After reinnervation the fibers group into the two types. There exists a definite period of time (approximately 1 year) after which a muscle is incapable of being reinnervated even if normal nerve fibers reach the muscle.

Simply placing a motor nerve into a muscle (neurotisation) can result in some recovery of motor function, but is unpredictable and not as good as recovery after a nerve graft.

Clinical Assessment

3 Primary Questions:
1. Is the injury isolated to the brachial plexus
2. Is it pre or post-ganglionic
3. Is the location supraclavicular or infraclavicular

Assessing Nerve Roots Clinically

C4 Intact diaphragm
C5 Intact rhomboids
C6 Intact serratus anterior

Differentiation of Pre- and Post-Ganglionic Lesions*
(See top of next page)

MRI evaluation of brachial plexus injuries:
Body or surface coil used to enhance images. Sagittal T-1 weighted images from spinal canal to the lateral end of clavicle and axial images from level of C4 vertebra to the carina are obtained. In addition, oblique coronal images oriented parallel to the subclavian artery are useful.

Signs of nerve root avulsion:
1) Non-visualisation of nerve roots
2) Pseudo-meningocoeles appear as masses extending from the neural foramen into the surrounding soft tissues. These masses have same intensity as CSF.

While CT-myelogram can detect the above, with MRI, neuromas can be identified as regions

of thickening on T-1 images and a high signal on T-2 images.

Differentiation of Pre- and Post-Ganglionic Lesions*

Procedure	Preganglionic	Postganglionic
Examination	Flail arm Horner's syndrome Winged scapula Paralysed Rhomboids Diaphragmatic paralysis	Flail arm
Myelography (Reliable in C-8 ; T-1)	Traumatic meningocoeles	No meningocoeles
Nerve Conduction	Sensory conduction intact Motor conduction absent	Sensory and motor conduction absent
EMG	Cervical paraspinal muscles denervated	Cervical paraspinal muscles normal
	Peripheral muscles denervated	Peripheral muscles denervated
Axon Response	Flare present	No flare in triple response

* Not all are 100% sensitive, hence a combination of tests is ue. The final word is by surgical, exploration and intra-operative electrophysical testing

Clinical Examination

Motor and sensory loss by root level

Prioritising Surgical

Root Level	Motor Loss	Sensory Loss
C-5-6	**Shoulder:** Ext rotation, flexion, abduction **Elbow:** Flexion **Wrist** : Extension	Thumb and index fingers
C-5-6-7	In addition to above: Extension of elbow, wrist, fingers and thumb	Thumb, index and middle fingers
C-8; T-1	Finger and thumb flexion, All intrinsics	Little and ring fingers; inner border of forearm
C-5; T-1	All of above	All of above

Root Values of Important Nerves Upper Extremity (Muscles)

Nerve (Muscle)	Spinal Root
Suprascapular (Supraspinatus and infraspinatus)	C-5-6
Axillary (Deltoid)	C-5-6
Musculocutaneous (Biceps, Brachialis)	C-5-6
Radial (Triceps) (ECRL, Brachioradialis)	C-6-7-8 C5-6

Nerve (Muscle)	Spinal Root
Ulnar (FCU) (½ FDP) (Intrinsics)	C7-8; T-1 C-7-8 C-8; T-1
Median (FCR, Pronator Teres) (FDS ½ FDP) (Intrinsics)	C-6-7 C-7-8 C-8; T-1
Supraclavicular lesions: C5,6 or C5,6,7 lesions: C8,T1: C5,6,7,8,T1:	75%of cases 25% 2-3% 75-80%
Infraclavicular lesions:	25% of cases

Procedures

♦ Restoration of shoulder function: Suprascapular and axillary nerve
♦ Restoration of elbow flexion: Musculocutaneous nerve
♦ Restoration of sensory function of the hand is based on motor function of hand. Medial cord is neurotised for protective sensation along ulnar border of forearm and hand. In a functional hand, the lateral cord is innervated to provide sensation to thumb and index finger.

Surgical Approach

♦ **POSITION:** Supine with neck, thorax, upper extremity and both lower limbs prepped.
♦ **INCISION:** The incision follows the posterior border of sternomastoid muscle, above the clavicle and then along the delto-pectoral groove.
♦ **EXPOSURE:** The clavicular insertion of sternomastoid is released and the scalene muscles are identified. The trunks of the plexus are identified between the scalene muscles. Clavicle is exposed subperiosteally and can be pulled down to expose lower trunk. If necessary, pre-drill and osteotomise clavicle.

For infraclavicular plexus, the deltopectoral groove is developed, pectoralis major is detached at its insertion into the humerus and pectorlais minor is divided. The cords of the plexus can be identified around the axillary vessels.

What to expect after Brachial Plexus Surgery

Excellent results are seen in almost 80% cases for recovery of proximal nerves- eg- axillary or suprascapular (grade 3-4 power). Elbow flexion results are fair, with 50% regaining flexion of grade 3-4 power.
Hand motor does not recover, but prognosis for recovery of protective sensation is good.

Neurotisation Procedures for Root Avulsion Injuries

¨ **Phrenic nerve:** Is mobilised distally down to the jugular fossa and directly neurotised to suprascapular nerve or axillary nerve. No significant respiratory problems are noted in adults.
¨ **Spinal accessory nerve:** Can be used directly to neurotise the suprascapular nerve for shoulder abduction or with a sural nerve graft for the musculocutaneous nerve to restore elbow flexion..
¨ **Intercostal nerves:** T3 and T4 are used by direct suture to musculocutaneous nerve.
¨ **Ipsilateral or Contralateral** C7 nerve root: Controversial- used on the premise that muscles supplied by C7 have dual innervation.

Late Reconstruction for Irrepairable Lesions

Restoration proceeds in a distal to proximal direction.

The shoulder:
1. *Flail shoulder:*
   Arthrodesis; 30^0 Abduction, 30^0 forward flexion, 30^0 int rot. Trapezius and serratus must be intact. Internal fixation desirable.

2. *Partial paralysis:*
   L'Episcopo Transfer: Release of internal rotation contracture with posterolateral transfer of Teres Major and Lat dorsi insertion.

The elbow:

1. *Steindler Flexorplasty*
2. *Clark's pectoralis major* muscle *transfer*
3. *Pectoralis major* tendon *transfer*
4. *Triceps transfer*
5. *Latissimus transfer*

Wrist :

Wrist arthrodesis
Tendon transfers

Treatment of Pain
Avoid narcotics
TENS unit

The Place of Amputation

Well motivated, counselled patient who will use prosthesis

Recurrent injury to insensate extremity.

No pain relief is obtained.

Mid forearm if some elbow motors or above elbow for flail limb

Notes

PRINCIPLES OF TENDON REPAIR AND TRANSFER
Mr R Bindra
Consultant Orthopaedic Surgeon
Pulvertaft Hand Centre, Derbyshire Royal Infirmary

1. TENDON HEALING AND REPAIR

Healing of tendon after a laceration or rupture continues to remain a focal point of research interest in hand surgery in an effort to better understand the process and improve the outcome. Successful tendon healing is not merely the process of restoration of continuity, but rather the ability of the healed tendon to glide in the tissue in order to restore active joint motion.

Although a part of the successful outcome after tendon repair may be attributable to surgical skill, other factors such as the nature of the laceration, surrounding tissue injury, and patient cooperation also play an important role. In order to perform a repair that is compatible with the best possible recovery of function, it is necessary to understand the structure and organisation of tendon, healing after injury and the factors that can influence the process.

1.1 Tendon Structure

Tendon fibres are largely made up of collagen fibres constituting about 70% of the dry weight of tendon. Interspersed in these bundles of collagen fibres are tendon cells or tenocytes that are structurally similar to mature fibroblasts. Type-l collagen is the main constituent (95%) with a little Type-III and Type-V collagen. Small amounts of elastin and mucopolysaccharides are also present in the extra-cellular matrix in varying constitutions.

Spiralling bundles of tenocytes and collagen fibres are arranged in fascicles. The various fascicles within the tendon are capable of gliding past each other covered by 'endotenon' that join together to form the fine fibrous outer layer of the 'epitenon' that envelops the tendon surface. Some blood vessels and nerves run within the tendon covered by endotenon but the majority are contained in the highly cellular epitenon. The structure of tendon varies in different regions of the body reflecting an adaptation of the tendon structure to the function they perform. On the flexor surface of the fingers the tendons are oval on cross-section whereas on the extensor aspect of the fingers tendons are flatter and thin out into a sheet-like extensor expansion over the digits.

In the palm a visceral and parietal adventitial layer surrounds the tendons and is referred to as the 'paratenon'.

There is synovial-like fluid associated with the paratenon and assists in gliding.

1.1.a Digital flexor tendon sheath

Starting at the distal palmar crease and extending up to the insertion in the distal phalanges the flexor tendons are covered in specially organised fibrous sheaths lined by double-layered synovial sheaths- the parietal layer lines the tube while the visceral synovial layer covers the superficialis and profundus tendons. The tendons glide freely within the sheath attached only by the thin vinculae that carry blood vessels to the tendon.

The flexor tendon sheaths over the fingers and thumb demonstrate a well-defined pattern with specially thickened segments referred to as pulleys. The thicker pulleys are referred to as the annular pulleys because of the largely transcircular arrangement of these fibres as they enclose the tendon. The intervening thinner parts of the sheath between the annular pulleys are arranged in a criss-cross fashion – the cruciate pulleys that allow the annular pulleys to approximate each other as the digit is flexed. Two pulleys have been shown experimentally to be critical in retaining excursion of the digit by preventing tendon bow-stringing. These are the A2 and the A4 pulleys attached to the periosteum of the proximal half of the proximal phalanx and the middle third of the middle phalanx. The A1, A3 and A5 pulleys are located over the volar plates of the metacarpophalangeal, proximal interphalangeal and distal interphalangeal joints respectively. In addition the distal edge of the palmar aponeurosis forms a pulley referred to as the palmar aponeurosis pulley.

1.1.b Tendon nutrition

Blood supply of a tendon is derived from various sources and essentially segmental with zones of relative avascularity. In the forearm longitudinal vessels run within the substance of the tendon right up to the palm where the blood supply is reinforced by the synovial reflection. Within the flexor sheath of the fingers the blood supply to the flexor tendons is provided by branches from the digital arteries that run to the tendons in the vinculae, entering the flexor tendons on their dorsal surface. Each tendon has a long and short vinculum with areas of relative avascularity in-between. The vascularity is reinforced at the bony insertion of the tendon.

A second mechanism of nutrition of synovial tendons is by diffusion of synovial fluid. The delivery of synovial fluid is accomplished by imbibition whereby synovial fluid is forced into the interstices of tendons by the pumping mechanism generated by finger flexion

1.2 Mechanical properties

The function of a tendon is to allow a transfer of muscle contraction to bone with minimal stretching and loss of force. The dense collagen fibres are arranged parallel to each other along the direction of the pull of the muscle providing one of the highest tensile strengths among soft tissues.

The stress-strain curve for tendons is similar to ligament and other tissues predominantly composed of collagen. As tendons have greater extensibility at low tensile loads, tendon deforms quite easily with little tensile force. This is followed by a linear rise in stress before eventual rupture as tendons have less extensibility at high loads like forces generated with finger movement.

The forces generated within the flexor tendons:

Passive flexion and extension without resistence	2-4N
Active flexion with mild resistence	10N
Moderate resisted flexion	17N
Strong composite grasp	70-120N

Tendons of the wrist demonstrate minimal gliding but digital flexors require considerable excursion obtain full range of motion. The tendons move almost 20mm in the palm, 15mm over the proximal phalanx and about 5mm over the middle phalanx.

1.3 Tendon Healing

A review of the literature in the subject of tendon healing reveals a longstanding controversy over the relative contribution of extrinsic processes versus intrinsic capabilities of the tendon to heal. It is now generally agreed that there is some contribution from both intrinsic and extrinsic mechanisms that can vary with the type of injury, mechanism of repair and postoperative regime selected.

While **extrinsic healing** provides tough scar tissue that envelops the injured tendon, it also has the deleterious effect of producing undesirable adhesions between the tendon and its surrounding soft tissues. **Intrinsic healing** on the other hand results in the formation of longitudinally aligned collagen fingers within the tendon substance with minimal adhesions.

The healing process in a tendon is not dissimilar to that of bone and can be differentiated into three phases: an inflammatory phase, a fibroblastic phase and remodelling phase.

Inflammatory Phase

In the inflammatory or cellular phase, cells from the periphery migrate into the wound site to provide fibroblasts and budding blood vessels. This phase starts as soon as three days after injury and the cellular sources for healing are both extrinsic and intrinsic. Extrinsic cells have been shown to arise by the proliferation and migration of granulation cells from the synovial sheath, surrounding soft tissues including periosteum.

Intrinsic cells arise from tendon cellular elements mainly from the outer layer of the epitenon and along with extrinsic cells migrate into and across the laceration site and form a "callus" between the tendon ends. The migration of fibroblasts is facilitated by the chemotatic effects of fibronectin, an important component in the early tendon healing process. The content of fibronectin begins to decrease after three weeks.

All of the connective tissue cells within the tendon participate actively in the healing process. The mature fibroblasts among the tendon cells are also capable of differentiation and migration, but this is a late feature, occurring 2 - 3 weeks into the healing process.

Fibroblastic Phase

By the fifth day, the production of collagen fibres is abundant and the proliferating fibroblasts lay collagen in a random fashion. The collagen content continues to rise for the first 4 weeks or so. The collagen fibres are initially laid down parallel to the cut surfaces of the tendon.

Remodelling Phase

By the end of the fourth week, collagen fibres begin to align themselves along the long axis of the tendon, in line with tensile forces. The process gets completed by eight weeks. The process is facilitated by subjecting the healing tendon to physiological loads and ultimately allows the tendon to regain its normal tensile strength. Complete maturation of the repair site and reversal of the active fibroblasts into quiescent tenocytes takes place by about three months.

Neo-vascularisation in tendon healing

Tendon healing depends on both intrinsic vascularity and diffusion of nutrients from the surrounding fluids. The latter has been demonstrated by experiments that have shown healing of avascular tendon segments placed within the knee joint and in tissue culture media. In addition, animal studies have shown that neovascularisation of the tendon occurs in previously recognised avascular zones. This vascularisation occurs by the penetration of new vessels into the repair site extending from the surface eiptenon vessels. This process of revascularisation is stimulated by early active motion of the tendon

1.4 The Effect of Motion on the Healing Process

Benefits of controlled motion on tendon healing:

1. Stimulation of intrinsic healing – The alternating stress and relaxation of the tissue with tendon gliding may help to induce the cellular response in the epitenon.
2. Inhibits the extrinsic response and may minimise adhesions - 3-5mm of motion of a tendon within its sheath has been shown to prevent the development of firm adhesions.

Basic Science for FRCS (Trauma and Orthopaedics)

3. Simulation of neovascularisation of the tendon
4. Earlier return of tensile strength
5. Minimises joint stiffness

Gelberman and co-workers have shown that controlled mobilisation of a healing tendon can induce significant changes in the type of healing response produced. Early controlled motion stimulates the intrinsic healing response. The main source of cells is the epitenon from where tenocytes and blood vessels active proliferate and grow into the area of repair. The healing progresses without significant adhesions between the flexor sheath and the repaired tendon. On the other hand, immobilised tendons heal by the ingrowth of repair tissue from the digital sheath with extensive scarring and adhesion formation between the tendon and its surrounding sheath. There is a contribution from the cells of the endotenon but this is late and does not contribute to the healing in any significant matter.

1.5 Principles of Tendon Repair

1. Best results usually can be expected from a primary repair done by a surgeon with expertise in dealing with these injuries.
2. Associated nerve injuries should be dealt with at the same time.
3. There must be adequate cover of the repaired tendon with vascularised soft tissues
4. Associated fractures must be stabilised adequately to allow early motion and gliding of the tendon minimising adhesions.

Surgical Principles

1. Use a tourniquet.
2. Follow usual principles of wound toilet.
3. Extend the wound as required.Proximal retraction of the tendons can be dealt with separate proximal incision and the tendon can be guided back using a narrow tube.
4. Preserve the vascularity of the tendon ends. Tendon handling should be minimal and should be restricted to the cut ends to avoid scarring on the smooth external surfaces.

Suture Technique
Various suture techniques have been described. Basic principles are:

1. The suture should be placed in the volar third of the tendon to minimise the disruption of the tendon vascularity as blood vessels enter the tendon on its dorsal surface.
2. Flexor tendons should be repaired with a core suture placed within the structure of the tendon and reinforced by an external circumferential suture

3. The strength of the repair is proportional to the number of strands of the core suture and is not significantly altered by the calibre of the suture material.In clinical practice a four-strand repair is easily achievable and is a good compromise between strength and excessive handling and foreign material across the repair site.
4. The tendon strength decreases to a fifth in the first week after injury.
5. The most common site of failure of suture is due to slippage or rupture.
6. The basic concept of placing a core suture is to have one or more transverse passes within the tendon substance to "grasp" the longitudinal collagen bundles.
7. Peripheral circumferential epitenon suture can add from 10% to 50% to the strength of the repair site. The epitenon sutures also inhibit gap formation

Recommendation for suture material:
A 3/0 or 4/0 or braided polyester suture (ethibond) is non-absorbable and inert, easy to handle, it is less plastic than polypropylene and has good tendon grasping and knotting characteristics.
When measured in vitro, a 2-strand Kessler repair with 4-0 ethibond has a tensile strength of approximately 30N, with an increase by about 50% in a 4-strand repair.

1.6 Post-Repair Rehabilitation
1. Early post-repair controlled motion is beneficial. It allows better tendon healing with more rapid recovery of tensile strength.
2. Fewer adhesions occur with early motion.
3. Improved tendon and joint excursion.
4. Passive motion produces minimal relative motion of the flexor tendons whereas active motion prevents bunching up of the tendons.

Principals of Rehabilitation

Passive Flexion-Active Extension Regimes (Kleinert)
Passive regimes use elastic bands to provide passive flexion of the fingers and the patient is expected to actively extend the digits. The drawbacks of such a system are that tendon gliding is not complete as the flexion is passive and the tendon may actually bunch up at the repair site. Furthermore, in an uncooperative patient, flexion contractures of the PIP may occur due to lack of active finger extension.

Controlled active flexion-extension motion regimes (CAM)
This is currently the favoured trend in rehabilitation. Active finger flexion encourages excursion of the repaired tendon. Apart from a protective dorsal splint, no elaborate traction system is required and it is easy to set up. The disadvantage is that the stress is placed across the tendon repair site and if the repair is not of adequate strength, failure is possible.

A variation to the above theme is the addition of a wrist movement to the exercise regime with specially constructed hinged splints. When finger flexion is accompanied by active dorsiflexion of the wrist, tendon excursion is nearly full. In addition, as less force is required to make a fist with the wrist dorsiflexed, the tension across the repair site may be lesser than a static splint. This method however, requires full patient co-operation and understanding of the composite movement of wrist extension with finger flexion.

2.0 Tendon Transfers

Definition

This is the procedure by which a tendon insertion is moved to a new destination in order to change its line of pull and thereby regain lost function or restore muscle imbalance.

2.1 Indications for Tendon Transfer

1. To restore lost muscle function when nerve repair has failed.
2. Restoration of function when nerve repair is not possible e.g. leprosy or in spinal cord injury
3. To correct muscle imbalance eg. in cerebral palsy

2.2 Timing of Tendon Transfer:

Primary:
1. Quadriplegia with irrecoverable cord damage.
2. Children with cerebral palsy.

Reconstruction:
1. Failure of adequate motor recovery after peripheral nerve repair.
2. High ulnar and median nerve injuries where motor recovery in the hand is usually poor.

N.B. After interruption of a largely motor nerve eg. the radial nerve, consideration may be given to a primary tendon transfer which can restore adequate function rather than nerve exploration and repair

2.3 Selection of Patient:

1. Sensible patient – the patient must be able to comprehend and cooperate with the rehabilitation programme and should be able to retrain the transferred muscle to perform its new function. Psychiatric or depressed patients will not yield a good result.

2. Sufficient age – As a general rule, tendon transfers should usually be preformed in children four years of age or older in order. If the transfer does not require retraining, the transfer can be done in children as young as one year.

2.4 Selection of Donor Muscle:

1. Sacrificable: The loss of the transferred tendon must have minimal' if any clinical impact. Neighbouring muscles must be able to compensate for the transferred muscle.

2. Strong muscle: The muscle can be expected to lose a grade or two in power after transfer. The donor must hence be least grade 4 power.

3. **S**ufficient excursion: In order to provide a reasonable range of motion, the donor muscle must have good excursion.
4. **S**ynergistic action to desired function: Although not absolutely essential, synergistic muscle transfers e.g. FCU to digital extensors require minimal retraining.

Muscle Work Capacity

Work capacity = Force x Amplitude
Force = 3.65 kg/cm^2 cross section

Work capacity (MKg):
PL, EPL, APL: 0.1
Wrist extensors: 1.0
Long finger flexors: 1.2 each
Brachioradialis, FCU: 2.0

2.5 Other Prerequisites:

1. Sensate hand except in conditions like leprosy. It is usually important to have some preserved sensation in the hand prior to restoring function.

2. Supple joints: The active motion of a transferred muscle cannot exceed that obtained by passive motion. If joints are stiff a tendon transfer is worthless.

2.6 Surgical Principles

1. Scar free tissues: the tendon transfer must be placed subcutaneously in tissues with minimal scarring to allow gliding.

2. Straight line of pull: The transferred tendon should be re-routed in as straight a line as possible in the direction of the desired pull of the muscle. If a change of direction is required e.g. for opponensplasty, it should be obtained by constructing a pulley or routing the tendon around the forearm.

3. Single action – tendon transfers can only exert pull in a single direction at a time. Splitting the tendon into two sites of insertion will only provide a single function at the tightest insertion

2.7 Choice of Tendon Transfers in the Upper Extremity

2.7.1 High radial palsy

Loss: Wrist extension
Thumb and digital extension
Thumb abduction

Transfers: Wrist extension – PT to ECRL and ECRB
Finger extension – FCU to EDC
Thumb clearance – PL to EPL or if absent add EPL to above

2.7.2 Posterior interosseous palsy

Loss: Thumb and digital extension
Thumb abduction

Transfers:

Finger extension – FCU to EDC
FCR to EDC may be preferable if there is a tendency to radial deviation of the wrist (intact radial wrist extensors)

Thumb extension – PL to EPL
BR to EPL
Thumb abduction – PT to APL

2.7.3 High median palsy

Loss: Thumb and index/middle flexion
Thumb opposition

Transfers:

Finger flexion - FDP of the index, middle to the ring and little or ECRL to FDP

Thumb flexion - BR to FPL
Thumb opposition: Use EIP or EDQ

2.7.4 Low median palsy

Loss: Thumb opposition

Transfers: Opponensplasty:

1. FDS to ring finger – this tendon has to be re-routed through a pulley in the flexor carpi ulnaris tendon (Riordan)
2. EIP – this has the advantage as it dispenses with the pulley. The direction of pulley is achieved by routing the tendon round the subcutaneous border of the ulnar before inserting into the thumb.
3. Palmaris longus provides an easily available but weak transfer usually reserved for elderly patients (Camitz procedure). Advantage is that it requires minimal additional surgery and can be combined with carpal tunnel decompression.Abductor digiti minimi transfer (Huber) – useful in children

2.7.5 High ulnar palsy

Loss: FDP ring, little
Less clawing of little and ring (ulnar paradox)
Adductor pollicis

Transfers: ECRB + free graft or EIP to Adductor pollicis
Claw correction

Transfer FDP ring, little to the intact middle, index.

Clawing of the fingers can be corrected by palmar or dorsal transfers

Palmar transfer

Active: FDS tendon is divided, split into two and transferred to the lateral band of little and ring fingers providing active MP flexion and aiding interphalangeal extension.

Passive: A slip of the FDS tendon in each finger may be turned back on itself and sutured to the A1 pulley thereby creating a flexion deformity of the MP joint and passively correcting the clawing. This does not add to the strength of the hand. Patient must demonstrate positive Bouvier manoeuvre preoperatively i.e. passive MP flexion allows IP extension by the long extensors.

Dorsal transfers:

Use muscles like the extensor indicis proprius on the back of the hand which are then re-routed palmar to the MP axis prior to insertion into the extensor apparatus. These add to strength of flexion. Other muscle that can be used is the extensor carpi radialis brevis lengthened with the palmaris longus.

2.8 Rehabilitation

The transfer is protected for 3-4 weeks in plaster followed by mobilisation. Some transfers, especially non-synergistic ones, require intensive therapy for re-education.

BIBLIOGRAPHY

Gelberman R H, Ven de Berg J S, Lundborg G N, Akeson, W H: Flexor Tendon Healing and Restoration of the Gliding Surface. An Ultrastructural Study in Dogs, J Bone Joint Surg 1983; 65A: 70-80.

Lindsay W K and Thomson H G: Digital Flexor Tendons: An Experimental Study, Part I. The Significance of Each Component of the Flexor Mechanism in Tendon Healing. Br J Plast Surg 1960;12: 289 - 319.

Manske P R: Flexor Tendon Healing – Review article. J Hand Surg 1988; 13B: 237-45.

Peacock E E: Biological Principles in the Healing of Long Tendons. Surg Clin North Am 1965; 45:2: 461-76.

Potenza A D: Mechanisms of Healing of Digital Flexor Tendons. Hand 1969; 1: 40 – 41.

Notes

Spinal Anatomy

Mr J Trivedi   Dr. S Roberts.

Consultant Spinal Surgeon.and Senior Research Scientist
Robert Jones & Agnes Hunt Orthopaedic Hospital Oswestry

1.   EMBRYOLOGY:

A.   Notochord Formation/ Induction:

Formation of the notochord is central to the development of the spinal cord and the vertebral system. The initial notochord forms as a rostral extension of cells from the primitive streak and then fuses to the endoderm. During the third week of gestation, the notochord induces cellular proliferation and aggregation in the overlying ectoderm and leads to the formation of the neural plate. The edges of the induced neural plate curve dorsally to create the "neural tube". This process begins centrally and progresses in a cranial and caudal direction. The notochord remains within the developing vertebral bodies but progressively diminishes in size during the foetal period. In the adult the nucleus pulposus of the intervertebral disc is the only remnant of the notochord.

Somites form in the mesodermal tissue adjacent to the neural tube. Cellular proliferation and differentiation within the somites results in the formation of distinctive cell masses. These cell masses subsequently result in the formation of the dermatome, myotome and skeletogenic tissue (sclerotome). The sclerotomes consist of loosely packed cells cranially and densely packed cells caudally. Each sclerotome separates at the junction of the loosely and densely packed cells. The caudal dense cells migrate to the cephalad loose cells of the next more caudal sclerotome. The space where the sclerotomes separate forms the intervertebral disc.

B.   Vertebral Development:

Primary centres of ossification for the vertebrae develop in the ninth or tenth week of gestation and may persist till adolescence. Usually one centre of ossification develops in the centrum and one in each neural arch of the vertebra. Between the sixth and the eighth years of life, the ossification centres of the centrum and the neural arches unite with one another obliterating the cartilaginous junction (neurocentral synchondrosis), thus completing the ossified vertebral body.

The first cervical vertebra does not have a body or a centrum. The equivalent of the primary ossification centre in the atlas develops in the anterior arch. This centre does not develop until the end of the first post-natal year. The second vertebral body (axis) is also atypical in that it develops from five primary ossification centres. Ossification commences in the lower thoracic and upper lumbar regions and then extends in a cephalad and caudal direction. The majority of the vertebral body is ossified at the time of birth. Cartilaginous remnants persist on the tips of spinous and transverse processes until puberty. Secondary centres of ossification develop within these tips at puberty. By the age of 25 years all secondary centres unite within the vertebral body.

Horizontal growth:

The vertebrae grow horizontally by the process of appositional new bone formation. The maximum horizontal growth takes place in the first 7 years after birth. Following puberty this growth slows and by the age of 25 years the vertebrae attain their adult size.

Vertical growth:

Longitudinal growth occurs through the superior and inferior growth plates. Maximum longitudinal growth occurs in the first 5 years of post-natal life. During this time the average vertebral height increases 2 to 4 times. The lumbar spine grows much faster than the thoracic and cervical spine. Differential rate of longitudinal growth accounts for the normal sagittal contours of the spine. In the lumbar spine the vertebral body grows faster than the posterior elements to give a lordosis. In the thoracic spine the reverse occurs to give a kyphosis.

Ring apophysis:

Around the age of 6 years in females and 8 or 9 years in males, foci of calcified cartilage develop along the periphery of the vertebral growth plates. Following the invasion of the growth plates by vessels, the calcified foci ossify to form a ring around the growth plate. This is the ring apophysis. Between the age of fourteen and twenty years this ring apophysis fuses with the vertebral body to signal the end of longitudinal growth. Note that the longitudinal growth occurs through the superior and inferior growth plates which are distinct from the ring apophysis. The latter does not contribute to longitudinal growth.

Applied Embryology:

A.   Neural tube anomalies:

The tubularisation of the neural tube may not be completed. This will lead to anomalies such as anencephaly and myelomeningocoele. The bi-directional pattern of neural tube closure in normal embryology explains the frequent concomitant occurrence of abnormalities at each end of the neural system (e.g., hydrocephalus in association with myelomeningocoele distally.

B.   Spina Bifida and Dysraphism

Dysraphism is basically the failure of formation of the posterior midline vertebral structures. Rarely this may occur anteriorly. This is caused due to the failure of the ossification centres of the neural arches to fuse. The spectrum includes spina bifida occulta, meningocoele and myelomeningocoele.

C. Lumbosacral Agenesis:

The syndrome involves a spectrum of morphologic disorders ranging from mild dysplasia to complete absence of components of the lumbar and/or sacral spine. There is a higher incidence of the condition in children of diabetic mothers.

D. Diastometamyelia:

Increased width of the pedicles may be associated with the presence of an osseous or cartilaginous mass extending from the vertebral body into the spinal canal. The cord or the cauda equina is divided around this mass. Neurological symptoms develop due to disparate longitudinal elongation of the spinal cord relative to the spine.

E. Congenital scoliosis:

This may be due to failure of formation of vertebrae (wedge vertebra, hemivertebra), failure of segmentation (unsegmented bar). Figure 1

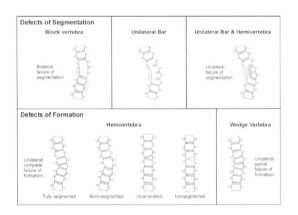

Figure 1

2. SPINAL ANATOMY:

A. Vascular anatomy:

Cervical Spine:

The arterial supply to the cervical spine is derived primarily from the paired vertebral arteries. The vertebral arteries arise from the first part of the subclavian artery. They ascend the vertebral column bilaterally within the transverse foramina of the cervical vertebral bodies. From each vertebral artery arise one anterior and two posterior branches. The anterior branches unite to form the anterior spinal artery which supplies blood to the ventral two-thirds of the cord. One posterior branch from each vertebral artery gives rise to the posterior spinal artery which travels along the posterolateral sulcus of the spinal cord.

The Salient features of the arterial supply of the spinal cord in the thoracic and lumbar regions are as follows:

1. The 3 main vessels are the anterior median longitudinal trunk and a pair of posterolateral trunks
2. The gray matter has a proportionately larger share of the supply in comparison to the white matter
3. At every vertebral level a pair of segmental arteries supplies extraspinal and intraspinal structures
4. The segmental arteries divide into numerous branches at the intervertebral foramen which may be referred to as the "distribution point."
5. **The Artery of Adamkiewicz** is the largest of the feeder vessels to the cord. It is located on the left usually at the level of T9 to T11.
6. The critical zone of the spinal cord is between T4 to T9. Here the spinal canal is the narrowest and the blood supply poorest.

Based on the above features the following clinical principles apply to anterior spinal surgery:

1) ligate segmental vessels only as necessary
2) ligate segmental arteries close to the aorta and away from the intervertebral intervertebral foramen
3) ligate segmental vessels only on one side of the vertebral body leaving the circulation intact on the other side.

B. Neuroanatomy:

The spinal cord fills about 35% of the canal at the level of the atlas and then about 50% in the cervical and the thoracolumbar segments. The remainder of the canal is filled with Cerebro spinal fluid, epidural fat and dura mater. Nerve roots and the blood vessels to the roots run through the subarachnoid space. The end of the spinal cord (conus medullaris), is most commonly located at the level of L1-L2 disc. Figure 2 gives the transverse view of the spinal cord in the cervical spine. From the figure it is clear that the sacral structures are most peripheral in both the posterior columns and the lateral corticospinal tracts.

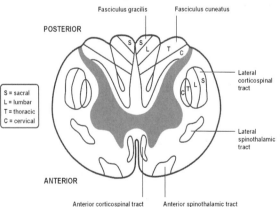

Figure 2: Cross section of the spinal cord in the cervical spine

Applied Neuroanatomy:
Figure 2 explains why there may be sacral sparing in patients with spinal cord injury. The sacral fibres being situated most peripherally may not be involved in incomplete injuries. Hence the importance of examination for sacral sparing in patients with spinal injury in order to differentiate between incomplete and complete injuries. Sacral sparing may be demonstrated by great toe flexion or the presence of anal tone.

3. BIOCHEMISTRY AND STRUCTURE OF THE INTERVERTEBRAL DISC

The intervertebral disc consists of the central gelatinous **nucleus pulposus** and the surrounding **annulus fibrosus.** In the adolescent, the nucleus is about 85% water and the annulus 78% water by weight. In the non-degenerate state the adult disc is avascular with a paucity of cellular content. The biomechanical behaviour of the disc is governed by the properties of the extracellular constituents.

The extracellular matrix is composed primarily of collagen and proteoglycans. The proteoglycans attract water to form a gel (see chapter 2, Articular cartilage) and this swelling is constrained within the collagen fibre network, forming a composite, load-bearing structure, particularly in compression. The collagen fibres bind the disc into the adjacent spinal structures, continuing from the disc and running directly into the cartilage endplates superiorly and inferiorly, into the longitudinal ligaments anteriorly and posteriorly and into the vertebral bodies, via Sharpey's fibres, at the vertebral rims.

The dry mass of the intervertebral disc ranges from 60% to 70% collagen in the annulus to 10% in the centre of the nucleus pulposus. The principal types of collagen in the disc are types I and II. Type II collagen predominates in the nucleus pulposus while type I is the more abundant collagen in the annulus. In the outer annulus the collagen fibres are aligned in parallel bundles, in concentric rings or lamellae. Within each lamella the fibres lie approximately 60° to the vertical axis, but in opposite directions. This highly organised structure is likely to be very important to the mechanical functioning of the disc. For example, it has been suggested that these lamellae can slide over one another, allowing the disc to stretch by more than 60%, for example in extension, whilst collagen molecules themselves can only extend by 3% of their length.

The main proteoglycan in the disc is aggrecan, which forms polymers or aggregates, of up to 100 molecules, by linking to long chains of hyaluronan, at least when it is newly synthesised. The aggrecans in disc are much smaller and more degenerate than in other tissues, for example in cartilage from the same individual, presumably because of the action of proteases such as matrix metallo proteinases (MMPs).

The nucleus pulposus has the highest proteoglycan content in the human body. The negatively charged glycosaminoglycans (GAGs) imbibe water and are responsible for maintaining the disc height under load. There is a diurnal variation of water content in the disc with a slow squeezing out of water during load bearing and a re-acquisition of it during rest. This is the reason that mankind is in general 1-2cm taller first thing in the morning than in the evening and 5cm taller on returning from space! Proteoglycans are also responsible for solute concentration in the disc. The concentration of small cations is much greater in the disc than in the plasma: concentration of anions and the larger solutes is lower in the disc.

Many other molecules are present in the disc matrix, some are structural, such as elastin and fibronectin, whilst others affect the disc's metabolism, such as growth factors or enzymes. Some of the structural substances, such as elastin, may only constitute 1-2% of the tissue but may influence its properties greatly. Elastin has been shown to exist in a highly organised network, running extensively between the lamellae, but also forming cross-bridges over or through the lamellae and lying radially within the nucleus.

Disc Metabolism
The activity of the disc cells determines the characteristics of the matrix and hence its mechanical properties. The cell density in disc is very low, particularly in the nucleus where it is only 10% that of articular cartilage. These cells normally synthesise the matrix macromolecules, albeit slowly. For example, proteoglycans are estimated to have a turnover time of 2 years in adult humans (although during growth and disease this can be quicker) and collagen is likely to be much longer.

Metabolism within the disc is mainly anaerobic, resulting in significant lactate production, particularly in the centre of the disc. Here the concentration of oxygen may be as little as 5% to 10% of that at the surface. This sets up very high concentration gradients within the disc. For oxygen and other small solutes transport is mostly via diffusion along these gradients, whereas for larger molecules, eg enzymes or newly synthesised matrix molecules, convective transport, or 'pumping' may be more important.

4. BIOMECHANICAL PROPERTIES OF THE SPINE

A. Viscoelastic properties.
Viscoelasticity is the time-dependent response of a material to the rate of deformation. The intervertebral disc is a viscoelastic structure. The viscoelasticity is a result of fluid flow in the nucleus pulposus under applied load, as well as due to the properties of the collagen network itself.

B. Disc Pressure:

The nucleus pulposus exerts a hydrostatic pressure within the disc. Lumbar disc pressure is lowest in the recumbent posture, higher in standing and highest in unsupported sitting. Disc pressure while sitting can be reduced by the following measures: 1) inclining the back rest to 110 degrees, 2) using arm rests and 3) using a lumbar support.

The load acting on a disc in the lumbar spine is related to the body weight as well as the forces produced by the stabilizing muscles. In the sitting position the average load on the L3/4 disc is 200% of the body weight. If there is damage to the vertebral end plates there is decompression of the nucleus pulposus and a subsequent increase in the stresses in the posterior annulus.

C. Spinal Instability:

Clinical instability is defined as a loss of the ability of the spine under physiologic loads to limit displacement so as to prevent damage to the spinal cord or nerve roots and, in addition, to prevent deformity or pain due to structural changes. The stability of the spine is dependent on 1) passive musculoskeletal system i.e ligaments 2) active musculoskeletal system i.e muscles and 3) neural feedback system. It is clear from observations where there is deficient muscular activity that muscles are important in stabilising the spine, as is neural proprioception.

5. DEGENERATIVE PROCESS IN THE SPINE.

Disc degeneration is generally more prevalent with increasing age, with the disc reported to degenerate earlier in life than any other connective tissue and occurring as young as adolescence. A decrease in nutrition is suggested as being a prime reason for this with vascular channels closing within the cartilage endplate soon after birth and the disc cells being greater distances from their source of nutrients (see Figure).

However, the link between disc degeneration and back pain is less distinct. Whilst there is no doubt an association between the two, the mechanism(s) remain unclear. The disc may be a direct source of pain in some patients but in others it may be an indirect cause, perhaps by altering the loading on adjacent, innervated tissues such as muscles or facet joints.

Biochemical changes in the degenerate spine

The major biochemical alteration in degenerate discs is a loss of proteoglycan, possibly loosing up to 80% of its content. There is a consequent loss of hydration and hydrostatic properties of the disc and initially an increased rate of creep (ability of viscoelastic material to deform, without loss of material, when subjected to a constant compressive force; in end-stage degeneration, however, this decreases).

The proteoglycans change by:
(i) a decrease in the number and size of aggregates forming
(ii) a decrease in the length of core protein of individual proteoglycan molecules
(iii) a decrease in the size and number of GAG chains on the proteoglycan molecules.

All of these are due to enzyme activity (eg MMPs or aggrecanases) which reduce the size of the aggrecan molecules, so they can be lost from the tissue more easily. These changes thus reduce the water imbibing capacity of the disc. There are also changes to the collagen in degenerate discs, but these are not as striking. More of the 'minor' collagens may be synthesied (eg types III, VI or X) and collagen molecules are also broken down by enzymes. The crosslinks that bind collagen molecules together change. Some crosslinks accumulate naturally with age (for example, pentosidine, a spontaneously occurring glycation product) and this can make the tissue more brittle.

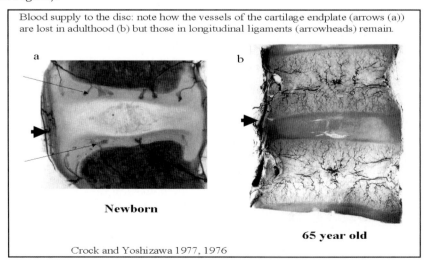

Blood supply to the disc: note how the vessels of the cartilage endplate (arrows (a)) are lost in adulthood (b) but those in longitudinal ligaments (arrowheads) remain.

a

b

Newborn

65 year old

Crock and Yoshizawa 1977, 1976

There are also associated changes in the vertebral end plates and adjacent marrow. Calcification may occur in the end plates which is likely to impede the delivery of disc nutrients and removal of toxins and could contribute to the structural changes outlined above.

Morphological changes in the degenerate spine

Beginning in the third decade of life, progressive morphological changes take place in the spine. However, microscopic degenerative changes to the intervertebral disc can be seen in the 2nd decade. Typically, as the disc degenerates it becomes more fissured. Cell clusters form, particularly in the nucleus. There are increased numbers and size of nerves, which occur more centrally than in normal discs. Vascularisation occurs and the annular lamellae become increasingly disorganised. The disc space narrows, due to loss of matrix and, or more bulging or focal extrusion of disc material results in a narrowing of the disc space. This then allows a closer approximation of the vertebral bodies. Facet joint arthrosis, with osteophyte formation occurs. The facet joint capsule thickens and the ligamentum flavum hypertrophies. The combined effect of these changes is a progressive decrease in the dimensions of the spinal canal.

Biomechanical changes in the degenerate spine

The structural and morphological changes which occur with degeneration, result in an alteration of the biomechanical properties of the intervertebral disc and the surrounding structures. Initially the elastic properties of the disc allow it to withstand a variety of deforming forces. The annulus receives the forces dispersed by the nucleus. These are then dissipated in a radial direction. With aging, the time dependent creep of the disc increases almost two-fold. This leads to diffuse bulging of the disc and narrowing of the disc space mentioned above. At the same time, facet arthrosis, subchondral sclerosis and loss of articular cartilage leads to laxity in each mobile segment. There is a change in the centre of motion of each mobile segment leading to segmental instability.

Other Clinical Sequelae of the Degenerate Spine

A. Disc herniation :
Prolapse or herniation of the intervertebral disc can occur in all directions: anteriorly, posteriorly, laterally or even through the end plates. The weakest part of the annulus is the posterior portion on either side of the midline; this, together with the neural components positioned here, means that the majority of symptomatic herniations are postero-lateral.

It is commonly acknowledged that there is a mechanical component to the pain due to disc herniation, ie bulging and pressure on the nerve roots. However, since 70% of individuals have posterior prolapses but no symptoms, there must be other factors involved also. It has been suggested that some component from the herniated disc can sensitise the nerve roots to the mechanical pressure. Potential candidates include TNFα, IL-1α, IL-1β, IL-6, monocyte chemoattractant protein or thromboxane, all of which can be produced by disc cells in the herniated tissue. Indeed the use of TNFα-antagonists may have great potential in the treatment of disc herniations, if they can alleviate symptoms until the natural process of resorption of the prolapsed tissue herniation occurs via endogenous MMPs.

B. Spinal stenosis:
The combined effect of loss of disc space, increased disc bulging, facet arthrosis, thickening of the facet capsules and ligamentum flavum hypertrophy leads to narrowing of the spinal canal as well as the lateral recesses. This narrowing of the spinal canal and the neural foramina leads to symptoms of stenosis. However, since the morphological changes are gradual in onset, many patients may remain asymptomatic until late in life and indeed some may never develop symptoms at all.

6 BIOMECHANICS OF SPINAL INSTRUMENTATION

The 4 most common types of spinal instrumentations include 1) wires 2) plates 3) pedicular screws and 4) rods and hooks.

Wires:
These have been shown to effectively reduce motion in the flexion-extension plane but not rotation. The addition of an anterior plate and interbody graft in addition to the wires posteriorly is shown to improve stability in rotation.

Plating:
Stability provided by posterior plates is dependant on the integrity of the anterior column. While a posterior plate can stabilize axial rotation and lateral bending, its effects on flexion-extension motion are less predictable.

Pedicular Screw:

These provide a high stiffness in all directions of loading. The stability of the bone–screw interface depends on the holding power of the screws, which in turn is shown to correlate with the bone mineral density. Other factors affecting the holding power of pedicle screws are 1) insertion torque and 2) screw length. In the sacrum the screws should engage the anterior cortex.

Rods and hooks;

These are increasingly being used in deformity correction. There are two broad types: the classic nonsegmental e.g Harrington and the multi-segmental e.g Cotrel-Dubousset. The latter is more stable on account of the multiple sites of attachment. Cross-linking the two rods, provides increased stability by creating a rectangular construct.

7. FUTURE TREATMENTS: BIOGENETICS?

As our knowledge of the aetiopathogenesis of spinal disorders develops it may allow for more biological therapies than surgery. This could be in the field of tissue engineering, utilising autologous cells to synthesise new, functional tissues (though this may be severely limited or inappropriate in patients, who for example, have blocked nutritive pathways with which to support any cells in the disc). Alternatively, genetic engineering may prove to be useful in some patient groups once the responsible genes have been identified (and some polymorphisms of aggrecan and collagens have been identified as being associated with disc degeneration already) and suitable genetic delivery systems established.

Selected Reading:

Alini M, Roughley PJ, Antoniou J, Stoll T, Aebi M. A biological approach to treating disc degeneration: not for today, but maybe for tomorrow. Eur Spine J 2002,11:S215-20.

Boos N, Weissbach,S, Rohrbach, H, Weiler, C, Spratt, K.F . Nerlich,A.G. Classification of age-related changess in lumbar intervertebral discs. Spine 2002; 27: 2631-44.

Crock HV,Yoshizawa H. The Blood Supply of the Vertebral column and spinal cord in man. New York: Springer,1997.

Ogden JA, Ganey TM, Sasse J, Neame PJ, Hilbelink DR. Development and Maturation of the Axial Skeleton. In: Weinstein SL.editor. The Pediatric Spine, Principles and Practice.Vol.1 New York: Raven 1994: 3-70.

Urban JPG. and Roberts S. Intervertebral Disc, in Comper WD. editor. Extracellular Matrix Vol 1. Amsterdam: Harwood Academic 1996: 203-33.

White AA. Panjabi MM. Clinical Biomechanics of the Spine, 2nd ed. Philadelphia: Lippincott JB. 1990.

Notes

Notes

Gait Analysis

Mr J H Patrick

Consultant Orthopaedic Surgeon,
Director ORLAU/Movement Analysis Service
Robert Jones & Agnes Hunt Orthopaedic Hospital
Oswestry

Understanding gait is made simpler if the various divisions of gait events are studied in detail. Remember that an analysis of these sections is rather artificial. Mostly, the events occur rapidly, blending one with another. The inter-dependence of muscle action (it's control system, feedback loops and group activity) and normal joint movement range must be present to allow a normal gait pattern. The latter condition involves constant intrinsic adjustments to keep the walking energy cost down.

There is always a 'carry-over' of energy from one step to the next in normal gait, to ensure maximal efficiency. The severely handicapped patient who takes one step as a 'single event' before halting, then taking the next step, is the most extreme case of squandering of this energy conservation.

A bipedal gait cycle is usually divided into a **stride** - measured from the moment a foot strikes the ground, until the same foot strikes the ground again. This means that the opposite leg will go through a stance phase, in sequence, as part of the stride.

A step is a one-sided event : it begins with the foot leaving the floor (on that side) and is the distance before it hits the floor again.

Normal stance phase is 60% of the cycle, swing the other 40%. Stability has be to assured for a reasonable stance phase posture - this requires stance phase stabilising muscles and 'balance' of the body segments over the plantigrade foot. Acceleration muscles function to drive limb and body forwards into swing phase. They are active, glycolytic, energitic, concentric muscles acting directly on joints. The concept of decelerative, eccentric-contracting muscles 'paying out the rope' to produce a controlled movement of the joint, to preserve progression forwards, but to absorb shock as well, is an important mechanism for us all.

Gait events

Initial contact (IC) : the instant the foot, or part of the foot, hits the ground. This used to be termed 'heel strike', but in disease many patients don't get the heel to the ground. If the heel does hit the ground, then shock absorption occurs in the heel fat pad, joints and synovial fluid, but the foot has to be actively dorsiflexed to get the heel down first (with the 'toes-up').

Loading response (LR) : This follows IC. The pre-tibial muscles contract eccentrically to allow a controlled 'let-down' of the fore foot to (what used to be called) flat foot. This is also the first ankle rocker. Whilst this foot activity occurs, the knee above is undergoing it's first flexion (controlled by eccentric activity in the quadriceps) and flexion also occurs in the hips (controlled similarly by gluteus maximus).

After LR response comes: **mid stance (MST)**. The inertial forces remain working on the body as a whole, and in the presence of normal joint ranges, the body moves forwards over the stance foot. At some stage all the body segments are balanced one over the other, over the plantigrade foot. At that moment there is **no** muscular action occurring. The body mass will move forwards of this 'top-dead-centre' position and the shank moves forwards at the tibio-talar joint. This movement is controlled by soleus contracting eccentrically (second ankle rocker).

As the opposite leg gets back into foot contact ahead of the 'old' stance foot, double stance phase (and thus better stability) resumes. This is called:-

Terminal stance (TST) phase - Even as this is occurring on the trailing-leg side, the gastrocnemii are contracting hard (concentrically) to produce plantarflexion : lifting the body forwards (and upwards). This is **Pre-swing PSW**. **Initial swing (ISW)** occurs as gastrosoleus concentric activity fades, the knee flexes, to allow a plantar and hip flexion 'couple' to occur. The powerful hip flexors contract at that moment to drive the leg into forwards flexion off the ground. Toe scuffing is prevented by a rapid contraction of the pre tibial musculature.

Mid Swing (MSW) occurs as the below-knee segment (shank) swings, under gravity, to lie vertically beneath the thigh section ; it's inertia will carry it forwards into:

Terminal swing (TSW) - This occurs as a separate event because the foot needs to be pre-positioned (in dorsiflexion) to allow another heel contact, and the knee extensors need to become active to straighten the limb to achieve maximum step length.

Notes

Orthoses

Mr. G.R. Gordon

Department of Orthotics
Robert Jones & Agnes Hunt Orthopaedic Hospital
Oswestry

The history of Orthotics is as old as the practice of medicine itself. From Galen to Dennis Browne and our own Robert Jones, many orthoses have been devised or associated with famous surgeons/physicians.

What is an orthosis and what functions can they perform?

It is a device applied directly and externally to a patient's body with the objective of **SUPPORTING, CORRECTING** or **COMPENSATING** for a skeletal deformity or weakness of any cause. Additional functions may be **ASSISTING, PERMITTING** and **RESTRICTING** movement of any part of the body. Orthoses today often perform a combination of these functions and below are listed some typical clinical examples:-

(1) **SUPPORTING:** weight of an arm with a hemiplegic sling.
(2) **CORRECTING:** a spinal deformity such as scoliosis with a Boston Brace.
(3) **COMPENSATING:** a leg length discrepancy with a shoe raise..
(4) **ASSISTING:** a paresis of ankle dorsiflexors with a drop foot splint.
(5 **PERMITTING:** a range of motion i.e. hip flexion & abduction with a Pavlik Harness.
(6) **RESTRICTING:** a pathological movement, anterior tibial shift with an ACL knee

How are Orthoses classified?

The American Academy of Orthopaedic Surgeons decided because of Eponymous descriptions of orthoses which often varied regionally in both their function, design and materials used to formulate a standardised system. As a result orthoses are described first by the principal joints that they encompass, examples being a long leg caliper/brace which became K.A.F.O., the acronym of the joints crossed. A below knee brace became an A.F.O., a wrist support a W.H.O. This terminology is endorsed by I.S.O. and accepted worldwide. Eponyms are still used in conjunction with the standardised terminology to clarify design or function i.e. a Boston type T.L.S.O. for management of scoliosis as opposed to other low profile T.L.S.O.s

What designs and materials do orthoses use and how do they work?

The current range of available orthoses are many and varied with the advent of materials such as carbon fibre and polypropylene and advanced manufacturing techniques. Early orthoses were made of metals and leather and were constructed with a conventional design of welding, rivets, screws and stitching. They were of poor cosmesis, heavy and offered only basic biomechanical control. Modern orthoses are of intimate conforming design often incorporating light thermoplastics and alloys for increased control, multi functional and greater cosmesis.

Orthoses primarily function biomechanically applying forces to a body or body segment. These forces are arranged in a fundamental 3 point pressure system:-

(1) In equilibrium to support or immobilise a segment or
(2) with imbalance in a desired direction and magnitude to produce a changed position of a body or body segment.

A simple example of 3 point pressure system employed in the provision of an orthosis is that of a KAFO used to stabilise a valgus knee joint in the frontal plane in the presence of weakened knee

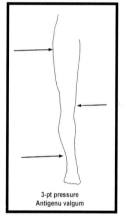

3-pt pressure
Antigenu valgum

collateral stabilisers as in the case of post poliomyelitis

Range and Provision of Orthotic Management in Britain:

Orthoses are available for all parts of the body and aid in the conservative and definitive treatment of many diseases, deformities and pathologies. They are used both for the very young and the most elderly patients as well as for the very mild to the most complex and disabling medical conditions. Devices may be fundamental and simple as a fracture brace or as sophisticated as a reciprocating gait orthosis for a paraplegic patient. They may be stock devices off the shelf or they may be bespoke custom made devices for the individual. Consultants are almost the sole prescribers of orthoses in Britain accounting for over £1 billion spend. The distribution by percentage of orthoses for various parts of the body illustrates that the majority are for the lower limb and aid in locomotion.

Head, Neck Spine	15%
Upper Limb Orthoses	5%
Footwear & Foot Orthoses	55%
Lower Limb Orthoses	25%

Notes

Orthotic Treatment for Lower Limb Muscle Paralysis is dependent upon Functioning Root Level

Mr J H Patrick

ORLAU
Robert Jones & Agnes Hunt Orthopaedic Hospital
Oswestry

It may seem obvious to state that orthotic provision for paralysed patients (including myelomeningocele) depends on the level of neurological involvement. For example, a lumbo-sacral level spinal dysraphism has lesions which produce unbalanced paralyses around the ankle/foot, treatable by ankle foot orthoses. Higher neurological levels of paraplegia, require more encompassing and complex orthoses. These examples can be used as a template to study possible orthotic treatments for other neurological handicap.

Myelomeningocoele Paralysis above L1:

The higher level lesions (eg. cervical, thoracic, low thoracic), have (at most) psoas muscle activity working because of the anatomical innervation. Thus hip flexion may be unopposed. If there is a flaccid paraplegia or paraparesis below this level, orthotic compensation to allow standing and walking compensations are needed for:-

      lack of limb acceleration into swing
      lack of stance phase stability
      lack of body advancement to move the
      patient forwards

(note: lack of lower limb sensation can allow ill-fitting orthoses to produce ghastly ulceration).

Orthotic treatment at above L1 level

This hip level paralysis is treated with a ParaWalker. It is a thoracic, pelvis, hip, knee, ankle, foot orthosis (THKAFO) (ie. each of the joints over which the splint works is mentioned). This is now an international nomenclature. Other examples include WHO - wrist hand orthosis and AFO - ankle foot orthosis).

The walking frame is very rigid to support the trunk and to keep that related to, and in balance, above each hip, knee and ankle. The latter are held 'stable' by 3-point fixation. Movement forwards for the leg is ensured by a patented hip joint, enabling the Orthotist to fix the required step length most suitable for the patient. The joint ensures correct planar movement. The rigidity of the orthotic apparatus allows gravity to be used positively, effecting a swinging leg, provided treat when one foot is released from the ground (by normal upper limb function through the ipsilateral crutch), that the leg released from the ground does not adduct towards the stance leg. The rigidity of the apparatus prevents this adduction. When the paralysed swinging leg, plus orthosis, has completed the step, normal upper limb muscle action brings the body forwards towards the grounded forward crutch, (ie. there is a reaction point at the crutch tip on the opposite side). Body advance is thus assured - provided that the upper limb muscles are of normal strength. Upper limb function to provide crutch grip is essential.

At lower levels, eg. in the high lumbar region, (L1, L2)

The addition of working and functional lower thoracic and upper lumbar muscle segments allows more activity and strength in the psoas muscle. But an unbalanced hip flexion deformity occurs, as the hip extensors (having a lower motor level innervation) are paralysed.

With neurological function to L3 level, useful action in the quadriceps (root value L2/3/4), and in the adductor group (similar root level) will be present. The latter situation may result in unopposed adduction action with hip dislocation. (although in myelomeningocele a neurological level at T10/T12 may also develop spontaneous hip dislocations before the age of 3 years).

Knee instability

In the sagittal plane persons with a high lumbar paralysis (L1, L2), due to any neurological dysfunction, have poor quadriceps power. Maintenance of a straight knee in single leg stance (whilst the opposite leg is swinging forwards) will thus need orthotic support with 3-point fixation. The knee buckles forwards otherwise.

It is much less clear why such children (and adults) are unable to orthotically walk well in a KAFO (knee ankle foot orthosis). Part of the problem is that they have to circumduct the swinging limb, since most KAFO splints do not have any knee bend facility for swing phase. Limb advancement is thus by hip circumduction and pelvic translation alone. Less obvious in these cases is the lack of hip abductor power on the stance side, preventing single leg stability in stance around the hip.

The resulting Trendelenburg allows the opposite hemipelvis to drop, and prevents clearance of the swing foot. The KAFO when used alone then has a disappointing effect, producing a high energy costing walk, with a need for a lot of upper limb action to counter the hip instability.

At lumbar level L4

Here quadriceps and adductor muscles are intact and functional by reason of normal neurological connections. This paraplegic patient will have active semi-membranosis (medial hamstring) action (L4 supply) and a working tibialis anterior producing adduction and inversion of the mid and fore foot at the sub talar joint and knee flexion contracture. Hip dislocation can occur as explained above.

An unbalanced paralysis is seen in the feet especially, and bizarre deformities can occur in myelomeningocele when there are intact lower segments present and more proximal paralysed segments. This is rare. An upper motor neurone type of spasticity is common in neurological disease allowing severe joint deformity when paralysed or weaker antagonists fail to achieve joint balance.

Paralysis of the L5 root

Because of the loss of the L5 root (which supplies TFL and gluteus medius), single leg stance stability is lost. The hip abductors are greatly important for walking and muscle or neurological disease produces a Trendelenburg gait. The body weight has to be shifted grossly over each stance leg by crutch use and upper trunk displacements. Since body mass needs to be moved through a displacement in such a walk, the patient has much extra work to perform with each step. This is different to the Trendelenburg occurring with hip arthritis

L5 Level paralysis below knee

This leaves both anterior and posterior tibial muscles working, so gross foot supination, inversion and adduction deformity usually results. The evertors and plantarflexors are paralysed. Walking continues if the foot is kept plantigrade (by surgery or with orthoses); since single leg stability in the hip abductors is assured. Unopposed dorsiflexor action produces calcaneus deformity. Although a later developing deformity it is difficult to treat orthotically, and surgical tendon transfers should be considered early on.

Ankle plantarflexion resulting from gravitational effects and weak dorsiflexors can be corrected with an AFO so that the toes do not scuff at the beginning of swing phase. Secondly the foot is pre-positioned for initial contact at the end of swing by the orthosis.

An L4 paralysis of the anterior tibial muscle (and peroneus tertius [L5]), often results in a drop foot deformity. This produces scuffing of the toe in initial swing phase, and a squandering of step length because of an early toe strike prematurely at the end of swing.

The 'drop foot' may also be caused by excess activity in the plantarflexors, if they are spastic due to Upper Motor Neurone (UMN) problems.

(S1), S2, S3:

Lower levels of lesion with paralysis of the below knee and intrinsic muscles (to the ankle foot) are usually well compensated for and accommodated within an ankle foot orthosis (AFO).

Any deformity correctable at ankle and sub talar joints can be held in the corrected position with an AFO. This can be a metal type with an iron and a T-strap, or a plastic AFO. (The title AFO is not synonymous with a plastic splint alone).

In these circumstances the peroneii (L5/S1/S2), and the gastrosoleus (L5/S1/S2/S3), may show variable degrees of paralysis. The AFO prevents an unbalanced equinus, calcaneus, varus or valgus deformity.

Deformities of the sub talar joint, if not fixed, can be effectively treated by reducing or correcting sub talar joint position with appropriate wings at the sides of a plastic AFO at ankle level. Providing that a comfortable shoe is worn, the AFO plus shoe prevents such sub talar joint deformity in stance phase and instability is overcome.

Notes

Notes

Clinincal NeuroPhysiology

Dr T Staunton

Consultant Neurophysiologist
Robert Jones and Agnes Hunt Orthopaedic Hospital

Most Neurophysiology Laboratories have a routine of investigation studying the major motor and sensory nerves of the Brachial Plexus and the Lumbrosacral Plexus. Theoretically, any motor or sensory nerve can be studied but in practice, 90% of the information is obtained from studying the Median Ulnar and Radial motor and sensory parameters in the upper limb and the Sciatic nerve with the Posterior tibial and Peroneal divisions, motor and sensory, in the lower limbs.

Needle EMG of individual muscles is used as a complementary technique which gives information about the number and nature of the activated motor units from the specific nerve root that innervates the muscle being tested. This can be used for anatomic clarification but also for pathophysiologic clarification and separation of radiculopathies from peripheral neuropathies and myopathies.

Nerve Conduction Studies
(Figs 1,2,3)

When studying a peripheral nerve, a nerve is stimulated electrically until it propagates an

action potential; one then measures the size of the compound muscle action potential (CMAP) in a motor nerve or the sensory nerve action potential (SNAP) of a sensory nerve and one estimates a conduction velocity.
This gives us 2 parameters:

(a) The amplitude(size)of the **evoked potential**

(b) a **conduction velocity**.

The amplitude of the response is a reflection of nerves or motor units recruited, e.g. if one loses half the nerve fibres in a peripheral nerve, the size of the elicited CMAP or SNAP will be reduced by 50%. This can be seen in trauma, vascular, compressive or any lesion that reduces the number of nerves carrying an impulse

From the **conduction velocity** one can determine if one is dealing with a demyelinating or conduction slowing neuropathy (e.g. Guillain-Barre Syndrome). If one has a focal entrapment neuropathy (with the pathology usually being focal demyelination) one will usually get focal slowing (e.g. in the ulnar nerve around the elbow) with normal velocities on either side. This can be demonstrated by stimulating the nerve at various sites and measuring conduction velocity over the area of interest, e.g. wrist in carpal Tunnel Syndrome, elbow in Ulnar Palsy.

Fig.1 Clinical Neurophysiology

Nerve Conduction/EMG	
Evoked Responses	VEP
	SSEP
	BAEP
EEG	
(Standard inter-ictal, intraoperative corticography)	
Intraoperative studies	EEG
	SSEP
	Nerve – Nerve
	Facial nerve
	Spinal Cord

Fig.2 Nerve Conduction Studies

	Motor	*Sensory*
Evokes	C.M.A.P.	S.N.A.P
Potential	Muscle (Twitch)	Nerve potential direct
Amplitude	5-10 mV	5 – 30 µV
Velocity	Indirect	Direct
Amplifier	Easy	Can be difficult Background and needs averaging

Fig 3. Motor Nerve Conduction

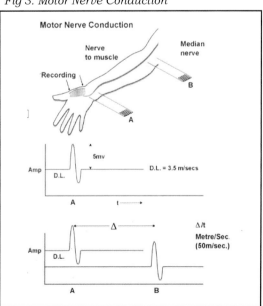

Motor Nerve Conduction, (Fig 2)

In this technique a muscle, usually distally (e.g. APB in the thenar eminence for a medial conduction study) is stimulated and after a distal latency one demonstrates the compound muscle action potential (CMAP).

Supramaximal stimulus must be delivered in order to ensure that all nerves and functioning motor units have discharged. Another stimulus is applied to the nerve at a proximal site and by measuring the difference in the size of the CMAP proximally and distally, one can estimate whether there is **conduction block**.

One can calculate **conduction velocity** by measuring the distance between the two sites of stimuli and dividing this by the time difference (latencies). The amplitudes are expressed in terms of millivolts, and the velocities in meters per second.

Sensory Nerve Conduction Studies.

The size of an evoked sensory potential (SNAP) is minuscule and sometimes smaller in amplitude than the background (usually muscle activity) noise. This requires therefore, technical expertise and good recording equipment. The size of the potential is measured in microvolts.

The nerve is stimulated over the nerve trunk and at a point either distally or proximally, usally 8-13 cm distance away. Recording electrodes, on the skin over the sub-cutaneous nerve pick up the SNAP. No distal latency is involved because no muscle contracts; one is recording directly the nerve action potential. This technique may require averaging of multiple recordings to separate the potential from the background noise.

E.M.G.

A concentric needle electrode contains two separated metal recording electrodes within the shape of a small hypodermic needle. This is inserted, usually quite painlessly in to the muscle to be studied.

At rest a normal muscle is silent. As the patient slowly with volition moves the muscle being studied, there is recruitment of one and then more and multiple motor units **(a motor unit** being defined as the anterior horn cell in the spinal cord, with its motor axon passing through the spinal roots and the peripheral nerve then innovating a variable number of muscle fibres spread through the body of the muscle being studied). A full recruitment pattern usually looks and sounds like "white noise

In a disease state the muscle **may not** be silent at rest and may demonstrate increased insertional activity and changes of **active denervation** represented by muscle fibres firing spontaneously. This represents the loss of control that the nerve exerts over the muscle fibre. These features may include **fibrillation potentials** which are the hallmark of denervated muscle fibres. It takes **7 to 12 days** for the changes of **active denervation** to be demonstrated in a neuropathy, acute or chronic. In a denervated muscle (e.g. the result of spinal root entrapment or other nerve injury) , the number of motor units recruited will be reduced and instead of "white noise" one sees a reduced pattern of isolated or scant muscle potentials. In a chronic neuropathy, with resprouting of remaining viable nerve fibres, any potentials elicited may be abnormal and **polyphasic** or even have a giant configuration.

Evaluation of the Patient and the data obtained
(Figs 4,5)

Obviously, the nerve studies and the interpretation of the electrophysiological findings will depend upon the clinical presentation of the patient. If one is investigating a specific root syndrome (e.g., C7 root) one will concentrate both nerve conduction and EMG studies around the C7 nerve root, often contrasting it to other nerve roots (e.g., C6 and T1) and comparing it to the contralateral usually asymptomatic limb.

In a peripheral polyneuropathy, one will need to study both upper and lower limbs.

To separate a radiculopathy from a peripheral neuropathy or a motor neurone disease, one may need to study multiple nerves, motor and sensory in both the upper and lower limbs demonstrating reduction in the evoked potential amplitude and/or conduction slowing.

A reduction in the amplitude of a motor or sensory response implies loss of nerves.

If the amplitude is reduced on proximal stimulation compared to distal stimulation, one is looking at conduction block (e.g. tardy ulnar palsy, when the potential in ADM stimulating above the elbow is reduced compared to the amplitude below the elbow (see EMG technique demonstrated at course).

Separating Root Disease from Peripheral Entrapment

Knowledge of the anatomy of the peripheral nerve, the motor unit and the spinal root is essential. For example, the **major** anatomic defining characteristics of a proximal root entrapment (e.g., by disc or osteophyte) is the **preservation of an intact sensory action potential**. This is because the lesion (e.g. the disc prolapse) interrupts the nerve root **proximal** to the dorsal root ganglion which is anatomically (and electrically) situated in the neural foramen, distal to the thecal sac. That is, the nerve is interrupted proximally within the spinal canal, resulting in the sensory deficit.

The dorsal root ganglion which is the **cell body** of the nerve keeping the peripheral nerve alive is intact and thus the sensory potential is normal.

The muscle potential may well be reduced as the motor nerve is separated from the anterior Horn Cell in the spinal cord.

In a wrist drop from a C7 root entrapment, the radial motor potentials are reduced or even absent, there is gross denervation on EMG, but the radial sensory potentials are preserved and entirely normal! **The presence of an intact sensory potential is what determines root and proximal disease from peripheral entrapment and plexus disease**

INTRAOPERATIVE MONITORING

Somatosensory Evoked Responses (SSEP)

This technique has been developed more recently using the basic principles as defined above and combining them with similar principles to electroencephalography (EEG). A peripheral nerve in the upper or the lower limb (usually the median and posterior tibial respectively) is stimulated but instead of recording from the nerve or the muscle twitch, one records from the scalp usually over the sensory parietal cortex. The evoked responses from the cortex is miniscule and one must average the obtained response 100 or 200 times at least, in order to differentiate the time linked evoked response from the background brain EEG activity.

Obviously this technique takes time, as 200 responses at a stimulus rate of 3 per second will only give us a measurable response or result, assuming all other factors are even and perfect, after 2 minutes or so.

As Orthopaedic Surgeons know only too well, much can be lost in the operating field over a period of 2 minutes!

Evoked brain potentials develop, e.g. the N20 response from medial nerve stimulation or the P37/N45 response from posterior tibial nerve stimulation. One can also measure potentials developed in the cervical spinal cord at C7 level and the L1 level as well as distally in the Brachial Plexus at Erb's point.

The measured parameter is usually the latency of the response, e.g. the N20 response is a cortical (brain) response occurring at approximately 20 milliseconds after stimulating the Median nerve at the wrist. In disease or if the spinal cord it damaged by surgical techniques, one will demonstrate a delay in the latency or a total absence or obliteration of the evoked response

	Most Informative Tests	**Classic Abnormalities**
Carpal Tunnel Syndrome	Sensory Nerve Conduction (NC) over Palm-wrist & finger-Wrist segment; terminal motor Latency (Median nerve)	Abnormal sensory NC over the tested segments; prolonged terminal latency
Ulnar compression Neuropathy at Elbow	Sensory NC over finger-wrist & mixed NC over forearm segments; motor NC across elbow	Abnormal sensory & mixed NC over finger-elbow segment; slow motor NCV across elbow
Peroneal nerve Palsy	Motor NC across fibular head	Slow motor NCV across fibular head
Tarsal Tunnel Syndrome	Sensory NCV in the plantar nerves; terminal Latency (posterior tibial N)	Abnormal sensory NC in plantar nerves prolonged terminal latency
Radiculopathy	Peripheral and Paraspinal needle EMG	Abnormal spontaneous potentials. Normal Nerve Conduction
Myopathy	Needle EMG	Short-small MUP's
Peripheral Neuropathy	Extensive NC Studies	Slow motor & Sensory NCV

Fig.4 NC/EMG Tests for Common Entrapment - Neuropathy and Neuromuscular Disorders

This should be "tailor-made" according to the procedure involved. It may include:

- **Nerve or nerve root stimulation** at various sites and measurement of either the distal nerve or muscle impulse. This may demonstrate conduction block or slowing or normal continuity of the nerve.
- **Intraoperative EMG** with needle in situ in the appropriate muscle (e.g., the face, quadriceps for L4, Abductor hallucis for S1 root) to assess the muscle contraction when the nerve is stimulated, either intentionally or otherwise.

- **Cord to cord stimulation** and cord to cortical potential measurement. Usually averaged, for evidence of spinal pathway disruption. Similar to SSEP.

Site of Entrapment, resulting in hand paraesthesia.

Fig5.	**Hand**	**Pins & Needles**
Median N	*Radial*	*Ulnar*
Digital Nerves	Forearm	Digital
Carpal Tunnel	Lateral elbow	Guyon
Pronator Teres	Spiral groove	Cubital Tunnel Tardy Palsy
Ligt of Struthers	Mid Humerus	Ligt of Struthers
Brachial plexus (Upper)	Plexus (Posterior)	Plexus(lower) (thoracic outlet)
C5-6/C8 root	C6,7 root	C8 – T1 root
CENTRAL (CORD)		

Fig.6 Needle EMG

Needle EMG

Detects and examines electrical potentials from multiple and occasionally single nerve fibres close to the "recording surface".

Used for

- anatomic correlation / diagnosis
- e.g. radiculopathy, M.N.D
- to examine nature of discharges e.g. myopathy

Resting Activity

- Fibrillations and PSW's: Denervation
- Increased insertional activity
- Rapid abnormal repetitive discharges (e.g. Myotonia)
- Fasciculations
- Recruitment -Type and fullness – appearance

These notes accompany a clinical demonstration of nerve conduction testing and EMG.

Notes

Notes

Statistics for FRCS (Trauma & Orthopaedics)

Mr P Cool

Consultant Orthopaedic & Oncological Surgeon
Robert Jones & Agnes Hunt Orthopaedic Hospital
Oswestry

Topics

- Epidemiology
- Statistics
- Curve Fitting
- Survival Curve
- Trials
- Paper Analysis

www.paulcool.com

Slide 1

Epidemiology

www.paulcool.com

Slide 2

Incidence

Number of NEW cases per Year
/
Population at Risk

www.paulcool.com

Slide 3

Prevalence

Number of EXISTING cases per Year
/
Population at Risk

www.paulcool.com

Slide 4

Prevalence

Prevalence = Incidence * Duration

(when population and disorder stable)

www.paulcool.com

Slide 5

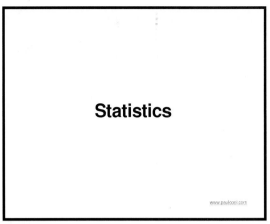

Slide 6

Data

- **Variable**
  – Actual property measured by individual observations

- **Variate**
  – Single score or reading of a given variable

Slide 7

Data

- **Nominal**
  – Different Classes
     Wedge Osteotomy / Dome Osteotomy
- **Ordinal**
  – Ranked
     Walking Frame / Stick / Unaided
- **Interval**
  – Number

Slide 8

Distribution of Data

- **Normal**
  – Parametric Statistics $\quad y = \dfrac{1}{\sqrt{2\pi}}\exp\dfrac{x^2}{2}$
     (Height)

- **Not Normal**
  – Non Parametric

Slide 9

Normal Distribution

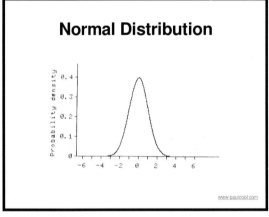

Slide 10

Normal Distribution

- **Mean / Average**

- **Standard Deviation**

Slide 11

Normal Distribution
Different Mean

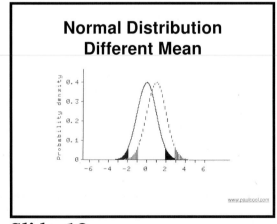

Slide 12

Basic Science for FRCS (Trauma and Orthopaedics)

Normal Distribution Different SD

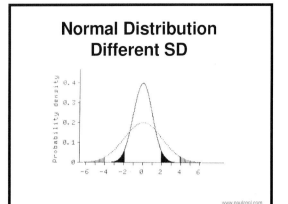

www.paulcool.com

Slide 13

Standard Deviation

1 * SD = 66 %
2 * SD = 95 % (1.96)
3 * SD = 99 %

www.paulcool.com

Slide 14

Variance

- Measure of the Spread of Data

- Standard Deviation Squared

www.paulcool.com

Slide 15

Non Normal Distribution

- **Range**
  – Highest and Lowest Reading
- **Median**
  – Equal Number results above and below
- **Mode**
  – Most common category
- **Mean / Average**

www.paulcool.com

Slide 16

Non Normal Distribution

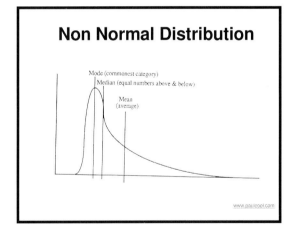

www.paulcool.com

Slide 17

Parametric Statistics

- **Interval Data**
- **Normal Distribution**
- **More Powerful**

- Large Sample Size: Normal Distribution
- Small Sample Size: Student t-Test

www.paulcool.com

Slide 18

Non Parametric Statistics

- **All Other Data**
- **Less Powerful**

- **Doubt**
  - Non Parametric Statistics
- **Transformation Data**
  - Make Distribution Normal (Log / Square)

Slide 19

Statistical Tests

Data	Sample Size	Test
Interval	> 50	Normal
	< 50 Normal	t - Test
	< 50 Not Normal	Mann-Whitney U Test
Ordinal		Mann-Whitney U Test
Nominal		Chi - Squared Test

Slide 20

Hypothesis

- **Null Hypothesis**
  - No Difference

- **Alternative Hypothesis**
  - Difference

Slide 21

Probability

P Value

Slide 22

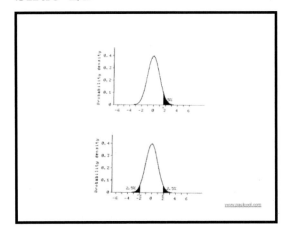

Slide 23

Errors

- **Population Standard Deviation**
- **Difference Desired to Detect**
- **Significance Level (Type 1 Error)**
- **Test Statistic**

Slide 24

Errors

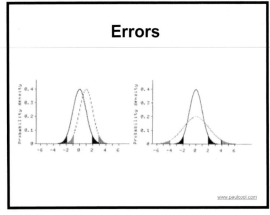

Slide 25

Errors

- **Type 1**
  - Null Hypothesis incorrectly rejected
  - False Positive
  - Controlled using Significance level
- **Type 2**
  - Null Hypothesis incorrectly accepted
  - False Negative
  - Controlled using Statistical Power

Slide 26

Basic Science for FRCS (Trauma and Orthopaedics)

Sensitivity

True Positive who are also Test Positive
/
All True Positive

Fire alarm

Slide 27

Specificity

True Negative who are also Test Negative
/
All True Negative

Speeding

Slide 28

Positive Predictive Value

True Positive who are also Test Positive
/
All Test Positive

Slide 29

Negative Predictive Value

True Negative who are also Test Negative
/
All Test Negative

Slide 30

		Arthroscopy	
		Positive	Negative
MRI	Positive	A	B
	Negative	C	D

Sensitivity	$\frac{A}{(A+C)}$
Specificity	$\frac{D}{(B+D)}$
Pos Pred Value	$\frac{A}{(A+B)}$
Neg Pred Value	$\frac{D}{(C+D)}$
Accuracy	$\frac{(A+D)}{(A+B+C+D)}$

Slide 31

Data

- **Precision**
  - Closeness of repeated measurements of the same quantity

- **Accuracy**
  - Closeness of a measured variate to its true value

Slide 32

Curve Fitting

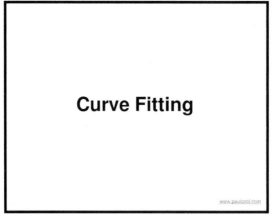

Slide 33

Curve Fitting

- **Type**
  - Linear
  - Non Linear (Log, Power, Polynomal)
- **Regression Coefficient**
  - Direction coefficient of the regression line
- **Correlation Coefficient**
  - Between −1 and +1
  - Measure of how close the curve fits the data

www.paulcool.com

Slide 34

Correlation Coefficient = 1

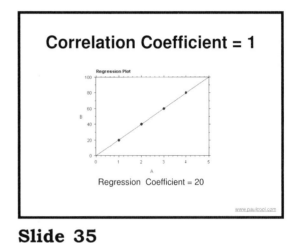

Regression Coefficient = 20

www.paulcool.com

Slide 35

Correlation Coefficient = 0

Regression Coefficient = 20

www.paulcool.com

Slide 36

Correlation Coefficient = -1

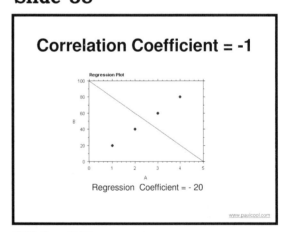

Regression Coefficient = - 20

www.paulcool.com

Slide 37

Basic Science for FRCS (Trauma and Orthopaedics)

Survival Curves

Slide 38

Survival Curves

- Order by length of observed survival time
- Hard 'End Point' required
  - Death
  - 'Revision' & 'Infection' are **not** hard end points
    - Surgeon can decide not to revise a loose prosthesis!
- Lost to follow up
  - Best and worse case scenarios
  - 95% Confidence Interval
- Tail end curve
  - Unreliable: only few patients

www.paulcool.com

Slide 39

Survival Curves - Methods

- Life Table

- Kaplan - Meier

www.paulcool.com

Slide 40

5 Year Survival

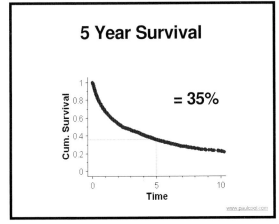

= 35%

Slide 41

Median Survival

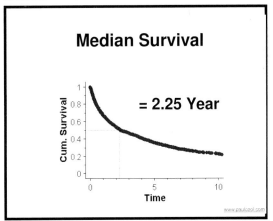

= 2.25 Year

Slide 42

Trials

Slide 43

Observational Trials

- **Cross Sectional (Prevalence)**
  - Performed on Survivor Population
  - Selection Bias
- **Case Control (Retrospective)**
  - Past Exposure to Risk Factor
  - Selection Bias
- **Cohort (Prospective or Retrospective)**
  - Minimal Observational Bias
  - Lost to Follow Up Bias

www.paulcool.com

Slide 44

Clinical Trials

Double Blind Randomised Trial
- **Gold Standard**
- **2 Arms**
  - **Control Group**
    - Placebo
    - Sham Operation
  - **Study Group**

www.paulcool.com

Slide 45

Hierarchy of Evidence

- Case Report
- Cross Sectional Study
- Case Control Study
- Cohort Study
- Randomised Controlled Trial
- Systematic Review & Meta-Analysis

www.paulcool.com

Slide 46

BIAS

- **Confounding (Factor)**
  - Effect from another variable (confounder)
- **Selection (Patient)**
  - Differences in characteristics between subjects who are selected and those who are not
- **Information / Observational (Outcome)**
  - Error in measurement of exposure or disease or misclassification

www.paulcool.com

Slide 47

Blinding

Reduces Observational Bias

www.paulcool.com

Slide 48

Randomisation

Reduces Selection Bias

www.paulcool.com

Slide 49

Stratification

- Modified Form of Randomisation

- Confounding Factors do not Distort the Groups

www.paulcool.com

Slide 50

Stratification

Reduces Confounding Bias

www.paulcool.com

Slide 51

Randomisation

External Randomisation

www.paulcool.com

Slide 52

RCT - Steps 1

- Null Hypothesis
- Inclusion /Exclusion Criteria
- Outcome Measure
  - Data: Nominal / Ordinal / Interval
  - Statistical Test
- Bias
  - Confounding / Selection / Observational
  - Blinding : Reduces Observational Bias
  - Randomisation : Reduces Selection Bias
  - Stratification / External Randomisation

www.paulcool.com

Slide 53

RCT - Steps 2

- Power Analysis
  - Variance / Standard Deviation
  - Significance Level
  - Difference in Means
  - ? Pilot Study
  - Estimated Sample Size
- Ethical Approval
- Informed Consent

www.paulcool.com

Slide 54

RCT - Steps 3

- **Collection of Data & Results**
- **Analysis**
  - Parametric / Non Parametric
- **Conclusions**
- **Publication**
  - Presentation of Data

Slide 55

Advantages of RCT

- Evaluation of Single Variable
- Prospective
- Reduces BIAS
- Allows for Meta-Analysis

Slide 56

Paper Analysis

Slide 57

Preliminary Questions

1. **Why was the study done**
   - What hypothesis is tested
2. **What type of study is done?**
   - Primary (first hand)
   - Secondary (summarise)
3. **Was the study design appropriate?**

Slide 58

Primary Studies

- **Experiments / Case Report**
- **Surveys**
  - Cross Sectional
  - Case Control
  - Cohort
- **Clinical Trials**
  - RCT

Slide 59

Secondary Studies

- **Overview**
  - Systematic Reviews
  - Meta-Analyses
- **Guidelines**
- **Decision Analyses**
- **Economic Analysis**

Slide 60

Hierarchy of Evidence

- Case Report
- Cross Sectional Study
- Case Control Study
- Cohort Study
- Randomised Controlled Trial
- Systematic Review & Meta-Analysis

Slide 61

10 Reasons for Rejection

- No important scientific issue
- Not Original study
- Study did not test hypothesis
- Different study should have been done
- Sample size too small
- Uncontrolled study
- Incorrect statistical analysis
- Inappropriate conclusions
- Conflict of interest
- Badly written

Slide 62

Download

www.paulcool.com

Slide 63

Notes

Metabolic Bone Disease

Dr R Butler

Consultant Rheumatologist
Robert Jones & Agnes Hunt Orthopaedic Hospital
Oswestry

HORMONAL REGULATION OF BONE TURNOVER

The actions of the main hormones which control bone turnover, namely parathormone (PTH) and vitamin D, are shown in Figure 1. Although calcitonin can be used therapeutically to reduce bone resorption, it seems to play a much less significant role in bone physiology than the other two hormones.

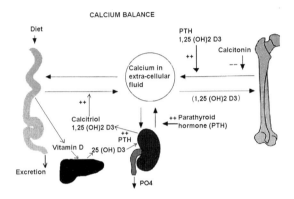

Figure 1. Factors involved in the control of serum calcium.

The calcium-sensing receptor plays a crucial role in calcium homeostasis (*Figure 2; adapted from Marx. N Engl J Med 2000, 343: 1863*). A rise in plasma calcium detected by the calcium-sensing receptor leads to reduced transcription of the PTH gene in order to normalise the calcium level. A gain of function mutation of the calcium-sensing receptor leads to the syndrome of hypocalcaemic hypercalciuria i.e. a lower calcium level is sufficient to switch off the stimulus for PTH production (*Pearse S. New Engl J Med 1996, 335: 1115*). Conversely a loss of function mutation of the calcium-sensing receptor leads to the syndrome of hypercalcaemic hypocalciuria (Thakker. Lancet 2001, 357: 974).

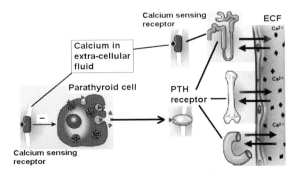

Figure 2. The calcium-sensing receptor on parathyroid and renal tubular cells controls the secretion of PTH (adapted from Marx N Engl J Med 2000, 343: 1863).

COUPLING OF RESORPTION AND FORMATION IN RE-MODELLING OF BONE

The bone remodelling process is described elsewhere in this volume. Recent advances in our understanding of how osteoblasts and osteoclasts communicate may help to explain how the processes of bone resorption and formation are usually coupled. Osteoblasts and stromal cells produce a molecule known as RANK-ligand, formerly known as osteoclast differentiation factor (ODF), which interacts with RANK expressed on osteoclast precursors to induce osteoclast differentiation and activate osteoclasis and the start of a resorption cycle (*Figure 3; adapted from Krane. N Engl J Med 2002 347: 210*). A soluble glycoprotein, osteoprotegerin (OPG) which is also produced by osteoblasts and stromal cells, can bind to RANK-ligand and act as a decoy receptor. This blocks the interaction of RANK-ligand with RANK and inhibits the differentiation of osteoclasts (*Aubin & Bonnelye. Osteoporosis Int 2000, 11: 905; Manolagas. Endocrine Rev 2000, 21: 115*).

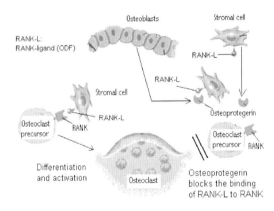

Figure 3. The roles of ODF, OPG and RANK in osteoclast biology (adapted from Krane N Engl J Med 2002 347: 210)

Many calcitrophic hormones and cytokines including 1,25 (OH)2 D3, PTH, PGE2, IL-1 and IL-11 have the capacity to both stimulate the production of RANK-ligand and inhibit the production of OPG and so promote bone resorption. By contrast oestrogens reduce the production of RANK-ligand and increase the production of OPG. Preliminary studies suggest that OPG may be a potent therapeutic agent in conditions characterised by excessive bone breakdown such as osteoporosis and juvenile Paget's disease.

INVESTIGATION OF BONE DISEASE

Routine biochemistry:	Serum calcium, phosphate & alkaline phosphate
	Urea & electrolytes; liver function tests
Where indicated:	Protein electrophoresis & free light chains in urine
	Parathormone (PTH).
	25-hydroxyvitamin D
	Gonadal hormones:
	Women: Oestradiol; FSH if hormonal status unclear
	Men: Testosterone, LH & SHBG
Formation markers:	Alkaline phosphatase
	Osteocalcin
	Procollagen type I peptide (P1CP)
Resorption markers:	Calcium: creatinine ratio in urine
	Deoxypyridinoline cross-links or collagen telopeptides
	(cross-laps; NTX; P1NP)
	TRAP (tartrate-resitant acid phosphatase)

Radiology ; Bone biopsy ; Bone density

BIOCHEMICAL FINDINGS IN METABOLIC BONE DISEASE

	Ca	PO4	Alk Phos	PTH
Osteoporosis	N	N	N	N
Osteomalacia				
Vit D Deficiency	Low	Low	High	High
PO4 depletion	N	Low	High	N
Hyperparathyroidism	High	Low	N or High	High
Hypoparathyroidism	Low	High	N	Low
Pseudohypoparathyroidism	Low	High	N	High
Renal osteodystrophy	Variable	N or High	N or High	High
Paget's disease	N	N	High	N

BONE DENSITY

Bone density can be assessed in different ways:

Plain X-rays: cannot assess bone density accurately but may suggest osteopenia and demonstrate fractures.

DEXA (dual energy X-ray absorptiometry): accurate and requires only modest radiation dose. Values in the spine may be falsely elevated by lumbar osteophytes or scoliosis.

Quantitative CT (QCT): accurate but relatively high radiation dose makes repeat examinations undesirable.

Bone ultrasound: Measurement of speed of ultrasound transmission (SOS) and broadband ultrasound attenuation (BUA) probably reflect not only bone density but also microarchitectural factors such as elasticity. Heel ultrasound machines can certainly predict risk of hip fracture and are portable and cheaper than DEXA machines but their precise role in comparison with DEXA is still being evaluated.

TECHNIQUES FOR MEASURING BONE DENSITY

	Bones measured	Examination time (minutes)	Precision (%CV)	Radiation dose(uSv)
Single Photon absorptiometry (SPA)	Wrist	15	4-6	<1
Dual Photon absorptiometry (DPA)	Spine, hip total body	20-40	4-10	5
Dual energy X-ray absorptiometry (DEXA)	Spine, hip total body	10-20	3-9	1-4
Quantitative CT (QCT)	Spine	10-15	5-15	50

Resnick D. Bone & Joint Imaging. Saunders, Philadelphia 1996, page 155

SPECIFIC METABOLIC BONE DISORDERS

OSTEOMALACIA

Definition: Specific childhood and adult defects of skeletal mineralisation, bone, cartilage and growth caused by inadequate activity of vitamin D. This results in the accumulation of increased amounts of unmineralised matrix (osteoid) and a decreased rate of bone formation.

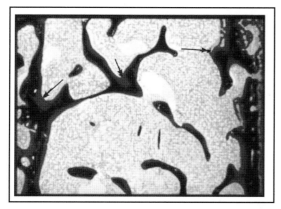

Figure 4. Osteomalacia: note increased quantities of unmineralised osteoid (arrowed) on bone surfaces.

This is not uncommon in the Asian community in the UK, and is probably under-recognised in the elderly white population, in whom diet is often poor and vitamin D deficiency common. In can also be seen in association with the various disorders below. A proximal myopathy and waddling gait are important clinical clues.

Causes of osteomalacia

Vitamin D deficiency:	**Dietary, malabsorption syndromes, lack of sunlight**
25OHD deficeincy:	**Chronic liver disease**
1,25[OH]2D deficiency:	**Chronic renal disease**
Hypophosphataemia:	**Familial hypophosphataemic rickets**
	Fanconi syndromes
	Oncogenic rickets
Drugs:	**Anticonvulsants**
Vitamin D-dependent rickets:	
	type I: reduced renal 1-alpha hydroxylase leads to low 1,25(OH)2D
	type II: end-organ resistance to 1,25(OH)2D due to receptor defect

Inherited rickets

1. X-linked familial hypophosphataemic rickets (also known as vitamin D-resistant rickets)
Caused by mutation in PHEX gene (phosphate-regulating gene with homology to endopeptidases on X chromosome)
(de Beur. J Clin Endocrinol Metab 2002, 87: 2467)
2. Vitamin D-dependent rickets type I: (also known as hereditary pseudovitamin D-deficiency rickets)
Caused by mutations in renal 1-alpha hydroxylase gene which lead to low 1,25(OH)2D

(Kitanaka et al. N Engl J Med 1998, 338: 653)

3. Vitamin D-dependent rickets type II (also known as hypocalcaemic vitamin D-resistant rickets)
Results from end-organ resistance to effect of 1,25(OH)2D due to mutated vitamin D receptor

(Malloy et al. J Clin Invest 1990, 86: 2071)

Radiological features of osteomalacia

Rickets:	Growth plate is widened, splayed and ragged. It is also concave and holds epiphysis in "cup". Metaphyses rarefied by secondary hyperparathyroidism.
Osteomalacia:	Pseudofracture (Looser's zone - Figure 5). Biconcave "cod-fish" vertebrae. Signs of secondary hyperparathyroidism.

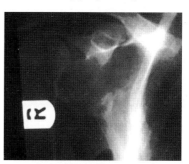

Figure 5. Osteomalacia: Looser zone in scapula.

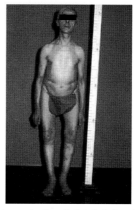

Figure 6. Osteomalacia: skeletal deformities in a man with long-standing untreated coeliac disease.

HYPERCALCAEMIA

Causes
Hyperparathyroidism.
Myeloma.
Other malignant disease +/- metastases.
Sarcoidosis.
Vitamin D excess.
Milk-alkali syndrome.
Paget's dise with immobilistaion.
Familial hypocalciuric hypercalcaemia.
Acute renal failure. (polyuric phase)

HYPERPARATHYROIDISM

(Marx. N Engl J Med 2000, 343: 1863; Silverberg et al. N Engl J Med 1999, 341: 1249)

This is usually discovered when hypercalcaemia is noted on a routine biochemical screen, but urinary calculi, chondrocalcinosis, fractures, abdominal or psychological symptoms can be presenting features. Hyperparathyroidism is sometimes part of the multiple endocrine neoplasia syndromes, and can be associated with adenomas of pituitary and pancreas (MEN-1) or with medullary thyroid cancer and phaechromocytoma (MEN-2)
(Brandi. J Clin Endocrinol Metab 2001, 86, 5658).

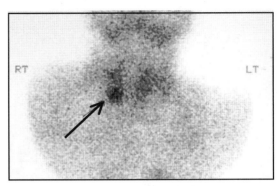

Figure 8. Parathyroid adenomas can often be demonstrated by a sestamibi isotope scan.

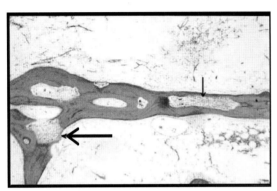

Figure 7. Hyperparathyroidism: note markedly increased osteoclastic activity with "tunnelling" (arrowed) within trabecula.

Hyperparathyroidism: Clinical features
Anorexia, vomiting, constipation & abdominal pain
Peptic ulcer
Pancreatitis
Polyuria / polydypsia
Renal calculi
Lethargy, depression, confusion & coma
Muscle weakness
Ectopic calcification of skin & eyes

Hyperparathyroidism: Presentation
(Mundy et al Lancet 1980 1: 1317)

	(%)
Asymptomatic biochemical finding	57
Acute hypercalcaemic syndrome	14
Lethargy / polyuria	8
Renal calculi	7
Psychiatric disorder	5
Hypertension	5
Gastrointestinal symptoms	4
Bone disease	0

Hyperparathyroidism: Causes

Single adenoma	80-85%
Multiple adenomata	5%
Hyperplasia	10%
Parathyroid carcinoma	1%

Hyperparathyroidism: Bony manifestations

Diffuse bone pain
Diffuse demineralisation
Subperiosteal resorption - Figure 9
Brown tumours
Fractures
Advanced changes known as osteitis fibrosa cystica

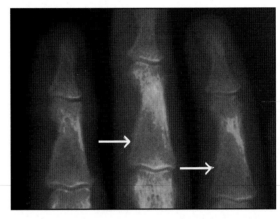

Figure 9. Hyperparathyroidism: typical subperiosteal erosions on the radial aspects of the middle phalanges.

Hyperparathyroidism: Treatment

Parathyroidectomy is the mainstay of treatment for significant hyperparathyroidism, but for milder cases, or elderly people who are not fit for surgery, alendronate may be an alternative
(Khan et al. J Clin Endocrinol Metab 2004, 89: 3319).

Hyperparathyroidism: Indications for parathyroidectomy
(Bilezikian & Potts. J Bone Min Res 2002, 17 (suppl 2) N57)

Age <50 years
Hypercalcaemia >2.85 mmol/l
Urinary calculi / nephrocalcinosis
Hypercalciuria: >10mmol/24 hours
Creatinine clearance reduced by 30%
Bone lesions and/or osteoporosis
Significant neuromuscular symptoms
Significant GI symptoms

Secondary hyperparathyroidism

Occurs in the following situations in order to try to maintain an adequate serum calcium. The serum calcium may be low or normal in secondary hyperparathyroidism, but not raised

Vitamin D deficiency	Malnutrition, malabsorption
Decreased calcium absorption	Old age, steroids, high phosphate intake
Hypercalciuria	Renal tubular acidosis
Hyperphosphataemia	Renal failure
Target organ resistance	Pseudohypoparathyroidism

RENAL OSTEODYSTROPHY

(Hruska & Teitelbaum. N Engl J Med, 1995, 333:166)

A complex form of metabolic bone disease:

A mixture of:	Osteomalacia Osteoporosis Osteitis fibrosa cystica Osteosclerosis
Resulting from:	Low 1,25[OH]2D; High serum phosphate; Acidosis; Aluminium toxicity secondary to dialysis

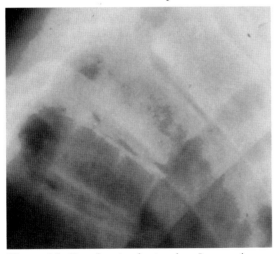

Figure 10: Renal osteodystrophy: "rugger-jersey spine" appearance of spine with alternating bands of sclerosis and osteopenia

PAGET'S DISEASE

(Deftos. N Engl J Med 2005,353:875; White. N Engl J Med 2006,355: 593)

This is often an incidental radiological finding but may present as bone pain, fracture or deformity. In a recent community study the mean age of people with Paget's disease was 75 with an equal sex ratio, and an annual incidence rate of about 1 case per 10,000, but this rises steeply with age (van Staa J Bone Min Res 2002, 17: 465).
Malignant bone neoplasms developed in 0.3% of these cases.

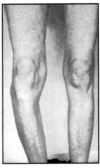

Figure 11. Paget's disease: skeletal deformity.

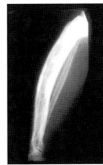

Figure 12. Paget's disease of tibia. The fibula is typically spared, as in this case.

Clinical features

Bone pain	
Fractures	
Deformity:	Skull Spine Long bones
Complications:	Tinnitus Vertigo Deafness Myelopathy High-output cardiac failure Osteosarcoma

Cause: Not known but possibly viral. Paramyxovirus-like particles seen on electronmicroscopy of osteoclasts and more recently evidence of canine distemper virus in Pagetic bone *(Mee Bone 1998, 23: 171)*

Pathology: Anarchic bone remodelling with increased matrix and numbers of both osteoblasts and osteoclasts. Major disorganisation of architecture and lamellar texture with overproduction of bone of poor quality.

Treatment: Bisphosphonates are the mainstay of treatment, although salmon calcitonin can be considered in people intolerant of bisphosphonates. Oral alendronate, risedronate and tiludronate are used most often, or intravenous pamidronate or zoledronate in people intolerant of oral preparations
(Whyte. N Engl J Med 2006, 355: 593).

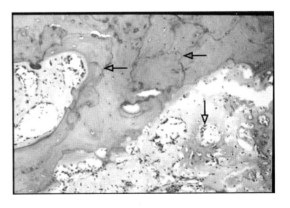

OSTEOPOROSIS

Approaching almost epidemic proportions as the population ages: at least one in three women older than 50 will experience an osteoporotic fracture during their remaining lifetime *(Sambrook & Cooper. Lancet 2006, 367: 2010)*. With increasing age less bone is formed than is resorbed at each site remodelled, leading to net loss of bone and structural damage *(Seeman. Lancet 2002, 359: 1841)*. In addition to the musculoskeletal consequences of osteoporosis, spinal deformity and loss of height can lead to dysphagia and abdominal bloating.

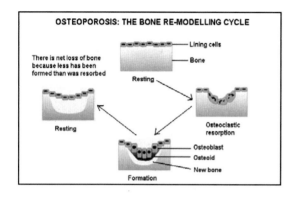

Figures 14. Osteoporosis: bone formation fails to keep pace with resorption.

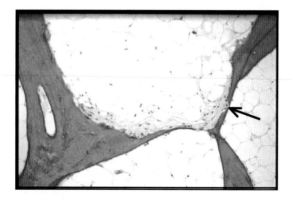

Figure 15. Osteoporosis: note fatty marrow with thin bone trabecula, one of which is about to be breached by osteoclastic resorption

Definition: "A skeletal disorder characterized by compromised bone strength predisposing a person to an increased risk of fracture. Bone strength reflects the integration of two main features: bone density and bone quality" *(NIH. JAMA, 2001, 285: 785)*. More practically it can be defined on the basis of bone density assessed by DEXA values *(Kanis. Lancet 2002, 359:1929)*:

Normal:	BMC not lower than 1 standard deviation below peak bone mass
Osteopenia:	BMC between 1 and 2.5 standard deviations below peak bone mass
Osteoporosis:	BMC more than 2.5 standard deviations below peak bone mass
T score:	refers to current bone density in relation to peak bone mass
Z-score:	refers to current bone density in relation to bone mass of age-matched people

The risk of fracture approximately doubles for each standard deviation decrease in T-score. The presence of a previous osteoporotic fracture greatly magnifies the adverse effect of a low T-score.
(Ross et al. Osteoporosis Int 1993, 3: 120).

Risk factors for primary osteoporosis

Genetic:	Female
	Positive family history
	White or Asian
	Thin
Hormonal:	Oestrogen deficiency
	late menarche
	prolonged amenorrhoea
	early menopause: ovarian failure
	hysterectomy
	oophorectomy
	Androgen deficiency
Lifestyle:	Smoking
	Excessive alcohol
	Inactivity
	Excessive exercise
Diet:	Calcium or vitamin D deficiency

Risk factors for secondary osteoporosis

Genetic:	Osteogenesis imperfecta
Endocrine:	Hyperthyroidism
	Hyperparathyroidism
GI:	Gastrectomy
	Malabsorption syndromes

Chronic liver disease
Chronic renal disease
Malignancy, notably myeloma
Drugs: Steroids
    Excessive thyroid replacement
    Anticonvulsants

Risk factors for fractures
(Cummings et al. N Engl J Med 1995, 332: 767; Kannus et al. Lancet 2005, 366: 1885)

Increasing age
Low bone density:
> Fracture risk doubles for each decreasing quintile of BMC

Previous fracture:
> One fracture increases risk of another x 5; three fractures x 25

(Ross et al. Osteoporosis Int 1993, 3: 120)
Force of impact
Increased risk of fall & poor protective reflexes:
> Neurological or musculoskeletal disease; use of hypnotics; alcohol or psychotropic drugs; poor vision

Treatment of Osteoporosis
(Delmas Lancet 2002, 359: 2018)

Calcium & vitamin D: Can help maintain bone mass but have very limited capacity to increase it. One widely quoted French study reported a reduced risk of hip fracture in elderly women when combined with vitamin D, but recent studies in the community reported no reduction in fracture risk *(RECORD trial group. Lancet 2005, 365: 1621)*. Calcium absorption from the gut decreases with age and the diet of elderly people, who often have little exposure to sunlight, is often deficient in vitamin D. All postmenopausal women should therefore have daily intake of at least 1g calcium and 400iu vitamin D to facilitate bone mineralisation.

Bisphosphponates: Will increase bone mass and reduce fracture rate *(Black et al. Lancet 1996, 346: 1535)*. They may however occasionally cause oesophageal ulceration.

HRT: Will increase bone mass and reduce the rate of hip fracture, but benefits for bone are lost rapidly when HRT is stopped. There is an increased risk of breast cancer with prolonged use and of uterine cancer unless progestogens are used as well, plus an increased risk of DVT/PE. The recent Women's Health Initiative randomised controlled trial of HRT showed that the hazards of HRT outweigh the benefits, and HRT is no longer recommended for the prevention of osteoporosis *(JAMA 2002, 288: 321)*.

Change in incidence of conditions in 1000 healthy post-menopausal women using HRT over a 5-year period *(Beral Lancet 2002, 360: 942)*

	Women 50-59	Women 60-69
Excess cases of:		
Breast cancer	3.2	4.0
Stroke	1.2	4.0
Pulmonary embolus	1.6	4.0
Total excess	6 (1 in 170 users)	12 (1 in 80 users)
Reduction in cases of:		
Colorectal cancer	1.2	3.0
# neck of femur	0.5	2.5
Total deficit	-1.7 (1 in 600 users)	-5.5 (in 180 users)

Raloxifene: This is a SERM (selective oestrogen receptor modulator). It will increase bone mass *(Delmas et al. N Engl J Med 1997, 337: 1641)* and will reduce vertebral fracture rate *(Ettinger et al. JAMA 1999, 282: 637)* but there are no good data on a reduction in hip fracture rate. It reduces the risk of breast cancer but like HRT it is associated with an increased risk of DVT/PE and stroke, and it is still unclear whether the benefits outweigh the hazards of the drug *(Barrett-Connor et al. N Engl J Med 2006, 355: 125)*.

Strontium ranelate: This increases bone mass as well as reducing resorption and it reduces the fracture rate *(Reginster et al. J Clin Endocrinol Metab 2005, 90: 2816)*. It is a useful alternative in people who cannot tolerate bisphosphonates. DEXA vaues are however unreliable in people taking the drug: as strontium is a heavier metal than calcium measurements over-estimate the increase in bone density.

Parathyroid hormone: Daily subcutaneous injections of PTH (1-34) can increase bone mass and reduce the fracture rate *(Neer et al. N Engl J Med 2001, 344: 1434)*. The drug is fairly expensive and inconvenient, and it is unclear how it should best be used in conjunction with other agents. NICE has ruled that it should only be used in the UK in people with severe osteoporosis who sustain fractures despite treatment with bisphosphonates
(NICE 2005, TA87)

Calcitriol (1,25 [OH]2D3): Will increase bone mass and reduce fracture rate but hypercalcaemia and hypercalciuria are sometimes a problem and it is rarely used.

Calcitonin: Will increase bone density and reduce risk of vertebral fractures. Was conventionally given by injection but the inconvenience of injections and frequency of side-effects meant that it was little used. A nasal preparation of salmon calcitonin is now available which can be useful in people intolerant of bisphosphonates and strontium.

Anti-fracture efficacy of different agents: strength of evidence*
(Royal College of Physicians / Bone & Tooth Society guidelines, 2000)

	Spine	Non-vertebral	Hip
Alendronate	A	A	A
Risedronate	A	A	A
Cyclic Etidronate	A	B	B
HRT	A	A	B
Raloxifene	A	-	-
Calcium + Vit D	-	A	A
Calcitriol	A	A	-
Calcitonin	A	B	B

* (A) 1+ randomised control trial; (B) 1+ well-designed descriptive or quasi-experimental study; (-) not demonstrated

STEROID OSTEOPOROSIS
(Canalis.   J Clin Endocrinol Metab 1996, 81: 3441)

Doses greater than 5mg daily have an adverse effect on bone but it is not clear whether lower doses are safe if taken long-term. Corticosteroids have various adverse effects on bone which contribute to osteoporosis including:

> Decreased bone formation
> Increased bone resorption
> Reduced calcium absorption and increased urinary calcium excretion
> leading to secondary hyperparathyroidism
> Decreased gonadal hormones
> Decreased muscle mass

Bone loss occurs quickly when steroids are started: lumbar BMD can fall by some 2% in 6 months and 3.5% in one year *(Adachi et al. N Engl J Med 1997, 337: 382)*. Although the most rapid rate of loss occurs in the first six months of treatment bone loss continues for as long as the patient remains on steroids.

Treatment
It is important to use as small a dose of steroid as possible. Bisphosphonates are the bone-sparing agents of choice and reduce the risk of fracture *(Adachi et al. Arthritis Rheum 2001, 44: 202; Nijs et al. N Engl J Med 2006, 355: 675)*. HRT will also reduce bone loss in post-menopausal women on steroids. Calcium and vitmain D have a only modest protective effect. Calcitriol and calcitonin are probably more effective, and may be options for patients in whom bisphosphonates, strontium or raloxifene cannot be used.

Guidelines on the prevention of glucocorticoid-induced osteoporosis have been produced (Bone & Tooth Society / National Osteoporosis Society / Royal College of Physicians guidelines, 2002). In brief, people who are going to be treated with steroids for at least three months and are aged >65 or who have already had a fragility fracture should receive osteoprotective therapy. Others should have a DEXA scan and if the t-score is -1.5 or worse, they too should be treated.

Reduction in bone loss and anti-fracture efficacy of different agents in steroid osteoporosis: strength of evidence
(Bone & Tooth Society / National Osteoporosis Society / Royal College of Physicians guidelines, 2002)

	Spine BMD	Femur BMD	Vertebral #
Alendronate	A	A	A
Risedronate	A	A	A
Cyclic Etidronate	A	A	A
HRT	A	A	?
Raloxifene	?	?	?
Calcium + Vit D	A	A	?
Calcitriol	A	A	?
Calcitonin	A	A	?
PTH	A	A	?

Notes

Notes

Bone Tumours

Mr D Williams, Dr A J Darby, Dr V N Cassar-Pullicino and Mr P Cool
Oncology Unit
Robert Jones & Agnes Hunt Orthopaedic Hospital
Oswestry

Benign Bone Tumours

1. Simple Bone Cyst
(Solitary Bone Cyst or Unicameral Bone Cyst)

Clinical Features
♦ Often present a pathological fracture in bone of child or adolescent

Investigation
♦ X-ray +/- CT scan
♦ Needle biopsy/aspiration

Treatment
♦ Steroid injection
♦ Curettage and grafting

Prognosis
♦ Can resolve spontaneously after fracture

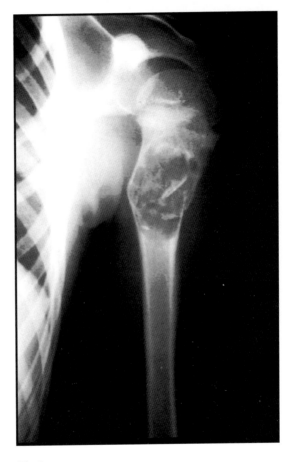

Fig.1

2. Aneurysmal Bone Cyst

Clinical Features

- Pain and swelling (variable time scale)
- Neurological symptons in spine lesions
- Pathological fracture

Investigation

- X-ray/CT Scan/Isotope bone scanning
- Needle biopsy

Treatment

- Curettage +/- bone grafting
- Low dosage radiotherapy

Prognosis

- Cured by complete removal
- More likely to recur in the younger patient

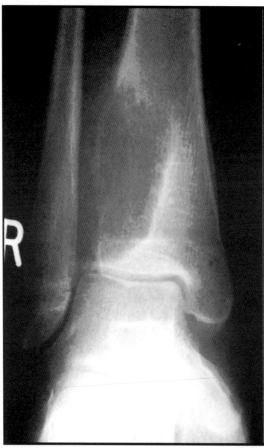

Fig.2

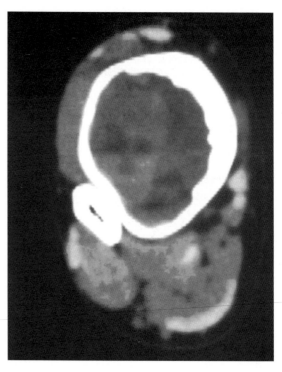

Fig.3

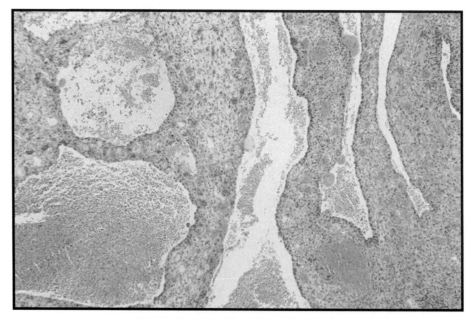

Fig.4

Basic Science for FRCS (Trauma and Orthopaedics)

Enchondroma

Clinical Features
♦ 60% occur in hand and feet
♦ Typical age at presentation: 35
♦ Pain - sometimes after mild trauma
♦ Mainly solitary

Special Features
♦ Olliers disease and Maffucci's syndrome

Treatment
♦ Curettage ± graft

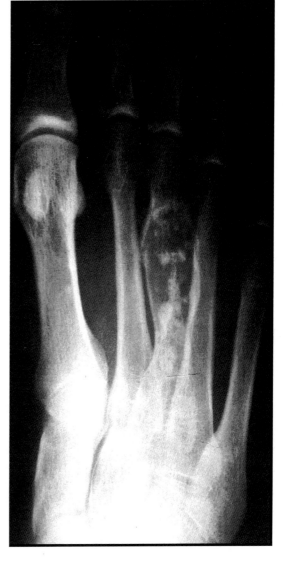

Fig.5

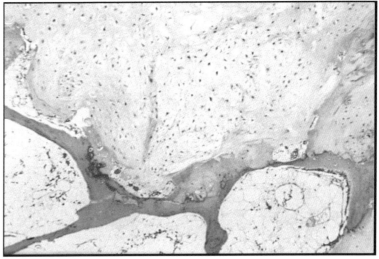

Fig.6

Osteochondroma

Clinical Features
- Presents as hard lump ± local discomfort
- Mechanical problems most commonly around the knee
- Can grow quite rapidly in the immature skeleton

Investigation
- X-ray ± Isotope Bone Scan ± CT scan

Treatment
- Basal excision

Prognosis
- Cured by complete excision

Special Features
- Less than 1% undergo malignant degeneration (to chondrosarcoma)
- Multiple hereditary = Diaphyseal Aclasia

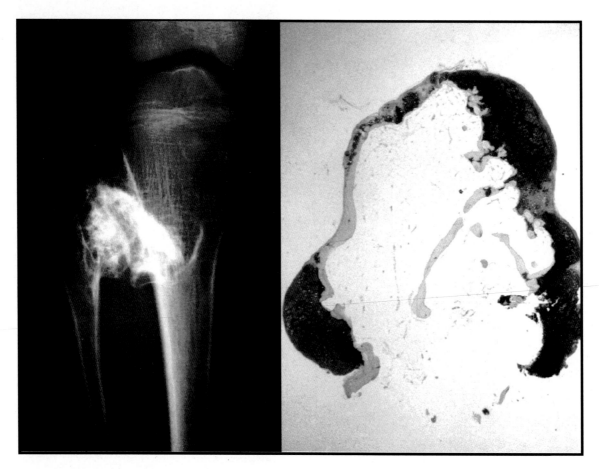

Fig.7

Fibrous Dysplasia

Clinical Features
- Asymptomatic or bone pain
- Usually present by age of 10 years
- May produce progressive bone deformity (curve)

Investigation
- X-ray (ground glass appearance, endosteal scalloping, shepherd's crook deformity in femoral neck)
- Needle biopsy
- Isotope bone scan
- CT-scan will define extent of lesion

Treatment
- Monostotic lesions may require no treatment
- Larger symptomatic lesions require internal fixation and bone grafting
- No role for radiotherapy

Special Features
- Albright's Syndrome = polyostotic lesions + precocious puberty + skin pigmentation

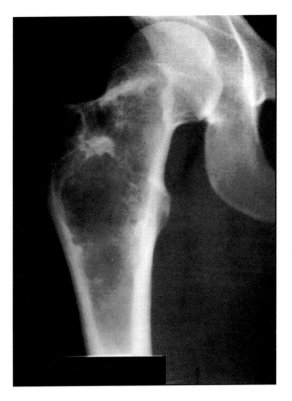

Fig.8

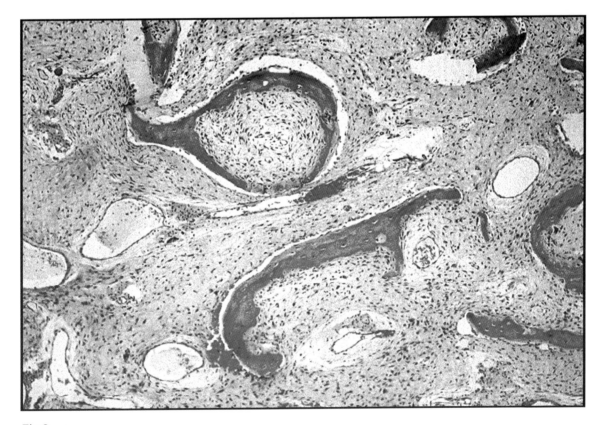

Fig.9

Chondroblastoma

Clinical Features
◆ Onset of local pain and swelling over several months
◆ Usually long bones; most commonly tibia or femur
◆ Epiphyseal lesion of adolescence

Investigation
◆ X-ray/CT-scan/MRI/Isotope bone scan
◆ Needle biopsy

Treatment
◆ En bloc resection and grafting
◆ Curettage and grafting

Prognosis
◆ Will recur after incomplete excision
◆ "Benign" lung mets have been described

Special Features
◆ Like Giant cell tumour is often more a "where it is" not "what it is" problem in management
◆ Rare; less than 1% of benign tumours

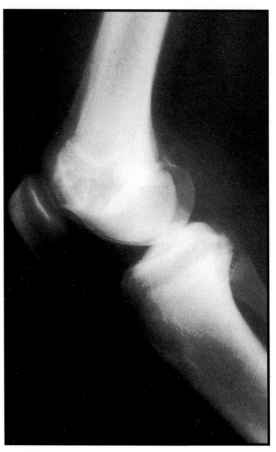

Fig. 10

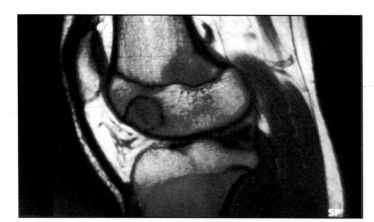

Fig. 11

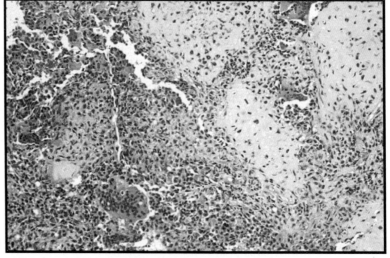

Fig. 12

Basic Science for FRCS (Trauma and Orthopaedics)

Giant Cell Tumour

Clinical Features
- Pain increasing over months
- Swelling
- Pathological fracture

Investigation
- X-ray
- Needle biopsy
- CT-scan/MRI/Isotope bone scan

Treatment
- Curettage ± Bone Graft ± Phenol ± Cement
- Block reaction and allograft
- Wide resection and prosthesis (especially for recurrence)
- Radiotherapy for inaccessible areas (scrum)

Prognosis
- Very liable to recur after incomplete removal
- Recurrence greatest in Grade 3 tumours
- Lesions of the distal radius may be most prone to recurrence

Special Features
- Tumour embolisation can be used effectively

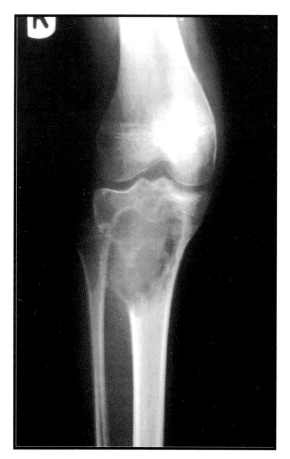

Fig.13

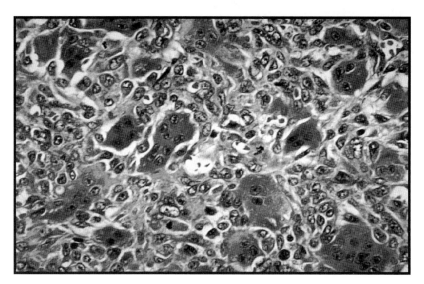

Fig.14

Osteoid Osteoma

Clinical Features
♦ Constant dull pain
♦ Most commonly tibia or femur
♦ relieved by Aspirin

Investigation
♦ X-ray/Isotope bone scan/CT-scan

Treatment
♦ Thermocoagulation/Excision

Prognosis
♦ Cured by complete excision
♦ No malignant potential
♦ Some may resolve spontaneously

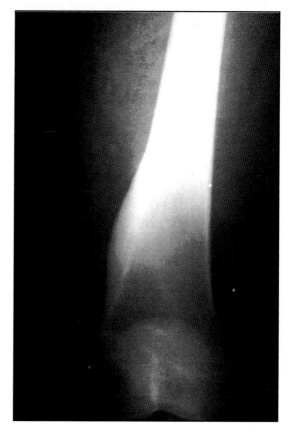

Fig.15

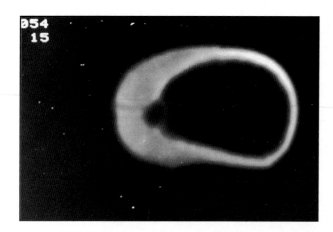

Fig.16

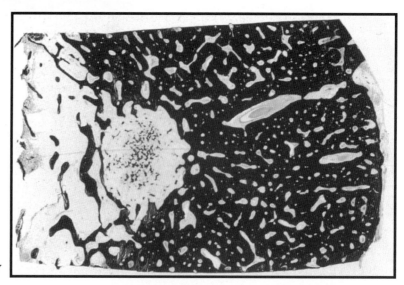

Fig.17

Basic Science for FRCS (Trauma and Orthopaedics)

Osteoblastoma

Clinical Features
♦ Constant dull pain
♦ Painful scoliosis in children

Investigation
♦ X-ray/CT-scan/Isotope bone scan

Treatment
♦ En bloc excision
♦ Curettage and grafting

Prognosis
♦ No recurrence when excision complete
♦ No malignant potential

Eosinophilic Granuloma

Clinical Features
♦ Typically a child (5-10 years) with pain of fairly acute onset in skull, mandible, humerus, rib, proximal femur or scapula
♦ No haematological changes

Investigation
♦ X-ray ("punched out" lytic lesions)
♦ Isotope bone scan/CT-scan
♦ Needle biopsy

Treatment
♦ Small solitary lesions resolve spontaneously
♦ Curettage and grafting for larger lesions
♦ Low dose radiotherapy occasionally used

Special Features
♦ Many form part of more extensive systemic histiocytosis (Hand-Schuller-Christian)
♦ Can present as vertebra plana

Malignant Bone Tumours

Metatastic Disease

Breast
Bronchus
Kidney
Prostate
Thyroid

Enneking Staging (1986)

Benign
♦ Latent
♦ Active
♦ Aggressive

Malignant
♦ **Low grade without metastases**
  ♦ (a) Intra-compartmental
  ♦ (b) Extra-compartmental
♦ **High grade without metastases**
  ♦ (a) Intra-compartmental
  ♦ (b) Extra-compartmental
♦ **Low/High Grade with metastases**
  ♦ (a) Intra-compartmental
  ♦ (b) Extra-compartmental

Staging

♦ CT Lung and Lesion
♦ Isotope bone scan
♦ MRI
♦ Biopsy

Surgical Margins

♦ **Intra-capsular**
  ♦ Within lesion
♦ **Marginal**
  ♦ Within reactive zone, extra-capsular
♦ **Wide**
  ♦ Beyond reactive zone in normal tissue
♦ **Radical**
  ♦ Extra-compartmental

Osteosarcoma

Clinical Features
♦ Gradual onset of pain and swelling
♦ Commonly around the knee of adolescent/young adults
♦ Often "contrived" history of trauma - no recognised trauma association
♦ Night/rest pain

Investigation
♦ X-ray
♦ Full staging
♦ Biopsy; preferably following referral to specialist centre

Treatment
♦ Must be in specialist centre to follow international protocol for oncological and surgical management
♦ Chemotherapy
  ♦ CIS Platimum, Adriamycin
♦ Surgery
  ♦ Limb salvage with prosthesis or graft, amputation, rotationplasty, bone transport for knee arthrodesi

Prognosis
♦ 50-60% 5-year survival
♦ At knee, 5-10% recurrence (AKA or limb salvage)
♦ Limb salvage does not compromise survival

Conventional Osteosarcoma

Conventional (Central) Osteosarcoma
♦ Telangiectatic
♦ Giant cell rich
♦ Round (small) cell

Surface Osteosarcoma
♦ Parosteal (juxtacortical)
♦ Periosteal
♦ High grade

Intra-osseous well-differentiated osteosarcoma

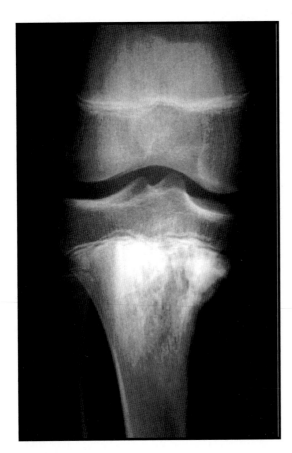

Fig.18

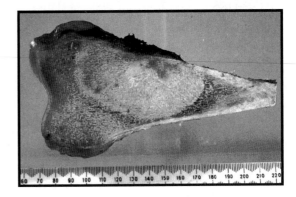

Fig.19

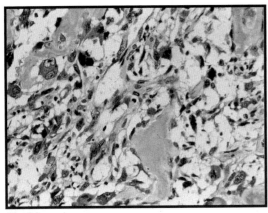

Fig.20

Response to Chemotherapy

Minimum of 30 fields within tumour inspected for extent of necrosis

Response graded
♦ Grade 1 - 50% viable tumour present
♦ Grade 2 - 50-90% necrosis
♦ Grade 3 - 90-99% necrosis
♦ Grade 4 - 100% necrosis

Tested in osteosarcoma and correlates well with survival
♦ Grade 4 responders have 95% 5-year survival rate

Parosteal Osteosarcoma

Clinical Features

- May present with mass only
- Long history
- Older age group (20s)
- 80% occur on posterior aspect of lower femur

Investigation

- X-ray
- Staging as for "conventional" osteosarcoma

Treatment

- Wide surgical resection
- No proven benefit from chemotherapy or radiotherapy

Prognosis

- Cured by wide resection

Special Features

- Prone to "careless" biopsy producing risk of local recurrence

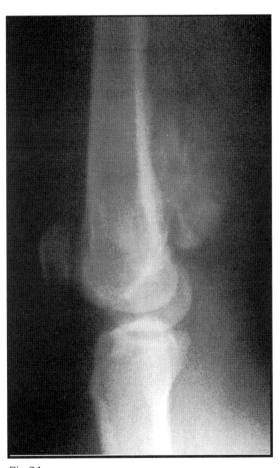

Fig.21

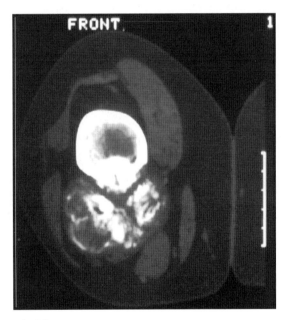

Fig.22

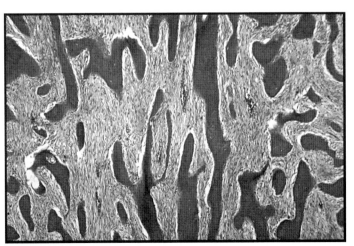

Fig.23

Chondrosarcoma

Clinical Features
♦ Typically a tumour of middle age
♦ Slow growing pelvic tumours may be very large at presentation
♦ Relatively mild local discomfort

Investigation
♦ X-ray
♦ CT-scan
♦ Staging protocol
♦ Open biopsy preferred (be kind to your pathologist!)

Treatment
♦ Wide surgical resection
♦ Prosthesis, hemipelvectomy, hind quarter amputation, Tickhoff-Lindberg at shoulder
♦ No role for chemotherapy or radiotherapy in primary treatment

Prognosis
♦ Depends upon resectability
♦ Tends to spread locally along blood vessels
♦ Metastases to lung
♦ 10-year survival 50%

Special Features
♦ Usually arises de novo (not form pre-existing benign lesions)

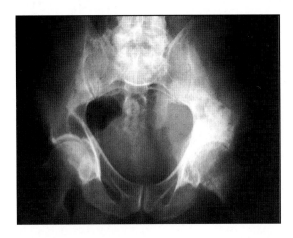

Fig.24

Fig.25

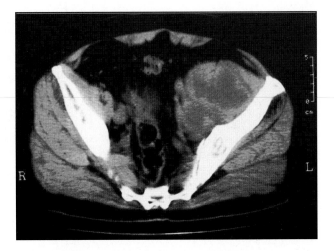

Chondrosarcoma

♦ **Central**
♦ **Periosteal (juxtacortical)**
♦ **Dedifferentiated**
♦ **Clear Cell**
♦ **Mesenchymal**
♦ **Secondary**

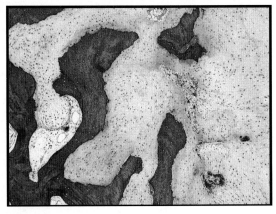

Fig.26

Basic Science for FRCS (Trauma and Orthopaedics)

Ewing's Sarcoma

Clinical Features
- Tumour of childhood and adolescence
- Pain and swelling
- Symptoms increasing over months
- Systemic symptoms (fever and malaise) common

Investigation
- X-ray (appearances vary, especially in adults)
- Full staging
- Biopsy; preferably following referral to a specialist centre
- This tumour is a great mimic of other pathologies (infection)
- Abnormal haematology (raised ESR, leucocytes, anaemia)

Treatment
- Province of paediatric oncology
- Both chemotherapy and radiotherapy are effective
- Role of limb salvage surgery incresaed in recent times
- Permeative tumour and clearance biopsy is essential

Prognosis
Much improved with modern chemotherapy
70% 5-year survival

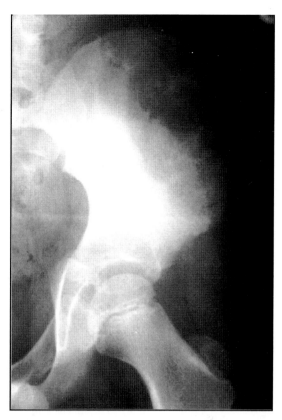

Fig.27

Ewing's Sarcoma

Differential Diagnosis

- **Primitive Neuroectodermal Tumour (PNET)**
- **Non-Hodgkin lymphoma**
- **Metastases**
  - Neuroblastoma
  - Rhabdomyosarcoma
  - Oat cell carcinoma

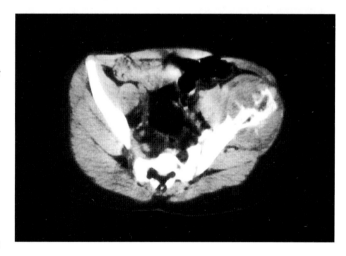

Fig.28

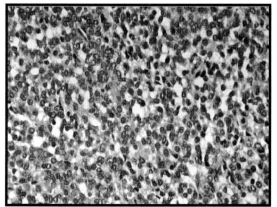

Fig.29

Basic Science for FRCS (Trauma and Orthopaedics)

Multiple Myeloma

Clinical Features
- Most common primary tumout of bone
- Predilection for marrow containing bones (spine, skull, ribs, sternum or pelvis)
- Most commonly inpatents over 50 years of age
- Twice a common in males
- Usually present with pin or occasionally with pathological fracture

Investigation
- Raised ESR, anaemia, hypercalcaemia
- Serum electrophoresis shows monoclonal protein
- Bence-Jones proteins (light chain sub-units) in urine
- Radiographically round lytic defects in bone

Treatment
- Haematological (chemotherapy/bone marro transplantation)
- Radiotherapy
- Treatment of hypercalcaemia
- Renal failure (hypercalcaemia, amyloid, uric acid)
- Fixation of fracture and impending fractures (IM nail)

Prognosis
- 5-year survival 30%

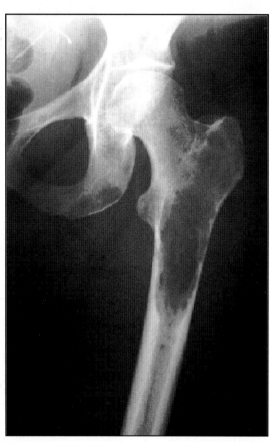

Fig.30

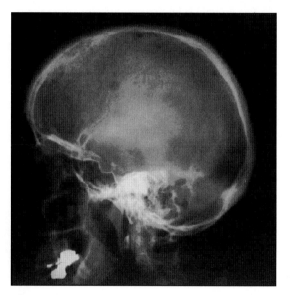

Fig.31

Fibrosarcoma/MFH

Clinical Features
- Pain and swelling of a few months duration
- Pathologial fracture not uncommon
- Long bones affected, rare in axial skeleton

Investigation
- X-ray
- Staging Protocol

Treatment
- Wide resection in true fibrosarcoma
- Permeative nature makes margins unclear, therefore amputation more favoured than limb salvage
- MFH more responsive to chemotherapy and radiotherapy

Prognosis
- Generally poor
- Fibrosarcoma worse than MFH
- 5-year survival 30% in Fibrosarcoma
- 5-year survival 50% in MFH with chemotherapy

Special Features
- Fibrosarcoma is rare
- May be associated with bone infarcts and Paget's

Lymphoma

Clinical Features
- Mainly adult tumour
- Pain, swelling
- Pathological fracture

Investigation
- Staging studies
- Mottled appearance on X-ray
- Poorly defined
- Bone marrow aspiration helpful

Treatment
- Radiotherapy is first line treatment
- Chemotherapy can be effective in systemic disease
- Role of surgery not well defined
- Wide resection or fixation for pathological fracture

Prognosis
- 5-year survival 50%

Notes

Soft Tissue Tumours

Mr P Cool
Consultant Orthopaedic & Oncological Surgeon
Robert Jones & Agnes Hunt Orthopaedic Hospital
Oswestry

Incidence

- Not known!
- ? 40/mill/year
- ~ 2000 Per Year in UK
  - No Registry
- Benign lesions ?? Many not send for Biopsy

Slide 1

History – warning

- > 5 cm
- Deep to fascia
- Increasing in size
- Recurrent
- Painful

Slide 2

Why Specialist Centre ?

- Swedish figures on LR
- 375 Patients
  - Primary Referral   18% LR
  - After Surgery   24% LR
  - Not Referred   45% LR
- **No** effect on survival

Slide 3

Oculo – Brachial Reflex

- A New Pathway with no discernible cortical connection
- Usually active in the presence of an unidentified lump
- Results in shelling out of lump
- Often followed by remorse
- Treatment
  - Try to obtain a cortical connection
  - Usually results in better treatment

Meirion Thomas

Slide 4

Diagnosis

Before treatment!!

Slide 5

Staging

- **S**oft **T**issue **S**welling
- **S**oft **T**issue **S**arcoma
  - **S**top
  - **T**hink
  - **S**tage

Slide 6

Staging

- X-ray lesion
- Chest X-ray
- MRI scan lesion
- (CT scan lesion)
- CT scan Chest

- *Bone scan usually unhelpful*

Slide 7

Biopsy

- In Tumour Treatment Centre
- After Staging
- Trucut (handheld / gun)
  - ? FNA
- Image guided (US/CT/MRI)
- Open Biopsy
  - Failed needle biopsy
  - Close to vital structures

Slide 8

Surgical Treatment

- Margins required depend on biological activity of the tumour

- High grade sarcoma
  - Compartmental excision

Slide 9

Further Treatment

- DXR
  - Omit in low grade lesions that are widely excised
- Chemo
  - Unproven
  - Trial

Slide 10

Survival

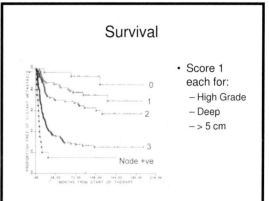

- Score 1 each for:
  - High Grade
  - Deep
  - > 5 cm

Slide 11

Soft Tissue Swelling

- **S**TOP
- **T**HINK
- **S**TAGE

Slide 12

Notes

Metabolic Response to Trauma

Dr R J Alcock and Mr JP Whittaker

Consultant Anaesthetist and Oswestry SPR
Robert Jones & Agnes Hunt Orthopaedic Hospital
Oswestry

Major trauma is associated with a complex sequence of metabolic events. An understanding of these phenomena is vital to the practicing surgeon because of the range of new metabolic therapies that are becoming part of clinical practice. The metabolic markers of these events may also influence the timing of operative intervention, so as to offer the patient the best prognosis.

70 years ago Cuthbertson described two distinct phases after injury. He called them the "Ebb" and "Flow" phases. For the purposes of this article we will call them "Early" and "Late". Ashen facies, thready pulse and clammy extremities are the earliest manifestations of the body's response to trauma. Later, after initial resuscitation, the patient becomes warm and pink with a bounding pulse. There would appear to be two distinct metabolic phases to match these clinical pictures.

The "Early" phase

Characteristics of the early phase are listed in figure 1. These are direct result of a dramatic neuro-endocrine response to tissue injury and possibly hypo-volaemia as a result of haemorrhage. Even with adequate resuscitation with fluids or inotropes, certain features such as fluid retention will continue for some days.

Fig. 1 Nine Characteristics of early phase following trauma

1.	Low core temperature
2.	Low cardiac output
3.	Poor perfusion of musculo-skeletal and splanchnic tissues
4.	Well-maintained perfusion of vital organs
5.	Decreased renal blood flow and urine output causing sodium and water retention
6.	High blood glucose
7.	Decreased energy expenditure
8.	Normal glucose production
9.	Mild protein catabolism

If we leave aside the response of the body to haemorrhage, the main trigger for these events is the afferent pain fibres from the site of tissue injury. A and c fibres carry pain sensation from the site of injury to the ventral posterior nucleus of the thalamus. The response is integrated in the hypothalamus and is largely mediated by two endocrine pathways:

1. Sympathoadrenal-medullary axis, where activation of the sympathetic nervous system causes release of Epinephrine, Dopamine and Nor-epinephrine from the adrenal medulla. Some of the relevant effects of this are listed in figure 2.

Fig. 2 Nine Effects of catecholamine release

1.	Narrowing of arterioles in skin, muscle, kidney and gut
2.	Coronary and pulmonary vasodilatation
3.	Increased heart rate and contractility.
4.	Decreased pancreatic Insulin secretion
5.	Renin release leading to sodium and water retention.
6.	Sweating
7.	Alertness
8.	Agitation
9.	Fear.

2. The hypothalamic pituitary-adrenal axis.

The hypothalamus triggers the pituitary to release ACTH, which causes the adrenal cortex to release glucocorticoids (principally cortisol). Effects of glucocorticoids in this situation are listed in figure 3. The magnitude of the glucocorticoid response correlates with the severity of injury.

Fig. 3 Five main effects of glucocorticoids

1.	Raised blood glucose by the stimulation gluconeogenesis and glycogenolysis
2.	Increased protein breakdown
3.	Lipolysis
4.	Suppression of inflammation
5.	Suppression of hormone release: Gonadotrophins and TSH

Although it can be seen that these endocrine responses can explain the clinical picture seen in the early phase after trauma, it is worth noting that the pituitary gland also co-ordinates rises in prolactin and growth hormone levels that contribute to the response, particularly by causing insulin resistance.

The "Late" Phase

After resuscitation the often swollen patient, now stable and well perfused will enter the late phase, during which profound metabolic interchanges occur. Some of the features are listed in figure 4.

Fig. 4 Twelve Characteristics of late phase following trauma

1.	Raised temperature
2.	Raised cardiac output
3.	Warm, pink peripheries
4.	Diuresis
5.	Increased energy expenditure
6.	Normal or increased blood glucose
7.	Increased glucose production
8.	Raised Insulin (insulin resistance)
9.	**Profound protein breakdown**
10.	Lipid breakdown
11.	Increased GH, Prolactin
12.	Decreased TSH & Gonadotrophins

The most dramatic and consistent feature of this phase is protein breakdown. After severe trauma, nearly one-fifth of the body's protein store may be lost over the first three weeks, most during the first ten days. The protein is largely mobilised from skeletal muscle.

This can lead to problems with weaning from mechanical ventilation and will frequently decrease the patient's mobility, delaying convalescence. The prime reason for the protein breakdown is the need for two amino acids, glutamine and alanine, as substrate. Glutamine is a fuel for the cells of the immune system, contributing to a rise in acute phase reactants, whilst alanine is the main gluconeogenic amino acid.

Although the endocrine response we looked at above will contribute to this catabolic state, this degree of protein breakdown cannot be explained by the neuro-endocrine responses alone. Indeed catecholamine levels frequently return to normal within a few days. Many people have observed that the changes that occur are very similar to those seen with sepsis and multi-organ failure. We will look at the other potential causes of these phenomena.

Cytokines

As we mentioned earlier one of the body's responses to trauma is the production of acute phase reactants by the liver. This is probably due to the presence in the blood stream of cytokines produced by leukocytes at the site of injury. It is likely that these cytokines are also at least partially responsible for the on-going metabolic changes that accompany the "late" phase. The main cytokines that have been associated with this process are interleukin 1, (IL1), interleukin 6, (IL6) and tumour necrosis factor, (TNF). Receptors for these substances are found throughout the body. The cytokine response to injury or indeed

sepsis can be monitored directly by measuring IL6 levels or indirectly by measuring the C reactive protein. Effects of TNF and the interleukins are shown in figure 5.

Fig. 5 Seven Effects of cytokines following trauma

1.	Pyrexia
2.	Hepatic production of acute phase proteins
3.	Leukocyte stimulation
4.	Increased metabolic rate
5.	Hepatic gluconeogenesis
6.	Whole body protein breakdown
7.	Stimulation of the hypothalamic-pituitary-adrenal axis

It appears that Cytokines work in synergy with the hormonal changes to promote the body's response to trauma.

Other inflammatory triggers

Neutrophils and macrophages that are attracted to the site of injury produce a wide range of substances in addition to the cytokines mentioned above. These include platelet activating factor, oxygen free radicals, nitric oxide, and arachadonic acid derivatives such as prostacyclin. There is activation of complement and the clotting cascade. All these mediators released from the site of injury have the potential to fuel this process. The relative importance of these substances is still not entirely clear.

Role of the gut

It is a widely accepted theory that the gut has a major role in the development of multiple organ failure. This is thought to be due to the translocation of bacterial endotoxin across the wall of the GI tract. This is fuelled by a number of factors including the systemic inflammatory response and ischaemia / reperfusion injury. As noted earlier there is a similarity between the body's response to sepsis and to trauma. It may be that the gut has a role in this common pathway of the body's response to insult, particularly where trauma is the precursor of multiple organ failure.

Role of immobility

Bed rest in itself causes protein catabolism and increased glucagon and cortisol levels. Whilst these changes are not of the magnitude of those after trauma, it may be that immobility does contribute to the process.

Timing of Surgery

Surgery in the trauma patient provides a second insult, which in at risk patients can precipitate multi-organ failure and worsen the prognosis. IL6 levels provide a good guide to the inflammatory response to the insults of both trauma and surgery. Following the work of several authors, Giannoudis has proposed the concept of "damage control orthopaedics". In many trauma patients early definitive fixation of fractures may be appropriate and may cause very little in the way of a secondary inflammatory response to the insult (as measured by IL6 levels). However, there is a group of at risk patients who benefit from early temporary stabilisation of their fractures using external fixation, followed by definitive surgery later. Factors that render patients at risk are listed below.

Fig. 6 Factors that render patients at risk of definitive primary surgery

Multiple injuries with an injury severity score (ISS) > 20 with thoracic trauma.
Multiple injuries with abdominal / pelvic trauma and haemorrhagic shock.
ISS >40
Radiographic (CXR or CT) evidence of bilateral pulmonary contusion.
Admission platelet count of < 95 X103/ml.
Admission temperature of < 32 C.
Initial mean pulmonary arterial pressure > 24mmHg.
PaO2 / FiO2 < 200 mmHg on admission.
Interleukin-6 level > 600 pg/ml.

The Injury Severity Score (ISS) applies the Abbreviated Injury Scale (AIS) to predict outcome. The ISS is calculated by adding the 3 highest AIS squared. The AIS for the six different body areas (head & neck, abdomen & pelvic organs, bony pelvis & limbs, face, chest, and body surface) are found in a code book for a multitude of injuries, with a minor injury scoring 1 to a fatal injury scoring 6. Therefore the ISS ranges from 3 $(1^2+1^2+1^2)$ to 75 $(5^2+5^2+5^2)$.

When should definitive surgery be performed? Pape demonstrated that both the rise in IL 6 levels and the incidence of multiple organ failure was decreased if definitive surgery was performed at 5 to 8 days as opposed to 2 to 4 days post trauma.

Conclusion

The body's response to trauma can conveniently be divided into early and late phases. These responses probably have different but multi-factorial and complex origins. Whilst neuro-endocrine responses are undoubtedly important in the early phase, cytokines, inflammatory mediators, altered gut permeability and immobility may also have a role in the late phase. Knowledge of these processes may help us to assess the optimum timing for definitive surgery following trauma.

References

Woolf P: Hormonal response to trauma. Crit Care Med. 1992;20: 216-26.

Hill A.G. Hill G.L.. Metabolic response to severe injury. Br J Surg, 1998;85: 884-90.

Giannoudis P.V. Aspects of current management. Surgical priorities in damage control in polytrauma. J Bone Joint Surg 2003;85B: 478-83.

Pape H.C, van Griensen M, Rice J et al. Major secondary surgery in blunt trauma patients and peri-operative cytokine liberation. Determination of the clinical relevance of biochemical markers. J Trauma 2001;50: 989-1000.

Notes

Basic Science for FRCS (Trauma and Orthopaedics)

Antibacterials

Dr Rod Warren

Director of Microbiology
Microbiology Laboratory,
Royal Shrewsbury Hospital,
Shrewsbury

Honorary Consultant
Medical Microbiologist,
Robert Jones and Agnes Hunt
Orthopaedic Hospital,
Oswestry

Bug & drug. The concept and implications of antibiotic spectrum and bacterial flora.

Human pharmacology is largely concerned with:
· an interaction between human enzymes that are target sites and the drug,
· drug pharmacokinetics, and
· any issues of specificity in the target site that may lead to unwanted effects: there is no significant issue that the drug target may change or be protected by mechanisms that can change by mutation or acquisition of new genetic information that protects the target site. Problems therefore relate only to two genomes - the patient and the prescriber!

With antibiotics and antiseptics, which are biocidal compounds, three genomes are involved - the addition of the microbe! The difference is that the generation time for division is 10 minutes and resistance can rapidly evolve or Darwinian selection by the antibiotic can change the bacterial population, even within the course of a single infection. The bacterial target site may:

· be innately differently accessible by bacterial species (i.e. Table 1 Innate spectrum) or
· rapidly mutate (e.g. one step single point mutation to resistance e.g. in staphylococci with rifampicin, fucidin and quinolone resistance.
These one step mutations are in the previous examples mutations in the target site for the antibiotic but one step mutations can be in the promoter and repressor genes that control regulation of the expression of the gene that controls expression of the resistance mechanism e.g. stable de-repression of the cephalosporinase, Amp C, in Enterobacter cloacae, a coliform, or the promoter gene that represses expression of clindamycin resistance in strains of staphylococci that are erythromycin resistant by the MLS ^{B} mechanism
· acquire single or multiple extrinsic genetic resistance mechanisms by genetic exchange with other bacteria e.g. plasmid acquisition, bacteriophage transduction, or bacterial transformation by free DNA. Examples of the first are the usual mechanism in Gram-negative species but all three occur in Gram-positive species. Plasmids often contain self- transferring cassettes of multiple resistances, which transfer between plasmids and chromosomes en-bloc and may further pick up further resistances by single self transmitting genes called transposons either from other plasmids or the bacterial chromosome or by small assemblies of genes called integrons. These resistance mechanisms involve many agents, not just antibiotics. Mercurial resistance has remained stably associated with the penicillinase plasmid for 60 years and dates back to the use of Mercurochrome as an early surgical antiseptic. Other metal resistances such as cadmium are also plasmid mediated. Low-level chlorhexidine and cetrimide resistance are plasmid-mediated resistances of unknown clinical significance that are common in MRSA

Table 1 Innate resistances
R-always resistant
U -not known at time of going to press!
No. Average% acquired resistance - may vary by species

DRUG/BUG	Group A,B,C,F,G/viridans streptococcus	Streptococcus pneumoniae	Enterococcus faecalis	Enterococcus faecium	Staphylococcus aureus/epidermidis	Leuconostoc/Pediococcus	Bacillus	Coryneforms and Propionibacterium	Listeria	Neisseria gonorrhoeae/meningitides	Moraxella	Haemophilus	Campylobacter	Escherichia coli
Colistin	R	R	R	R	R	R	R	R	R	R	0	0	R	0
Sulphonamides	R	A	R	R	A	U	R	U	0	10-20	U	R	R	A
Trimethoprim	R	R	R	R	20	U	U	U	0	R	U	10	R	30
Quinupristin/Dalfopristin	0	0	0	0	0	U	U	U	U	U	U	U	R	R
Tetracyclines	20	5	80	90	10	U	U	U	U	U	U	5	U	A
Cipro/Nor/O-floxacin	U	R	R	R	50	U	0	U	U	0-10	0	1	20	10
Nitrofurantoin	R	U	0	0	0	U	U	U	R	U	R	R	U	0
Clindamycin	5	8	R	R	40	U	U	U	R	R	R	R	U	R
Erythromycin	5	12	80	80	40	U	0	U	U	R	0	R	0-5	R
Fusidic acid	R	R	U	U	0-10	U	U	U	U	R	R	R	R	R
Chloramphenicol	U	U	R	R	U	U	U	U	U	U	U	5	U	30
Linezolid	0	0	1	1	0	U	U	U	0	R	R	R	R	R
Rifampicin	0	0	R	R	1-5	U	U	U	U	U	U	U	R	R
Vancomycin/Teicoplanin	0	0	1	20	0	R	0	0	0	R	R	R	R	R
Ertapenem	0	1	R	R	50	U	U	U	R	U	U	U	U	0
Imipenem	0	1	0	R	50	U	U	U	R	0	0	U	U	0
Cefotaxime	0	1	R	R	50	U	U	U	R	0	0	0-1	R	10
Ceftazidime	0	5	R	R	50	U	U	U	R	0	0	0-1	R	10
Cefuroxime	0	5	R	R	50	U	U	U	R	0	0	5	R	10
Piperacillin/tazobactam	0	U	0	R	R	U	U	U	0	0	0	5	U	10
Flucloxacillin	0	5	R	R	50	U	U	U	R	R	R	R	R	R
Coamoxiclav	0	5	0	R	50	0	U	U	0	0	0	5	U	10
Amoxycillin	0	5	0	R	95	0	0-90	5	0	0-5	0-80	15	R	40
Penicillin	0-5	5	0	R	95	0	0-90	5	0	0-5	0-80	R	R	R
Aminoglycosides (gentamicin)	R	R	R	R	10-60	U	0	U	0	R	0	0	0	1

Basic Science for FRCS (Trauma and Orthopaedics)

Table 1 Innate resistances
R – always resistant
U – not known at time of going to press!
No. Average% acquired resistance – may vary by species

DRUG / BUG	Klebsiella	Citrobacter	Salmonella	Enterobacter	Serratia	Proteus	Providencia	Morganella	Pseudomonas	Stenotrophomonas	Acinetobacter	Bacteroides fragilis	Clostridium perfringens
Colistin	0	0	0	0	R	R	R	R	1-5	0	U	R	R
Sulphonamides	50	50	U	50	R	A	A	A	R	10	A	R	A
Trimethoprim	30	10	0-30	10	R	0-30	10	10	R	R	80	R	R
Quinupristin/Dalfopristin	R	R	R	R	R	R	R	R	R	R	R	R	U
Tetracyclines	A	A	A	A	A	R	R	R	R	R	U	30	U
Cipro/Nor/O-floxacin	10	10	0-30	10	10	0-5	0-5	0-5	10	R	50	R	U
Nitrofurantoin	10	U	R	U	U	R	R	R	R	R	20	U	U
Clindamycin	R	R	R	R	R	R	R	R	R	R	R	0-5	0
Erythromycin	R	R	R	R	R	R	R	R	R	R	R	U	U
Fusidic acid	R	R	R	R	R	R	R	R	R	R	R	U	U
Chloramphenicol	U	U	0-30	U	R	U	U	U	R	U	U	U	U
Linezolid	R	R	R	R	R	R	R	R	R	R	R	R	0
Rifampicin	R	R	R	R	R	R	R	R	R	R	R	0	U
Vancomycin/Teicoplanin	R	R	R	R	R	R	R	R	R	R	R	0	0
Ertapenem	0	0	0	0	0	5	5	5	R	R	5	0	0
Imipenem	0	0	0	0	0	5	5	5	10	R	5	0	0
Cefotaxime	10	20	0-10	20	0-10	5	5	5	R	R	20	R	0
Ceftazidime	10	20	0-10	20	0-10	5	5	5	R	R	20	R	0
Cefuroxime	20	R	0-10	R	R	10	0-90	10	R	R	20	R	0
Piperacillin/tazobactam	10	10	0-10	10	10	10	10	10	5	50	U	0	0
Flucloxacillin	R	R	R	R	R	R	R	R	R	R	R	R	R
Coamoxiclav	20	90	0-10	90	R	10-100	0-90	R	R	R	5	0	0
Amoxycillin	R	R	0-30	R	R	10-100	0-90	R	R	R	20	R	0
Penicillin	R	R	R	R	R	R	R	R	R	R	R	R	0
Aminoglycosides (gentamicin)	5	5	0	5	5	0	5	0	10	R	20	R	R

DRUG/BUG	Clostridium septicum	Peptostreptococcus	Mycobacterium	Mycoplasma	Chlamydia	Legionella	Spirochaetes inc. Borrelia
Colistin	R	R	R	o	R	U	R
Sulphonamides	U	U	R	R	R	R	R
Trimethoprim	R	R	R	R	R	U	R
Quinupristin/Dalfopristin	U	U	R	U	U	U	U
Tetracyclines	U	U	R	0-10	o	U	o
Cipro/Nor/O-floxacin	o	U	10	o	o	o	U
Nitrofurantoin	U	U	R	R	R	R	R
Clindamycin	o	o	R	R	R	R	U
Erythromycin	U	U	R	0-90	o	o	o
Fusidic acid	U	U	R	U	R	R	U
Chloramphenicol	U	U	R	U	U	R	U
Linezolid	U	o	U	o	o	U	U
Rifampicin	U	o	1-5	U	o	o	R
Vancomycin/Teicoplanin	o	o	R	R	R	R	U
Ertapenem	o	o	R	R	R	R	U
Imipenem	o	o	R	R	R	R	U
Cefotaxime	R	o	R	R	R	R	U
Ceftazidime	R	o	R	R	R	R	U
Cefuroxime	o	o	R	R	R	R	o
Piperacillin/tazobactam	o	o	R	R	R	R	U
Flucloxacillin	R	U	R	R	R	R	U
Coamoxiclav	o	o	R	R	R	R	U
Amoxycillin	o	o	R	R	R	R	o
Penicillin	o	o	R	R	R	R	o
Aminoglycosides (gentamicin)	R	R	R	o	R	o	R

Table 1 Innate resistances
R-always resistant
U -not known at time of going to press!
No. Average% acquired resistance - may vary by species

Genetic resistance transfer mechanisms therefore exist at the level of:
· plasmid
· cassette
· INTEGRON
· transposon.

Proteomic mechanisms of antibiotic resistance include:
· Target site change
· Prevention of access to target either by specific enzyme degradation of the drug or permeability change in external bacterial membranes or both
· augmented efflux mechanisms for drug transport out of the bacterium, which may involve multiple antibiotics

For any one drug multiple mechanisms of resistance may occur.

Bacterial receptor interactions of the antibiotic and other drugs may affect the inhibitory effect. For example the B-lactamase inhibitors clavulanic acid and tazobactam permit respectively amoxycillin and piperacillin to have activity against anaerobes, staphylococci and some but not all B-lactamase producing coliforms. Human receptor interactions are also important. Methotrexate a dihydrofolate reductase inhibitor used frequently in rheumatoid arthritis shares a renal tubular excretion mechanism with Trimethoprim a bacterial dihydrofolate reductase inhibitor. Using the drugs together can result in methotrexate accumulation and agranulocytosis.

To summarise each antibiotic and antiseptic has a spectrum of innate activity against different bacterial groups, genera and species and in addition the spectrum is influenced by prevalence of acquired antibiotic resistance.

Acquired antibiotic resistance relates to previous exposure of bacteria to a drug and is rare in the early life of drugs when they are undergoing clinical trial but commoner later when there has been widespread exposure to the drug. This means early and published clinical trials are often an unreliable guide to subsequent usage and that cross infection of bacteria is also important in affecting the usefulness of an antibiotic. The likely species in which acquired resistance will emerge also depends on the natural ecosystem in which a particular bacterial species lives and its exposure there to antibacterial agents. Common ecosystems important in infection in orthopaedics include both the skin and the oro-gastrointestinal tract. The principle of selection in the ecosystem by the local antibiotic concentration for emergent acquired antibiotic resistant strains applies equally to innate resistant species selection in the ecosystem.

The normal skin flora consists of a variety of staphylococci includes both the large numbers of coagulase-negative staphylococci of which S.epidermidis and S haemolyticus are important, S aureus, and anaerobic and microaerophilic Gram positive bacilli commonly called diphtheroids and including Propionibacterium acnes and Brevibacterium sp. At different sites there are different organisms. Staphylococcus capitis as the name implies is found on the scalp: Brevibacterium is found where there are apocrine glands in axilla and groin. All these skin bacteria are accessible to both lipophilic antibiotics such as tetracyclines and macrolides (e.g. erythromycin) excreted in sebum and hydrophilic antibiotics such as quinolones (e.g. ciprofloxacin, levofloxacin, moxifloxacin, norfloxacin) excreted in sweat. For new antibiotics the selective site may be predicted. Linezolid in labelling experiments reaches the surface of the skin well. The bacterial population of the skin, like the oro-gastrointestinal tract is very large and resistant forms occurring even with, for example, mutation rates as low as 1 in 109 may be rapidly selected with antibiotics even used for infections at non-skin sites. Even in normal patients from the community, resistant bacteria are said to be frequent. In hospital environments quinolone and macrolide resistance are very frequent. Exogenous agents such as topical antibiotics are now supplemented as selective agents by a range of antiseptics incorporated into everyday products ranging from Chlorhexidine (Microban) in chopping boards to quaternary ammonium compounds related to cetrimide etc in fabric softeners and hand-soaps. Some antibiotics are polar and do not penetrate well onto the skin surface from systemic use e.g. gentamicin, tobramycin, vancomycin, teicoplanin. Data on cephalosporins and penicillins is thin but there is suggestive but not conclusive data that widespread overuse of quinolones and cephalosporins in hospitals selects for high prevalence of MRSA. Some patients receive long term topical or oral tetracyclines, erythromycin or clindamycin to treat skin flora and reduce acne and are selective for resistant acne bacilli and staphylococci. Patients with chronic atopic dermatitis have increased S aureus colonisation rates and there is some controversy over whether this also is the case in psoriasis and related conditions.

The gastrointestinal flora contains a very diverse mixture of anaerobes including bacteroides, clostridia and anaerobic streptococci and also aerobes, which includes staphylococci and enterococci as well as the diverse Gram negative bacilli (e.g. Escherichia coli, Klebsiella sp, Enterobacter sp, Proteus sp, and Pseudomonas aeruginosa). It is affected by exogenous acquisition of organisms from food, drink and anything else put into the mouth, and by antibacterials that are not completely absorbed e.g. penicillins, and quinolones - or are excreted by the biliary route in sufficient concentrations to select in the small and large bowel flora e.g. quinolones second and third generation cephalosporins. Compounds with high innate activity (therapeutic index) such as quinolones, cephalosporins and penicillins and biliary excretion are likely to have a selective effect whereas those with low therapeutic indices (e.g. gentamicin) and low biliary excretion (e.g. vancomycin and gentamicin) are less likely to be selective. The therapeutic index for an antibiotic is the ratio between the effective concentration reached at a site and the antibacterial concentration (commonly termed the minimum inhibitory concentration or MIC. It is worth considering that there is a selective index in any body fluid compartment: the maximum MIC of a resistant isolate and the local concentration of the drug. High local concentrations can produce a low selective index and avoid selection of resistant isolates.

A number of key issues with antibacterial use emerge from this.
· What are the likely infecting organisms at a site?
· What antibiotics are they likely to be sensitive to (dependent on knowledge of spectrum)?
· What is the most certain and appropriate single drug or combination to cover this spectrum without emergence of resistance on treatment?
· Does the drug reach the site of infection and how must it be administered to do this?
· What unwanted effects does the drug have including selection of resistant flora that imperils future use of the antibacterial again if organisms from the flora spread to other patients?

Conventional antibiotic sensitivity testing applies to rapidly growing free planktonic bacteria rather than slow growing organisms in bio films where, with penicillins, cephalosporins, aminoglycosides and glycopeptides, it is difficult to demonstrate any antibacterial activity. Rifampicin seems to be an exception that has some 3 logs of activity against the very slow growing Gram-positive organisms in bio films. Despite widespread speculation that this is the case, there is as yet no evidence that bio films exist on orthopaedic implants or bone matrix although they are demonstrable in intravascular implants and in respiratory secretions. Having said this, clinical trials that show special benefits of rifampicin in prosthetic infection may suggest that bio films are present.

Drug and bug classes

Some limitations about antibiotic testing also apply to the antibiotic concentration reached in a particular site. Nitrofurantoin only reaches adequate antibacterial concentrations in the renal tubule and is ineffective in systemic infection and so well absorbed it does not appear to select in the gut flora. There are also restrictions on antibacterials relating to killing of bacteria within phagolysosomes of polymorphs and macrophages and within abscesses. These low pH environments make drugs such as aminoglycosides inactive. Large polar molecules such as aminoglycosides and glycopeptides do not penetrate into the neutrophil well whereas small lipophilic molecules such as rifampicin and teracyclines do. One important anti-tuberculous antibiotic, pyrazinamide only shows anti-tuberculous activity at the very acid pH of the phagolysosomes.

Conventional antibiotic susceptibilities are now tested by disc and automated methodologies or by the reference method the Minimum Inhibitory Concentration of the antibiotic. Beware that there is US and national variation in the concentrations considered to be inhibitory and this may make comparisons of clinical response when an agent is said to be active against the cause of infection different in each country!. The usual UK premise is that the MIC should relate to a concentration of the drug that is achieved at the site of infection for 60% of the inter-dose interval but lower percentages are sometimes relevant. These guidelines are published by most countries but are only slowly reaching a consensus and agreed position due the desire for exactitude in predicting clinical response in patients from in-vitro tests against bacteria. Some US publications seem to relate more to peak concentrations! Similarly there are variations in how the percentage of strains is recorded as resistant. Sometimes the MIC^{90} is recorded - the MIC for 90% of strains - but it is more useful for clinicians to refer to the percentage of strains below a breakpoint MIC determined as above - although this may not always correlate with a resistance mechanism

Bacterial groups can be crudely but usefully classified on their spectrum when Gram-stained and whether they a re obligate anaerobes or can grow aerobically. See Table 2. The Gram-stain reaction of an antibiotic is determined by its cell wall structure and permeability

Table 2		Aerobes	Anaerobes
Cocci			
	Gram-positive	Staphylococci	
		Streptococci	Peptostreptococcus
		Enterococci	
	Gram-negative	Neisseria	Veillonella
Bacilli			
	Gram-positive	Bacillus	Clostridium
		Corynebacterium / Propionibacterium	
	Gram-negative	Escherichia coli	Bacteroides
		Klebsiella / Citrobacter	Porphyromonas
		Enterobacter / Serratia	Prevotella
		Proteus / Morganella	
		Salmonella / Shigella	
		Pseudomonas / Acinetobacter	

Basic Science for FRCS (Trauma and Orthopaedics)

Drug and bug classification make it easier to describe the spectrum and discuss the use of individual antibiotics. Some indications of spectrum are given in Table 1.

Drug classes include:
- B-lactams -
    cephalosporins,
    penicillins,
    carbapenems (Imipenem, ertapenem, meropenem)
- B lactams plus B lactamase inhibitors (coamoxiclav & tazobactam)
- Aminoglycosides - gentamicin, tobramycin, amikacin
- Glycopeptides - vancomycin, teicoplanin, (oritovancin,ramiplanin,dalbovancin not yet marketed in UK)

- Lipopeptides - daptomycin (not yet licensed in the UK)
- Macrolides - erythromycin, clarithromycin
- Lincosamines - clindamycin
- Streptogramins - quinopristin/dalfopristin
- Steroids - fucidin
- Quinolones - ciprofloxacin, ofloxacin, norfloxacin, levofloxacin, moxifloxacin
- Nitroimidazoles - metronidazole
- Tetracyclines - oxytetracycline, doxycycline, minocyline
- Oxazolidonones - linezolid
- Rifamycins - rifampicin, rifabutin
- Pseudomonic acids - mupirocin.

The site of action of these antibiotics is shown in Figure 1 and Table 3.

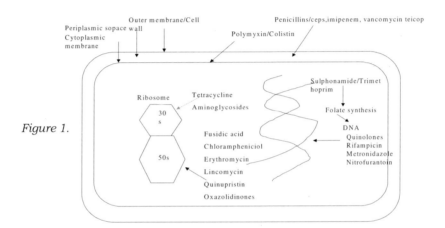

Figure 1.

Table 3. Agents and targets

Agent	Target	Effect
B-lactams (penicillins/cephalosporins/carbapenems	Cell wall transpeptidase	Blocks cross-linking of cell wall and cell wall division/growth
Glycopeptides (vancomycin/teicoplanin)	Cell wall acyl-0-alanyl D alanine	Block interstitial growth of bacterial cell wall
Antifols (suphonamides/trimethoprims	Folate synthesis -Pteroate synthetase/Dihydrofolate reductase	Blocks tetrahydrofolate synthesis and 1 carbon transfer into pyrimidine synthesis
Quinolones	DNA gyrase and toposiomerase 4	Blocks packaging and coiling of DNA
Rifamycins (rifampicin)	DNA dependent RNA polymerase B unit	Blocks RNA transcription from DNA
Metronidazole	Electron transport & DNA damage	At low redox potential generates reduced nitro compound that damages DNA
Fusidic acid	Elongation and peptide translocation on ribosome	Blocks peptide movement on ribosome
Chloramphenicol	Ribosomal peptidyl transferase	Blocks polypeptide elongation
Macrolides and lincosamines (erythromycin and clindamycin)	Interfere with peptide binding sites on ribosome	Block peptide binding and movement on ribosome
Streptogramins (Quinopristin/dalfopristin)	Block attachment of t- RNA and peptide bond formation	Block polypeptide elongation
Tetracyclines	Block 30s binding of tRNA	Block polypeptide elongation
Oxazolidonones (Linezolid)	Block ribosome 50s association with 30s	Prevent ribosome function
Aminoglycosides (Gentamicin, tobramycin, streptomycin, amikacin)	Make ribosomes inoperative in translation of mRNA	Bactericidal as protein synthesis totally irreversibly stopped

Some antibiotics do not penetrate across the Gram-negative cell wall and are only active against Gram-positive bacteria. These include glycopeptides, fusidic acid and oxazolidonones, streptogramins and for practical purposes rifamycins.

It is important to note that drug-bug classes need to be considered when considering dosing intervals and what the key factors are in assaying antibiotics for adequacy. This is because of the existence of post-antibiotic effect. For most drugs and particularly the bacteristatic agents, the organism will start regrowing immediately the antibiotic concentration at the site of the organism falls below the MIC. This means that trough concentrations are the key measure of efficacy. For vancomycin the trough must not fall below 5mg/l and to avoid any peak concentration that has conceivably been described as toxic should not be above 12mg/l (although these toxicities are only described with older impure compounds and higher concentrations may not be toxic. For teicoplanin many authorities consider trough concentrations should exceed 20mg/l and this can only be achieved if a loading dose is given. For aminoglycosides such as gentamicin it takes the organism time to recover after a peak dose. The higher the peak the longer the post-antibiotic effect. For this reason once daily dosing is preferred in most but not all cases in preference to the previous thrice daily dosing. Drug concentration should be measured 6-14 hours after dosing and if 7mg/Kg is used can be interpreted from a validated nomogram. The lower concentration of 5mg/Kg has not been validated as regards efficacy and toxicity nor have bd schedules. Measuring trough levels on once daily dosing is below the sensitivity of assays used in the UK and is not advised. Catching a peak level is difficult to time. If tds doses are used then peaks should lie between 5-10mg/l and the trough should be <2mg/l. Penicillins and cephalosporins have modest post-antibiotic effects.

It has become fashionable to use antimicrobials in combination. This originated in the need in empirical therapy whilst awaiting laboratory results to cover the spectrum of microbes that might be responsible for the infection with a range of agents with complementary spectra of activity. It was also known that endocarditis often required use of two agents for a successful outcome. Extensive work was done on whether specific combinations were synergic, antagonistic or produce no additional effect (indifference) and regimens were assessed for synergic activity. For example penicillins and gentamicin are often synergic because the damage to the cell wall produced by the penicillin permits gentamicin to get across the cell wall and reach its ribosomal target. It has since become clear that in most cases synergic antibiotics do not improve therapeutic outcome per se and that single agents determine the outcome of treatment and can be used just as effectively. There are reasons to use two antibiotics together if there is the possibility of one step mutation to resistance with one of the agents and also issues where antibiotics do not penetrate to the same sites where organisms are present. It is often stated that large molecules do not penetrate well but there is evidence more that penetration of certain agents is erratic for reasons that are not understood. Care should be taken with using certain agents together. Bacteristatic inhibitors of protein synthesis such as tetracyclines can block the synthesis of the enzyme targets for penicillins for example and render the agent of choice for the infection ineffective - permitting regrowth of the organism when the bacteristatic antibiotic is stopped, whereas if the bacteristatic agent had not been used the bactericidal antibiotic would have killed the organism.

Antibiotic combinations in definitive as distinct from empirical therapy is an area where microbiological advice should be sought.

Antibiotic resistances of note

Antibiotic resistances are constantly emerging and once emerged usually increase inexorably in prevalence even if the antibiotic is withheld. Because of linkage of resistance to other agents that continue to be used.. Examples of diminishing resistance rates are rare but include the association of declining tetracycline resistance in staphylococci, pneumococci, and Haemophilus associated with a drop in community use in England and Wales, a drop in erythromycin resistant Group A streptococci in Finland associated with decreased use, and the disappearance of early highly prevalent clones of MRSA in the UK in the period 1968 to 1977 for unknown reasons. Other resistances have persisted. Sulphonamide resistance in E coli persists although sulphonamides are effectively never used. The resistance mechanism persists on many plasmids in association with Trimethoprim resistance mechanisms associated with trimethoprim resistance and different dihydrofolate reductases. Streptomycin resistance persists although the drug is now hardly used in England because of linkage with tetracycline and sulphonamide resistance in Esch.coli.

Important resistances that have become prevalent in the last 10 years include:
• MRSA / MRSE (Methicillin-resistant-Staphylococcus aureus or M-R-Staphylococcus epidermidis). MRSE are often (60-80%) gentamicin resistant, MRSA gentamicin-resistance depends if the strain is EMRSA 15 (commonest in UK and normally susceptible, EMRSA 16 (next commonest and usually gentamicin resistant). Gentamicin resistance is usually due to an acquired bifunctional acetyl- and phosphor- transferase, which is also active against tobramycin, kanamycin and netilmicin but rarely amikacin. The same gene confers high-level resistance in enterococci. These enzymes were rare (<10%) at the time gentamicin cements were trialled. It is probably gentamicin and tobramycin cements no longer have prophylactic

activity against staphylococci and enterococci although they remain effective against Gram-negative organisms - coliforms.

• GISA/VISA/TISA & GRSA,VRSA, TRSA. (Glycopeptide/Vancomycin/Teicoplanin intermediate or resistant Staphylococcus aureus) - These strains are rarer than initially thought, are described almost exclusively in MRSA and have been a worrying threat until the recent emergence of new drugs for MRSA and the realisation that the thickened cell wall which is the phenotypic expression of the resistance mechanism appears to place the organism at a survival disadvantage. This cell wall mechanism is not plasmid-mediated. TISAs are relatively common in the SE of England and to a lesser extent elsewhere. EMRSA 17 is usually a TISA. Some strains of MRSA segregate low frequency mutant glycopeptide resistant forms with up to 4 fold greater resistance -so called hetero-resistant VISAs. Those with a vancomycin MIC of less than 6mg/l are usually regarded as sensitive - if not normally so - to vancomycin.

• VRE (Vancomycin-resistant enterococci) - These strains which in the UK are usually the imperilling, tobramycin and gentamicin resistant Enterococcus faecium rather than the commoner Enterococcus faecalis have one of three classes of transferable plasmid-mediated vancomycin and teicoplanin resistance of high level which is in vitro transferable to staphylococci. This resistance has not yet become prevalent in staphylococci but may yet do so. It is important to note that some 15% of MRSA carriers carry the organism in faeces, the natural habitat of enterococci. Selection of all enterococci is associated with cephalosporin, trimethoprim and quinolone use. Vancomycin resistant strains are selected by the use of these antibiotics. Enterococcal prosthetic infection is an emerging very difficult therapeutic problem and vancomycin resistant strains may be impossible to manage by salvage or revision options.

• ESBL producing Escherichia coli, Klebsiella and Enterobacter sp (Extended-spectrum Beta-Lactamase producers). From the days of the TEM1 enzyme detected 6 months after the introduction of ampicillin myriad families of different B-lactamases have emerged. There are now TEM, SHV, and CTXM enzymes resistant to all cephalosporins, which are becoming highly prevalent in the UK and USA. These strains appear to be particularly arising in quinolone-resistant bacteria leaving few therapeutic options for deep infections with these strains . Many are resistant to gentamicin and Trimethoprim. The carbapenems are usually active but new carbapenemases are becoming more frequent and potentially will leave coliforms only susceptible to colistin in terms of drugs useful for cements or parenteral use. There are now new Gram negative antibiotics n the therapeutic pipeline which has a 15 year lead-in. These organisms may become problematic in orthopaedics.

Some controversial issues in newer antibiotics and changing resistance.

Choosing between teicoplanin and vancomycin

Teicoplanin is a newer glycopeptide antibiotic than vancomycin. It has no FDA license for US use. In early trials it was used at inadequate dose and failed more frequently than vancomycin in serious S aureus infection. In later trials it was given at higher dose with loading - Two 400mg doses 12 hours apart should be given in the first 24 hours to ensure adequate blood levels. Many authorities consider that the levels are less predictable than vancomycin and that trough levels should be measured or a greater than usual dose(400mg once daily) routinely given i.e. 800mg. At either 400mg or 800 mg the drug is considerably more expensive than vancomycin. Later studies suggest that teicoplanin is as effective with these caveats as vancomycin. The drug can be given i.m. or into tissues because its pH is neutral not 3.5 as with vancomycin hydrochloride. It can also be given by bolus injection rather than infusion. It has been used in single dose prophylaxis trials but it is not clear how it would achieve adequate concentrations without the loading dose. In knee replacement regional prophylaxis after tourniquet application might be the best way to be certain of adequate concentrations. Teicoplanin is less likely than vancomycin to cause red man syndrome by histamine release with rapid infusion but cross allergenicity can occur. Nephrotoxicity is more likely if vancomycin is used intravenously in combination with gentamicin than if teicoplanin is used in combination with gentamicin. In the difficult scenario of prolonged therapy for enterococci there might therefore be an advantage in teicoplanin use bit many enterococci are now resistant to the synergic effect of a glycopeptide and gentamicin. Inducible resistance to teicoplanin not vancomycin occurs in the second commonest infecting coagulase negative staphylococcus, Staph. haemolyticus. Resistant S aureus do occur whereas this remains very rare with S aureus. In general in Oswestry we have continued to use vancomycin and see some disadvantages in teicoplanin use.

Using glycopeptides in prophylaxis

Guidelines often state that these agents should not be used in prophylaxis for arthroplasty. This is for a number of reasons. Firstly comparative studies with prolonged follow-up have not been done. Centres with low sepsis rates would need enormous studies with prolonged follow-up: centres with high sepsis rates where small trials would be expected to show an advantage are unwilling to publish high sepsis rates! Secondly, when glycopeptides were the only effective agents for MRSA there was fear that overuse would select for resistance either of the VISA variety or transferred resistance from vancomycin resistant enterococci. Thirdly meta-analysis of comparative studies with cephalosporins may not take into account the emergence in later years of MRSA as the major orthopaedic pathogen because early studies when cephalosporins were effective against sensitive S aureus are over-represented. Many units now use glycopeptides but the evidence base is poor. Patients with primary total joint replacement have often not been in contact with healthcare for other reasons and have not therefore acquired MRSA or MRSE. In general these patients can still be given anti-staphylococcal cephalosporins or penicillins safely. There is no evidence that cephalosporin prophylaxis against Gram-negative infection is important. Patients having conversions of hemiarthroplasties or revision arthroplasty generally have often had prolonged opportunities to acquire MRSA and MRSE and it is not unreasonable, and indeed is Oswestry policy, to give these patients glycopeptide single dose prophylaxis for revision. Subject to assessment of its usefulness in your clinical practise the British Society for Antimicrobial Chemotherapy and Hospital Infection Society recommend screening the nose for MRSA at pre-assessment clinics. Nasal carriage is a good predictor of carriage elsewhere. A process of risk reduction for MRSA infection can be initiated on receipt of a swab. Nasal mupirocin against susceptible strains (not Mupirocin resistant strains) will eliminate carriage. It is not proven that it will reduce the incidence of orthopaedic infection but in other situations there is evidence of a reduction in the likelihood of MRSA bacteraemia. Patients who are persistent MRSA carriers (and possibly all patients known to have MRSA at some time in the past) should have glycopeptide prophylaxis for surgery. There is no evidence that MRSA carriage is a contra-indication to surgery if adequate prophylaxis is used.

Using vancomycin in therapy of S aureus sepsis

In the UK between 30 and 50% of S aureus infection in hospital is now due to MRSA. The mortality from S aureus sepsis in the era before this and for methicillin susceptible Staph. aureus was usually 30%. There is evidence that there is an additional 30% mortality from S aureus septicaemia if the organism is MRSA. Fifty per cent of MRSA septicaemias seem to come from intravenous line infection. For these reasons flucloxacillin and cephalosporins or carbapenems cannot be used safely in the urgent empirical treatment of line infection or serious S aureus sepsis. If the strain is known to be susceptible, or when antibiotic susceptibilities are available showing the strain is flucloxacillin susceptible then flucloxacillin can and should be used. There is evidence that if dose is adequate (20mg/Kg repeated 4 times daily) flucloxacillin has better results against susceptible strains than vancomycin or teicoplanin. So switch therapy is justified in definitive as distinct from empirical treatment of S aureus infection. There may be a caveat in arthroplasty situations if it is possible there is co-infection with coagulase negative staphylococci. These cannot be reliably susceptibility tested by non-molecular means to flucloxacillin and resistance is common. Real time PCR is now available on an experimental basis in some centres for the detection of methicillin resistance, and of staphylococci, enterococci and Pseudomonas. The tests take approximately 2 hours to run.

Using linezolid or quinupristin/dalfopristin as new anti MRSA agents.

Linezolid is a member of the oxazolidonone class of antibiotics the first new chemical entities as antibiotics for over 40 years. Linezolid is a small bacteristatic molecule with useful activity only against Gram-positive organisms. It has the same dose orally and intravenously and is very expensive. It has not been formally comparatively trialled in bone infection and has no license for the treatment of bone and joint infection. In soft tissue infection it generally has equivalent activity to vancomycin. There is some evidence that it is more effective in MRSA pneumonia in ITU. There is evidence that it does not eliminate MRSA carriage - as with vancomycin the organism commonly reappears in mucosal sites when the drug is topped. The antibiotic penetrates onto the surface of the skin and can be expected to have a selective effect on the flora. In the gastrointestinal tract Linezolid resistant enterococci are easily selected for and such selection can also occur in enterococcal infections that are being treated. A very few Linezolid resistant staphylococci have already been described. The drug has a license for only 4 weeks use, which limits its use in orthopaedics. Thrombocytopenia, neutropenia and hypoplastic anaemia were all described during trials of the drug and were the reason earlier compounds in the class were not marketed. Pre marketing rates of 1% of marrow suppression were quoted but it is now thought to be closer to 5% and to relate to duration of therapy perhaps rising to 10% at 4-6 weeks use. Marrow suppression is normally reversible on drug withdrawal. It is recommended that full blood counts are performed weekly in the first two weeks and twice weekly thereafter. The drug is clearly too expensive to use in other than serious infection. In Oswestry we use the agent as a 2-week oral follow-on in situations where a serious MRSA infection has or is being treated and the patient is now fit for home therapy but it is important to realise that the use of this compound in orthopaedics is not evidence based. Given the apparent markers that emergence of resistance may be a problem and that this is a useful oral reserve drug, use should be restrained.

Quinupristin/dalfopristin (Synercid) is an intravenous antibiotic with activity against MRSA, MRSE and vancomycin resistant enterococci. It is an antibiotic, which is a combination of two streptogramins, which are a class related to the macrolide antibiotics. They are derivatives of pristinamycin which has been available in Europe but not the UK or USA. Pristinamycin has been used in animal feeds in Europe with emergence of resistance but then avoparcin a glycopeptide was similarly used and led to the emergence of vancomycin resistant enterococci in Europe. This agent is active against erythromycin- resistant Gram-positive organisms i.e. there is no cross-resistance. There is essentially no reported orthopaedic experience but in general use for MRSA sepsis is has reported efficacy rates of up to 57% (slightly less than vancomycin or Linezolid - 70% - in courses of up to 14 days duration fro skin and soft tissue associated MRSA bacteraemia. There is better and more successful data for its use against vancomycin resistant enterococci. Unwanted effects include phlebitis and jaundice and the drug also has interactions because of P450 enzyme induction in the liver. This for all these reasons is probably seldom the drug of first choice even as a reserve agent.

Daptomycin is a new lipopeptide class related to vancomycin. It as yet has a US bit not European license. It has a very long half-life permitting twice weekly dosing and may be a suitable agent for home therapy as may other newer vancomycin related compounds in clinical trial. There is as yet little published data on its use.

Further Reading;

Finch RG, Greenwood D, Norrby SR, editors. Antibiotic and chemotheraphy: Anti-infective agents and their use in therapy. 8th ed. Edinburgh: Churchill Livingstone, 2003.

Notes

The Microbiology of Working in a Theatre.

R E Warren.

Consultant Microbiologist, Royal Shrewsbury Hospital.

Introduction

Much of theatre practice evolved from custom and practice or ritual and this accounts for much existing variation in procedure and often for strongly held attachment to protocols which others regard as rituals or out-dated. An increasing base of evidence to support standards is now available. One should always be critical of the evidence-base and not overestimate the importance of any single study. Playing safe by serially adding layers of complexity to one's practise or adding to myths by accepting less than reproducible evidence is not advisable as it may generate neglect of important practises as well as being expensive. However, it is particularly important that surgeons are aware of the need to design instruments that are easily cleaned and sterilised in theatre sterile supply departments and have at least once in their career visited the department and asked detailed questions about instrument cleaning and sterilisation conditions. They need to be aware of the minimum times for sterilisation and the principles of delivery of latent heat on which steam as distinct from dry heat permits sterilisation of instruments at lower temperatures and shorter durations in autoclaves than hot air ovens. They consequently need to understand that wet packs are not made safe by drying and that flash sterilisation procedures for dropped instruments may not remove bacterial clostridial and bacillus spores effectively. They should alos be aware of sterilisation conditions appropriate to fibre optic arthroscopes and the hazards of chemical sterilants. They also need to understand the desirable features of instrument design from a sterilisation viewpoint. Surgeons who take an interest in sterile supply are now rare but it is important to support sterile supply departments and ensure their adequacy if safe surgery is to be practised.

The origin of organisms in the dry environment and air.

98% of the organisms (mostly Gram-positive) on the floor originate from skin scales but no more than 15% of air-borne organisms in a conventional theatre originate from the floor. Obsessions with the floor as a source of organisms in theatre that will cause wound infection are therefore mis-placed. Sticky mats to take fluff and dirt off wheels coming from the ward increase counts on the wheels by acting as a source. Porters washing wheels on trolleys is also an unnecessary or infrequently required activity. Putting on overshoes to go into theatre accommodation is unnecessary and indeed taking off the overshoe is a good way of getting organisms onto the hands from the floor -

something that is undesirable. Washing the floor other than to keep it aesthetically clean is unnecessary and it is important to use floor cleaners that are appropriate rather than those with caustic or severe chemical properties. Neutral detergents are adequate. Bonded finishes can be de-glued, and terrazzo finishes damaged by alkalis and abrasives admitting moisture and Gram-negative contamination of the floor from washing mops etc can become heavy and contaminate other items in the theatre.

The organisms on the 12u skin scales are often abraded off by clothing. The concept that clothing stops this is open to question. A cotton weave may have 80-100u gaps! On average an individual disseminates between 100 and 5000 bacteria carrying particles per minute, 70 % of these from below the waist. Woven gowns reduce this dissemination by only 30%. However the shedding is usually below the operating table. Of course clothing design does affect dissemination. Leotards are better than trousers that are better than skirts in terms of dissemination. High counts are obtained if you sample at the bottom of trouser legs and it is probably better to tuck these into boots than leave them flapping on clogs. The organisms distributed into the environment depend on the skin flora and on perineal carriage. Interestingly on average, heavy dispersers of S aureus are ten times as frequently male as female, according to twenty year old and older studies. The function of changing into cleanly laundered theatre clothing is to avoid contaminating your own clothes but also to avoid bringing organisms from the wards into theatre - an extension of the principle recognised by Semmelweiss in Vienna and Budapest that going from autopsies to the wards without washing your hands in chlorinated lime led to puerperal sepsis. Going back to wards wearing theatre clothes or appearing in the dining room in theatre clothes indicates a failure to understand the principle of theatre clothing.

Efforts have been directed to make clothing into a barrier to skin scales as well as a barrier the other way to blood strike-through to the skin. The initial attempt to restrict perineal distribution and breakthrough over the table by using a 20u pore Ventile gown bib and underpants was both ineffective and very hot. A gown made of woven Gortex with an incorporated polytetrafluoroethylene impermeable membrane with 0.2U pores in the weave was also found to be ineffective when worn over cotton and when incorporated into short and trousers merely contrived to pump a greater concentration of organisms out of trouser legs .

and arm holes. Specific fabrics such as Seeguard T85392 which had low weave porosity were effective but the fabric was easily damaged by normal laundry and became ineffective after more than 4 uses unless special laundry techniques were employed. The evidence is good that non-woven fibres made of cellulose are the best available gowns for excluding skin organisms from breakthrough.

Fabrics and paper are also used in surgical drapes. There is almost no evidence that these make any difference either to theatre air counts or wound washout counts, which seem to be a predictor of surgical sepsis. Use of adhesive drapes, iodophore impregnated drapes and wound edge drapes do not seem to make a significant difference to bacterial counts in the wound and all are expensive. Most drapes are for modesty purposes and to provide a clean (?sterile) surface against which sterile gowns and gloves may rest and on which instruments may be placed occasionally. There is no evidence that their design is important in sepsis and they are an obvious target for cost-cutting in theatres. Drapes are important in orthopaedic implant work to cover opened sterile instrument packs. If instruments opened before a procedure are exposed to normal air there is a risk that sizeable numbers of organisms will settle on them from the air. In solid wall clean air enclosures with High Efficiency Particulate Air (HEPA) filters this is not the case and trolleys of instruments can be safely unpacked in these. Air curtain clean air enclosures must be large enough to incorporate all unpacked instrument trolleys with surgeons, assistants and patient clear of the turbulent air flow at the edge of the curtain (approximately 15 inches inside the top canopy). If instrument trolleys project or are outside a small enclosure and brought in in sequence they must be covered with a sterile drape before being brought in.

Drapes should not be used to occlude openings in solid wall clean air enclosures. They raise the air-pressures in the cabin and increase airflows under cabon walls - into adjacent cabins in a barn design!

Some surgeons have taken to use Stryker hoods for surgery. These are designed for protecting the operator not protecting the patient and their effect on air-flows and counts in a clean air enclosure is conjectural although their supply fan makes them cool. The use of Charnley water cooled exhausted suits reduces bacterial counts by voiding them outside the clean air enclosure. These are documented to reduce air counts in older theatres but their use in a modern theatre with high airflows (400 airchanges) has not been shown to reduce sepsis rates

The importance of clean air.

This remains a controversial area with interventional studies producing differing answers. The problem of mutifactorial control and randomisations is extremely difficult to arrange. The key study to be familiar with is the analysis of the 1973 MRC study of hip arthroplasty involving 19 hospital theatres and 8052 operations. This was neither a randomised nor controlled study and sepsis rates varied with the use of clean air antibiotics and exhaust suits as shown in Figure 1.

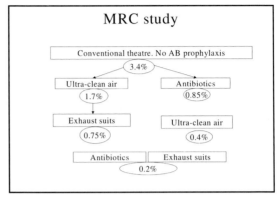

Figure 1.

There are a number of papers on this but the analysis of Lidwell in 1988 is key. In this analysis he provides data that shows that sepsis relates to air counts and is best if these are <10colony forming units/cu.m. Early wound sepsis was associated with 4-30 times increase in late S.aureus sepsis and sepsis rates doubled in patients with rheumatoid arthritis. Sepsis rates of wound washouts at the end of surgery and air counts of bacteria which relate to settling into the wound were all inter-related.(See Figures 2 & 3).

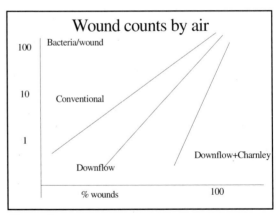

Figure 2.

Air and wound counts and sepsis rates in arthoplasties

	Ops	Samples	Air Median cfu	Wound wash-out Median Geomet. cfu	Joint sepsis
Conventional	1793	127	142	4.5	1.5%
Ultra-clean	686	86	7.3	1.5	0.9%
Ultra-clean + body suit	1129	141	0.47	0.57	0.3%

Figure 3.

Lidwell reports the micro-organisms causing sepsis in this study. There were 86 infections and 68 organisms were recovered.

- 31 S.aureus (2/12 from patient)
- 19 Coag.neg.staph
- 6 Propionibacteria
- 5 Enterococci
- 6 Gram positive mixture
- 10 Gram negatives

Low virulence organisms such as coagulase negative staphylococci and propionibacteria can take years to declare themselves. The origin of Gram negative and some S aureus infections can be by post-operative infection or may in some cases be haematogenous or lymphatic but classification as haematogenous infections is not included in the MRC study analysis.

Air filtration and airflow

All modern theatres have continuous positive pressure ventilation plant with solid ducting, which must be cleaned of construction dust before theatre commissioning, have exit grilles to exclude birds nesting in or in front of the ducting, and coarse pre-filters - usually bag filters - to exclude leaves and other gross contamination. Air counts depend on the sort of theatre. See Figure 4.

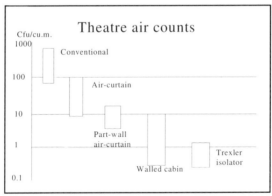

Figure 4.

A major function of the air supply is to dilute bacterial counts generated from activity in the theatre. The standard of <35 bacteria or fungal particles /cu m of air has remained in British operating theatre commissioning practise for over 20 years but is only relevant to conventional theatres. A conventional theatre should have 20 air changes /hour. Clean air theatres have much higher air delivery rates (up to 400 air-changes/hour) with corresponding improved dilution. In clean air theatres HEPA filters are seated in the air-flow. These are 0.3u filters that exclude bacteria and fungal spores. They are very easily damaged and almost always there are pre-filters to protect them. They must be checked with discharge of particles into the duct and scanning with a particle counter across their theatre face to ensure they are properly seated in an airtight manner in their frame mounting and have no holes or pin holes caused by high velocity dust. In the absence of effective tough pre-filters demolition works or helicopter dust outside air intakes can destroy HEPA filters.

Because of the need for theatre comfort all theatres must have in their air supply humidification - preferably steam rather than spray to avoid any hazard from Legionella, and heating and refrigeration coils. Because of the energy loss and expense from such conditioning all clean air theatres have a recirculating design with air exhausted either from the outside of the canopy of air curtains or from the outside of barns back through the HEPA filters. It is important to ensure that the filters do not become blocked by paper or linen lint or airflows will be reduced and theatre washout of activity-related particles abolished. Designs vary but downward facing air flows are more secure than horizontal air-flows. Cross flow to ground level balance flaps, which permit air exit, are safer than straight across exits for air. Checks need to be made that diffusers direct air in the direction intended by using smoke. Straight across ventilation in conventional theatres may not ventilate the operative filed and circular roof-mounted diffusers are preferable to produce turbulent flow in conventional theatres. Laminarity as a concept in clean air theatres is unrealistic. Any obstruction will divide the air-flow and thermal convection currents over the skin always bear air upwards in the microenvironment of the skin. Nevertheless air direction should carry air away from the operator and patient. Air flow control is important to avoid both excessive flow that bounces from the ground and entrains floor particles back up the sides of the clean air enclosure and recirculates them downwards, and inadequate flow. Care with light design is important to avoid light shadows, which obstruct airflows over the operating table.

Air flow rates should not be perceptible as drafts to the operator. In conventional theatres air delivery rates of 0.65 cu.m./second in the theatre and 0.15cu.m./sec in anaesthetic rooms, lay up areas, preparation and store areas are normal. Having said that recent guidance suggests air-change rates of 37 in instrument lay-up areas which is probably not achievable with these velocities. Some ask for lower airflows in handscrub areas or negative pressures but these are not necessary now brushes and even scrubs are being replaced by alcohol hand-rubs. Normal linear airflow in clean air theatres is a more sophisticated matter. The clean area should be marked out as a 30cm grid. The air flow in each of these squares should be measured using a hot wire anemometer 2m high and should exceed 0.38m/s for partial wall air curtains or 0.3m/s for full wall enclosures. These results can be averaged across the enclosure. In the inner 6X6 squares the air velocity should be rechecked 1m above floor level and each reading should exceed 0.2m/s. If particle tests of the filters are done in clean air enclosure it is unnecessary to do microbiological test and evenundesirable as they have tobe very stringent calling for bacterial counts of <1 bacteria/2 cu.m sampled. Agar media dries if >10cu.m is passed over it and becomes inhibitory, and agar media can be contaminated before it is used!

The commissioning of theatres or their re-commissioning after filter change is a specialist matter. It is normally conducted with empty theatres 1 hour post tenancy. There is an argument that this does not stress the theatre with a standard particle or bacterial load and therefore does not truly measure ventilation. For example in conventional theatres the normal bacterial air count may be <4 colony forming units/cu.m., whereas the same theatre in use may have a count 100 times that. In commissioning clean air theatres the standards for industrial clean rooms by particle counting can be usefully used - although this has not generally been advocated. Electronic particle counters are essential for this.

Medicines Control Agency Class A rooms have counts of <3,500 0.5u particles/cu m and no 5u particles or greater /cu.m. US Federal standard 209E Class M1 has 0.1u particles <350, 0,2 and 0,3u <10 particles and 0.5u 0 particles/cu.m. British Standards Institute
Class C standards are <100 0.3u particles,<35 0.5u particles, and 0 5u particles. Class A room standards can be met in most clean air theatres and certainly particle counts above 0.5u should be close to zero if filters and dilution are working effectively.

Hand antisepsis

Antisepsis is well understood and badly practised.

Lowbury et al showed in volunteers in the early 1970s that 6 washes with povidone-iodine scrub produced a greater than 97 % reduction in surgeons hand flora and chlorhexidine detergent scrub 99%. Single washes produce reductions with povidone iodine of 68%, Chlorhexidine scrub 87.1% and alcoholic chlorhexidine hand-rub 97.9% reduction. The findings of the equivalence of alcoholic hand rub have been confirmed in surgical trials. Chlorhexidine's superiority to povidone-iodine has not been overturned by later studies. Antiseptics have a residual effect on regrowth of the skin flora. This has been assessed under the gloved hands of volunteers after 3 hours. The residual reduction is as follows:

Bar soap 12.3%
Povidone 89.4%
70% spirit 90.9%
70% isopropanol 93.8%
0.5% chlorhexidine in 70% ethanol 96.2%
0.5% chlorhexidine in 70% IPA 96.9%
4% Chlorhexidine 4% IPA detergent 97.4%

Chlorhexidine shows the best cumulative effect with no difference between alcoholic and detergent based application. Bar soap removes this cumulative effect from the hands as its stearic acid binds to Chlorhexidine and renders it insoluble. Bar soap should not be used to wash hands once chlorhexidine scrub is in use in the course of the day. The cumulative effects of chlorhexidine continue to increase if bar soap is not used. Neutral detergents can be used. Larson in 1986 compared bacterial counts at first wash, the end of 1 day and the end of 5 days with an average 15 hand washes/day and meaning results over 10 people. Count results are shown in the accompanying table.

	Mean log bacterial counts		
	1st time wash	After 1 day	After 5 days
Bar soap	6.41	6.19	6.31
70% isopropanol	5.89	4.26	3.92
0.5% chlorhexidine in 70% isopropanol	6.11	3.47	3.03
4% Chlorhexidine in 4% isopropanol and a detergent base	5.93	4.29	2.68

Similar independent studies performed with povidone iodine suggest a reduction of 1-1.5 log orders

Operation site antisepsis

The same principles of skin antisepsis apply to wound sites as to hands. Preoperative antisepsis is not effective in the form of pre-operative showers and use of chlorhexidine and in big trials has no effect on sepsis rates. The use of povidone iodine and alcoholic compresses (Lowbury 1973) to reduce skin spore counts on the lower limb is a redundant practise now prophylactic antibiotics are used. It was always a relatively ineffective practise basedon very few patients.. In theatres particular care is needed if alcoholic preparations are applied to the operation site that the amount of preparation is not excessive and does fully dry without involving diathermy pads as otherwise burns and fires may result. It is wisest not to apply with the gloved hand but with a swab to avoid excess.

Taking and processing operative samples
It is important to remember that the knife and instruments you have used for the skin will be contaminated with skin organisms and should not be used to sample suspected infection in prostheses or the presence of metalwork. For independent results from each biopsy a separate clean knife and forceps should be used for each sample.
The appropriate samples from a prosthesis are
- swab of any joint fluid
- biopsy of the proximal and distal prosthesis/joint junctions either side of the joint "the membrane"
- joint capsule
- surrounding inflammatory tissue

Samples are best sent in a sterile nutrient medium containing sharp-edged Ballotini beads that can be shaken for 10 minutes to thoroughly macerate the tissue, releasing organisms. The broth can then be aseptically subcultured after maceration and the broth reincubated. Prolonged incubation for up to 7 days and prolonged incubation of subculture plates is necessary. 48 hours is inadequate. Using grinders and blenders may accidentally heat the sample and sterilise it by pasteurisation. Culture plates need examination with a plate microscope but even so small colony variant organisms can be missed

In addition to microbiology the gold standard is to examine membranes for quantitative neutrophil infiltration (Athanasou 1985) . Atkins et al (1988) have validated the interpretation of the above broth cultures by reference to the histological gold standard - although neutrophil infiltration can also be seen in inflammatory arthritides such as rheumatoid disease.
The interpretation is that recovery of an organism from only one sample (common with Propionibacteria) predicts infection in only 10.6% of cases. >1 sample predicts infection in 41% cases and >2 samples in 96%. Frozen sections may be helpful in showing neutrophil infiltration and as a decision making tool as to 1 or 2 stage revision arthroplasty.

Bone bank microbiological issues

Bone and tissue banking is since April 2001 an activity that must be specifically licensed through the medicines and devices agency in the Department of Health. The process requires accreditation to ISO 9000 standards. Stringent precautions to avoid transmission of viruses, tumours and other diseases must be followed. Microbiology is covered by the DH publication on the Microbiological Safety of organs and tissues for transplantation guidelines and subsequent DH circulars. It is currently recommended that bone donors are tested for HIV, Hepatitis Bsurface Antigen, Hepatitis C Virus, Syphilis, and Human T lymphotropic Viruses 1& 2. Tissue should be quarantined for 6 months and then the donor re-tested before bone is released. There are additional contraindications to donation involving risk of vCJD and lifestyle, including lately travel to the US in the summer months when West Nile virus is prevalent. Femoral heads collected in clean air enclosures do not need terminal sterilisation but it is usual to culture material prior to freezing. Cadaver bone is used by NBS and commercial bone banks and should be sterilised by gamma irradiation after washing and drying as it is frequently bacterially contaminated prior to this.

Further reading

Athanasou NAR, Pandy R, DeSteiger R, Crook D, McLardey-Smith P. Diagnosis of infection by frozen section during revision arthroplasty J Bone Joint Surg 1995;77B: 28-33.

Atkins BL, Athanasou NA, Deeks JJ, Crook DWM, Simpson H, Peto TEA, McLardey-Smith P, Berendt AR. Prospective evaluation of criteria for microbiological diagnosis of prosthetic-joint infection at revision arthroplasty. J Clin Microbiol 1998; 36: 2932-9.

Bryce EA, Spence D, Roberts FJ. An in-use evaluation of an alcohol-based pre-surgical hand disinfectant. Infec Control Hosp Epidemiol 2001; 22:635-9.

Girou E, Loyeau S, Legrand P, Oppein F, Brun-Buisson C Efficacy of handrubbing with alcohol based solution versus standard handwashing with antiseptic soap: a randomised clinical trial. BMJ 2002; 325: 362-5.

Hambraeus A. Aerobiology in the operating room - a review. J Hosp Infect 1988; 11 (Suppl A); 68-76.

Health technical Memorandum 2025. Ventilation in healthcare premises. NHS Estates,1994.

Hoffman PN. Microbiological commissioning & monitoring of operating theatre suites. J Hosp Infect 2002; 52:1-28.

Humphreys H. Operating theatre ventilation standards and the risk of postoperative infection. J Hosp Infect 2002; 50:85-90.

Kramer A, Rudolph P, Kampf G, Pittet Dl Limited efficacy of alcohol-based hand gels. Lancet 2002; 2:1489-50.

Larson EL, Eke PI, Loughan BE. Efficacy of alcohol-based hand rinses under frequent-use conditions. Antimicrob Agents Chemother 1986; 30: 542-4.

Leonas KK, Jinkins RS. The relationship of selected fabric characteristics and the barrier effectiveness of surgical gown fabrics Am J Infect Control 1997; 25:16-23.

Lidwell OM. Air, antibiotics and sepsis in replacement joints J Hosp Infect 1988; 11 (Suppl C):18-40.

Lowbury EJL & Lilly HA. Use of 4% Chlorhexidine detergent solution (Hibiscrub) and other methods of skin disinfection. BMJ 1973; i:510-5

Lowbury EJL, Lilly HA, Ayliffe GAJ. Preoperative disinfection of surgeon's hands: Use of alcoholic solutions and effects of gloves on skin flora. BMJ 1974; 4:369-374.

Lowbury EJL Skin preparation for operation. Br J Hosp Med1973; 627-634.

Parienti JJ, Thibon P, LeRoux Y, et al. Hand-rubbing with an aqueous alcoholic solution vs traditional surgical hand-scrubbing and 30-day surgical site infection rates: a randomised equivalence study. JAMA 2002; 288:722-7.

Recommendations of the Healthcare Infection Control practices Advisory Committee and the HICPAC/SHEA/APIC/IDSA Hand Hygiene taskforce. Guidelines for hand Hygiene in Health-care settings. Morbidity and Mortality Weekly Report; Vol 51 October 25th 2002. Atlanta: Centres for Disease Control and Prevention.

Ventilation of operating departments:A design guide. Department of Health, 1983.

Woodhead K et al (HIS working party) Behaviours and rituals in the operating theatre. J Hosp Infect 2002; 51:241-255

Notes

Notes

Personal Experiences from the FRCS Orth

Mr JP Whittaker and Mr R Roach

Oswestry Trainees
Robert Jones & Agnes Hunt Orthopaedic Hospital
Oswestry

The Exam is both exhaustive and exhausting. It covers a great breadth of orthopaedics, with a large number of subjects covered. It pays to know something about everything, rather than everything about something. They want you to be a safe DGH Consultant in the middle of the night.

Mechanics of the Examination

Section 1

Paper 1
Single Best Answer MCQ
2 hours 15 minutes

First 15 Questions relate to a published paper.
One best answer from 5 possibles.

Paper 2
Extended Matching Questions
2 hours

approx 135 questions
with 10-15 stems

Candidates must meet the required standard in Section 1 in order to gain eligibility to proceed to Section 2. Currently the intercollegiate website stipulates that candidates will have up to three attempts to pass Section 2 after which candidates would be required to re-enter Section 1 (www.intercollegiate.org.uk).

Section 2 (Clinicals)

Long Case (30 mins)   History / examination / discussion 10 mins each

Short Cases (30 mins)   Lower limb & spine / upper limb 15 mins each
                             5-8 cases 3-4 mins per case

Vivas in 4 topics   Basic Sciences
(2 hours)   Adult and Pathology
                             Trauma
                             Paediatric and Hands
                             25 mins each with 5 mins break between each.

How Much Do I Need to Know?

Stats MCQ's (first 15 single best answer questions)

◆   Statistical Methods - learn how a paper is constructed
◆   Very limited number of questions possible
◆   In the new format exam they are not negatively marked
◆   Read the questions first. Some can be answered without even reading the paper for example a p-value of 0.05 means......."

Long Case

◆   Take in as good a history as you can, the examiners will be present.
      name, age, occupation, family details. Then well or unwell generally. Then presenting diagnosis or problems with functional history to support the problem/s
◆   Examine the patient as history suggests (no need to look exhaustively at elbows if the patient has only an infected TKR)
◆   Examiners are unlikely to repeat a whole examination, just important segments (" how would you assess this man's leg length discrepancy ?")
◆   Discussion of X-rays, management, cause of disease etc.
◆   Don't forget a myelopathy in a RhA patient
◆   Don't lie. Be honest

This mimics very nicely the presentation you do to the boss in clinic.

Short Cases

♦ Large sports area/ physio gym. Pts all around edge in various states of undress you will be pushed to go faster: be polite, listen, talk sense.
♦ Don't take a history unless asked to.
♦ But you should ask questions that are important for examination is it tender?, can you feel this? etc.
♦ Look, feel, move, special tests.
♦ You may be asked just to perform special tests alone.
♦ Provide a sensible running commentary for what you have done. Don't examine in silence.
♦ Bilateral - start at the neck for upper limb or back for lower limb
♦ Look at spine / skin in all children

Vivas

Remember all the examiners must be practising Orthopaedic Surgeons. You will be more comfortable with questions if you know to "A level" standard, but you will fail if you know "A level" stuff but not "O level". e.g. understanding every type of flap but not remembering the basics of wound care eg: Irrigation, betadine dressings, tetanus status, swabs, antibiotics, analgesia, splintage etc.

So remember to keep it simple...stupid !

♦ The Question Chain: Almost every question (except perhaps in Basic Science) will have a prop, X-ray slide to Tee it off. Some slides are older than the examiners but the pathology will be evident.
♦ Examiners try to calm the candidate by first asking an easy question before progressing to the more difficult questions.
♦ Each prop generates a series of questions, usually very obvious.
♦ A good candidate will answer the first few questions before they are asked.
♦ Describe what you see.
♦ Stay on the question chain and the subject will be completed in less than 2 minutes then on to the next prop.
♦ Typically 6 or more topics per viva.

♦ You will take around a piece of paper detailing the previous examiners questions to avoid duplication.
♦ Try not to appear too excited that the examiner has asked you a question to which, it appears, you know the answer.

♦ The Complexity Ladder: A question chain may lead to an ever-increasing level of complexity on a particular subject. The examiner is trying to push to find the ceiling of your knowledge.
♦ If you talk for more than a minute on a subject and you don't know the answer, say "I don't know", don't waffle as you have scored all the points you need.
♦ The Idiot Loop: If you say something daft - you may get flustered and spend 2 or more minutes justifying yourself, you are not scoring points and you are off the question chain. To get back onto the question chain, say "I'm sorry, I don't know" and you are no longer wasting your precious time.

Frequently Asked Questions

Question: Do I need to quote papers?
Answer: No, not unless specifically asked - but it is good to say 'there has been a recent review in the JBJS that has tried to clarify this....they suggest ....' You should really be up to date with the journals. It is the cream on the cake if you appear to have read around and it will help you score a few extra marks. Don't try and remember 10 papers and all the results/ cross reference each and confuse the examiner. Ask around as to which papers are the key ones and learn one per topic.

Q.   Should I quote the practice of my boss or institution?
A: Not unless you wish to appear forever a registrar or unless specifically asked.

Q: Should I always look at the date and name of the patient on X-rays?
A: It's good practice to do it for the first case, but slows down your viva scoring, but is should be done if you're looking at a sequence of X-rays particularly in the long case. It is not wise to appear to be dragging out the time.

Q: What I would take with me ?

♦   Goniometer
♦   Tape measure
♦   Small objects e.g. coin & key for grip testing
♦   Pen torch

♦   Don't need...   Stethoscope
♦   May need...   Small tendon hammer

Don't assume anything will be provided, although it usually is.

Summary

There is no doubt that the FRCS (Trauma & Orthopaedics) is a stressful experience, even for the most well prepared candidate. However, the exam is very fair since you will be discussing subjects in which you are genuinely interested with like minded people, rather than having to force feed trivial and boring facts into your head, to regurgitate to specialists in esoteric subjects; an experience we all had to endure for in earlier surgical exams.

Finally

It is not a competitive exam and that clever looking chap in the corner who seems to know all the answers is neither going to show you up or take away the one remaining pass place.

Before exam:
Visit your orthotics unit.
Run through all past papers.
Team up and test each other.
Visit wards every morning starting 6 weeks before the exam.
Stay at a good hotel.
Get sleep.
Know the route to the exam areas if you are going by taxi ie: times.

During the exam:
Look forwards.
Don't ponder on your bad bits.
Be more aggressive and determined to put the record straight if you made an error.
Try not to talk in too much depth about the exam unless you know what the person is like you are talking to (ie a clever dick/ know all/ basic knowledge guy etc).
Relax.
Keep hydrated
Comfortable thin suits to keep cool/ short sleeves okay-you don't want to sweat it out!

GOOD LUCK!

Sample Clinical Cases from a

FRCS (Trauma & Orthopaedics) Examination

Long Case

Hip Arthrodesis post SUFE, leg length discrepancies.
THR Primary arthroplasty then Peri prosthetic fracture.
Also Aortic Aneurysm discussed.

- ◆ Position of arthrodesis.
- ◆ Aortic aneurysm repair.
- ◆ Work up of infected hip.
- ◆ Classification of periprosthetic fractures.
- ◆ Management of periprosthetic fractures.
- ◆ Taking down Arthrodesis.
- ◆ TKR with hip arthrodesis.
- ◆ Risk of back pain.
- ◆ Other joint arthrosis

Short Cases

Dupuytren's:	Discussed bands, cords , management, surgical approach.
Claw toes:	Discussed differential diagnosis. (I have no idea what was wrong with this lady!)
Patellectomy:	Demonstration of full power of extension.
Long head Bicep:	Rotator cuff Pathology, demonstrated active power.
Rupture:	In all cuff muscles. Impingement tests.
Gouty Tophi:	Over both lateral malleoli.

Basic Science

Growth plate:	Changes seen in SUFE in Rickets. Epiphyseodesis.
Free body diagram of elbow:	Joint reaction force.
Structure and ligaments:	ACL, anatomy proprioception for ACL principles of repair.
Fracture healing:	Stages. Arrest leading to non-union. BMP: effect on bone. Cytokines involved.

(Examiner said he was pushing me)

Bone graft:	Types of bone graft. Auto/Allo/Vascularised. Storage. Sterility. Antigenicity What is bone graft used for?
Statistics:	Why? Confidence Interval.

Describe how MRI works:

Hands

Non union at scaphoid:

X-ray.
Approaches to scaphoid.
Bone grafts.
Fixation.

Swelling in thenar eminence:

Tumours.
Examination.
Ix, Mx.

Giant cell tumours:

What processes have giant cells.
GCT of bone, common sites.

Thumb proximal phalangeal fracture:

Intra- articular.
Management.
Natural Hx.

Brachial Plexus:

Upper trunks: pre post ganglionic.
Erb's point, Weakness patterns.
Operations for: transfers, cable grafts.

Paediatrics

Chondroblastoma of humerus:

Malignant change of cartilage tumour histology.

Club Foot with contralateral polydactyly:

What to discuss with parents.
Early Mx: strapping and manipulation.
Postero-medial release.
Teratogenic causes.

Fibrous Dysplasia of humerus:

Diff.Diagnosis of X-ray.with pathological fracture management.

Type III and I Salter Harris fracture of ankle:

Management.
Growth arrest of above.
Other possible complications.

Adult and Pathology

Central Disc:

Exam,Hx,Ix,Mx.

Spinal Stenosis:

Definition.
Indications for Surgery.
Natural Hx.

Pathological fracture mid shaft femur:

Ex, Hx, Ix, Mx.
Non-union.

Multiple myeloma shoulder + skull:
Old pathological fracture of humerus
with known breast Ca:

Ex, X-ray.
Rational of prophylactic nailing.

Eosinophilic granuloma at spine:

Synovial chondromatosis:

Diaphyseal aclasia:

Ankle Sprains:

ATFL, LCFL + Snydesmotic Injury.
Ex + Mx.

Bone density

Dexa scan, T & Z scores.

Trauma

Lisfranc fracture dislocation:	Vascular complications.
Complex 4 part proximal femoral fracture:	Poor fixation. Redo surgery.
Distal paediatric femoral fracture:	Initial management in casualty. Traction set up. Three point fixation. Flexible intra medullary nails. Leg over growth/AVN of femoral head.
Galeazzi fracture:	Unstable DRUJ management.
Paediatric clavicle fracture: Adult clavicle fracture:	Threaded pin, plates. Non-union rate. Indications for ORIF.
Pathological fracture:	Again!